From
Arab Spring
to
Islamic Winter

From
Arab Spring
to
Islamic Winter

Raphael Israeli

Transaction Publishers
New Brunswick (U.S.A.) and London (U.K.)

Library of Congress Catalog Number: 2013011223
ISBN: 978-1-4128-5259-3

Printed in the United States of America

Library of Congress Cataloging-in-Publication Data

Israeli, Raphael.
  From Arab Spring to Islamic winter / Raphael Israeli.
      pages cm
  1. Arab Spring, 2010-   2. Islamic countries--Politics and
government--21st century.   3. World politics--2005-2015. I. Title.
  JQ1850.A91I85 2013
  909'.097492708312--dc23
                                                                    2013011223

To my son Avi and his family,
for their happy return into the fold

Contents

Acknowledgments

This volume was born out of two sets of lectures I delivered, the first at the Jerusalem Islamic Museum in the spring of 2011, when the process of revolution was young and the enthusiasm and hopes of overthrowing once-entrenched governments it raised were at their highest and most euphoric stage. The general educated and informed public, eager to comprehend the import of those momentous events, was confused, on the one hand, by the revolutionary and violent sights it watched on television, but even more so by the cataract of expert commentators who said one thing one day and contradicted it the next. I delivered the second set of lectures in the fall of 2012 before a private club in Mevasseret Zion, a suburb of Jerusalem, and it reviewed the earlier impressions and information in view of what had happened in the intervening sixteen months.

In this book, as in my work of the past three decades, I have benefited from the generosity of the Truman Institute of the Hebrew University. I am also indebted to my colleague Ronnie Shaked, a journalist and expert in the Arab world, who encouraged this project from the very outset. Especially helpful has been my research assistant, Adi Shiran, a gifted student of Arab and Islamic affairs who assisted in collecting the materials, putting them together, and providing many insights and ideas that have added to whatever quality can be attributable to the end result. But all responsibility for any errors of fact and interpretation rests wholly and squarely on my shoulders alone. The time-consuming and exhausting task of writing this, under the pressure of constantly keeping up with data and runaway developments, was considerably facilitated by the hospitality of my relatives and friends: in Sweden, Estrid Dahlstrom (Stockholm), Eva Zlatin (Gothenburg), and Ake and

Brith Aspenlind (Malmo); and in Switzerland:, Gisele Littman (Bat Ye'or). My ability to turn the summer of 2012 into a working vacation was due to their warm encouragement, comfortable homes, and inspiring atmosphere.

Jerusalem, Fall 2012

Introduction: The Transition from an Arab Spring to an Islamic Winter

This is the third year that the world has been watching in wonderment on television screens the unfolding of what international politics and media have dubbed the "Arab Spring," which connotes renewal, revival, a flourishing of thought and deed. It should have signaled a promising and creative new beginning for the Arab world, a promising road of no return toward progress and plenty that should have resolutely directed it toward liberal democracy, peace with its neighbors, and the end of confrontations and tensions internally and with the Western world. But in all its manifestations and ups and downs, unfortunately, all these hopeful signs were missing, remaining only the wishful thinking of diplomats and media people still hopelessly shackled to their political correctness. And like Oslo, which by now has fallen victim to similar false hopes, the Spring in question—which was erroneously connected to some imaginary democratic process that had, as it were, suddenly swept through the Islamic world—has gradually died out, as it becomes clear that a democratic endeavor is not taking place here but rather a power struggle to disinherit the long-standing tyrants who ruled Islamic countries and to replace them with something better, legitimate, popular, and representative of the masses, something that would bring salvation to the alienated youth and to the desperate crowds from the depths of their social, economic, and identity crisis.

This struggle is far from its conclusion, and it would smack of intellectual arrogance to pretend to predict either its longevity or its outcome. But judging from the places where the dust seems to have begun to settle—like Tunisia—and from the balance of power that seems to be in the making in others—like Egypt, Yemen, and maybe also Syria and Libya—it appears that Islam has been emerging as the winner from this Spring turbulence, while the other governing alternatives, comprising the democratic, liberal, and secular forces, which have been cultivated by the West, have been badly beaten and discarded. It is always positive to think and to act imaginatively, if one remains wary of the other derivative of *imagination*: the imaginary. For in reality, all those putative options have gone with the wind, or have been fighting for their lives in the midst of the present whirlpool in the Islamic world. Worse, it seems that the West has relinquished its hopes of seeing democracy and freedom prevail and has made peace with the idea that Islamic governments must be accepted as the least of all evils. The result has been that the tyrants who had barred the way of the rise of Islamic governments were removed, and Islamic regimes are being set up as the only viable alternative.

It is noteworthy, however, that even when defining the "Islamic Spring," there is controversy about its significance, both within the Islamic world and outside of it. Hence the lingering debates about its course, its nature, and its consequences—even on the very effect it is having on the various Muslim societies that have experienced it. For, not only would the application of shari'a law mean depriving women of their basic human rights, imposing death on heretics or anyone who dares to insult the Prophet or his memory, and flogging alcohol users in public, but clouds of tension and war would gather over the skies of the Middle East as incitement and jihad rise to new heights, directed against the West and, more specifically, Israel. In other words, instead of the peace, progress, development, democracy, and stability that the (Arab) Spring was supposed to have triggered, we are entering an era of uncertainty, tumult, instability, unrest, and deprivation caused by the unfolding Islamic Winter.

In the world of the Islamic Winter, the choices that are presented to the public are sharp and dichotomic: between preserving the current tyrannical, corrupt and oppressive regimes, which in some places are still fighting for their lives, or vying for a new order of the shari'a, which seeks a restorative revolution. For, unlike the Western revolutionary movements that have placed their utopia in the future, to be attained through certain prescribed social and economic policies—a viewpoint that has meanwhile collapsed in Eastern Europe—Islam has always turned its eyes to the example of the Prophet in the far past. Since he was the most perfect of men and the chosen Seal of the Messengers of Allah, the regime he set up in Medina in the seventh century is the ideal one, and it can hardly be emulated by anyone; therefore, any Muslim rule thereafter can only strive to approximate it. In the Islamic setting of today, any revolutionary movement based on a theoretical and rosy set of ideals will always retreat if confronted by a restorative Muslim ideal anchored in the personality of the Prophet or modeled on his times.

The temptation then presented to the Muslim public is to adopt an Islamic regime that was tested and emerged with flying colors in Muhammed's times—therefore there is nothing more guaranteed to succeed than to revive it or a close simulation of it. One can hardly detect arguments about the modalities of that regime, its ideal parameters being carved in stone in the Islamic tradition. Indeed, the Muslim Brothers in Egypt, Syria, Jordan, Algeria, Libya, Sudan, and even in Europe and the United States, or east of there in Asia, or throughout the rest of the world among the supporters of Hizb-ul-Tahrir (the Liberation Party), and various Salafi tendencies, all profess the revival of the caliphate, the regime that was installed by Muhammed's righteous successors, the caliphs, and has become the iconic model to be emulated by all future generations of Muslims. And to the extent that more militant Islamic movements like the Salafiya (the Rule of the Predecessors), Islamic Jihad, al-Qa'ida, and their sisters in Asia—like the Taliban in Afghanistan and Pakistan and Hamas among the Palestinians—are viewed as more extreme or radical than the others, this is more a matter of temperament and pace than any real doctrinal gap between them, which does not actually exist. To wit, they all advocate the revival of the caliphate as the ideal Islamic state to be attained under shari'a law, and all endorse jihad as the means to attain that goal.

However, in the wider world, this artificial distinction, unknown in the Islamic world, is maintained between moderate Islam and extreme Islam, or standard Islam versus the fundamentalist brand, or pragmatic Islam to contrast with the militant/radical/confrontational/political kind, as if these were two rival doctrines competing for the souls of their followers. In the real world, apart from personal jealousies and peripheral doctrinal matters that distinguish (but do not separate) these various factions, there are truly no contentious arguments between them regarding the need to reach a shari'a state. There might be nuances as to whether to take power by force when peaceful ways are blocked, as the Wahhabis did in Arabia in the nineteenth century and their likes (al Qa'ida, Hamas, the Taliban) also tried for a time when the opportunity was open to them—or by peaceful means, as the Muslim Brotherhood in Algeria, Egypt, Tunisia, Jordan, and their likes have attempted constantly through the existing political system. At one time or another, they all tried, but since they were crushed by the existing rulers, whom they wished to eliminate, and since they feared for their very survival, they embraced the peaceful way of propaganda (*da'wa*), social welfare, education, and participation in the democratic game to gain legitimacy among their constituents until they are able to take over the rule and impose the Islamic way of politicking.

There are, however, no salient doctrinal differences between the two tendencies. The fundamental principles, like the Five Pillars (*Arkan*), or the obligation of aggressive jihad that has been revived by the Muslim Brothers, are equally sacrosanct in the eyes of all brands of Islam. Certainly, the existence of moderate Muslims, who are distinguished from the fanatic ones, cannot be denied. However, both advocate the same Islam, respect its same tenets, more or less practice its requirements, and devotedly walk in Allah's path. But those who have chosen the moderate way to practice their Islam do so patiently and with a long-term vision, awaiting the right moment. In the meantime they may be lax on the practice of daily duties, while the others want everything now and have no time for delaying tactics or patience for democratic niceties. The latter are also usually the militant types, those who demonstrate, often violently, call for jihad, and often participate personally in the jihad. The former belong to the silent majority, who would hail Islamic successes when they occur but usually would prefer to stay on the sidelines and deal with their personal business. Even those who entertain relatively liberal or semi-democratic ideas, by instinct or because they had lived in the West, usually elect to keep quiet, knowing what it cost their peers who had the temerity to air their more moderate views in public.

Some misguided Westerners have even gone as far as quantifying the putative difference between the two kinds of Islam, presumably as a way to gain credibility by announcing supposedly "precise and scientific" data. There are claims that about 15 percent of Muslims are radical—militant and jihad supporters. Even if this were true, this amounts to more than two hundred million out of the general Muslim population of 1.5 billion. This in itself would constitute a worldwide threat, thus undoing the intentions of the theory to minimize the impact relative to the otherwise "peaceful and quietist bulk of Muslims," as some misguided politicians (like President Bush and Prime Minister Blair) have dubbed world Islam. Or, perhaps in order to avoid confronting the charge of Islamophobia, these well-meaning theoreticians have elected to limit their criticism of militant Islam to 15 percent of the whole, letting the politically correct do-gooders comfort themselves that the rest of the 85 percent are ideal neighbors who seek only peace and tranquility and therefore can be accepted with open arms in the West when they come in hordes, financed by Saudi Arabia and Qatar, to open mosques and Islamic centers, educational networks, and even hostile and subversive organizations that militate against the very foundations of Western culture and of their host countries.

These naive people are not even awakened by the fact that following every major slaughter of Westerners and/or Jews, the Muslim world celebrates, as when the Twin Towers collapsed in September 2001,[1] and Muslims of all countries, all walks of life, old and young, educated and illiterate, distributed sweets and danced in the streets, boasting about their "outstanding achievements." At the same time, many of their spokesmen shamelessly denied that any Muslims could have committed those heinous acts and attributed them to the CIA, the Mossad, or such. Could anyone who watched those mind-boggling events live or on the TV screen identify—among those children and the worked-up demonstrators in the streets of Casablanca, Paris, Quetta, or Gaza—who was radical, part of those 15 percent, and who was moderate, belonging to the 85 percent majority? One has to remember that the al-Aqsa Brigades, who belong to the supposedly moderate PLO, have performed no fewer acts of Islamikaze[2] against Israelis than the fanatic radicals of Hamas.

Another issue that has been brought up for debate in the context of the Spring has been the question of stability. As conventional wisdom has it, one should not disturb stability, even at the price of abstaining from intervention in areas of conflict or human-rights violations. NATO chose to intervene with air bombing against Qaddafi in Libya, but it has been reluctant to act similarly in Syria. In both places, stability evaporated into a distant memory before the beginning of the turmoil, as it has been in all countries where this drama is unfolding and producing new surprises every day, causing more casualties than occurred during the international wars in the area prior to the Spring. It is then ludicrous when the great powers intervene in the Spring, one way or another, but find ideological justifications to interfere or to refrain from interfering, usually under the same banner of stability. For example, America and the West state their support for democracy and human rights, rushing to apply those principles when one Palestinian complains about a violation by an Israeli act of self-defense, even when those complaints refer to events happening within Hamas territory, where violation of human rights is rife. But at the same time, the West keeps silent when those violations occur on a daily basis in Saudi Arabia, the darkest and most regressive regime in the Arab world.

In Bahrain, where a Spring uprising against the monarch broke out rather early in the process, the autocratic regime—which is backed militarily by Saudi Arabia—did not raise any protest or objection from the West in support of the sacred stability that had to be preserved. But in Libya, NATO airplanes bombed until Qaddafi was removed. How about stability there? If the powers were at least consistent in their support of their friendly, moderate, or pro-democracy allies, for the sake of stability, one could still understand. Prior to the Spring, Qaddafi again became the darling of the West after he gave up his nuclear program, despite having perpetrated the greatest horror by permitting the Pan Am plane to be blown up above Lockerbie, Scotland. But the perpetrator of the horror was released by the British for "humanitarian" reasons. No one in the West questioned Qaddafi's legitimacy after forty-one years of tyranny, because he had provided stability. So, what happened when the rebellion against him erupted, first in Benghazi and then in Tripoli? Did he suddenly lose the legitimacy that he never had? Why did those same powers that befriended him, sold him weapons, and allowed him to plant his extravagant tent in the heart of Rome and Paris end up bombing him to his bitter end?

Similarly, Mubarak—who served the West loyally for three decades, never condoned terrorism, and provided stability in Egypt,—was well known to the Americans. They were aware that he had converted the peace with Israel into a cold peace and that he rigged the elections in his country, at every turn, to get "reelected." But the Americans kept silent for fear that an Islamic alternative might be worse. And then, suddenly, when the Spring broke out, Mubarak became illegitimate, lost favor with the West, and was ejected like a "squeezed lemon," to use an expression of another champion of democracy, Josef Stalin, who was in the custom of using his allies until he needed them no more. The fate of Ben Ali, the president of moderate, stable, and pro-Western Tunisia where the entire process was kindled (literally) was not different. And in order to precipitate the replacement of those tyrants by others, the West did not hesitate to delegitimize its allies of yesteryear, to ally with the new rulers whom they had shunned all those years,

thereby undoing the famous stability they had supposedly been trying to preserve. Ali Saleh, the Yemenite president, suffered the same
lot, while Bashar Assad, the son of Hafez Assad—both of whom were
courted to be brought into the Western loop despite the slaughters
they committed against their own people—were tempted by the most
liberal American administration in a century (Obama) to pursue their
tyranny with impunity. In fact, the Bush presidency had boycotted Syria
and isolated it, forced it to evacuate its troops from Lebanon, cut off
diplomatic relations with it, and threatened even harsher measures,
while under Obama's watch, diplomatic relations were restored to
facilitate "engagement," and Assad's isolation was lifted, so the signal
to the tyrant became clear that he might move as he wished—and he
did—as long as stability was preserved.

When the Spring erupted, the Western supporters of yesteryear
suddenly began demanding the departure of their old protégés before
they could ensure the identity of the successors, and before understanding that stability should not be a blind mantra and that not any stability
was worth pursuing at any price, anywhere and at any time. For there
is a positive stability that supports democracy, legitimacy, and peace;
and there is an evil stability that should be fought and opposed and
shunned. The Soviet regime had provided stability in Eastern Europe
for forty-five years; nevertheless President Reagan had called it "evil"
and acted successfully to bring it down. And so were the regimes of
Mubarak, Asad, Qaddafi, Saddam Hussein, the Iranian ayatullahs, and
their ilk, in spite of being stable and enduring. It is no coincidence that
only regimes that lack total legitimacy, like the Russian and the Chinese,
continue to support recalcitrant tyrants like Assad without worrying
about their legitimacy, which they never had in the first place. Who has
given shelter to Ben Ali, and who is defending Bahrain from the turmoil
of the Spring? Saudi Arabia, whose government also lacks legitimacy—
but due to its illusory stability, the West keeps silent about it, especially
since both Bahrain and Saudi Arabia provide oil to the West.

In sum, the Western delusion that by supporting the Spring they
are preserving stability and cultivating democratization does not have
any legs to stand on. It appears that the winning orientation in many
of these countries will be in the direction of Islamization, which, if it
completely materializes, does not promise either stability or democratization. The reaction so far in the Islamic world is nourished by either
the confused initiatives of the Western world and the deeply seated
suspicions toward it, or conversely by the determined refusal of Russia

and China to accept the seemingly zigzagging and hypocritical nature of Western policies: they support stability and instability, negotiate with civil governments and Islamic fundamentalists, deal with autocrats and revolutionaries, all at once. Developments on the ground are affected by both the domino and the snowball effects. The domino came into play in Tunisia when an unknown peddler set himself on fire because he sensed that his government did not care for the plight of its citizens, something that signaled to next-door Egyptians, Libyans, Syrians, and Yemenites that they might try the same against their respective tyrants to make them flee the country. All those people had watched twenty years earlier, live on television screens, the autocrats of the Soviet Bloc fall one after the other, but they needed a courageous example to remove the obstacle of fear and launch the process—and that happened in Tunisia. The snowball effect worked the moment the flame was kindled in every one of those countries, and others followed suit, while there was no one able to stop it. So far—except for Tunisia where things seem to have settled, though not completely, and in Egypt, which has embarked on that rocky process—in all other countries, twenty-six months after the initial explosion, with the autocrats removed and the realization of the change sinking in, domestic disagreements have been raging as to the alternatives to choose from. Destruction is by nature much faster than construction, and it will take time before we know where this Spring is going to take us, before the enormous task of reconstruction is launched.

These are the issues that we will have to tackle, combining two simultaneous approaches: on the one hand examining thematic problems that cut across all the Muslim states that are experiencing this unrest, thematic problems such as the tribal structure of society, the Ottoman heritage, the impact of globalization and of social networks, authoritarian and caliphal rule, and the like. On the other hand, all Muslim countries in question will be grouped in various blocs according to their shared characteristics (tribal, Shi'ite, revolutionary, monarchical, and republican) in order to discuss them one by one. We shall also check whether the liberal-democratic option is viable in those countries, what kind of regime would be considered legitimate and stable there, and what sort of final settlement would provide the incentives for creativity and development, and perhaps lead the new regimes to placate their innate divisions and rebellious zeal and produce a new peaceful and constructive mood both internally and toward their neighbors outwardly.

Notes

1. See, for example, R. Israeli, *Islamikaze: Manifestations of Islamic Marty-rology*, Frank Cass, London, 2003, especially Chapter 1, which samples the reactions in the Muslim world to the 9/11 horror.
2. For the significance of the term see ibid.

1

The Structure of Arab Society: Tribes and Artificial States

Modern nationalism, which sorts out peoples and nations according to their national belonging and which often cuts through ethnic, religious, linguistic and interest groups, for two centuries has been an invention of the West, which exported it to its previous colonial possessions across the world for emulation as the ideal model for political and administrative organization of people who wished to live autonomously of others under their own sovereignty. These processes have had their impact on the emerging modern Muslim countries as well, when they rid themselves of foreign occupation as colonial possessions of other powers. Today they number some fifty-seven Muslim-majority countries, which are all members of the Conference of Islamic nations across Africa and Asia. But it is far from a forgone conclusion that the new nation-states have been able to cultivate well-rooted, homogeneous, and harmonious Islamic societies. Rather, as evidence in some of these countries suggests, their ancient tribal makeup, their subordination willy-nilly to different Muslim or multicultural empires (the Umayyads, the Abbasids, the Fatimids, the Mameluks, the Mongols, the Ottomans, and the Persians in the Middle East; the Almoravids and the Almohads in North Africa; or the Moghuls in India) left an indelible mark on their history and identity.

Judging by the incredibly easy and rapid collapse of long-standing countries like Libya and Yemen, with Syria to follow, one suspects that this artificial entity of nation-state either did not go deep enough yet into the fiber and consciousness of Arab citizens, or that the ancient tribal identity simply refuses to die out. The idea of nation-state that was born in the West presupposed a collective of individuals who share the same history, territory, culture, and language and are willing to surrender voluntarily some of their individual freedoms and pay taxes to the state, which in return keeps peace and order and governs the

1

country according to the will of the people, who periodically choose the government of their taste. Governments come and go, but the structures and institutions of the state still provide continuity, and every individual regards himself as directly linked to the state and its machinery. But when the will of the people does not count, as under autocracies, and the rulers impose their will without being legitimately delegated by the people to do so—and especially when the artificial state is composed of a medley of various ethnic groups that share little else except territory—then the entire survival of the state is ensured only as long as the tyrant ruler holds the reins. As soon as he dies or is reversed, the pecking order will change, the estrangement between ruler and ruled will grow, and people will naturally revert to their basic tribal fealty, having never felt any belonging and close identity with the state. This seems to have been the case with the countries most typically comprised in the category of the tribal model (Syria, Libya, Yemen), though almost no Arab/Islamic country is totally immune to various degrees of tribalism (Iraq, Morocco, Algeria, Pakistan, Afghanistan, Somalia, and more).

Then add to that the tremendous mosaic of religions—beginning with the major divisions between Sunnites and Shi'ites, and then the sects and subsects that derived from the Shi'a but then went so far afield that they were excluded from Islam (like the Druze, the Alawis, the Bahai), or the members of the many Christian denominations (Copts, Armenians, Greek Orthodox, Maronites, Assyrians, and others)—that are out of place in the Islamic world that had conquered them and evicted them from their lands or assimilated them into the dominant culture. And also add the many ethnic/national groups that inhabit the vast Islamic world (Kurds, Alevis, Turkemans, Assyrians, who despite their Islamization have kept their separate cultures, languages, and customs, and continue to aspire to autonomy). All together, you have a foolproof and fatal recipe that contradicts the requirements of a modern nation-state and makes for perennial political, social, and religious conflicts, jealousies, competitions, and tensions in the lands of Islam, as we have been watching during this Spring.

Thus, to detect the sources of the divisions, differences, and inability in the lands of Islam to bridge these gaps and create harmonious societies where all groups consent to one social contract common to the entire population and share one state of law, under one steady constitution not given to the whims of any dictator, and the judiciary is independent and inspires awe—we have to clarify the fundaments of government common to all Muslim countries that have been surfacing with various degrees of intensity and making any permanent settlement difficult or impossible. Autocracy, the only method that worked so far to keep those countries together, no longer works, and a Western-style democratic and voluntary system seems unattainable in the short run. These fundamentals are historical, traditional, political, psychological, and religious. They were molded for centuries and came to be sanctified; therefore they cannot be changed overnight and have to be recognized and gradually adapted into the modern world. These fundamentals are: the tribal organization of old; the utopia that looks backward; the Islamic political ideology; the all-encompassing nature of civilizational Islam, which has set standards and established yardsticks to gauge everything from political regime to artistic taste and from social activity to individual conduct both at home and outdoors; and, finally, the authoritarian rule that did not permit the development of participatory democracy in the Western style. Some of these aspects will be tackled here.

Tribal Organization in the Prophet's Era

Life in the desert was nearly unbearable in the pre-Islamic era (*jahiliya*); therefore no individual could survive unless he leaned on his family, clan, and tribe, and sometimes on the even wider base of an alliance of tribes. Tribal federations were necessary in order to strengthen one's party in the constant wars for meager pastures in the vast and hostile deserts, or as a measure of defense against threats from the outside. Dependence on the tribal structure was so absolute that a tribal culture was developed with its own laws, traditions, and value systems, which were personified by the head of the tribe (the *sayyed*, the very word for sir or master in modern Arabic) or the sheikh (old man, old age being coterminous with wisdom), who was always expected to be wise in leadership, courageous in battle, judicious in mediating quarrels, and generous as a host at home, all qualities of machismo (*muruwwa*) worthy of emulation. All these qualities were manifested by the chieftain, making him a nearly perfect gentleman, (or a *Junzi* in the classical Confucian tradition). These lofty qualities made the reputation of the leader within his tribe and of his tribe outside of it. The greater and wider the renown of the tribe, the more outsiders would flock to the tribe to seek its protection (*jiwar*), something that would further increase its fame. This ideal, which preceded the time of the Prophet, was incorporated into the Islamic tradition and came to be

3

typically expressed in the persona of the Prophet, the most perfect of men ever living on earth, and this won him his election by Allah as his messenger and as the Seal of Prophets.

In modern times, this ideal model was picked up by many Arab and Islamic leaders, from Sadat of Egypt to Arafat of the Palestinians, for if they were recognized as enjoying one speck of those qualities, they would also be acknowledged as sharing Muhammed's unequalled wisdom and divinely guided leadership. Latter times' federations of Arabs (like the Arab League) and of Muslims (like the Organization of Muslim Cooperation)—and the Arab and Muslim forums in the UN, the African Unity Organization, and the Group of 77—are but an echo of the tribal federations from the times of Prophet, which Arabs and Muslims regard as part of their heritage, with a view of aggrandizing their collective impact in the world and their bargaining power in any world forum. But as in old times, these forums are flimsy and fragile and can be dissolved or rendered impotent (like the Islamic Congress and the Islamic League in the 1930s and 1940s) due to personal or tribal battles and jealousies, with others replacing them, to fit in with the pace of the shifting sands of the desert.

In that illiterate society, where the holy scripture of the Qur'an was transmitted from God to an illiterate messenger, the Prophet's lack of literacy and education did not hurt his reputation but on the contrary enhanced it, for it showed that his genius was so overwhelming that it overcame his technical deficiency in writing and reading. This turns the transmission of Allah's word to him, via the angel Gabriel, into a miraculous event unparalleled in history and never destined to recur. The Prophet's illiteracy could not have encouraged learning, intellectual curiosity, and scholarship among his followers, who grew to believe that everything there was to know was told by the Prophet and about him in the holy book and in the vast literature about him and his life. Hence, whenever there is talk of reform, change, advancement of knowledge and science, intellectual and spiritual development, reference is invariably made to the revival and application of that corpus of traditional knowledge that Muhammed brought to its peak and that constitutes the core of the Islamic shari'a. World Islamic movements, from the Muslim Brotherhood to the international Hizb-ul-Tahrir, from Hamas to the Pakistani Lashkar-e-Taiba, profess the same slogans/mantras, which advocate that "Islam is the solution," or proclaim, "Muhammed is our leader, the Qur'an our constitution, jihad in the Path of Allah our way, and death as *shahids* (martyrs) our most sublime goal."

In general, Islamic societies, which have remained at the bottom of the international scale of human development according to UN surveys, owe that status in no small measure to their fixed ideology, having turned the Prophet and his life in distant Arabia a millennium and half ago into the ideal that cannot be improved upon, thus erecting obstacles on the way to modern and progressive state and society building. In consequence, the emerging alternatives to the crumbling tyrants of the Spring do not seem to hold much promise of extricating those societies from their accumulated multigenerational backwardness. This is only one aspect of the perennial contradiction between the principles of democracy and progress and the revival of political Islam, should free elections produce Islamic parties that would further dig in the past and strive to emulate it. Certainly, Islamic societies also include bourgeois sections that have lived in or visited other countries and have grown modern and Westernized enough to recoil from the prospect of seeing their countries thoroughly Islamized and thrown backward (e.g., Egypt, Turkey, Tunisia, and Iran). It is precisely in those countries that a mammoth struggle has been unleashed between these forces of change and the new Islamic forces that threaten takeover, over the back of the masses, via democratic means of participatory elections—which if successful can also be the last.

The chieftain of the tribe was not alone in the leadership spot. At his side there was a poet (*sha'ir*), who acted as a kind of public relations man and spokesman for the tribe. His role was to preserve the oral records of his tribe, which essentially played and replayed its days of glory. Paradoxically, the *jahiliya* (Era of Ignorance) collections of poetry, known as *Ayyam al-'Arab* (The Chronicles of the Arabs) have been recognized as one of the pinnacles of poetry and literary creation. For want of better, they have also become one of the important sources for the history of that period before the emergence of the Prophet. Again paradoxically, despite its sublime beauty and the richness of its expression, this literature was also stigmatized for smacking of the *Jahili* atmosphere and culture in which it evolved, when humanity was sunken in sin, loss, and disorientation until the messenger of Allah came to bring it salvation. In our context, critiques of contemporary Muslim societies, precisely some of those who kindled the Spring and led it, have accused their countries of having relinquished Muslim values to the point of reverting—Allah Forbid!—to a *jahiliyya*-like condition. Therefore, the remedy today, as of old, has been to readopt the thinking of the Prophet and to migrate, as he did from Mecca to Medina in

AD 622, traveling spiritually if not physically to a purer Islamic society where the revival of Islam might become possible. This is the sense that Islamic Spring leaders wish to give to their popular movements, implying that like the Prophet, after they have revitalized the Shari'a state, the entire world would open up to a world Islamic revolution. Many of those Muslim fundamentalists had tried for years to precipitate this process through violence, but as they were crushed by their tyrannical rulers who were supported by the West, they metamorphosed into peace- and legitimacy-seeking parties, as during the Spring in some countries, and gained as a result the support of world public opinion.

The poet was also the living oral archives of his tribe, for lack of written record. He stored in his mind his tribe's literature, stories, legends, and tales of heroism, in order to raise the morale of his kin, together with tales of other tribes' history that denigrated them as cowards who yielded to his own people's courage. He also was the author of the never-drying fountainhead of new epic tales and poems unfolding as the history of the tribe evolved, whether or not those events occurred or were inventions. In our days, Arab poetry readings still attract masses, and national poets enjoy a great reputation (Darwish and Ziyad, for example, were worshipped by Palestinian nationalists). And often the leaders of Islamic countries use poetry to mobilize the masses. Some of them, like Nasser and Sadat of Egypt, delivered speeches for hours in public squares, acting not only as the chieftains of their countries but also as poets of their tribes, who accuse their enemies of cowardice and heap praise on their own noble people and heroic armed forces. Only in more recent times, due to the increasing requirements of security and the threat of terrorism, did tyrants retreat to their palaces (or tents in the case of Qaddafi) and content themselves with spreading their messages through the state media.

The difference is that in old days the chieftains and poets grew organically out of the tribal milieu, due to their natural gifts, because in that situation it was nearly impossible for anyone to impose himself upon his kin. From many respects, this was a kind of meritocratic order, but instead of the public servants being tested and approved by the authorities (as in ancient China and modern England), the order evolved and was accepted by the elders' consensual silent agreement. Over time, however, as the Umayyads (AD 661–750) and the Abbasids (AD 750–1253) took over and imposed a dynastic order, Islam absorbed the idea of blood inheritance, which received a further boost from the emerging Shi'ites, who based their religion on the concept of the

Twelve Imams. In dynastic succession beginning with Ali, these imams had imputed to themselves the sole right of inheritance of the rule of Islam. The idea of inheriting power rather than competing for it peacefully has taken such deep roots in Islam that even in republican regimes today, the tyrants who saw their masses rising against them during this Spring had destined their sons to inherit their rule after many years of autocratic power: Mubarak of Egypt, Saleh of Yemen, Qaddafi of Libya, Saddam of Iraq. Even in Syria, where the transition of power between Hafez Assad and his son was complete ten years prior to the Spring, it was that continuity that enraged the rebels, among their other grievances.

The chieftain of the tribe and its poet were bound to the concept of honor (*sharaf*). The violation of honor could not be ignored, for otherwise an undefended honor could appear as unworthy of defense and fatally harm the reputation of its owners. Honor was also related to the possession of assets and women, and a violation of either could trigger a chain of hostile acts between the contending parties, because leaving a violated honor unpunished would leave the matter hanging, yearning for a settlement, tied to compensation, or taking the life of a killer (*lex talionis*). This is quite different from the modern idea of retaliation for wrongdoing, or inflicting punishment for it, that derives from the Roman legal tradition. For in ancient Arabia, and in the Islamic world today, the very act of vengeance—for example in case of the violation of a woman's honor or of the killing of someone of another clan—is supposed, *eo ipso*, to calm down the boiling blood of the victim or of the owner of the defiled honor. (Honor killings among Muslim communities are well known not only in the Islamic world, but also in the West.) The idea of retaliation in the modern world, by contrast (e.g., bomb Berlin and Dresden as retaliation for London and Coventry, or Tokyo and Hiroshima as punishment for Nanjing and Manila), is to chastise for what is known as a war crime and to deter recurrence. This retaliation is not motivated primarily by a primal desire to take revenge, but by a calculated consideration to make the enemy pay such a high price for his deed that he is deterred from repeating it. On the personal level, or in cases of inter-family, inter-clan, or inter-tribal rifts, honor killings for a woman's immoral conduct can be accepted and understood in Islamic societies, and these killings occur all too often. But European societies and Israel, where large Muslim populations live, cannot take these murders indifferently, for they are bound in their Roman and Jewish traditions by their civil codes of law to punish any murder. However, when they punish murders as criminal acts of manslaughter, clashes unavoidably occur between the authorities and Muslim minorities, who, based on their own history and tradition, consider themselves entitled to follow their customs. These minorities consider the insistence of the law enforcement agencies on imposing the criminal code to be Islamophobia.

The idea of justice ('adala) in Arab and Islamic societies is also derived from the ancient Bedouin culture of Arabia. Then, it meant the balance between the two sides of the saddlebag on the camel's back. Just as the camel—so essential for the survival of the Bedouin in the desert—should have its saddlebags balanced on its back lest it limp and be unable to stride through the sand, so no Arab can function in daily life if the wrong done to him in his eyes is not redressed. In such societies, justice has never had, and does not have today, objective yardsticks to gauge the damage caused by the enemy or the compensation required to achieve redress. It used, and still uses, only a subjective criterion for measure, and that is the self-satisfaction of the wronged party. Only if he feels that the proper compensation was paid, or a ritual of conciliation (sulha) is held, and his honor is upheld and not humiliated, would he agree to accept the redress. The result is the concept of a "just peace" that is largely unparalleled in other cultures, as if justice had absolute parameters, when in reality what is just for one can seem unjust to another. For example, today, Arabs and Muslims demand a just solution for the Palestinians, which means, in their terms, the elimination of Israel and its replacement by them. And since no country would agree to commit suicide, and a compromise on that cannot be achieved, no peace can be expected.

When President Sadat spoke at the Israeli Knesset in November 1977, he insisted on a "just peace," which should return "every grain of sand of Sinai" to Egyptian possession. It was not because sands are important in themselves, but because what he considered to be *his* should be returned without argument or bargaining, regardless of who started the war where that territory was lost, regardless of who lost the war, and regardless of who should make redress for the damages of the war. Indeed, Sadat would not even have come to Jerusalem had the return of the Sinai Peninsula not been pledged to him a priori. On another occasion, Sadat said that in the Egyptian countryside where he came from, clans used to fight for generations over a useless patch of rocky land, solely because without the justice of returning that land to its owner, peace could not return to the village. On the international level, any Arab leader Israel who engages in early negotiations demands as a first step the return of the entire claimed land (for Syria the Golan, for the Palestinians the West Bank and Jerusalem), short of which no process can even begin. Arabs often demand that justice should be done for their prisoners in Israel by releasing them, regardless of their criminal convictions. They also demand that any incarcerated Palestinian should be set free on Ramadan, because those are days of *haram* (forbidden warfare), regardless of the fact that they launched the October 1973 war on Ramadan, and not to speak of Temple Mount in Jerusalem (*haram al-Sharif*), where they allow no Jew to set his foot, because it is now an exclusively Islamic site, regardless of the place's history. That is justice in their eye. In other words, Muslims are the only ones to determine what is Muslim territory, including Temple Mount, regardless of archeological digs, history, and the claims of other religions. For only Muslim conquests (*futuh*) lend legitimacy to the status of a place, and any other takeover of the same territory by anyone else is ipso facto illegitimate and unjust.

In ancient Arabia there were market towns—like Mecca and Yathrib (turned Medina after the Prophet moved there in AD 622), where Muhammed established his rule; Khaybar, where a thriving Jewish community was deeply rooted well before the times of Muhammed—that were managed by councils of elders (*shura*), in contrast with the wandering tribes that were ruled by their *sheikhs*. The Prophet's friends and closest companions (*sahaba*) also implemented such a *shura* around him, to dispense counsel and comfort, though his final say as the messenger of Allah was binding for all. When he was dying, and more so after his death, this council was the pool from which the first vicars (caliphs) were selected, and until the first ruling dynasties were established, it acted as the supreme authority in the fledgling Islamic state, under the leadership of the serving caliph. This patrimony is still so powerful that any contemporary Muslim state, movement, or organization nominates a *shura* to lead it as its supreme institution. Hamas and the Muslim Brothers in Egypt and Jordan are led by such a council. Many of them regard this institution as the ultimate expression of democracy Muslim style, refusing to listen to Western preaching about the need for democracy, because they claim that the idea of collective leadership was invented in and by Islam. Saudi Arabia—which does not allow any sort of elections, not even rigged ones—preserves the institution of the *shura* (appointed by the king, not elected) as a high manifestation of democracy. Countries such as Egypt, which ran elections under their tyrant regime for many years (rigged at every turn, to be sure) also maintained an appointed *shura* as an upper house, to balance the authority of the parliament in case it was not rigged enough to surrender to the will of the ruler.

And finally, when we look at the complicated tribal situation in the countries affected by the Spring, we can see that in certain places that old structure and those old norms are time resistant and repel the pressure for change in the modern world. In Iraq, where the Spring preceded by one decade its outbreak elsewhere, the Saddam Hussein regime, ended by the American incursion, was replaced by a weaker and less cruel regime that no longer controls the tribes as did the departed tyrant, either through soothing statements or ruthless measures. Add to that the dismantlement of the Ba'ath's extremely coercive rule and of the army that had been the main arm of control of the Saddam regime, and questions have started to arise about the new democratic games that the Shi'ite revolution brought about by the Americans has been trying to enforce, and about the revival of tribalism under its aegis as never before. When Iraq was the Mosul and Basra Districts of the Ottoman Empire, the Shi'ites regarded the other minorities, like Kurds and Turkemans, who were also Muslims, as subjects of the sultan in Istanbul, while the Christian and Jewish minorities' status fell within the general Millet arrangements that applied to the entire extent of the Empire, which meant that the non-Muslim minorities were regarded as autonomous communities in managing their religious affairs. Now that an Islamic Empire is no more, and even the Ba'ath framework has collapsed, minorities are left hanging insecurely in the air, and in the general atmosphere of insecurity, no one can guarantee their future—especially in light (or rather, obscurity) of the massacres of Assyrians in northern Iraq, which the Shi'ite government is unwilling or unable to check. Only the Kurdish situation has improved in the post-Saddam era, since the Kurds have upgraded their autonomous status from the weak central government and have even ensured the presidency of the federal republic through their coalition with the ruling Shi'ites. There is also a question about the longevity of the present system, which through elections has toppled the Sunnite minority rule and, for now, turned over the decisive power in the country from the bullet to the ballot.

In Egypt, which was one of the first sites of the Spring revolution, it turned out very quickly that the Muslim movements of all brands took control of most events, while the military, who took over power in the intermediate period, were trying to rein them in and diminish their increasing demands: first to run to Parliament, then to take it over, then to run to the presidency, then to claim it and hold on to it. To Tahrir Square they rushed the venerated Sheikh Qaradawi, the most important and popular Muslim preacher in the Sunnite world, who did not hide his restorative message to revert to the ancient mold of Islam, thus widening the gap between the Muslim fundamentalists, who constitute the vast elected majority and represent the old conquerors and rulers of the country, and the ancient natives of the land, now the 10 percent minority of the Copts, who are scared stiff of the imposition of a Shari'a law in their land. The rift between the two is not strictly ethnic or tribal but religious, but since the two groups do not intermarry due to religious barriers, they have grown into two rivaling ethnic groups, with Copts fearing increasing harassment by the Muslim fanatics, as in the last years of the rule of Sadat (1970–81) when his image began to fade. In Syria and Lebanon, where communal and religious diversity was managed by the Millet arrangement under the Ottomans, the French Mandate that followed continued to distinguish among the various groups so as to facilitate *divide et impera.* For example, persecuted minorities like the Druze and the Alawites, who were no longer considered part of Islam, were encouraged to embrace military careers in the colonial army so as to be used to control the Sunnite majority. Those minorities, which usually had strongholds, like the Latakiya area on the Syrian coast or the Shuf Mountains in Lebanon, also ensured their survival through their appointment to key posts in the army. After the independence of those countries following World War II, the appointed minority chiefs held onto their military positions in the national armies, and they often reached even the top leadership, like the Alawites of Syria, who were reluctant to renounce their positions during the Spring turmoil lest they be exterminated by a revengeful Sunnite majority rebelling against them. Their world of options does not include the Syrian national interest, but first of all Alawite sectarian interest, which they have been pursuing in the coalition of minorities with various Christian and Druze groups. The Alawites know that if they free the tiger which they are holding tightly, they would be immediately devoured by the enraged animal, hence their apparent readiness to fight to the finish. This is how the tribal tradition, which has been preserved in Syria due to its basic diversity, might enhance the reversion of the country to its tribal origin.

In Libya and Yemen, as in Syria, a very prolonged and destructive civil war was necessary to bring down the tyrant. These countries provide the proof that in tribal societies there is a zero-sum game wherein when some group wins the upper hand, another loses. In Egypt and Tunisia, which are less marked by tribalism, the struggle was shorter and less fierce, because the stakes of survival of one party or another were not as high, and no matter what happened, the country remained one, under one regime or another. But in tribal situations, the elimination of tyranny can also produce the breakup of the political entity. Certainly, the advocates of stability would support the continuity of the nation-states as they were prior to the Spring, but it is not certain that can be achieved. It is a fact that Islamic troublemakers and stability breakers such as al-Qa'ida have infiltrated these tribal countries, seeking to gain something from their dismantlement—but not into the solid nation-states like Egypt, where the local strong armies can still maintain security and resist any foreign challenges. However, it is noteworthy that while Egypt proper can still deal with its security in spite of the Spring, the Sinai Peninsula, which is part of its sovereignty, has been relinquished to those forces of instability that seek confrontation with Israel. Indeed, numerous terrorist attacks have already been launched against Israel from there, and the gas pipeline from Egypt to Israel was blown up fifteen times in the space of one year, before it was finally disconnected in contravention of the long-term gas supply contract between the two countries. The discovery in Israeli waters of vast offshore gas deposits has in the meantime turned the situation around.

The Past as Ideal

The Islamic instinct for restorative reforms every time a revolution looms harks back to the ancient Islamic heritage, with at its center its Prophet, who combined his prophecy with his actual rule of Medina, thus creating, by the grace of Allah, the perfect model of a ruler of the first organized Muslim community, by the most perfect of rulers, who received via the Qur'an, the word of Allah, divine guidance to the ideal way of governance. During his early prophecy in Mecca, all the chapters of the Qur'an that were revealed to him were of an apocalyptic import, predicting that the end of the world was at hand, on the model of the great Jewish prophets, but the moment he migrated to Medina in AD 622 and began serving as the local ruler, the burden of government obliged him to tailor-make new revelations that more resembled the legislative character of Leviticus and Numbers. But once those revelations were sanctified by inclusion in the Qur'an, after the passing of Muhammed, they could no longer be changed or improved upon, especially after the Prophet himself had followed their guidelines. Since then, those prescriptions for good government have been engraved in stone as the ideal Islamic rule for all generations to come—ideal since the Prophet himself practiced them. For, unlike the prophets of Israel who were giant intellectuals, usually inimical to the royal rule and its greatest critiques, Muhammed was himself the ruler, some kind of philosopher-king, who understood the requirements of government and found solutions to them. Moreover, since he practiced that rule under divine inspiration and was himself infallible, his style of government could not have been afflicted by major errors or deviations that would require redress today. Quite the contrary, pretending to amend today what the most perfect of men did, would amount to insulting the wisdom and integrity of the messenger of Allah.

No wonder, then, that the era of the Prophet has become the perfect model for emulation, both spiritually and politically. Granted, after him no one can claim the gift of prophecy since he was the Seal of Prophets; his tradition (sunna) became the ultimate model of emulation, and the greatest scare of all in Islam has been innovation (bid'a—doctrinal, not technical). We change things in order to improve upon them, but if it is determined that the best occurred in the time of the Prophet, then what is the incentive to alter anything? The rationale is that the generations away from the Prophet keep deteriorating. In his time, the companions (sahaba) were second in perfection only to the Prophet himself, but their followers (tabi'un) and more so the followers' followers (tabi'u al-tabi'un), and so on ad infinitum, can only continually decrease in quality the farther they get from the Prophet's times. Therefore, people can no longer attain the hereafter thanks simply to their proximity to the Prophet, but due only to their own piety and good deeds. This is the basis for the doctrine that has been adopted by the two most puritanical schools of law (the Hanbalites and the Malikites), which reject the bida' and claim that after the worthy men who founded all four schools of law had passed away, the inspiration that moved them to legislate and innovate was terminated (namely the gates of ijtihad had been closed); therefore any innovation after them would be hazardous and against good counsel.

Hence the precedents and verdicts of the past remain the exclusive reference for any judicial pronouncement, something that obviously precludes any free and open thinking, divine inspiration having been exhausted on earth. Paradoxically, then, the more the new generations become distanced from the Prophet and in need of new interpretations to meet the challenges and requirements of new modes of life, the more they are denied any such opportunities and have to rely on the irrelevant judgment of the ancients. A classical example is Egypt, which in the 1920s and '30s was more liberal, open, and democratic than today. Indeed, in these days of the Spring, as Islamic opinions and sentiments are reasserting themselves, the remnants of the liberal and democratic voices can hardly go on blocking the dam with their thumb to hold back the threat of the Islamic flood. To this trend there is one major exception, and that is Shi'ite Islam, where the ayatullahs, due to their ongoing link to the Hidden Imam, can still get divine inspiration. This is what enabled Khumeini to lend innovative interpretations to the rule of the mullahs, as part of his *ijtihad* endeavors (see following).

Looking backward at the past and finding in it all sources of wisdom and references to action, all that good and devoted Muslims can strive for today, is to attempt to recreate, in as close a replica as humanly possible, the time of the Prophet, and this is exactly the meaning of the Salafi movements: pious Muslims who strive to emulate the ancestors (*aslaf*), from the generation of the Prophet onward. In Egypt, the Salafiya gained 30 percent of the votes to Parliament and came second only to the Brothers, who secured 45 percent of the electorate. These Muslim tendencies profoundly believe that the truth is embedded in the sayings and deeds of their predecessors, and that pretending to improve upon them is blasphemous—a baseless and vain thought. Hence the tremendous magnetic appeal of those movements throughout the Islamic world that do not advocate any new doctrine, but simply to revive the ancient, venerated, but neglected and forlorn precepts that made the glory of Islam in the past. And unlike the legendary Muslim Brothers, who are equipped with long-term patience and invest in welfare to prepare a solid base for their future rule, the Salafi movements and their likes (the Algerian Armed Groups of the 1990s, the Egyptian Gama'at of the 1970s and 1980s, the Taliban, al-Qa'ida, and their ilk of the 1990s and 2000s) want everything and now, and are often violent in their demand for immediate application of their rule. The Brothers had in the past also embraced that road of impatience and violence in Egypt, Syria, and Jordan, but when they were crushed by the authorities and risked annihilation, they elected to lower their profile and pretend that they had been moderated, giving the false impression to uninitiated foreign observers that they had indeed changed their ways. But now that Muslim Brothers are gaining legitimacy as a consequence of the Spring, they will also gradually revive the venomous discourse of their founding fathers—Hassan al-Banna and Sayyid Qutb, who continue to be deeply venerated throughout the Muslim world—and in practice merge with the Salafis, there being no significant doctrinal and operational gap between them.

No less detrimental for the obstruction of the future by the past, when considering the era of the Prophet the best of regimes and the most perfect of societies, has been the pessimistic state of mind this creates among Islamic peoples when they grow up to believe that the best existed and is gone and is irretrievable; therefore things can only get worse. This does not encourage effort for betterment, initiative, entrepreneurship, but a spirit of fatalism and doom that leaves the individual apathetic, lacking in incentive to move and change, and not attaching hopes to learning, science, and advancement. Even as the Spring proceeds, we watch the rebels against their tyrants not only cursing their oppressors and removing them from power but also doing that in the name of Allah, shouting war cries of *Allah Akbar* (Allah is the greatest) in response to bombardment and shelling by their rulers' artillery and jet fighters. That means that they leave the revolution in the hands of God, while they, who expose themselves on the fire line, are only tools in his hands. It is doubtful whether Lenin or Mao could have achieved their grand revolutions if they had counted on any god instead of taking matters in their own hands, risking their lives and the fate of their nations in the name of the alternative ideologies they pursued.

The Islamic revolutionary passivity, as much as it sounds like a contradiction in terms, continues to lay at the base of the Islamic Spring today. The pessimistic view that all has been decided from above also stands at the foundation of the annual UN reports on social and economic development, which have invariably cast the Muslim countries at the bottom of the world scale, in spite of the fact that these surveys are made by Arab and Muslim scholars who know and understand this hopeless situation—for otherwise the accusation would have smacked of Islamophobia on the part of scholars, who would be accused of ill intent. In these annual surveys, the same sad themes are recurrent; this built-in chronic backwardness is due to Islam and its ramifications—namely the status of women, the lack of human rights and freedom, and the Islamic form of government. The young people who have risen in rebellion in this Spring are aiming specifically at illiteracy, poverty, unemployment, and sickness, which only if eliminated could salvage the situation. Paradoxically, however, the desperate people who ignited the rebellion also support the success of the Islamic parties, whose regressive views and worship of the past have helped generate this accumulated national lagging behind, which it has become urgent to change.

The Foundation of the *Umma*

The tribal structure discussed above, which connoted the absolute dependence of the individual on his family, clan, and tribe for survival, was an almost impassable obstacle for the Prophet when he began spreading his message among the tribes of Arabia. Why would any individual who felt secure and comfortable within his tribe risk his very existence by following a preacher to an uncertain future? The conditions of the desert did not encourage anyone to leave the protective wings of his tribe, hence the meager success of the Prophet at first, except for the first disciples, who followed him in Mecca and then in Medina, and who lived in his proximity and learned to know him as a man they could trust. This is where the genius of the Prophet came to full expression: when he convinced the tribal heads to accept the Islamic call, most members of the tribe followed suit, a sort of collective undertaking. In the beginning this facilitated the process of conversion in Arabia, but later it caused the bloodiest war in the history of early Islam upon the death of the Prophet, when most of the tribal chieftains reneged on their personal fealty to the deceased messenger of Allah and refused to transfer it to his successors. Then, the first caliph of Islam, Abu Bakr, had to sink his two years of rule in a bloodbath against the renegades (*murtadd*), which became the basis for the death penalty against any Muslim who relinquishes his faith.

The *ridda* (apostasy) war has remained carved in the consciousness of all Muslims to mean that rebellion against the ruler is harshly punished by death, something we observe every day as the Spring unfolds. Since *Islam* means literally submission (to the will of Allah), anyone who seems to defy that principle cannot escape death. We have seen many heads cut off by fanatic Muslim groups (like al-Qa'ida, the Taliban, abu Saif in the Philippines, and the Janjaweed in the Sudan, or the Armed Groups in Algeria, who ruthlessly killed even other Muslim rivals who were accused of *ridda* or heresy). The ongoing massacres in Syria, which are perpetrated by the opposition in the name of Allah and by the ruler in the name of his prerogative to rule—like the terrible slaughters in Libya until Qaddafi fell; the tribal strife that is still brewing in Yemen; the almost daily explosions against other Muslims in Pakistan, Afghanistan, and Iraq, with hundreds of victims in all those places, which do not seem to bother anyone, and which are perpetrated without regard to human life and met by silence and indifference in the rest of Islamic world—seem to express the continuity of those mass killings in Islamic history. That is the reason why instead of looking inward into their atrocities, of which they are unable to cure themselves, they direct their ire against America and NATO for their slaughters in Iraq and Afghanistan and against Israel, for its claimed "massacres" of the Palestinians, even when, in comparison, the horrors they purposely commit of their own volition against their own people generate tenfold the victims that the West or Israel, as a rule, cause unintentionally in collateral damage to other Muslims.

The second stroke of genius by the Prophet was his creation of the universal *umma*, an integrated supra-tribal community that guaranteed those who joined Islam that they would be protected and provided for, just as in their original tribes, thus encouraging them to relinquish their tribes and follow him. The growing Muslim community was no longer a matter of tribe or locale, but an all-encompassing and in the course of time universal community, which like the ancient ecclesia—where every new Christian convert became a member—turned into one organ in its body. In the outset, when the community was confined to Medina, all Muslims felt close, like members of the same city; they knew and trusted one another like the members of their original tribe to which they felt committed. And in order also to rely on them economically, the *umma* created a fund, called for the *zakat* (alms, which was in reality a tax) to be imposed on all members, which provided a public treasury to sustain the community. The *zakat* became the fourth Pillar (*rukn, pl. arkan*) of Islam (the others are the declaration of Allah's unity, prayer, fast and pilgrimage), which, when repeated daily by each believer, became a sort of validation of their membership in the *umma*. This revolutionary device, which entrusted to the leadership of Islam a permanent source of income for the needs of the community, both encouraged and hastened its growth and also serves today as a powerful argument in the hands of fundamentalist Muslims who refer to it as the first democratic endeavor by the Prophet of Islam, establishing the first social welfare system. It constitutes an incentive to return to the early days of Islam as a model of an ideal regime, as Salafi Muslims would have it.

These days, as modern taxation systems have replaced *zakat*, the latter is no longer levied in most Islamic countries; it became voluntary alms contributed to the treasury of Muslim associations for their charitable activities, real or as a cover to terrorist organizations, or disbursed by donors for specific needs, like hospitals, orphanages, mosques, and the like. Muslim associations have also learned to accommodate donors who are short of cash by accepting their payments in kind: building materials from builders, food and clothes from merchants, expertise from professionals like doctors, lawyers, and accountants, and labor by skilled workers. In this way, organizations like the Muslim Brothers and their affiliates could finance and run their operations in the days when they were banned from power and often persecuted by the authorities. In this fashion, they and other Muslim associations could accumulate the large pool of public goodwill toward themselves, which paid off when the Spring was launched. The masses that appeared in the public square and celebrated Islam and mobilized a million people to welcome Sheikh Qaradawi in Tahrir Square at the outset of the Spring, came from these social strata, which had known poverty and despair and owed much to the Muslim associations for their survival. Naturally, these are also the masses that stream into the streets to voice support for the Brothers or shout: *Allah Akbar*!

The Islamic Political Theory

We have looked at several aspects of the tribal society preceding Islam, which have marked Muslim societies down to the turbulences of the Spring. But we must also be aware of the crystallization of some of these customs and practices when Islam began its conquests and expansion immediately subsequent to the death of the Prophet (AD 632), when the political theory of Islam united all the bits and pieces into one doctrine. The need for a doctrine grew out of the imperative of determining what should be done with the vast territories that were overrun by the Muslim zealots who sprang out of the desert to conquer the world, and with the medley of populations that were encountered, subjugated, and had to be ruled according to the new standards set by the victorious religion of Allah. The doctrine created an entire new political vocabulary of international relations that thereafter came to govern the relationship of Islam with the world. It is still being evoked today by the fundamentalist Muslims who dream of renewing the momentum of Muslim conquests as of old. It goes without saying that the champions of the Muslim Spring are at the forefront of this revival of the terminology and symbols that Islam had created in its heyday.

The Spring has also been harking back to the beginnings of Islam with regard to the internal functioning of the Muslim state, which is the main theme discussed among the leaders of the Spring: who will hold the reins of power, what is the source of legitimacy of the ruler and the legislation, will Shari'a law and its experts among the clerics have the upper hand over civil law and institutions, and whether and how much should be retained from civil legislation in the projected Shari'a state. From past experience and history, Muslim jurists and historians have learned that the more puritanical the Muslim state was, the more it depended on the clerics. For while the state provided protection and finances to the clerical establishment, the latter assured in return the legitimacy of the ruler and the ideological underpinnings of the state, while also controlling public morality in the public square. In this fashion, the renowned Muslim dynasties (Umayyads, Abbasids, Fatimids, Mamluks, Ottomans) had operated in the Middle East, the Western Umayyads in Spain, and the Almoravids and Almohads in North Africa. In more recent times, the Hanbalites in Saudi Arabia and the Shi'ites of Iran, and for a time the Taliban of Afghanistan and the Turabi-Bashir alliance in Sudan, also functioned in a similar fashion, when the symbiosis between secular rule and religious doctrine seemed operational.

On the international level the newly shaped Islamic doctrine spoke in imperial terms about conquest and expansion as of a right, compared with today when all countries have to pay lip service to the world order, which does not justify overstepping other countries' borders. Only movements like al-Qa'ida, which do not have any governmental responsibility, can emit bold and aggressive noises against others, while governments, even those subordinated to clerical rulers, fear that defying the rules of international conduct can result in their ejection from the world community. Thus, all emerging Islamic movements who have attained power or are vying for it have announced their respect of all international obligations of their country, though in private they had declared their intentions to revise those commitments—for instance, to abrogate their peace treaty with Israel. For them, Israel is a minor actor in world affairs; therefore there is no great risk in challenging her, in pledging to wipe her off the map, as Iran has repeatedly done, or in boycotting her—for no one has moved to exclude from the UN those intransigent Islamic members who proffer those threats.

The particularly hostile attitude of the Islamic world toward Israel has also been founded on the time of the Prophet, when during his rule in Medina he encountered four Jewish tribes which had lived there from time immemorial, and whom he hoped to convert to his cause.

As they refused, some of them were slaughtered, others were Islamized, and others were expelled from the city. These historical memories are preserved in the Qur'an and other Islamic writings, and even in Islamic countries that have made peace with Israel (Egypt and Jordan), Imams in the mosques keep repeating every Friday the quotations from the Qur'an that evince a deep and foundational hatred against Jews, and contempt of them and their culture, or cite abominable words of incitement against Jews and Israel, words that in any civilized country would be considered racial hatred and prosecuted accordingly. It is only natural that the rank and file of Muslims, including the more educated among them, keep repeating those insults as facts and keep transferring those heinous anti-Semitic stereotypes into Zionism and Israel. Bin Laden, for example—like Yussuf Qaradawi, the most respected Muslim scholar and preacher in the Sunnite world—usually spelled out anti-Semitic broadsides against Jews, Zionism, and Israel, and drew endlessly from the delusory pool of anti-Jewish hatred that has accumulated in the Islamic tradition and became part of the Islamic heritage. So much more so during the Spring.

2

The Ottoman Heritage

For four long centuries the Ottoman Empire ruled most of the Arab space where the Spring is taking place today; therefore it is essential to examine the heritage of that rule as it plays out in contemporary events. This is especially true given that the Ottoman government from Istanbul has become fixated in Middle Eastern minds as the last imperial system under which the entire area was one—divided into various districts (*vilayet*) to be sure, not necessarily overlapping the present-day geographical and political boundaries. At the same time, like the preceding Umayyad and Abbasid dynasties that ruled the core of the same space, the Ottomans had entertained the ambition of extending their dominion over all Muslims, in order to bring under their umbrella the entire *umma*. Under Muslim empires the ambition was also cultivated among Muslims, which developed into a precept, that Muslims should endeavor to live in a Muslim state, because only there can the ambition of realizing the will of Allah in everyday life come to full fruition. But it became evident that the more expansive the territory under Islam, and the larger the volume of peoples, cultures, religions, and languages it came to dominate, the more difficult it became to maintain one central rule in those vast areas.

It then became inevitable for the Emperors to appoint trusted governors to represent them in far-flung areas. Due to the distances and the slow and difficult means of communication of the time, these governors tended to accumulate local power for themselves, and when they became enamored with it, they sometimes rebelled against their sovereigns and declared their own sultanates, or even attempted to launch attacks against the capital of the Empire. Thus, when the first kingdom was founded in Damascus, it did not last beyond ninety years (661–750) before the Abbasids of remote Iraq and Persia took over and moved their capital to Baghdad. That dynasty nominally ruled for five hundred years (750–1259), but practically for only two hundred years, before its authority was gradually eroded by small principalities that turned the once awesome caliphs in Baghdad into puppets in their hands, until the Mongols took over and brought down the entire structure. At the same time that those first two dynasties constituted the center of gravity of the Muslim empire, rivals rose to challenge its authority—in north Africa and Spain, then in Egypt and Persia, who regarded themselves as equal and worthy challengers to the caliph. Thus, throughout the generations, the tension persisted between the central caliphs and the peripheral sultans, whose dominion extended from Central Asia to the Atlantic Ocean and created such sultanates as the Almohads of Morocco, the Mamluks in Egypt, the Timurids in Bukhara, or the Samanids in Persia.

Similarly, Turkish tribes invaded from Central Asia after they converted to Islam, thus injecting new energies into Islam's tired and vanishing stamina, and gradually gnawed at the Anatolian plateau, then under the Byzantines, until they occupied illustrious Constantinople and converted it into Istanbul. From there they advanced into the Balkans and came ultimately to encompass the entire Arab space under their rule, until due to the extent of the territory, and perhaps following the example of the Roman Empire, they came to divide their vast territories into the East (*mashreq*), which included Asian lands, and the West (*maghrib*), in north Africa. The Ottomans were not, however, left to monopolize on their own the Muslim empire. Contemporaneous with them, and apart from the many other smaller sultanates and principalities in the Middle East, Central Asia, and North Africa, another powerful and fabulously rich Muslim empire rose in India, known as the Moghul (sixteenth to nineteenth centuries), which lagged in nothing behind the Ottomans either in conquests and empire or in splendor and glory. Its mighty and illustrious emperors, Akbar, Shah Jehan, and Aurangzeb, were in no manner inferior to Mehmet the Conqueror and Suleiman the Magnificent—so much so that to this day, it is still difficult to say which of them left a longer trail of fame and legend.

There is little doubt that much of the essence, stamina, and inspiration of the Spring draws from the Ottoman patrimony, whose traces are still identifiable in practically all those countries in all administrative, organizational, conceptual, constitutional, and social domains a full one hundred years after its end. During the Ottoman rule (sixteenth to twentieth century), there were no signs yet of the emergence of modern nationalism in the territories that constituted part of the faltering empire since the nineteenth century. People's identity then focused on locale (town or village, or area of pasturage) and on the

Muslim empire that encompassed them all. Any Arab from Palestine, Egypt, or Iraq who was asked to identify himself would certainly have responded that he was Muhammed the son of Mustafa, from a certain village, and subject of his majesty the sultan in Istanbul. For him, the legitimacy of the sultan's rule, and his natural disposition to accept it and swear by it, all stemmed from the knowledge that it was an Islamic Empire, headed by a Muslim sultan, which was there to care for the entire Muslim community. Whether Turk, Arab, Kurd, or Bosniak, he would have considered the incumbent overall ruler as an heir and continuation of the previous Muslim dynasties whose name and glory was preserved in folktales and popular culture.

Indeed, save for Morocco and a few other exceptions that preserved their independence thanks to their closure to the outside world, the rest of the Maghreb (Algeria, Tripolitania, Cyrenaica, and Tunisia)—once they fell under the attacks of the Spaniards and Portuguese after the Muslims were finally expelled from Granada (1492)—appealed to the Muslim power of the time, which sat in Istanbul, to come to their aid. Thus, the Arabs of North Africa, who sat on the far fringe of the Empire, not only were ready to accept the Ottoman yoke, but they cried for it as the only way to avoid Christian occupation from Europe. The Ottoman sultanate at the time of Suleiman the Magnificent (1520–1566) had developed the best and most powerful Mediterranean fleet to defend its territories, which included the entire eastern shore and most of the southern coast, almost turning that sea, as in Roman times, into a Turkish *mare nostrum.* Is it a coincidence that two of those North African countries (Tunisia and Libya) became the launching pads of the Spring? There is no doubt that the strong Islamic base built there by the Ottomans (and the local powerful dynasties of the Almoravids and the Almohads) was a key element in the outbreak of the Spring.

In the Middle East, when the Mamluk governor of Yemen surrendered to the Ottomans in 1517, the entire Arabic-speaking East fell to the Ottomans, although in 1630 the Yemenite-Zaydis fighters once again achieved their independence. It was not a national, nor even proto-national revolution to achieve independence, but rather a religious uprising, because the pro-Shi'ite Zaydis could not accept the rule of a Sunnite dynasty. Even the Sherifs of Mecca who claimed descent from the Prophet, had recognized the suzerainty of Istanbul, though Ottoman forces did not have to occupy the holy cities of Islam to enforce their rule. However, the Bedouins outside the Hijaz remained rebellious as in the Prophet's days, keeping their autonomy in the inaccessible desert. By contrast, Egypt and Syria gained the status of a privileged district, even though they were ultimately included in the Empire, and their former Mamluk rulers were defeated by the Ottomans while their Arab population looked indifferently on the change of government. The Empire itself tended to regard its Arabic-speaking peoples as somehow privileged due to their use of Arabic, the holy language of the holy book, and due to most of them being pure Sunnite Muslims. This feeling of privilege in Egypt survived the fall of the Ottoman Empire for nearly one century, and Egypt is still considered the main Arab country. For the past millennium it has been the location of al-Azhar, which is still venerated in the Sunnite world as the most authoritative spiritual institution, and as the headquarters of the Arab League since in foundation in 1945. Egypt has also remained the main arbiter in matters of war and peace, that no other Arab country would dare to undertake without her, and also the supreme standard-setter of film, theater, the arts, science, literature, and the media. Syria, by contrast, always saw itself as the capital of Arab nationalism, the heart of Arab revolution, the champion of Palestinian rights, and part of the main front of confrontation with Israel.

The privileged attitude toward Arabic as the language of the holy book was also the reason why the Ottomans did not Turkefy the Arabic-speaking areas of the Empire. Even though Arabic was the official language of the administration, many young people from across the Empire studied Turkish and went to Istanbul to pursue advanced studies. The state did appoint its own Turkish officials to high positions like provincial governors to the Arabic-speaking areas, but unlike their Mamluk predecessors, who settled in their governorate and soon assimilated, the Turkish bureaucrats kept apart and cultivated their dominant Turkish identity. Upon completion of their tour of duty they either moved to their new appointment or relocated to the Turkish heartland, which following its occupation from the Byzantines underwent thorough Turkification and Islamization. Moreover, in view of the fact that local government remained in the hands of the local Arab *sheikhs* and *ulama* (*'umda* in Egypt), Arabic kept its position as the language of the notables in the villages and of the adjudication of personal affairs. It was only in the nineteenth century, when central government began to falter, that antagonism developed between Turkism and Arabism, as ethnicity and linguistic and cultural identity started to develop into nationalism, and into the centrifugal forces that would ultimately dismember the Ottoman Empire. Only then, while the Turks were trying to force Turkish as the language of education (except for religious studies, where Arabic remained unchallenged) at the expense of local languages (as they have been doing in Kurdistan since the beginning of the Republic), did the contention between Arabic and Turkish erupt full-blown. It was precisely the previous coexistence between Turkish and Arabic that permitted smooth Turkish rule over Arab lands for four centuries, and which was facilitated, to be sure, by the proximity of many ethnic groups under the protection of Islam and by the feeling of being subjects of the mighty Ottoman Empire which the West feared so much at the time.

That situation would reverse only in the nineteenth century, bringing to its culmination a slow process of deterioration following the Ottoman defeat at the gates of Vienna (1683) and the emergence of the European powers that threatened Ottoman possessions in the West. Western intervention in Ottoman affairs started with the status of the Christian minorities throughout the Empire. Indeed, when the Empire had conquered its vast territories, it encountered large populations of Christians, who felt they had become strangers in their own country, but at the same time they were not counted as equal subjects of the sultan since they were not Muslim. Those minorities came under the device of the *Millet*, which was not much different in essence from the *dhimma* under which scriptuary peoples had been treated under all earlier Muslim governments, from Morocco to India. Namely, they were considered second-rate citizens and had to pay a poll tax, the *jizya*, in return for protection (*dhimma*) by the Islamic ruler in place. Similarly, the *Millet* enabled them to run their communal life and to enjoy autonomy regarding their personal status and the administration of their communities, for any legal clash with a Muslim was bound to end in the Muslim's favor. However, one has to observe the difference that existed then between the Muslim and the Christian worlds. While Christians relentlessly and cruelly persecuted their dissidents and minorities, for they recognized no independent existence except within the Catholic Church, Muslims had adopted a theory that divided society into three slices: the dominant Muslims, who were full-blown subjects; the scriptuaries (Christians and Jews), who occupied an intermediate position and were protected as long as they submitted to the *dhimma* rules; and then the pagans, who could choose only between conversion to Islam or extinction.

Based on these distinctions, the Ottoman state sorted the non-Muslims according to their communal faith into various categories, or

Millets, while under other Muslim states, like the Mamluks and the strict dynasties of North Africa, Christians and Jews were forced to convert or were so harshly persecuted that in some locations they were totally eliminated. It all depended on the mood of the ruler or the style of the ruling dynasty, in spite of the Islamic doctrine that in theory recognized their existence and obliged the ruler in place to protect them as long as they accepted their inferior status under Islam and paid their poll tax. In the Ottoman Empire, though the laws of the *dhimma* were part of the Shari'a and could not be formally repealed as far as second-rate nationality and payment of the poll tax were concerned, the *Millet* framework enabled Jews and Christians to go on with their own lifestyles, and even succeed and flourish, and sometimes even attain the highest corridors of economic and social influence, while remaining impervious to the passing negative whims of the ruling sultan. Conversely, in times of crisis and uncertainty, like when war broke out, uncontrollable horrors could also occur, like the massacre of the Armenians in World War I, or the arrest, execution, or expulsion of Jews from Palestine during the same period, or transfers of populations from the Caucasus to the Middle East, and other such calamities.

The Turks, who had adopted Islam relatively late, about half a millennium after the Prophet, escaped unscathed from the major misfortunes that had afflicted Sunni Islam with the fall of Baghdad to the Mongols and the clashes with the Crusaders. It is possible, as it is widely believed today, that thanks only to that injection of fresh Turkish blood into the moribund Sunni Islam has it evaded sharp decline. One can imagine how today's Muslim world would have responded had it been rescued not by Sunnite Turks but by a Shi'ite dynasty like the Fatimids of Egypt or the Isma'ilis who have found refuge in the Indian subcontinent. It was only thanks to the constant rebellious struggle of the Shi'ites of Iran against the Ottomans that those few enclaves of the Shi'a survived in Iran, Iraq, and the Gulf coast, while throughout the Empire the Sunnite consensus grew so predominant that the few centers of Shi'ism that had existed in Egypt under the Fatimids were almost wiped out. Moreover, the Sunna-Shi'a controversy, though not symmetrical due to the huge disproportion of 85 percent to 15 percent between the contenders, went on escalating once the determined Shi'ites showed their capacity to establish their own dynasties (the Fatimids in Egypt, the Safavids in Iran)—so much so that *taqiya*, the precaution of adopting a low profile by the minority Shi'ites among the Sunnites so as to survive, grew into a tenet in the Shi'a that assured its self-preservation.

In our days of the Spring, Iran is the main country where it all started, with the uprising against the shah, thirty years prior to its explosion in the Arab world. And despite Iran's continuing alienation by much of the rest of the Islamic world, the Islamic Revolution of 1978 in Iran was accompanied by an amazing overture toward the Sunnites, declaring a World Islamic Revolution that was supposed to unite the entire Muslim *umma* against the West, which had been the main pillar of support of the departed Shah. The Revolution marked some successes too: in Lebanon; in Iraq; in the Gulf, where large Shi'ite communities reside; and even in Egypt, the largest Arab-Sunnite country, where the number of converts to Shi'ism was estimated at one million since the Iranian Revolution. Then, as the Shi'a became a menacing challenge, and no longer only an annoying tease, the Sunni-Shi'i competition grew fiercer, turning into open hostility, especially due to the nuclear weapons that Iran is determined to build. Sunni clerics have characterized the Shi'ites as "worse than Jews," a compliment that no Iranian would find laudable.

The bottom line is that despite the fact that the Ottoman state was founded and managed by Turks—and despite being dubbed by Europeans, in an insulting way, as the Turkish Empire—it was founded as and remained to its last day an Islamic Empire, encompassing all the Arabic-speaking world of those days, in addition to the Turks and many other Muslim peoples on its fringes, though like any empire it aspired to universal rule. In day-to-day business, there was no mention of Turk, Arab, or other, because the identity focus was Islam. Some Spring countries of our days, which pride themselves on their Arabism, previously considered *Arabs* to be the nomadic Bedouins in the desert, exactly as the Ottomans regarded the *Turks*—with the same disparagement—as the nomadic people of Anatolia. At the same time, the ruling elite, who spoke Turkish, regarded itself as Muslim, and a servant of the Muslim Ottoman Empire first and foremost. Moreover, since the sultanate was the central institution of the Empire, the idea of *"L'etat c'est moi"*—usually attributed to Louis XIV of France—had been implanted there well before, as had earlier been the custom in the Byzantine Empire, which the Ottomans had gnawed at until its final collapse with the fall of Constantinople. Today it is difficult to establish with certainty whether in the previous Arab world, or in the one now emerging as a result of the Spring, there has ever been a desire to put any Ottoman ruler on a pedestal as a model to emulate—not even the greatest among them like Murad I, Bayazid (the Lightening), Mehmet II (the Conqueror), or Suleiman the Magnificent. Many now-deposed

Arab dictators pretended to take Attaturk as their model of moderniza-tion, Westernization, and self-strengthening, geared to turn their own countries into local powers. But they were probably more impressed by the iconization of the mythical father of their own new republic; they put him at the apex of power and admiration, with attending personality worship, even if that implied a return to an ancient history not their own, in order to legitimize their rule by drawing from the deeply rooted civilization that preceded the Ottoman Empire. Thus did Saddam Hussein skip with agility over the Ottoman heritage and directly connected himself to the Hammorabi tradition, and Sadat did the same with the pharaohs of Egypt, claiming to preside over the most ancient civilization on earth, while Arafat kept referring to his Cana'anite "ances-tors." But when the Spring broke out, and the new propensities toward Islam surfaced, then the Islamic traditions of the Prophet, the caliphate, the Salafiya, and in time also the Ottomans became fashionable.

The Ottoman Empire had also established a lasting precedent, usu-ally followed by the states that stemmed from it, of striking a balance between Shari'a laws and state laws dubbed *Qanun*, trying all the while to create the impression that no contradiction existed between them, though everyone knew that one originated from Allah and therefore could not be amended or questioned and certainly not abrogated, while the second was man-made and therefore subject to change, amend-ment, and abrogation. Thus, without coming out publicly against the Shari'a as Attaturk had done, Arab leaders of the pre-Spring era had to walk three parallel paths, depending on the degree of Shari'a dominance they cared to emphasize and to carry out in practice: The most pious and puritanical states—like Saudi Arabia, Yemen, and others—continued to swear by the Shari'a as the only source of legislation; that is, they obligated themselves not to innovate, all having been said and written already in the Qur'an and the sunna, thus candidly acknowledging that there was no need for parliaments or other elected bodies. The less conservative, who wished to at least appear modern and innovative to a point, have elected parliaments, under certain restrictions of rigging and appointing people to carry out the rulers' legislative plans. They stated that the Shari'a would be the main source of legislation, leaving some leeway to deviate from Islamic norms according to the needs of the ruling tyrants. This was the policy of Sadat of Egypt, some North African countries, and part of the Gulf states. At the lowest level oper-ated revolutionary regimes, like those of Nasser, Assad and Saddam, or Westernized ones like Tunisia, who adopted Shari'a only as one of the sources of legislation, taking liberty to act as they deemed fit, while in the sensitive field of personal status (marriage, divorce, inheritance, adoption) the *qadis* (religious judges) were left free to act as of old. Now that Islam has been gathering strength as a result of the Spring, one has to assume that Shari'a-based legislation might be enforced, though gradually, in order to prevent the rage of the bourgeois urbanites who got so used to the comforts of modern life and to the relatively lax policies in the public square that they will be first required to return to the fold, as a prerequisite to the much-hailed reconstitution of the universal caliphate. Only then might the Ottoman model take its place in the gallery of options open in the post-Spring era, to show that a revived caliphate can act as a powerful Muslim country for centuries, together with adopting the trappings of modernity and inspiring international awe and respect.

The Ottoman Empire also bequeathed as part of its heritage the personal fealty of the military men that it cultivated, through the *devshirme*, and the military education they received in the Janissaries corps, where the administrative and military elite was recruited, and some of whom have even attained the position of wazir (the head of the executive branch of government). Most of them served as infantry battle–hardened fighters in the elite units, and their numbers consistently grew from thousands to tens of thousands, and paradoxically, the deeper the Empire began to sink at its decline, the more recruits enlisted. The Young Turks, who from 1909 practically managed the affairs of the state, were themselves military officers, who in spite of their universal imperial tradition were also aware of the national sentiment that emerged among them. Some of them also developed a special relationship with Germany, especially under Mahmud II, into a strategic and ideological concept, as a countermeasure to the expanding Russian takeover of Turkish-speaking territories. For example, Central Asia and the Caucasus, which were taken over by the expanding Russian Empire and annexed to it, came to be regarded as a hostile entity, which eventually dragged Turkey into alliance with the Axis Powers in World War I. On the other hand, it was this new and young national movement that provided an option to the survival of the new Turkey after its rout in the Great War. That tradition of the military taking over the rule of the country, or at the very least participating in it, especially in time of crisis, was pursued in most Arab countries that gained independence following the collapse of the Empire. For it turned out that in the Empire, as in the Arab countries that emerged from it, the army was the most modern, organized, and strong element that could draw the land together and maintain it as one unit, and at the same time could encourage local nationalism (*wataniyya*), in Egypt, Iraq, and Syria, the moment the all-encompassing ethnic/tribal Arab nationalism (*qawmiyya*) started to evaporate when Faisal bin Hussein was expelled from Syria by the French and crowned in Baghdad under British protection instead.

Practically all the revolutions and coups mounted in Islamic countries following World War II—from Egypt to Iraq, from Libya to Yemen, whose peoples were to rise up in the Spring of 2011—were generated by military elites who took over the rule of their countries and were in no hurry to return it to civilian hands. When they did, they ensured that strong parts of the government remained under their control. In republican Turkey, the army kept the constitutional right to dismiss the elected civilian government and replace it when it considered the Attaturk heritage violated or endangered. Indeed, since the 1960s the army removed the elected government and took over the rule on four occasions, and in 1998, after less than two years in government, the elected Islamic government of Necmettin Erbakan was dismissed and his party outlawed. And yet, that government was dubbed "democratic," meaning that words do not necessarily reflect reality. Only when Tayyip Erdogan's party ascended to power in 2002, he took the precaution of removing the army from its privileged position and charged the military of mounting a conspiracy to take over the elected government. This resulted in lower esteem toward the army in the eye of public opinion, and its replacement with his own people, who would not dare to contradict their leader's political line. That too was called "democracy." In Syria and Yemen, the army's loyalty to the regime caused the Spring to last so long, resulting in so many casualties. Only when the army crossed the lines in Egypt, Tunisia, Libya, and Yemen and started to show cracks in its absolute loyalty to the regime were the previous rulers inclined to yield to the Spring or to negotiate their future. In Bahrain, it was only the direct intervention of the Saudi military that has quelled, for now, the uprising of the Sh'ite majority, and in Saudi Arabia itself, only the appointments to the high bureaucracy among the Saudi family have so far prevented a long-overdue explosion there too. For the moment, the Saudi regime is surviving, despite its oppressive nature, because neither the United States nor any other Western country vying for human rights has firmly expressed itself in favor of a change.

While Iran and Iraq have preceded the current Spring by a few decades, in Egypt the awakening came one and a half centuries earlier, in the times of Muhammed Ali, who understood that the Ottoman Empire was disintegrating. He took the initiative to cause a revolution in that country against the powerless Ottomans who were losing their grip on their rule. It is no coincidence that Egypt also remained in the forefront of the Arab awakening in the 1950s, with the Young Officers leading up front, and again in the 2011 situation, which had its roots in the nineteenth century, as unrest never completely vanished there. Ali was an Ottoman official, not even of Arab origin, but he took advantage of the vacuum left by the temporary Napoleonic occupation, aided by many Egyptians who had had enough of the constant competition between the weakening Ottomans and the vestiges of the vanishing Mamluks, to build an impressive military power. This allowed him to rid himself of the Ottomans and launch a rapid modernization, which enabled him to hold to power for forty years and achieve the dramatic advance of his adopted country, and even expand into Palestine and Syria. Nominally, he was only the governor of Egypt, but having achieved the unchallenged rule of those territories, and since the Empire was unable to dethrone him, he was able to establish a dynastic rule that only ended during the Officers' revolution in 1952. His successors had become Egyptians for all intents and purposes, and their removal was not caused by their alien roots, but by their corruption and unduly privileged rule. There is no doubt that it was Ali who eliminated the Mamluk rulers before he embarked on the strengthening of Egypt and its acquisitions, in a fashion that would have generated admiration today, as it did then. He enforced economic reforms in agriculture, industry, especially military, and introduced a series of administrative reforms that made his country's bureaucracy more effective. Militarily, he set up his modern army and in 1833 the first foreign office in Egypt, in practice detaching himself from the sovereignty of the monarch in Istanbul. That is, even though today's Egyptian leadership does not openly acknowledge the precedents established by Ali, they cannot deny them, nor the revolutionary spirit he courageously and imaginatively introduced.

Even since the Empire disintegrated after World War I, and the idea of the caliphate was laid to rest (the sultan being the last of the caliphs), a mighty instinct remained among the Muslims to restore their corporative power of bringing together under one umbrella hundreds of millions of Muslims through an international Muslim institution of some sort. For years, fruitless attempts were made to establish an Islamic League or an Islamic Congress in order to bridge the gap between the reality of division and weakness and the dream of power and unity. But in every instance the attempt was scuttled due to personal or regional competition between various Muslim leaders and states, each of which had good reasons to wish to head the organization: either they were stronger, larger, the most populated, the curator of the Holy places, or headed by the most prestigious rulers. In 1969 all that changed when a lunatic Australian Christian, Michael Rohan, tried to put fire to the Aqsa Mosque in Jerusalem and caused a worldwide Muslim outrage against Israel, despite the fact that it rushed to extinguish the blaze and to punish the culprit. Then, the Morocco king convened a Muslim conference in Rabat in which only half the Muslim states participated, but the corporative feeling of the Islamic world was rekindled by the sight, on television screens, of the heads of Muslim states walking side by side and putting up a show of unity. The importance of that conference did not lie only in its convening but in the fact that it was institutionalized, and since then an annual meeting of the representatives of fifty-seven Muslim states comes together to proclaim Muslim power in world affairs. Since that first meeting at the level of heads of state, the annual assembly has brought together the foreign ministers of Islamic countries, who convene in one Islamic capital or another, from Rabat and Tehran to Lahor and Kuala Lumpur, constantly adding new members from Africa and Asia (like Uganda) that had hitherto not been recognized as Muslim states.

Civilian Republican Turkey, especially its successive governments that protected her against the rule of Islam and insisted on the separation of state and church, yielded in 1976 and held the annual Islamic conference in Istanbul, thus joining the Islamic bloc at large and dramatically impacting the world political agenda via the organization of Islamic countries in the UN, which controls about one-third of the UN members and can win UN votes through that organization. Simultaneously, the Turkish political leadership slowly abandoned the civil agenda and veered toward an Islamic one, after the civil heyday of Inonu, Menderes, Ozal, Ecevit, and Ciller. At that time, the rise of Islam was more marked in the countryside, which was the main power base of the Islamic parties, first under Erbakan and then under his disciple Erdogan. Then, the leadership of the government was still under the sway of the Westernized and modernized urban bourgeoisie. The reversal started in the 1970s, and the Turkish government then suggested Istanbul as the venue of the Islamic Conference in 1976. Concurrently, Turkey joined the Islamic conference organization, until under Erdogan a Turk became its fanatic secretary general. Though the heyday of Turkish relations with Israel happened in the 1990s, Ankara also began its slow rapprochement to the Arabs and Islam. Erbakan's government was dismissed and outlawed by the army in 1998, as the final gasp of the manifestation of its privilege in public affairs, when it was still empowered to remove an elected Islamic governement and facilitate the reversion to a civilian one. But then Erdogan came to power in 2002, and that was the beginning of the Spring in Turkey, admittedly by peaceful and democratic means.

One can assume that the policies of the civil governments were adopted as a way to temporarily placate their Muslim opponents, but the writing was on the wall in 1996 when Erbakan won the plurality in the elections, though not the majority, and he was called upon to form a government. He was removed by the army two years later when he edged dangerously closer to Iran. It is noteworthy that when Erdogan's party won the elections, he himself was in prison for incitement, as the mayor of Istanbul, while Abdullah Gul, the second-in-command and now the president, then ran at the head of the party. The rules of the game changed in the 2002 elections in Erdogan's favor, with the results reconfirmed in 2006 and 2010. In the Erdogan-Gul government signs were emerging of a revival of neo-Ottoman tendencies, with ambitions to regain a sort of imperial influence through Pan-ethnic/cultural policies (in Central Asia and the Caucasus) and Pan-Islamic/religious policies (toward other Islamic countries, especially the Arabs). Hence the special relationship that Erdogan created with the newly independent countries of Central Asia, his special visits to Cairo and Damascus when the Spring broke out, his ambition to lead the Syrian solution, his generous aid to Syrian refugees, and his adoption of the Palestinian issue as his own, though Turkey has nothing directly to do with it. Even his Gaza flotilla in 2010, which brought his relations with Israel to a crisis, and strained relations with the United States, were risks he was willing to take. It all looked and sounded as if he again felt in charge of the old Ottoman Empire, where he aspired to become the supreme sponsor responsible for managing the problems of his subordinates.

Similarly, Erdogan immediately showed support for the Spring in Tunisia and Egypt once it showed pro-Islamic tendencies, and he expressed his ambition to quiet down the disturbances and killings in Syria. At first, prior to the Spring, Erdogan favored Iran and Syria over

Israel and objected to the sanctions against nuclearizing Iran. Only when he realized that he was losing prestige with that support did he turn against the Syrian tyrant and cool his relations with Tehran, which threw all its weight behind Assad for fear that his fall might mean the ayatullah's regime's decline too. Erdogan had probably hoped that when things settled in Syria, especially if the Brothers took over there, then Turkish influence might regain some importance, this time tinged with Neo-Ottoman coloring. For it is clear from his denial of the Armenian massacre during the Great War, the cruel attitude of his country toward the Kurds, 20 percent of its citizenry, and from the heaps of lies that he invents to incite his ignorant constituents against Jews and Israel, that he does not aspire to live in peace with the countries next door. Instead, he aims to lead power struggles and to inspire hatred and the revival of Turkey's centrality in the affairs of the Middle East and the Islamic world.

What has been happening today with the Christian minorities during the Spring also has some characteristics inherited from the Ottoman Empire. When the modern states rose after the collapse of the Empire, the situation of the Christian communities worsened from what it had been under the sultan and the *Millet* system that he had instituted. While it was bad enough under the intervening Arab and Islamic states in the last century (Christians in Sudan, Copts in Egypt, Maronites in Lebanon, Assyrians in Iraq, etc.), things further deteriorated under the Spring, expanding to include ethnic issues, since during periods of upheaval every minority regarded itself as struggling for its survival amid the uncertainty that reigned over the country. Indeed, the Alawites and Druze in Syria, the Kurds in Iraq and Syria, the black Christians of Sudan, and the Copts of Egypt, who do not usually intermarry with the Arab-Muslim majority, have become ethnically distinct. This was because it was one thing to feel oneself sharing the inferior status of the many non-Muslim groups under the *Millet* ticket within the Empire, and quite another to find oneself confronting the Muslim majority in one's own postindependence state.

As long as socialist and revolutionary states dominated those countries, as they did under Nasser or the Ba'ath, the very participation of the minorities in the regime and their very identification with it shielded them from extermination, while the Muslim Brothers were shoved to the sidelines, due to their menace against both the regime and the minorities. Even under the tyrannical regimes that followed those revolutions, rulers continued to protect their minorities, as Mubarak did in Egypt, or minorities were fending for themselves by holding power, like the Alawites in Syria. But when the Spring broke out, with propensities to veer toward Islam, minorities were once again alerted, like the Copts and the Maronites, to protect their survival, and they feel compelled to go out into the public square and voice their fears about Islamic regimes that threaten to take the helm, or they ready themselves for the last stand like the Alawites, the Maronites, the Kurds, and the Druze, or stand in queues near the Western consulates to ask to emigrate. No wonder, then, that when the Syrian regime was desperately and cruelly battling for its life as the crisis raged, its best, closest, and most devoted allies were the Christian and Druze minorities who supported the Ba'ath, realizing that they would rise and fall with the regime. But as Assad's situation got graver, the minorities began to distance themselves, in order to let him sink without dragging themselves down with him. But should the Brothers or other Islamic groups take over in Damascus, and perhaps the Hizbullah in Beirut, the Christian minorities would either have to submit or run for their lives.

It is quite surprising to realize that while the Arabs regard the four hundred years of oppressive Ottoman rule as far from a golden era, they nevertheless view them as less troublesome than they could have been, and therefore they accepted submission to powerful, Islamic, protective, and stable Istanbul. By contrast, today the Arabs are steeped in constant turmoil, are fighting and removing one tyrant after another from power, and are ready to make sacrifices to attain that goal. Is that only because the Ottoman Empire looked, after all, like the other ancient Muslim empires that had succeeded each other in the days of glory (Umayyads, Abbasids, Fatimids, Mamluks, Moghuls), and it made no difference who headed the Empire? Or were they so desperate, oppressed, and ignorant that they simply dared not confront that awesome empire that even the Western powers had feared? Or perhaps was it that they felt so neglected and forlorn, and were so convinced that the Empire was declining and yielding to Western powers at the end of its rule, that the decline of Islam and the East and the ascent of the Western Christian world were inevitable? Or else, maybe they were not aware of the emergence of their own nationalism until the Empire was crumbling? During all that painful process, could they only recall the glory of past Muslim empires and dynasties and feel humiliation and frustration, while previously they had seen Allah favoring them, making them the conquerors the world and subordinating other nations to them, and they began questioning what had happened and where they had gone wrong? How was it that the progenitors of a large, feared, and respected world civilization suddenly found themselves defeated, humiliated, and lagging on the sidelines?

Maybe the answer they were looking for could be found in the fact that since the fall of the Abbasids to the Mongols in 1258, and Mamluk Egypt to the Ottomans in 1517, which put an end to the Arab primacy in the Islamic world, Arabs had stopped pondering the huge successes of other non-Arab Muslims (Turks, Persians, Moghuls), and sank into their own grievances and inextricably hopeless situation. Since then, the Arabs made many attempts to revive themselves and to reoccupy their previous place in Islam, through revivalist movements and revolutionary coups, and all manner of social and political experiments that failed dismally, because they were nipped in the bud by tyrants and military juntas which took them over. Conversely, the current Spring ought, therefore, to be tested in historical perspective as the first major, serious, and all-encompassing attempt in the post-Ottoman era to revive the lost glory days. This attempt does not have to be viewed, in consequence, only as made merely within the boundaries of each Muslim state separately, but as a comprehensive effort to bring in many Muslim countries under the lead of radical Muslims, with a view of restoring the great and united caliphate, which alone can also revive the reputation and impact of the Islamic *umma*. This is precisely what the fundamentalist movements of the Brotherhood, the Salafis, Hamas, Hizbullah, Hizb-ul-Tahrir, al-Qa'ida, Lashkar e-Taiba, and their likes are aspiring to.

3

Authoritarian Rule
in the Islamic World

From its inception, Islamic government had to learn from the great imperial experiments of its time: the Sassanids in Persia and the Byzantines in Anatolia, which combined empire and religion. The Prophet Muhammed, consciously or not, adopted this model in his ten years of rule in Medina (AD 622–32), for without his experience as a preacher in Mecca he would not have been invited to Medina, and without his ruling experience in Medina, it is doubtful whether his prophetic experience in Mecca would have served any practical purpose and accorded him his fame as the founder of Islam. The mold of government developed by Muhammed through his Medina experience while he was setting the first example of rule in the first Muslim polis consisted of five functions: prophecy, legislation, administration, judiciary, and military.

Muhammed's prophecy was his value-added quality over all humans, and when he moved from Mecca (where he was a mere apocalyptic soothsayer who predicted the end of the world and had not much to offer except to sermonize the bourgeois merchant population of his clan in his city) to Medina, where he was an invited ruler, his career changed completely. Now he had to care for the city's affairs, to deal with personal, clan, tribal, and commercial issues that sought settlement before him. His prophecies continued, but this time tailor-made to respond to the arising problems he had to resolve. As he and other Muslims came to see them, those revelations—being imprinted in the holy book—served later as the precedents and the base for the Prophet's legislation. But when he died, leaving no successor as a prophet, it was clear that no caliph could legislate after the Prophet, that the Prophet and his sunna already contained all necessary legislation for all humanity for all time, and that only 'ulama (doctors of the Holy Law) could henceforth tell what was the law. Hence the important role the doctors of Islam have in the state as interpreters of the law (faqih = jurist), as religious verdict renderers (mufti) or as *quda'* (singular qadi = judge). Theoretically, the caliphs could not legislate, because they lacked the understanding of the scholars, but they could make other scholars who obeyed them pronounce the legal sanctions they wanted.

In Muhammed's time, legislation was narrowly related to prophecy; since the Prophet's revelations were laws, and when later included in the verses of the Qur'an, they became laws by definition. But after his death, who else could legislate who did not possess the power of prophecy? In theory, the jurists retained that right for themselves, of legislation via interpretation—but not anymore via divine inspiration, since the gates of *Ijtihad* had been closed, and most certainly not via innovation (the *bid'a*, Allah forbid!). Except for periods of truly righteous and pious rulers, who would consult the scholars of their time to determine right or wrong, most rulers could not resist the temptation of ruling daily on current matters and then asking their scholars to find rationalizations for their decisions. In our days, there is supposed to be a modern legal code that is partly based on the Islamic sources and party on the civil code. But the body of laws in both systems is there to be violated by the rulers, who continue to play by the Islamic rules in public, but in private they do much what they like. Therefore, though no Arab dictator prior to the Spring would admit that he was the legislator, and would assert that he made sure that every item of legislation passed the parliament, everybody knew that even the king of Jordan and the president of Egypt, who were among the mildest dictators, could suspend the parliament at will; conversely, anything they wished the parliament to pass was done without much foot-dragging. That meant, in fact, that the dictators were also the legislators.

As far as executive power was concerned, the Prophet was truly limitless, even though the Medina Treaty that he signed (metaphorically, since he was illiterate) prior to his arrival had stipulated certain conditions and obligations of him. In fact, after he Islamized the city and subjugated it to his will, and as his lifestyle had become the model for all Muslims to emulate, who could question his wisdom in his executive functions, especially since, under the constant blessing of his divine revelations, he could not be contradicted or disobeyed. And so the Prophet, using his charisma and his leadership skills, could unite the Arab tribes; deal with the Jewish tribes quite harshly, expelling some of them, executing others, and Islamizing still others; subjugate his rivals from within; launch military campaigns against other tribes;

reform the inner structures of the city; launch the new religion; and much more, all in the space of ten years. Executive powers are the area where the present tyrants excel too: they make their own constitution upon ascending to power, thus taking over something from the legislative branch when there is one; they monopolize the appointments of all ministers and their prime ministers; they hold the reins of power at all levels; they decide upon the budget, the rate of taxation to be levied, and the persons and institutions who enjoy public budgeting; they determine what the people will eat and at what price; and they hold all the entrances and exits to and from public power. Is this a continuation of the old privileges that the Prophet had enjoyed, or simply the place where all dictators are bound to slide? It does not matter, as long as there will always be people who find justification to their deeds in Muhammed's exemplary life.

The sociopolitical conditions of those days had indeed required that all those powers be concentrated in the Prophet's hands, regardless of whether or not he knew that his style was not different from the authoritarian rule that he saw or heard about in his environment. The only model he was familiar with was the tribal one, where the *sheikh* concentrated all authority in his hands; thus he could not deviate much from what was known without producing controversy around him. Naturally, the *sheikh* was also committed to his tribe and its values, and to the consensus among the notables to preserve his dominant rule; therefore he could not turn his rule into a heartless and unrestrained tyranny without incurring the risk of losing it. There was an unwritten social pact, worded in terms of the classical *muruwa*, which included ruling justly (the judiciary aspect), managing wisely and effectively (the executive part), and leading heroically in battle (the military aspect). In return, the ruled undertook to obey him and his orders and to follow his lead in all his endeavors. In other words, when the messenger of Allah was asked to proceed to Medina and take over the rule there, it is reasonable to assume that he knew what was expected of him.

The authoritarian rule in Islam naturally followed in the footsteps of the Prophet, who was, and still is, considered infallible and the most perfect of men who could commit no fault, in government or in anything else. It is also reasonable to assume that while establishing the fundamentals of Muslim rule according to his needs, he also learned something from the imperial models he knew or learned about. Possessing an acute sense of obedience to his example, the Arabs have always felt that the great precedents he set had necessarily grown to become valid for all times, especially after Muhammed died and the Arabs sprang out of Arabia to conquer the world, and needed to find a Muslim style of government that would respond to their growing and pressing needs. One has to assume that they were convinced of divine assistance to their vast and exciting enterprise of conquest, which was done under the authoritarian regime of the time. Therefore, after the death of the Prophet they pursued the same route, which was common to them and to the enemies they fought against. Moreover, at a time when their Sassanid and Byzantine rivals were tyrannical rulers dipped in luxury and opulence, in addition to authoritarianism, to the point that one spoke of the legendary Byzantine Court and Sassanid ostentation, the Muslim court was managed much more simply and modestly. At least this was the way in the beginning of Islam, for the authority of the ruler was institutionalized in the *bay'a* (oath of fealty), without a need for all the paraphernalia that had inspired awe and authority in the rule and succession of those ancient imperial houses. That meant that the ruler in place, who had been designated by the *shura*, as in the times of the righteous caliphs, or later inherited his mantle through dynastic inheritance, was recognized and accepted in the public square, as if the oath of allegiance to him were given personally by each Muslim. For any time of rebellion or dissatisfaction with the ruler, dubbed *fitna*, meant that the oath (*bay'a*) lost its validity. Then, worshippers no longer mentioned the name of the ruler at Friday's prayers, as if the weekly validation of the oath no longer held. Thus, the outside symbols of power were very much personal and direct, needing no elaboration.

The charisma of the Prophet in his time was beyond doubt. Nobody put into question his sublime qualities and natural propensity to rule, as if he were a prince who inherited those qualities. But what about those who followed him as rulers? Did they inherit his charisma? How was the balance preserved between their nature as pious and righteous men and their ability to govern the people, for the people, and make their rule appear as just and beyond reproach as possible? Allah's messenger, apart from serving in all the functions cited above, also created and enforced a systematic ritual, repeated daily and many times a day, that became one of the sources of his power, in addition of being the messenger of Allah and his last Prophet. The first pillar of the faith, the *Shahadah* (bearing witness)—which repeated at the start of each prayer the formula that "there is no God but Allah and Muhammed his Prophet"—made inextricable the connection between the messenger of Allah and the very belief in the religion. When repeated many times over, every day, in prayer and preceding each important act, this accorded a central place to the Prophet in one's life. As long as the Prophet lived, and his contemporaries felt privileged to be around him, they could see in front of them the perpetual expression of Allah's grace in sending to them the Seal of the Prophets and the most perfect of men to serve them and to guide them. There was never a possibility that anyone could question that charisma. Even in moments of friction with his closest companions, like with 'Umar in Hudaibiyya, Muhammed's unique and prevalent quality remained, because he always had the last word.

When the Prophet suddenly died in AD 632, there was an urgent need to appoint a successor, lest his entire heritage disintegrate. The *shura* elected Abu-Bakr, probably by order or seniority since he was the older compared to the other candidates, but also the Prophet's father-in-law. What to make of his attribute of *Siddiq* (the righteous)? Probably not much, because it was accorded to him after his death. After him came the three others (Umar, Uthman, Ali), every time following huge controversies and forceful lobbying for each candidate, which ended with compromises, horse-trading, bargaining, and pressures. The main issue was to elect a successor, lest the charisma of the Prophet be discontinued and the authority of the caliph be so diminished that there would not be much left to inherit. At the same time, it was clear that prophecy was sealed forever by Muhammed, and so were the divine legislative powers that emanated from it. Therefore, all that could be passed on to the caliphs were the remaining four functions of the Muslim ruler: civil legislation, executive, judiciary, and military command. This combination of so many top functions made sure that the caliph would be no less omnipotent than the Prophet in the practical domain of rule, while the special and unique level of prophecy would remain sealed. Hence the attribute of *Khalifa* (caliph) imputed to him, meaning a human figure—as the Prophet had insisted upon characterizing himself—who served as a replacement (or vicar in Christian parlance for the replacement of Jesus on earth). But in Christianity the vicars became infallible popes who had inherited a divine figure, while the caliphs remain human all the way, with righteous qualities to be sure, but nothing divine, otherwise the doctrine of the unity of Allah (*tawhid*) would be seriously compromised.

After the Four Righteous, many Islamic dynasties followed, often simultaneously and struggling against each other. Sometimes the sons of the same ruler fought to succeed their father, as with the bloody struggles between Aurangzeb and his brothers for the succession of Shah Jehan. While these struggles unfolded, the imprisoned ruler was helplessly watching his sons butchering each other. This war to the finish proceeded with every generation, for a new king cannot feel safe on his throne, as an absolute ruler, unless all the rival contenders are eliminated. In the Arab monarchies today, there are families on the throne that try to ensure an orderly succession, and there is no telling when someone down the line might rebel and reverse the order, as happened with the Nasser and Qaddafi revolutions in North Africa or the Islamic Revolution in Iran. There are certainly various degrees of absolutism, like the one perceivable between Saudi Arabia—without any institutions to palliate the royal house, and where even the *shura* is appointed by the monarch—and Kuwait or Jordan, who have some kind of parliament. Some kingdoms, like Jordan and Morocco, boast of their constitutional monarchy, but either they do understand the difference between their kingdoms and those of Benelux, the Scandinavians, and England and they continue nonetheless their fraudulent pursuit, or they don't understand and they just play with words. But absolutism in these countries is not confined to monarchies, for in Saddam's Iraq, Assad's Syria, and Qaddafi's Libya there was also an extreme sort of absolutism, which surpassed even monarchies in cruelty and egotism of the rulers. Some of them were/are so full of themselves that they designated heirs among their sons to succeed them (Saddam for Iraq, Mubarak for Egypt, Ali for Yemen, Qaddafi for Libya, Assad for Syria, where Bashar had actually inherited from his father in 2000).

More moderate and human, and less cruel and absolutistic authoritarianism was offered by Ben Ali of Tunisia and Mubarak or Egypt, and, paradoxically, it was they who fell first at the beginning of the Spring, but their lives were preserved or they escaped to a protective exile. It seems that the more cruel among them, who were also ruthless in defense of their rule, like Assad, Qaddafi, and Ali of Yemen, had to fight the longest and kill the most of their own citizens to remain in place, or before they lost their lives. Islamic history had known both types, of tyrants who ran away and of others who were killed under their watch. But even the more benevolent type like Mubarak, when too long in power (thirty years) tended toward corruption and monarchic rule. In effect, Mubarak was elected and reelected every time anew, by an obedient parliament, with no rival candidate allowed to run, lest he caused "division among the people." Lately, when an old and tired Mubarak announced that his son would run for office after him, his people rebelled, because when they agreed to a republic in 1952, they did not mean a monarchical or dynastic republic. In Lebanon, too, despite the full-blown election campaign, Sa'd Hariri ran to replace his father who was murdered by Hizbullah on behalf of the Syrians. This is exactly as, to replace legendary Pierre Jumayel, the founder and commander of the Phalangs, his two sons followed to the presidency: Bashir first, and when he was slain by the Syrians, his brother, Amin. Kamal Junblatt, the Druze leader, was replaced by his son, Walid, who is far from reaching his stature and has even shown subservience to Bashar Assad, wrongly betting on the leader of Syria who began to stagger to his disappearance.

All these examples show that when it comes to authoritarian executive power, all the Arab countries of the Middle East have some affinity to it, one way or another. Only lust for power in this fashion can instigate a father to wish to bequeath his rule to his sons. It is not known what the Prophet himself would have done had he had a son. But since only Fatima, his daughter, survived, and she married his cousin Ali, who also became a contender for power, it is difficult to conclude from that anything about the pre-Spring present-day rule of succession in the Muslim world. One strong suspicion has to be mentioned, nonetheless, and that is that the tyrants in place are/were so much afraid of what might happen to them or to their memory after their death that their only way to guarantee the posthumous survival of their reputation is/was to ensure rule of their sons after them. This is because (a) only the son can preserve the memory of his father, by making sure that he is properly commemorated and his heritage is respected and even worshipped (just imagine what would have happened to Hafez Assad's Memorial in Qardahah had his son not been around to defend and cultivate it); and (b) without prearranged succession, fathers, especially those from a minority group, could not even ensure that their children would or could succeed, or even survive. Imagine that Assad the father had been killed as a president-dictator; then his son Bashar would at best have remained an optometrist, or continued to seek shelter in London, and his father's memory may have been totally erased. Conversely, had the successions of Saddam, Qaddafi, Saleh, and Mubarak succeeded, the dictators could still be in power, or put on a pedestal as elder statesmen, and in any case allowed to die naturally.

As far as the judiciary is concerned, judges, who were all religious (*qadi*) in old days, served under the various caliphs and dynasties, and since they depended on the royal court for their appointment to the job, they were also usually obedient, though they were supposed to enforce Shari'a law. But since the Ottoman rule, which established the distinction between Shari'a and civil law (*Qanun*), all independent Muslim countries then gradually adopted such a system, and pressures began as to the degree and extent to which the law of each country ought to depend—entirely, to a large degree, or partially—on religious law. In any case, the two systems exist side by side, and both are appointed by the administration in place. But under dictators the system does not matter and things are usually decided according to the whims of the rulers—if the problem in question is important to him to the point that he cares to intervene. As we mentioned above, the first legal document that every ruler in the modern Muslim world introduced was a constitution, which, instead of being left to the public or to assemblies of representatives to put together, is made by the tyrant or his underlings. Rather than constituting a legal framework that limits the dictator's power and promises protection to the citizens and their rights, this sort of constitution only draws the guidelines for the future action of the ruler, which will not necessarily be respected, and will be altered by a new document when the next dictator comes along.

And finally, there is the military field, fulfilled with distinction by the Prophet, who launched periodical wars of expansion in Arabia or seized the holy shrine of Mecca, which he had not been allowed to enter by his fellow tribesmen of the Qureish. Through his raids throughout Arabia, where his Medinan followers never hesitated to tread, he ensured for himself the title of *Amir-al-Mu'minin* (commander of the faithful), a title he seemed to like in particular due to the frequency of its usage when other Muslims addressed him. This was also the title preferred by all the caliphs and sultans who followed throughout the generations. There were even cases of Muslim minority rebellions, where the local commanders who wished to rally larger Muslim troops around them summoned their public using this title or one similar to it.[1] In the modern Arab and Islamic worlds, most dictators also put themselves at the head of the high military command in their country, either because they had themselves mounted a coup as military men or because they wish to appear as generals or marshals or admirals in their military uniform. (Sadat was killed in a general's suit while watching a military parade; Idi Amin dressed like a marshal; Qaddafi liked to parade in either his officer's suit or his clown outfit.) In that fashion, they seem to send a clear message that whatever their generals' ranks, the uniforms they wear are superior. For all these dictatorships, the army is their main sustenance in power, and it is worth recalling that when the Egyptian army abandoned Mubarak, he collapsed; in Syria, Bashar's army supported him, so he could fight for a long time before he faltered.

Even though dust is far from settling on all those countries, it is clear that what was will never be again and that new and uncertain paths are being carved into the rock, and we cannot yet ascertain their directions. It is also clear that the masses of Arabs and Muslims are loath to sustain the tyrannical rule that has ruled them before. Yes, they all shout *Democracy!* as if they knew what it was, but what they mean is that they are tired of dynastic and absolute rulers. On the other hand, it is not easy to imagine in the Islamic world powerless, vegetarian monarchical regimes like those in Europe, because for them a ruler is a ruler, a king is a king, and an executive without authority is nobody. Thus, Saudi Arabia, Morocco, or Jordan, or the Gulf states—who are proclaiming their wish to adopt reform, for example by instituting constitutional monarchies—will ultimately have to go, because neither can they relinquish their power totally, without which there is no constitutional monarchy, nor would their nations (which were enslaved by them for many decades) let them continue their rule unchecked. For then, instead of being the symbol of the state the monarch remains a power broker, which is a recipe for friction and future crises.

The most amazing aspect of this is the fact that after years of intimate knowledge of the heads of states of the Spring, and business dealings with them, and official representations in each other's country—during which they had the chance to examine the regime, gauge its feudalistic and dictatorial dimensions, evaluate the degree of oppression, suppression, corruption, and exploitation that sustained it—Western powers, including their politicians, diplomats, intelligence, and scholars, hardly ever voiced a word of alarm, warning, and fear of things to come. They allowed things to deteriorate to their maximum, and only when open rebellion broke out and blood started to spill in the streets did they have the decency to say "Oh yeah, we knew all along but were ordered not to speak up," or "We knew it was coming," or "We never believed this rule would be so easy to remove." We could even have expected someone to cry out, "Remember the shah's island of stability," which Carter turned into a swamp of Iranian hostility. Where were all those presidents and foreign ministers who invited those dictators, like the King of Saudi Arabia or the President of Libya, to their capitals, sold them weapons, defended them in the United Nations, formed alliances with them, pardoned their violations of every law, forgave their crimes, and allowed them to plant their tents (literally) in the hearts of Rome, Paris, and London? Didn't they know they were corrupt tyrants? If they did not know, they should have dismissed their ambassadors and heads of intelligence, who submitted false and biased reports, and if they knew and refrained from action, they should themselves resign from office. Their late reaction would expose them now to two sorts of accusations that they would find difficult to refute. First, that they now admit their faltering policies in the previous years, that lent support to all sorts of corrupt and dangerous dictators and enabled them to survive for decades, knowing that they were robbing and exploiting their peoples; and secondly, if that is, or was, the situation, why expect the countries of the Spring to have confidence in the Western powers whose conduct has disappointed them in the past?

Many secondary questions pop up in the public squares of all those countries that have chosen to change course, all leading to the main question of trusting once again the powers that betrayed them more than once before. For example, America and the West now promise to support democracy. What democracy? How can we be sure we are talking about the same democracy? For years they let Mubarak (and the others) rig elections, so how can they be trusted to ensure fair elections now? They let Saudi Arabia and Libya do without elections at all, and they were never heard urging those rulers to conform. What has happened now? Did Westerners suddenly mend their ways? Why did they let Egypt suppress the Copts for decades, let Syrians impose a regime of terror and interfere in their neighbor's affairs, and let Hizbullah take over the rule in Lebanon, in submission to the Syrian and Iranian tyrannies? And when the West intervened in oil-rich Libya, dropping bombs without taking any risks, everyone expected to see the same in Syria. But NATO members knew the difference, because the Syrian army was and still is large, larger than the number of divisions NATO could field (except for the Americans). Its air force and air defenses are formidable enough to challenge any Western air power save the American, while Libyan forces did not exist as a fighting force. No major European power could stand the domestic disaster of bringing home plastic bags with corpses, therefore no country volunteered to fight there. America, who could have done it, had its hands full in Afghanistan, and previously in Iraq, and a presidential election approaching, and it was clear that America would not take any additional risk.

The faults that the awakening champions of the Spring can detect and complain about in the West are not only on the military level, but on the diplomatic front as well. When America stated one year into the Syrian crisis that Assad had "lost his legitimacy," it simply revealed in public what it refused to overtly recognize before: that Assad never had any legitimacy for power, exactly as with the other dictators. His father, who took over the rule by a coup and then bequeathed it to his son, had never been elected by anyone either. Bashar Assad's role in power has been sustained by Iran and by Hizbullah, two outlaws that never got legitimacy from anyone to rule. Obama's administration stated a policy of engagement, which failed dismally. Before him, the Bush administration had successfully isolated Syria, cut off relations with it, put it under political siege, forced it to evacuate its forces from Lebanon—all this to punish it for the al-Qa'ida forces that were allowed to infiltrate Iraq's Anbar Sunni region and cause damage to the American forces there. Then came Obama with his new policy; he went to Riyad to prostrate before the king of that primitive and obscurantist country, a notoriously corrupt denier of human rights, and then proceeded to Cairo, where he made an incredibly hypocritical speech to the Muslim world, which produced no positive result, apart from the Spring of 2011, which Obama did not want in the first place. Then he enlisted Turkey to also sponsor Syria back into the fold, by granting her back her place among nations and re-establishing diplomatic relations with her. Assad and others came to believe that America needed them more than they needed America, and felt free to act at will on their domestic front.

Within one year, Mubarak was urged to go; he no longer represented the Muslim world, nor the much-solicited stability. Assad was again boycotted; his legitimacy had gone, and as he engaged in more killings of his own citizens, suddenly America discovered that he had formidable allies in Moscow and Beijing, even more so in Tehran and in Beirut, and that his allies would not let him fall, exactly as America and Turkey had tried to boost him one year earlier. Who could take that zigzagging policy seriously? Least of all the countries of the Spring, who look at pathetic Obama one week supporting Mubarak, the next negotiating with his sworn enemies the Muslim Brothers; one week America boycotting and besieging Assad, then giving him long leashes with enthusiastic Turkish support, then banning him again and acting for his demise. Do they know whom would they support instead? Of course not, and they call that "foreign policy," as if it were all measured, calculated, and considered. They publish the State Department report about human rights violations, where the most liberal and most staunch human-rights guardian, Israel, is censured, but Saudi Arabia, the most grievous violator of those rights, is kept hidden behind the scenes. One wonders what is going on. In Bahrain, an uprising of the Shi'ite majority was quelled militarily, with several casualties, but no word of delegitimation, censure, condemnation, or blame came out of the State Department.

We have seen several elements of authoritarian rule in Islamic tradition, which have all found expression in this Spring. For example, the tradition of the *sheikh,* which generated the caliphate and the dictatorships still extant today, and, by contrast, the other tendencies that palliate that harsh aspect, like the *Ijma'* (consensus in religious practice), the *shura* (principle of the council with notables participating), the lack of hierarchy in the clerical system, and the mystical equality between all, on the floor of the mosque, from the king to the last worshipper. We are suggesting here a contradiction, as it were, between principles that look proto-democratic, down to earth, and popular, and harsh autocratic principles of government. There is a tradition in Islam that the Prophet and the first caliphs were simple, accessible, and wary of elevating themselves over the masses, in contrast to the later kings, emperors, and sultans, who hid in their palaces hardly to be seen by the public. Partly that stemmed from the size of the growing Empire and its bureaucracy; it had to grow impersonal for the state to fill its pressing needs. But partly it was due to the changing interpretations of things. For example, in the beginning of Islam coffee was considered a drug, or equivalent to alcohol or narcotics, and there were people who were arrested for using it. But popular custom was stronger, and at last coffee was not only permitted but became an essential tool of socialization. But one has also to pay attention to the fact that while *Ijma'* did gather momentum as a social and religious consensus, it was no longer possible to implement it in practice when the *umma* grew beyond the city-polis of Medina, to extend over large parts of the medieval world, and then over the entire globe. It was then necessary to confine its validity to the scholars of each community, since it was impossible that a consensus between all world Muslims be attained, especially under the conditions of transport and communications at the time. But that too was too vast for a practical consensus, and in time it became imperative to consult the main scholars of each generation.

Of course, there was neither democracy nor anything resembling it. But this was the closest one could come to some kind of representative body. Moreover, unlike the *shura* and other councils of appointed notables, the consensus of scholars was, and still is, meritocratic in essence, because it is self-selected—just like the ayatullahs in the Shi'ite system—and elitist due to the participation of a select few. There is another limitation here: suppose a consensus requires at least a majority, if not the totality of the main scholars—namely that the minority does not even have the right to express its minority view, let alone implement it under the sweep of the majority. In other words, to seek democracy in this society is equivalent to sending a blind person to a dark room to look for a black cat that is not there.

In the West, legitimacy is achieved by freely electing a parliament and a government at the end of each term specified by law, upon which power is smoothly transferred from the incumbent to the elect. In the Islamic world there is no democracy of the Western type, though in Saudi Arabia one could hear arguments in favor of the *shura* as the mother of all democracies. So, in what way would those who seize power justify or rationalize it? Except for the Prophet himself, who ruled by the grace of Allah who dispatched him as his messenger, all his successors had to prove their legitimacy one way or another. One way to gain legitimacy today is to follow the spirit of the time and hold "elections," whose results are preprogrammed and whose unfolding is choreographed in such a style as not to betray the rigging. In the communist world, there were also elections, but with candidates from a single party, namely the ruling party, and they were "elected" without opposition. This pattern has been generously and uncritically copied by most Islamic countries if and when elections were held at all. In Iran, there is a Supreme Screening Commission, which decides whom to permit to run for elections and whom to ban. In that system, there is a permanent Supreme Spiritual Leader, who does not run or stand for election; he supervises from above, and nothing can be done without his agreement. The entire bureaucracy, from the president down, is supposed to be guided by him, due to his aura of sanctity. This system was launched by Khumeini and allowed to continue even though no one has been found so far to fill that position adequately.

In monarchic systems, kings and princes are not elected, and when they don their crowns they act as authoritarian and sometimes as absolute rulers like the other sorts of dictators. They preserve their clan's laws of succession, going first through the collateral members of the family, brother by brother, and only when they are all exhausted, usually in their eighties, does the crown skip one or two generations forward to start a new list of kings, heirs, and princes, the others becoming ministers, governors, military commanders, court councilors, ambassadors, and senior officials. In that system, proximity to the king and loyalty to him, rather than skill or proficiency for the job are the main criteria for senior appointments. In other systems, like Qaddafi's, Saddam's, Assad's, there was no pretense of election or legitimacy; they simply took over and ruled, with the help of a military clique that supported them, in return for benefits that accrued to them after the success of the coup. After they take over power, they organize "elections," to signify to the world that the Arab Middle East is no different from the American Midwest. Very often, misinformed and naive correspondents report about those "elections" with enthusiasm and statistics, as if the data were ironclad and authoritative. This grotesque farce continued for decades while the West kept its silence, pretending it did not know and did not hear. The Islamic regimes also pretended that all was well, since very rarely did any Western country protest against any disorder in the "elections" or in the transition from fake elections to rigged power. Quite the contrary, every president who was thus "elected" was met with a cascade of Western greetings upon his election.

Even before the coming of the Spring, the autocrats in place started feeling the push from the bottom, through the Internet and social networks, to open up and democratize, something that compelled them to devise new rationalizations for their illegitimate rule, because they realized that their previous pseudo-democratic measures had encountered only contempt and anger in the street. So, they at first reverted to their rusty pretexts. The president of Egypt boasted the strongest military force in the area, which would stand fast in defense of all Arabs; the Syrians were proud of their resolute Arab nationalism and their unconditional support of the Palestinians; the king of Morocco invoked his descent from the Prophet; and so did the king of Jordan, who also added to his arrows the title of the curator of Al-Aqsa, which he obtained from his peace deal with Israel; and Saudi Arabia boasted the curatorship of the Two Mosques of Mecca and Medina, the holiest in Islam. They thought that if they all were so wonderful, idealistic, and caring about their countries and peoples, and other Arabs and Muslims, who would want to replace them? But in fact, they were all illegitimate, because no one chose them; they took power either by royal inheritance or through succession of revolutionary leaders (Nasser, Sadat, Mubarak). If not for the Spring, which discontinued that chain, successions would have gone on to the sons of the leaders in place.

In World War II, Giuselmo Ferrero wrote his book *On Democracy*, which became a classic, where he coined the idea of "fraudulent democracy" to describe the fascist regimes in Europe (Hitler, Mussolini, Franco, and some of their short-lived supporters in the Arab world like Rashid Ali in Iraq, the Brothers in Egypt, and Haj Amin in Palestine). Some of these states had experienced something of the democratic system, but simply ended up borrowing its rules in order to distort its substance. For example, elections were held technically, but only to leave the arena open to the autocrat, and to him alone. In the Arab and Islamic world, which had almost never experienced democracy (even in Turkey, the classic border case, the elected governments were removed by the army on several occasions), one can suspect not a fraud, but ignorance of the essence of democracy. Indeed, how could they know what it meant if they had never experienced it? If the UN wants to extend assistance to a new country to organize elections, it should not dispatch as its messengers the delegates of Syria, Sudan, or Iran, but those of Sweden, Britain, and Luxemburg, who have knowledge and experience in working democracy. In any case, democracy has, even prior to the Spring, become a mantra repeated by every leader as if it were part of his platform, his belief, or his understanding. In fact, it was meaningless, not only because those autocrats did not mean it, but also because they did not comprehend it.

Mubarak's party was called National Democratic, which like the popular democracies in Eastern Europe—namely Bulgaria, Rumania, Poland, East Germany, and Czechoslovakia—purposely added to their names the appellation *democratic*, knowing full well that they were not. Britain, France, or Sweden never needed to underline that they were democracies, because everyone knew it. China, similarly, boasts its attribute of being "popular," intending to distance its image from the autocracy that it actually is. The bottom line is that where there is a democracy, autocrats cannot rise, and vice versa: where there is an autocrat there can be no democracy. When Ariel Sharon headed the Israeli government in the 2000s, President Mubarak was interviewed by the international press, and he stressed, that unlike "Sharon the dictator," he himself was a "real democrat," voted in by 90 percent of the parliament. It was clear that Mubarak never understood how democracy worked, nor the very stringent rules and controls over Israeli elections, so that there should be no doubt or question over their results. What he said indicated more his ignorance than any flaw with the free and democratic elections in Israel, which are supervised by an impeccable supreme court judge. Or take Bashar Assad. He inherited his father in 2000, following a speedy process of amending the constitution (as if it mattered) to make the successor eligible for the presidency despite his young age (thirty-four). But the members of Parliament and the public at large who were interviewed after the amendment all pointed to the democratic process that regulated the succession. No one dared to raise the issue of an inexperienced son inheriting the mantle of his murderous father, proving once again the case of a very simple-minded fraud rather than a sophisticated and effective system of succession of rule.

We have already mentioned the fleeting constitutions, introduced by every new tyrant as a way to lay his future plans before his constituency, whom he did not consult when he seized power. He and everyone else knew that he would not be restrained by those rules and will pursue autocracy with or without a constitution. But lacking any other legitimacy, he feels that his proclaimed goal serves as some kind of justifier, and he would hold on to it throughout his term and show it as his achievement, even if there is no real substance to it. That constitution was aimed at replacing the previous one, which had been written by the previous ruler, full of rosy wordings and sublime pledges, but when the day comes and the autocrat is removed, another paper of that sort will replace it. A plurality of constitutions, one succeeding the other, means that there is no one binding constitution. Only now, in view of the changing realities under the Spring, since public commissions were established to assemble, discuss, and formulate a new constitution, is there any chance that it would be more open and liberal and not reflective exclusively of the ruler's whims. Two more obstacles stand in the way of removing tyrants: returning the armies to their barracks, as has been done by Erdogan in Turkey and Mursi in Egypt, and searching for some working compromises between the fundamentalist Muslim governments, who are getting the majority but are almost totally shorn of any governing experience, and those parts of the civil population that fear them, lest the entire infrastructure erected by the tyrants in the past decades come to total paralysis.

Note

1.   During the Muslim Rebellion in Yunnan, China, in the nineteenth century, its leader, Du Wenxiu, assumed the title of *Qa'id Jami' al-Muslimin* (the commander of all Muslims).

4

The Caliphate and the Ideal of the Islamic State

There is almost no Muslim fundamentalist movement in the Islamic world that, in spite of the uncertainties of the Spring, does not put forward its dream of establishing its Shari'a state as part of the ultimate caliphate. What is the magic of this utopian state that is so much talked about? We have already explained above the contribution of the caliphate to the authoritarian state in Islam, and we have now to become aware that a caliphate would mean two contradictory trends: on the one hand, this is the ideal Islamic state that any Islamic society, in fact all Islamic society, should strive for; but on the other hand such a regime is only a replacement (*Khilafa*) of the truly ideal one that existed at the time of the Prophet. The time of the Prophet was unique in human history and will not repeat itself; therefore the ideal will never recur, since the era of the Prophet has revolved and the past has passed. But at the same time, the peak of human ambition cannot possibly surpass the original human endeavor as expressed in and by the caliphate. Thus, it is agreed that the caliphate is the most adequate regime to govern the *umma*, provide for its needs, and defend it. In the pre-nationalist world, when the caliphate succeeded to Muhammed's rule, it was designed to become a universal Muslim administration, like the contemporaneous Sassanid and Byzantine Empires, which were regarded as governing all Zoroastrians and all Christians, respectively.

The great questions remain: since no one could possibly emulate the Prophet, in spite of his unmistakably human nature, does one focus on the example of the caliphs only, and spot among them those particularly worthy of admiration and imitation? Secondly, will the agreed-upon model remain applicable to all future generations of Muslims, in view that the Shari'a is itself eternal and immutable? And thirdly, are there other ways than the *bai'a* to legitimize the rule, creating a lasting social pact between the ruler and the ruled? At the beginning of Islam, the four righteous caliphs who succeeded the Prophet ad hoc (Abu Bakr, 'Umar, 'Uthman, and 'Ali) were elected by the *shura* based on their personal merit, though admittedly also on nepotism, lobbying, tensions, competition, and quarrels. But, exactly as the Prophet was the most perfect of created men and he could not sin or act indecently, so too the Righteous, known as second only in sanctity to the Prophet, came closest to perfection, though differences existed between and among them in Islam during their lifetime and certainly after their death. The fact is that three of the four were assassinated/killed in the middle of their term, creating a precedent of responding to disagreement by taking the lives of those who were thought to deviate from the norm in the making of government in post-prophetic Islam. The last of them, 'Ali, absorbed the most criticism, because unlike others who accepted the choice of the *shura* and served under the elected caliphs, he and his followers bitterly protested discrimination against him, since on three occasions he was skipped over, until he was elected as the fourth successor.

When Ali was elected, his election remained questioned and challenged by others, so much so that his brief caliphate of five years (656–61) was in itself controversial and ended with his death in battle, thus bringing to its close the Rashidun era of thirty years (632–61). Ali was supported throughout his repeated candidacy by a faction (Shi'a) of well-wishers and disciples, who brought out his personal and family qualities (*Ahl al-bayt*), rather than his governmental skills to fill the function of caliph, for he was the Prophet's cousin and also son-in-law, since he married Muhammed's sole surviving daughter, Fatima. The Shi'a also propagated an unconfirmed claim that on his deathbed the Prophet had designated Ali, his son-in-law, as his successor. It would have had a tremendous impact on the inheritance of government in Islam, had the Prophet had a son who might have succeeded him, which would have meant more of a reliance on blood succession than on merit. This complication was further aggravated when Mu'awiya, the nephew of the slain third caliph 'Uthman, accused Ali's people of the murder and seized power in Damascus, ostensibly to avenge his uncle, but in fact to vie for himself and for the establishment of the Umayyads, the first dynastic house in Islam. Thus, it was not only Ali's life that ended in battle, but with him also the Era of the Righteous Caliphs, who remain nevertheless sublime and deeply respected in Islam, second only to the Prophet himself.

As explained above, the Ali faction was created and maintained to sustain their patron's claim to the caliphate; it was a political expectation and demand to start with. It is well possible that had Ali received what he wanted, and had the enormous opposition been neutralized, there would have been no major schism in Islam. However, as it happened, right after 'Uthman's murder in 656 and Ali's appointment to succeed, the mounting opposition led him on a collision course with the mainstream. For a great innovation was there, when Ali and his people claimed that family qualifications overrode personal merit. But Mu'awiya, who led the battle against Ali, did exactly what his sworn enemy wanted: to lend family priority to the rules of succession, when he instituted his royal house of the Umayyads. For decades in that house, rule passed from father to son, thus opening the road thereafter to blood succession in Islam, as in other royal dynasties in other cultures, lasting until the decline of the Ottomans in the twentieth century. Nonetheless, Ali was accepted and venerated in Sunni Islam as the fourth caliph, while the Shi'ites continued to curse the first three as usurpers. The Sunnites, who made many efforts for the Shi'a to join Islam as a fifth school, naturally predicated the union on the Shi'ites' acceptance of the first three Rashidun, but the followers of Ali categorically refused. As years passed, the two parts of Islam have grown so far apart, both politically and theologically, that it is impossible to see how they can get closer, or how the gap between their principles can be bridged. The Spring has further deepened and dramatized the gap, to the point of turning them into bitter rivals on both sides of the divide.

The main sect of the Shi'a, the Twelvers who rule Iran, is founded on the principle of the Twelve Imams, the first of whom is Ali himself, followed by his two sons, Hasan and Hussein, and another series of nine imams. The last of these disappeared as a child in the tenth century, and as the Hidden Imam who rules the world from behind the scenes, he will reappear as the savior at the end of time, rescue humanity from misery, and inaugurate an era of justice and plenty. As long as this doctrine existed as an eschatological vision, it was not disputed so openly and bitterly, and the Shi'ite minority could live side by side with the Sunni majority with a low profile, though no love was lost between them. But the 1979 Islamic Revolution of Khumeini shuffled the cards, in fact unwittingly serving as the precursor of the Islamic Spring. Khumeini in his time, and even more so Ahmadinejad, the president of Iran in the 2000s, pressed for the acceleration of the messianic process. Like Rabbi Kook in religious Judaism, and unlike Ultra-Orthodox Jews who prefer the quietist approach of waiting and expecting the Messiah, the Iranian leaders have elected to aid the process and hasten salvation through acts of piety, like the declaration of the Revolution; the aid they extend to Syria, Hamas, and Hizbullah to fight for the cause of Islam; the convening in Tehran of the Terrorism International organization to struggle against the West and Israel, and more.

Khumeini professed that his Islamic Revolution was intended for export. He also revived and operationalized the doctrine advocated by the senior ayatullahs (ayatullah uzma). They are in constant contact with the Hidden Imam and get their guidance from him; therefore they are the best positioned to know how to manage the affairs of the state until his reappearance, and how to hasten his return. President Ahmadinejad, who despite his high position is not a cleric, is nevertheless one of the most zealous believers in hastening the coming of the imam. When he was the mayor of Tehran he undertook the widening of the main avenues of the city to accommodate the large crowds projected to flood the streets when the imam reappears. When he spoke at the UN, he said he sensed and was aware of the aura of the imam that enveloped him, all meaning that the return of the Hidden Imam was no longer an apocalyptic event to occur at the end of days, but a concrete and imminent affair to be expected any day. Thus, when these visions and delusions are spelled out, coupled with the nuclear power that Iran has been frantically deploying a supreme effort to attain, they cause extreme concern in Israel and the world. Moreover, due to the historical division in the world of Islam between Sunna and Shi'a, Iran's current doctrinal precipitation of the end of days, when declaring the immediate return of the Hidden Imam, instead of what was traditionally an eschatological long-haul thought, coupled with its stepped-up military preparations, nuclear and missile armaments, and unbridled bellicose statements, has raised deep security concerns among Iran's Sunnite neighbors and heightened the arms race in the region.

Another aspect is also added to these worries: Unlike policy considerations of give and take, gains and losses, the desirable and the possible, which are usually made within rational boundaries, the apocalyptic motive of Iran's leaders may distort their capacity to weigh pros and cons once they are persuaded that the worse the situation, the closer the Day of Judgment and the return of the imam, which are foretold and signaled by the "Pangs of the Messiah." In such a situation, they will not be deterred by the threats they incur in pursuing their policy, but may even wish to precipitate them, knowing they would thus hasten the return of the imam. In other words, all the international reasoning based on accepted norms of restraint, diplomatic custom, rational debate, and logical argument are turned on their head. The Iranians, who launched their Spring thirty years before all others, have in the meantime acquired some valuable allies in Iraq, Syria, Hizbullah in Lebanon, and Hamas in Gaza, thus forming the Shi'ite Crescent (despite the fact that Syria and Hamas are consummately Sunnite). This alliance has become a real threat to its neighborhood, with its well-armed one hundred million inhabitants who can sustain their own long-term bellicosity without risk of depletion or exhaustion. They are perceived as so dangerous to the Sunnite countries (except for Syria, their ally, but that too can change with the eventual fall of Assad) that for many clerics in the Sunnite world they are "worse than the Jews," no mean compliment for both. That means that this is no longer a matter of bridging the doctrinal gaps between them, but bridging a widening gulf that can produce a confrontation between the parties and push the Sunnites to develop nuclear weapons too. Turkey enjoys a special status in this regard, because as a senior Sunnite state that wishes to lead the rest, it also abhors the idea of a nuclear Iran. One has to recall that the removal of the Erbakan government from Ankara in 1998 was due to its rapprochement to Iran, and that Syria, which Turkey wished to co-opt into its alliance with Iran to form a new Middle Eastern front, has slipped into chaos and caused increased tension with Iran. For now, as the balance in the new Middle East seems to turn toward the Muslim Brothers and their ilk, and as they are busy showing their smiling face, it is difficult to predict what policy they might adopt after the dust settles.

This deviation from the main narrative to explain what has happened in modern Iran impels us to return to the main course in order to pursue the story of the caliphate. Shi'a continued after its schism from the sunna, inhabiting the eastern mountainous regions of Islamdom, in Persia/Iran and Central Asia, with one exceptional foray into North Africa—the Fatimid Empire of the time of the Crusades. Most other Muslim territory was Sunni. Namely, when we talk about Muslim empires, we mean Sunnite. For the Shi'ites that means that if three out of the four first caliphs are rejected as usurpers, then the entire model of the caliphate as the ideal form of rule collapses. After those four, Mu'awiya's family literally took over by force the kingship of the Arab/ Muslim world, establishing the first dynasty of the House of Umayya, thus not only enforcing dynastic hereditary succession of rule instead of the previously meritocratic system but also determining that since no dynasty can survive forever, wars of succession would follow. After the Umayyads came the Abbasids, some of whose legendary rulers were immortalized in the *Thousand Nights and One Night* tales, and they were themselves demoted by the Mongols in 1258 when Baghdad was occupied and destroyed. But before it crumbled under the weight of its years, the dynasty had grown more Islamic than Arab, and its capital moved eastward to the Iranian area. However, the vast uncontrollable territories of the dynasty and the huge distances between them could not prevent new centrifugal forces from rising in the periphery: the Iberian Umayyads, the successive North African dynasties, the Fatimids, and then the Mamluks in Egypt, and then slowly the penetration of the Turkish Seljuks and Ottomans, who, once Islamized, contributed to the revitalization of the Islamic Empire.

We are shown by the historical experience with so many caliphates—from the Righteous to the Ottomans, even if we should include the mighty Moghuls who paralleled the Ottomans chronologically—that only seldom was the ideal of one Shari'a Law state inclusive of the entire *umma* close to being realized. The record also shows that the more *dar-al-Islam* expanded, the less was the caliphate able to exercise power over it. For example, when Islam reached East and Southeast Asia, and Black Africa, and took root in places like Indonesia, Malaysia, Mali, Kenya, and Nigeria, it was clear that aspiring to one all-encompassing Muslim caliphate had become impractical. Then, why the persistence of the single-mindedness that this kind of regime was the ideal one, while in the real world it could almost never enforce itself in view of the geographical, ethnic, linguistic, cultural, and political diversity? Maybe the modern dreamers of the renewed caliphate hope that the improvements in communications and transport could make possible what was not in the previous centuries. In any case, this mythical ambition persists. Take for example the platform of Hamas, worded in 1988, which was supposed to respond to the Palestinian aspiration to rid themselves of what they saw as Israeli occupation, but ended up peddling the idea of the caliphate, which larger and more secure states like Turkey and Pakistan, who had experienced empire, do not dream of. The reason is that Hamas, being a branch of the Muslim Brothers, who have made the caliphate one of their main tenets, is bound to raise it as one of its principal goals. Now that Egypt itself, the homeland of the Brothers, has come under their aegis, it may be that this item will no longer be confined to a platform and will grow to become a political blueprint.

The following references in the Hamas charter are worth mentioning and remembering, bearing in mind the great strides the Brothers and their affiliates have been making in the world:

1. Article 11 of the charter refers to the land of Palestine as an eternal *waqf* (holy endowment). Therefore it is not negotiable, even not by Arab kings, presidents, and other leaders, because the ban to negotiate it away is part of the Shari'a. This formula leans on the caliphate of 'Umar (634–44). When the caliph was asked about the fate of Syria and Iraq, which had just been conquered, he answered, after consultation with the rest of the Prophet's companions, that the land had to stay in the hands of those (not yet Islamized inhabitants living on it at the time) as a *usufructus*, but its ownership and domination must stay as an eternal Muslim *waqf* for all generations to come, until the Day of Judgment. It is clear that by recruiting such a prestigious source among the Rashidun to back their uncompromising demand for the entire land of Palestine, Hamas was addressing the entire Muslim audience and expecting their help. Knowing how much 'Umar was an exemplary caliph among caliphs, and remembering the image he created of a righteous and just ruler, it is clear why they chose his reputation and the institution of the caliphate to back their claim.

2. In Article 22, the Jews are presented as the enemies of the caliphate, because they triggered World War I in order to wipe out the caliphate, a hint to the Anglo-French conspiracy against the Ottoman Empire. This kind of accusation had been propagated by none other than Sayyid Qut'b, the great guide of the Brothers until his execution in 1966 by Nasser. He had spent time in the United States and returned obsessed by hatred of the West and its values, which he viciously attacked in his writings. Prominent among them was his book *Our War with the Jews*, in which he dubbed them the enemies of Allah and of Islam, and imputed to them—like other anti-Semites, Muslim and non-Muslim—all the evils of the world, including the dismantling of the caliphate.

It would seem unrealistic today—after the division of the Islamic world into fifty-seven separate countries, languages, and ethnic groups, and in view of the prevailing personal, regional, and national jealousies among them—that they could all possibly unite under one rule. But it is a fact that the ideal persists, in any case among the fundamentalists who aspire to *shari'a* law in their countries. But among these groups that champion the caliphate there are different orders and different paces of execution. The Brothers, including Hamas, advocate the takeover of government in their countries and the enforcement of Shari'a there, as they did in Gaza, before all countries who would have achieved the same could unite into a caliphate. But the Salafis and the Taliban profess the creation of a caliphate first, one that would by definition be mighty and comprehensive enough to impose Shari'a on all Muslims. The Brothers in Egypt have embraced a cautious and gradual method of introducing the holy law to all citizenry, lest sudden and all-encompassing Islamization deter and frighten hesitant and uncertain souls who had been corrupted by modernization, secularization, and Westernization. But there are also some aggressive currents, such as the Taliban when they held the helm of power in Afghanistan in the 1990s; the Gama'at in Egypt before they were wiped out by Mubarak; or the armed groups in Algeria, who mercilessly fought and killed their countrymen in order to impose their way. Only now, as the Spring is beginning to show its fruits—for example in Tunisia and Egypt—will we be able to detect the way and method chosen by the new leaderships of those countries to implement their Islamization blueprint. Where there is no decision yet, as in Syria, Libya, and Yemen, it is too early to know who will rise and who will fall, and for how long. One can imagine, however, that everywhere a settlement is agreed upon, the emerging ruler will have to explain where his legitimacy comes from. In Egypt and Tunisia we saw a genuine effort to conduct a fair election campaign, to keep restraint, and to distance the military from the election process. These are signs of legitimization of government.

Conversely, in places where the struggle is going on, there is no telling how it might be decided. But one thing is certain: the previous illegitimate rulers will not be back; in other words, there is necessity and urgency to replace them by others who can inspire legitimacy. But who are they? What do they stand for? Who can guarantee their behavior as long as the democratic game is not digested well enough to become an organic part of the local politics? And what is legitimacy after all? It can follow the Ferrero model of democracy or the caliphate precedent, as the fundamentalists would have it. Democracy has never been tried to its full extent in the Islamic world, and we are hardly watching its first steps and holding our breath for it to succeed. It is true that most current Spring movements in the Islamic world advocate slogans of democracy, but it is not clear at all that any of them knows what it is talking about, for none of them ever experienced Western-style democracy . Democracy is not only elections, because beyond a given method of electing the leadership, it also means a state of mind that lets the media act freely, respects the majority but protects the minority, does not pursue investigative journalists who publicize the corruption of the system (as is the case in Pakistan and Turkey today); respects human rights; gives top adjudicating power to an independent judiciary; does not arbitrarily arrest its citizens, accusing them of plots against the government; refrains from incitement against its citizens and neighbors; advocates an open and liberal mode of government; and pursues a policy of good neighborliness. Where was there ever a paradise like this in the Islamic world? And where could such a regime materialize after so many years of oppression, corruption, and travesty of justice? For a regime to be able to operate on such a standard, it first has to be legitimate. It is obvious that the Spring broke out precisely in countries where the young people have had enough of tyrannical rule for decades, with no chance of change, for the rule of the fathers was to be taken up by their sons. Namely, the hopelessness of change was what pushed the young people to rebel. The demonstrators shouted, "Freedom! Democracy! Expel the tyrant!" But we do not know what they meant, nor did they indicate what ought to be done to alter the situation. In most places we saw the same hypocrites and servile aides of the previous rulers, who had served them for years, suddenly turn over to the rebels. So, people are suspicious and confused, not knowing whom to trust, convinced that whoever steals for you today will steal from you tomorrow.

At the height of the crisis, the only alternative to the crumbling rulers has seemed to be the Islamic state that the Muslim Brothers consistently preached since their inception. They are on record as opposing democracy for being a human-made system that cannot compete with divinely inspired shari'a. Thus, despite the latter's problems and anachronism, the caliphate, after a millennium and a half of experiments that never lasted, still looks to the Believers as the most trusted, known, and promising avenue. In other words, that was the only system that could still lend legitimacy to the rulers, being based on Islamic tradition. For that reason, each time an existing system threatened to crumble, the caliphate alternative loomed on the horizon as the only acceptable alternative. But when we begin comparing it with democracy, we immediately realize that not only are they incompatible but they contradict each other in some very fundamental respects. Some believe that fundamentalist movements that totally negate democracy would step immediately into a shari'a caliphate-like state, as did the Taliban during their short stint in power (1996–2001) in Afghanistan. But the masses in the world of Islam have become so open to world media, to television, to the customs and standards of living in the West, to Internet and the social networks, and to the benefits of liberal democracy and human rights that they cannot be easily deprived of all that after decades of exposure. They are no longer prepared to accept oppression as a divine calamity; therefore the idea of a caliphate, which would be another kind of oppression from their point of view, would not be readily accepted without question.

Therefore, pragmatic Islamic movements like those in Egypt and Tunisia are compelled to pretend to behave democratically, just long enough to accustom the public to their style of rule, before they begin imposing restrictions and gradually trapping their public with the incontrovertibility of *sharia* law, which no individual in an Islamic society can resist without incurring the wrath of his environment. This method has already been dubbed "one man, one vote, one time," meaning that following the one voluntary vote that lent legitimacy to their rule, such fundamentalists would need no more legitimacy to rule, because they would be applying *sharia*. For this reason, the early experiments we are witnessing in Egypt and Tunisia, as the test cases of the Spring, could be decisive for the fate of the entire Spring. For if these tests succeed in establishing a modern and efficient Muslim society that enjoys freedom, without the harassments that accompany puritanical Muslim societies—like restrictions on women, public morals police, and fair elections to all levels of government and the like—then the new reformed style of the Muslim Brothers, which will be more moderate and sensitive than what they have been preaching for almost a century since their foundation, can perhaps produce a new, softer, feasible, and foundational Islam, a sort of revolutionary reform, instead of the restorative reform that they have advocated since their beginnings.

However, if, as one is entitled to suspect, the eternal values of Islam prevail, with their conservative and fundamentalist leanings, as in the days of Ibn Taymiya in Egypt and Syria or the Wahhabis in Arabia, or the days of Banna and Qutb in Egypt again, and the clerics once again regard themselves as the watchdogs of the integrity of their faith in the face of the Western cultural and civilizational onslaught, then major confrontations are to be expected between two lifestyles, where the winner is not necessarily the stronger but the more doggedly committed to his version of Islam in the world, as has already been evident in many arenas of the Spring today. The days of the Spring have shown that even in Islamic societies that had taken large strides toward civil government, like Turkey and Tunisia, it was still possible to arrest the process with the help of the backward societies of the conservative and illiterate countryside, while the urban bourgeoisie was watching with horror, but helplessly, as its great modernizing achievements rolled back toward abrogation. What model of Islam will these countries choose when the dust settles? Only time will tell.

5

The Globalization of Information and the World Media

In the past decades, we have gotten used to the fact that important international events are dubbed "breaking news" and covered ad nauseam from top to bottom, much more than a well-informed person would need. So we watched that intrusive report on Tiananmen (1989), and the popular revolutions against the tyrants of Eastern Europe (1989–90), including the executions of their leaders, minute by minute, to the point that we felt as though we were taking part in the news, not just watching them. This was also the case at the beginning of the Spring, when it was still considered an Arab Spring, and the hopes attached to it reached the sky. After Tunisia, Egypt rapidly drew our attention to the point that the large gatherings in Tahrir Square (which is in fact a roundabout), the cascades of messages in social media, the ceaseless demonstrations in the streets under the open eyes of the international networks, and the takeover by the army—which brought an end to the thirty-year rule of Mubarak—all became part of our daily schedule. The waning away of Mubarak, who had grown synonymous with government in Egypt and became a permanent fixture in his palaces, was somehow subsumed under the cataract of events. Then, that very same image rolled on to Libya, Yemen, Bahrain, Syria, and back. It seemed that the entire Arab world was in turmoil and that after some weeks of disorder, order was bound to fall back into place. Little did we know that even the second year of the upheaval did not see the turmoil end, and what seemed a transitory phase of rebellion pending a settlement seemed to stabilize into a permanent situation of unease, uncertainty, and rage.

It is evident that if it were not for the media revolution that shook the Arab world a decade ago and introduced Qatar-based al-Jazeera as a new standard of relatively free and critical reporting into the Arab world, maybe the Spring could not have broken out, and if it had, it might have been quelled without the outside world even knowing about it. For until al-Jazeera, most of the Arabic press reported only what it was told or allowed to report; the rulers considered the press a tool to shape their public opinion rather than reflect it. To this day, only countries like Saudi Arabia, which do not permit al-Jazeera to operate within their borders, can continue to cover up what they wish and cut off any news not to their liking (without any Western protest or sanctions). After this breakthrough in the Arab media, and the outstanding reputation al-Jazeera achieved for its newly revealed authoritativeness and credibility (though it has also been accused of inciting anti-Western sentiment and pro-Islamic fundamentalist support), other international media followed suit: CNN, BBC, France 24, al-Arabiya, Fox News, Sky News, and others, which lent worldwide resonance to anything happening in the Arab world, especially in the context of the Spring. That intense reporting, which was constantly accompanied by commentaries, round tables, and special bulletins of breaking news, brought every detail of what was going on in the Arab world, minute by minute, to all the living rooms of the world, acquainting everyone who wished to listen or watch with names of people and places that they had never heard before, and with the histories of those remote places that most people did not know existed. The very fact of reporting so intensely and so frequently on the same part of the world had a snowball effect, because the moment a major event was recorded somewhere, parallels were sought in other parts of the Islamic world, in the understandable quest to complete the picture with similar events that were unfolding elsewhere. To that were immediately added expert views of commentators who were asked to predict the future of the Spring in this or that part of the world, and what consequences could be expected from these events. In other words, the Spring became a self-nourishing and self-perpetuating topic, which could keep busy all the international media for months to come. To this were added the side stories and anecdotes that had nothing to do with the Spring, but with the adventures or mishaps of the foreign correspondents who tried to cover it. These included journalists trapped under bombardment in Aleppo or Hama, a female journalist who was dragged into Tahrir square and raped by the incited crowds, another reporter who was wounded in the exchange of fire and could not be evacuated, or UN observers who could not be deployed on the ground for fear of being injured, as if firefighters were not supposed to act where fires raged, and the like. Back in their own countries, the readership of these war reporters became more interested in hearing what happened to them and how they did survive their mishaps, than in the continuing saga of the Spring, which was now temporarily shoved aside or reduced in volume in those Western news outlets.

The unfolding developments also created their own industry of news: for example, when NATO began to bomb Libya, the question immediately arose whether the same would be applied to Syria, and speculation began about whether in the face of the much more formidable military defenses of the latter, any European power would dare to risk the lives of its soldiers to advance its foreign policy. It was impossible to predict, on the basis of a single event, what would be happening the next day, but there were always daring and imaginative commentators who *knew* precisely what this leader or that movement would do or how they would react. The message of the Spring became so prevalent in the news networks that the international media focused all eyes on the central squares where things happened or on the battle fronts where government and rebel forces were confronting each other. The rebels, confident of the international sympathy that their democratic pretensions drew, took comfort from the growing circles of fighters who joined their ranks, and from the prominent personalities among their compatriots who announced periodically their desertion from government offices in order to join the opposition. More than a grain of opportunism was there, because if all those who wished to rebel and oppose government policies had been there from the outset, they should have joined the rebellion at its inception. To join it only when it seemed to win, and the government seemed to wane and lose, looked more like a convenient way to ensure themselves high positions after the Spring than ideological support for one side or another. Certainly, the rationale could always be used that they were hesitant in the beginning, not knowing whether the rebellion had any chance, but when its success firmed up, they took the daring step of joining it after their help became redundant. But an expedient Spring without ideology, just relying on the good judgment of moving from a losing side to a winning side, is hardly the sort of upheaval that could be expected to unfold or to emerge victorious.

The Western countries also sat on the sidelines, waiting for a decisive trend to emerge before they took sides. They behaved as if they had no other considerations than their narrow interest, and they peddled those interests cynically, coldly, so as not to inspire—Allah forbid!—any sense of morality, justice, humanity, or good thinking. Europeans who had just traded with Qaddafi the release of the Lockerbie terrorists in return for some commercial benefits, or had just sold him weapons to enable him to oppress his people, suddenly switched sides and began to bombard him and seek his destruction, while in the preceding months they had been cultivating him and praising him for relinquishing his nuclear program. Those ugly turnarounds did not escape the scrutiny of the rebels who were trying to unseat him and then kill him. "How was it possible to support the tyrant and then turn against him when his fortunes were reversed?" So asked the Egyptian rebels of Tahrir Square, who for decades saw their dictator bolstered by the Westerners—and suddenly, as he seemed to lose support in the army, they demanded his ouster? "Who can take the West seriously and who can count on its support or encouragement?" they asked. It was as if the Western leaders had been blinded for years by the tyrants who were now being shot down one by one, and now that they discovered, to their dismay and disarray, the fallacy of their judgment, they were trying to urge everybody to open their eyes and see the sight they had themselves ignored for so long. New phrases began to figure in the media, where they were absent for too long, phrases like: "pictures are like weapons; they can totter a regime." What is more, most of the pictures that caused the sympathy to shift to the rebellions were taken by amateur cameras embedded within mobile phones, incidental shots that no one had intended to take, much less to spread around the world.

In short, this entire upheaval has been the fruit of the media revolution that has unfolded among the young individually, only by accident, not by design, while each was attending to his own concerns; it was coincidence that all of these young revolutionaries unwittingly came together to amplify the public message into one big, loud, and clear voice of the revolution. Thus, the affairs of state, economy, and society, toward which the rebels had evinced indifference a year earlier, were pushed to the frontline of the public agenda. Then, the pictures that shook the world, of the young man burning in Tunisia and of thousands streaming to Tahrir Square, were soon spread to other parts of the universe, thus multiplying the effects worldwide, commensurate with the tremendous resonance that social networks like Facebook, Twitter, talkbacks, blogs, and the like can afford. Now, these new networks were no longer only a matter of social expediency serving a cause of gossip and small talk, or advertising a party or a concert, but had become a tool of momentous importance, to help oppressed people to organize, to urge scattered individuals to defy the tools of oppression that controlled them, and to offer to the world alternative avenues of free information other than the narrow options of official data that they had been fed for years, or the biased versions that major news organizations were collecting to respond to their own needs and interests. In spite of the paradox involved, media created immediacy.

These rapid developments have created in each location a wider circle of interest in the Spring, inasmuch as not only local people in each country cared about what was happening in their immediate environment, but groups of the fans of the Spring were created everywhere. These groups not only began to form contacts and channel help, advice, and encouragement to a place in need but also to show interest in the comparison between various sites of the Spring, to investigate the common traits between them, to learn from each other, and to extend assistance from a place that had passed through similar experiences to another country that was about to face them. Names of people and places that had been anonymous and beyond the experience of common people who go about their daily business suddenly became a matter of course (Mursi, Tantawi, Ghanouchi, Tahrir, Hama, Tartus, and the like). They all flowed daily through our living rooms, and the images in flames emitting smoke hung before our eyes constantly. And everyone had an opinion about who did what, what should be done, who were right and who were wrong, who are the righteous to be encouraged and the evil to be condemned and fought against.

The deep significance of the revolution did not consist in the fact that every oppressed on earth could suddenly demand justice, as if he knew what that meant, and as if doing justice was something so absolute and well defined that it was only necessary to bend and pick it up from the street. Now justice, rights, revolution, democracy were discussed as if everyone knew what they meant, along with who should advance the demands, from whom and to whom. Everyone saw fit not only to feel the suffering and describe it in his or her own words, but also to report it in detail, amid explosions of emotion, and outside the allowed state media that had previously set the boundaries of what could be said and seen, when, how, and by whom. Now, there was a torrent of information pouring in from every direction and course, a state of affairs that suddenly moved the international media from measured and rationed information into this gushing wellspring of news and gossip, fact and legend, eye-report and hearsay, as if to compensate for all the years and decades of news constipation, censorship, oppression of information and of the soul. A good deal of daring was necessary on the part of the new unprofessional journalists who were eager to report and be part of the news flow in spite of the risk of being caught and shot as a traitor for exposing to foreign propaganda what should have remained patriotically hidden from the eye. Those who took the risk viewed themselves as contemporary historians, in charge of telling and documenting the history that was being made in their presence, like Thucydides and Josephus Flavius in their times. For lack of skill and training in writing, and acceding to the state media, they stealthily took pictures that became their visiting cards and made their reputation by their sheer widespread distribution.

A sizeable part of the media revolution, triggered by al-Jazeera during the Spring, has been to enlist and encourage those informal reporters to become its affiliates, thereby widening the scope of its representatives on the ground, while events were erupting everywhere; by gaining free and instant amplification, these events turned into world events. Syria, Yemen, and Libya later followed that example, enriching the reports on the ground as they were unfolding. One amateurish movie tells the story of a few young people who became underground reporters and dispatched tweets during the shelling, relating the "true story" of what was going on. *True story* is inside quotation marks because what these inexperienced reporters saw or heard was not necessarily what happened. One of those young people reported from Cairo, for example, about a violent demonstration opposite the Israeli Embassy there, with Egyptian security forces standing by and not showing any intention of interfering. Israel was forced to evacuate its people from the building, under emergency measures, after the United States had to intervene with the highest Egyptian authorities. That Egyptian reporter, however, narrated a story of a tranquil and nonviolent demonstration, a story that did not concord with the way the Egyptian army got violently involved, thus acting against the Egyptian people whom it was supposed to defend, according to reports one heard continuously in the field. This clip, which was also edited by al-Jazeera, showed that during those chaotic moments someone was interested in blaming the Egyptian armed forces for having defended the cause of the Israelis, instead of naturally extending their protection to the Egyptian people. In fact, it was the Israeli Embassy's personnel who were exposed to imminent danger, and if not for the firm intervention of the armed forces, under American instigation, there could have been a serious threat to their lives. In other words, one had to take those reports with a large grain of salt, because the reporters also had an axe to grind or were hired to serve the interest of others.

The new actors on the media scene became a topic of interest unto themselves, independently of the Spring cause they were representing. The tweets themselves turned into an item for reports and video clips. Later they developed into full-fledged films and background stories, like those of February 2012 that purported to sum up a year of revolution in Egypt, eliciting reactions from people who a year earlier would not have cared to react to the events. Some of them thought that one year after Mubarak, nothing had really changed, since everything, even the elections, was still under the same military control as since the 1952 Revolution. Mubarak, who was now indicted for his "crimes" had yet to receive the punishment he deserved for what he did, they complained, while ten thousand commoners who had demonstrated against the tyrant were tried and convicted by military courts. It was said that only through Twitter could one gauge the true scope of the revolution and follow minute by minute the events that were not reported by the state media. In the minds of the unprofessional field reporters, this pointed to the courage of the people. They surveyed the eighteen months of euphoria that preceded the revolution and the twelve difficult months that followed. In a film made on that period, the narrative of events conformed to the points of view of the young and frustrated narrators, and the innovation was that those young people themselves, not the events of the rebellion, had become the major focus of the investigation of the film. Why was it so, and why was international attention suddenly turned on Egypt, while previously Egypt was a backwater sunk in poverty? Wide-ranging reports of this sort were broadcast on al-Jazeera about Tunisia and Libya, indicating the network's support of the revolutions and of the military governments that had risen against the tyrants. Take two examples of this never-before-seen coverage of those momentous events:

a. In an early account of the first days of the Tunisian revolution (December 31, 2010) it was said that a Tunisian demonstrator died of his wounds after he was shot by police in the town of Manzil Bouzien The international human rights organization blamed the use of live ammunition by the Tunisian security forces and called for an independent investigation to find out what had happened. It also urged that the right to demonstrate peacefully be observed. The unusual revolutionary conduct of all concerned was noticed at once, when the human rights organizations in Tunisia dared to give interviews and condemn the government for its conduct. Lawyers were arrested and beaten harshly, both in the capital and in the city of Monastir, when they protested government violence. The government had indeed ordered the lawyers beaten; some were arrested, and the rest dispersed. The lawyers also complained that their mobile phones had been confiscated, in order to prevent them from photographing the events. Attorney Abd al-Rahman Aidi complained that he was tortured by police after he was arrested on December 28. Helpless in the face of the situation, President Ben-ali dismissed the governor of Sidi Bouzeid, where the turbulences had broken out, as well two other governors and three government ministers, including the minister of communications. The demonstrators claimed that instead of responding to their demands for reforms, the administration prevented them from any public debate. They also complained that the Tunisian media, obedient to the government, did not properly report on the disturbances. They bitterly mentioned that unlike the angry reaction of the Western media against the Iran government for quelling the 2009 demonstrations against it, the same public opinion was indifferent with regard to Tunisia, proving that it was not concern about freedom and democracy, but some other narrow interests that left Western media apathetic toward Tunisia.

When demonstrators started to feel self-confident and free to lash out at the subject of their wrath, nothing could stop them anymore, after all the obstacles of fear, embarrassment, and good manners were removed. In their interviews with the press, people complained about unemployment for university graduates and aired grievances regarding the oppression of the freedom of speech, the government domination of the state media, and the tight control by the Ministry of Communications of all the printed and electronic media. To their mind, that left the Internet as the only channel of communications through which young people could express their views, especially when the government, which faced this wave of complaints, banned al-Jazeera within Tunisia. This left YouTube and Twitter as the only accessible means for reporting on the protests and rebellions within the country. Many of the writers in these avenues expressed dissatisfaction with the international networks for failing to report more adequately on the events in Tunisia, compared, for example, with the more fluent, detailed comments and breaking news that all of them had reserved to cover the Iran demonstrations in 2009.

b. On May 11, 2012, al-Jazeera disseminated a series of portraits of the Libyan leaders, materials that under Qaddafi would have been impossible to collect, let alone to distribute. There was an entire treasure of information on the leader himself and his heirs, especially Saif-al-Islam, who was trying to project a more sophisticated image than his primitive, eccentric, and deranged father. For that purpose, he is said to have purchased a doctorate in London and placed himself at the head of high-level and complicated diplomatic missions for his father. During the fighting, he appeared in two alternative images in the Western media: on the one hand, he urged his soldiers to fight and quell the rebels against his father; but on the other hand, he firmly denied that his men were killing civilians. Several times he suggested that elections should be held in his country, but his offer was rejected by the rebels. These aspects of Libyan politics were taboo, and no one dared to bring them up until the Spring broke out and the media started to take liberties. Al Baghdadi al-Mahmudi, who was appointed by Qaddafi as his prime minister in 2006, was in charge of Libyan diplomacy during the Spring, and kept in contact with the secretary general of the UN. But when the rebels laid siege to Tripoli, he ran away to Tunisia, where he was arrested for illegal entry into the country. Libya asked for his extradition, but legal procedures lingered on and on. Abdallah Sanusi was another mysterious figure who served in the much-feared security apparatus suspected of wide-scale killings for Qaddafi. Sanusi was convicted in 1999 in France for the downing on a French plane over Niger (a repetition of the Lockerbie horror), and was sued for crimes against humanity in the International Criminal Court. Finally, he was arrested in Mauritania's international Airport as he tried to escape. Other key personalities, like Tayyib al-Safi, were also exposed by the media, and they would have remained in the shadows, leading a living of corruption and cruelty, had they not been unmasked in this fashion by the rebels.

Nothing revealed more about the incomplete revolutions in all countries concerned than the continuous demonstrations even after the immediate goal of reversing the tyrant was achieved. The initial demonstrators were one thing, but the free riders who took over the revolution were quite another. Take Egypt, for example, where the young (and frustrated) militants—who spontaneously kindled the uprising in Tahrir and sustained losses when the regime reacted violently—were set aside by the better organized and long-term planners of the Muslim Brothers, who ultimately emerged as the winners. The latter, not sure of their ultimate triumph, and reluctant to scare off the Egyptian public by images of an Egypt gone Islamized, assured and reassured the public that they would compete for less than 50 percent of the seats in Parliament and would not run a candidate for the presidency. But enamored of their own successes in the street, they escalated their ambitions as they went along, until they came to emerge victorious in both the legislative and the executive branches of government. These demonstrations—including the one-million rally in Tahrir convened by the Brothers for Sheikh Yussuf Qaradawi, the victory rallies after the elections for both branches of government, and the much publicized swearing in ceremony of President Mursi—could not have happened without the "breaking news" appellation given to them by the world media and al-Jazeera, making the Brothers not only the determining factor in Egyptian politics, but also a new player of consequence on the world scene.

However, for the young people who took part in the demonstrations that tottered Mubarak, little if anything had changed in the past year and a half, popular celebrations notwithstanding. It is a fact that, at variance with the overwhelming victory of the Brothers, some 48 percent of the vote went to their rival, Ahmed Shafiq, who after the result was announced fell into obscure insignificance, instead of heading the strong opposition of almost half the population. That meant that the powers at work were not truly reflected in the media. And until the added drama, played out in the media, of Mursi's dismissal of the army and the top defense command of the country, the initial movers of the revolution were not impressed by its course, because it seemed to them that the same military people who had ruled the country since the 1952 revolution were still in charge of the affairs of the state. Mursi's secret weapon for success has been a series of publicly acted dramas, reported live by the world media, under the unbeatable title of "breaking news."

The Spring afforded many intellectuals, professionals, and artists—in addition to the common people who filled the function of reporters and photographers of their own initiative—the opportunity to speak up, while previously they had been advised to keep quiet or to sing the praise of the regime. For example, the trial of Bahraini policemen over the death of a blogger would have never occurred, nor the event even been heard of, had it not been for the Spring. That trial became an international cause célèbre when it opened in the Bahrain capital of Manama. On trial were five police officers implicated in the death in custody of blogger Zakariya al-Ashiri on April 9, 1911, seven days after he had been arrested as part of a crackdown on pro-democracy activists in the kingdom. The authorities originally said that he died from complications of sickle-cell anemia, but photos showed significant bruises on his body, consistent with beatings. Expectedly, Ashiri was a Shi'ite member of the oppressed majority who ran an online news with a focus on human rights, business, and culture, and he was charged with inciting hatred against the government and promoting sectarianism. His death, a routine misfortune in all the countries of the Spring, provoked an international outcry due to the Spring and the attention of the global media.[1] Under international pressure, two officers were charged with administering the beating that led to the blogger's death, the three others with failure to report a crime to the authorities. The important thing is once they admitted the wrong, the authorities were forced to deal with more reports of this sort: on April 12, when Karim Fakhrawi, the publisher of independent paper *Al-Wasat*, was reported dead in detention. The government tried to misrepresent the cause of death as kidney failure, but again photographs showed clear signs of beatings.

An important study of the media performance during the Tunisian crisis revealed that Facebook fell victim to serious hacking, which required a firm and prompt reaction from the social media site.[2] The security officers of Facebook were discovering, between Christmas 2010 and New Year 2011, that Ammar, the government authority that was censuring Facebook, was in the process of stealing the entire country's worth of passwords. Though there is disagreement about the role of Facebook or Twitter in spreading the uprising that forced Ben-Ali's removal from power on January 14, 2011, there is no doubt that it was the social networks that made the difference this time. It is said that back in July 2010, Mark Zuckerberg, the Facebook founder and president, was shown on his network holding up a sign with a slogan for the freedom of expression campaign. Later, Zuckerberg's image appeared on a sign outside the Saudi Embassy in Tunis, carried by Tunisian protesters, demanding the arrest of Ben Ali. In other words, the young inventor of Facebook had become a symbol of freedom so powerful that merely his picture on signs of protest had become a major mobilizer for the cause of freedom. In that regard one can say that, even if he did not intend to do so, he easily attained something that political, clerical, artistic, academic, scientific, military, or business leaders could not achieve—this young man in his early twenties, with no other record behind him than the huge mobilizing power of a social medium. One can surmise that thanks to that success, by force of circumstance in that country where it was relatively easy to succeed (for Ben Ali was no Saddam Hussein and no Assad), the barrier of fear was broken, and for the rest of the Islamic audience to copy that became a matter of course. That is the power of precedent that Tunisia firmly set up, and that is its importance as the pioneer in the process.

The videos that were shot with camera phones created a link between the demonstrators in the streets and the rest of the Tunisian population, and with the rest of the world in general, and in particular with the Islamic world, which was vying for a model and precedent to emulate. In one video, a young man was lying on a stretcher with his skull cracked open and his brain oozing out. Cries were heard all around. The picture focused on the young man's face, and as the camera withdrew, it captured other people with cameras recording the same injury. That, of course, amplified that event, making it emblematic of the Spring, although such events were probably, and fortunately, rather rare. And so it also happened with each death, atrocity, destruction, injury, and what have you was brought instantly to the attention of the many, but inflated beyond measure. The effect also served to arouse the common people and the world media against the oppressive authorities who caused those horrors, but also to frighten the rest of the victims and prompt them either to run for their lives or to hold firm with determination in their stand against the evil. Besides cameras and cell phones, Facebook tracked minute-by-minute developments of the situation, so that by January 8, 2011, the small country of Tunisia had several hundred thousand more users than it had ever had before, within a week since the outbreak of the disturbances. It is easy to calculate how many times that number must have multiplied for countries twice or ten times Tunisia's population. Also, the average time spent on the site more than doubled what it had been before.

While clashes in the streets went on, bloggers and other watchers sat in their homes and exchanged videos, causing small protests of fifty participants to draw fifty more, who would share them with fifty more, ad infinitum. It was through the instant transmission of these videos that the idea of the need to change the regime began to spread, involving not only the street protesters themselves but also the peaceful middle class who avoided public trouble. The idea took hold so much so that from January 13 onward, rumors began to fly as to the kind of retaliation the government was preparing: to shut down Facebook, or electricity altogether, in order to incapacitate all computers. In any case, a Facebook security investigation found out that the country's Internet providers were concocting a malicious code to record users' login information on sites like Facebook, so that by January 5 the entire country's worth of passwords were being stolen right in the middle of the great political upheaval that shook the Islamic world. That meant that the very tool that people were using to express their discontent was becoming the means of compromising their identities. Facebook implemented technical tricks to protect its viewers, but this is beyond our interest here.

In Libya, where Internet connectivity was already spotty when the violent clashes began, it was completely paralyzed at one point in an attempt to stifle information about the uprising, since the government controlled the country's primary Internet service. In the beginning of March 2011, all online traffic in and out of Libya had ceased. Egypt had taken the same measure several days into the nonviolent protests, when it shut down Internet access for almost a week. Antigovernment protesters there had been using social media services such as Facebook and Twitter to organize and share personal experiences of the unrest. But in Libya the story was a little different, because relatively few people had Internet access prior to the Spring, something that is expected to change after the introduced changes. Only 6 percent of Libyans had Internet access either in their houses or in Internet cafes, compared with 24 percent of Egyptians and 81 percent of Americans. In consequence, Facebook and Twitter played a marginal role in galvanizing antigovernment protesters in Libya. Nonetheless, because the Internet was not central to everyday life in Libya, the few who could get online were the educated and influential, people who used the web to keep informed about the course of the rebellion and the world's reactions to it. In Egypt, by comparison, millions of people used the web, and it was not only the few with access who reported the news; many communicated via blogs that described all sorts of feelings. But in Libya the few who communicated focused on political news, knowing how the masses depended on them for information. So, the blackout made it impossible, especially in the capital Tripoli, for Libyans to receive updates about the revolution in other parts of the country. In particular it made it almost impossible for people outside the country to know how the uprising was unfolding, which was probably the government's main reason for shutting down the web, thus limiting communication to cell phones. Libya had then, and will probably retain, one of the highest rates of cell phone usage in Africa, but the country's two mobile phone operators were owned by government, so even though there was no evidence of phone disruptions, there were occasions when coverage was spotty.

Amazing in itself is the array of slogans that kicked off the revolution, especially in Tunisia, which despite the repression was more open than elsewhere for such a medium as street advertisement. Larbi Sadiki[3] has

shown the poignancy and impact of several such public pronouncements on the unfolding Spring in Tunisia. The simple heartwarming
declaration "Love you people" (*Ahibbak ya-sha'b*), written in black paint
on whitewashed walls, was one of the most striking pieces of graffiti.
"Just imagine," wrote Sadiki, "loving 10 million Tunisians at once. That
would include the tens of thousands who were trained and deployed
to kill the Revolution, the rapists, the opportunists and the butchers of
Tala, Sidi Bouzid and Kasserine." He questions whether before January
14, 2011, when that slogan was born, there was any *people* per se, who
then became the core of what happened in that revolution; namely, it
became a dictator-less people, a more human one. A new meaning of the
people was born, he said, which made it sovereign, sublime, ennobled,
and scared. A corollary of this slogan, also reported by Sadiki, was the
phrase "The People's Will" (*al-Sha'b Yureed*), which became one of the
live sites of the revolutions. That will was expressed by people choosing,
opining, parleying, opposing, approving, voting, electing, demonstrating, speaking, writing, and being—novel usages of existing verbs never,
or seldom, used before. It reverberated when chanted in unison by
the masses and echoed the will and determination, invincibility, and
peoplehood of those who were united in chanting it. Nearly the same
wording was used in Tahrir Square in Cairo, in the half-ruined and
besieged neighborhoods of Hama, Der'a, and Aleppo, in the oil fields of
Bregga and the alleys of Tripoli, by the tribes of Yemen and the Shi'ites
of Bahrain. They were all one voice, one people, one will.

"*Tunis Hurra*" (Tunisia is free), was a ubiquitous phrase adorning
the walls of every locality, expressing elation at the departure of the
dictator, while in Damascus calls for the dismissal and execution of
Assad echoed the protracted chants of determined crowds in San'a
for the departure of Saleh, in Tripoli for the execution of Qaddafi and
his corrupt family, and in Cairo for ridding Egypt of ailing Mubarak
and his corrupt and abusive gang. Other slogans urging democracy
or justice, or calling the world for help, weapons, food, medicine,
action, and what have you, were either scribbled on walls or shouted
by demonstrators to foreign journalists or UN observers or written
on signs and waved in the face of anyone who could see or hear. The
shouts of freedom, even if not yet fully experienced positively due to
the predominance of the state of chaos, were very expressive negatively
of the total rejection of the state of slavery, exploitation, misery, and
contempt the masses felt they were treated with by the departed tyrants.
Sadiki also brought up a series of moving images he captured during

the Spring in Tunisia—for example, a man in shooting posture using a baguette to spray imaginary bullets at a long line of riot police officers, all symbolically at the boulevard named after Habib Bourguiba, the man who had installed the civilian authoritarianism that followed the long reigns of the royal *beys*. In another metaphorical image, birdcages were lifted high, their doors open, giving their residents an outlet for freedom; opposite the notorious ministry of the interior, the area was teeming with courageous demonstrators, many draped in the red and white national flag, who constituted the critical mass that triggered the Spring, the revolution that changed Tunisia, the Islamic world, and the world. At the final stages of the upsurge, hundreds of thousands of demonstrators had stood there opposite the Interior Ministry that symbolized the reign of terror, producing an axial shift in history. One year later, the new minister in charge of the interior was Ali La'rayd, one of its former inmates.

When the masses of demonstrators took the risk of confronting their repressive tyrants, one of their fundamental demands was to put an end to online censorship, and ensure freedom of expression. As Yasmine Ryan of al-Jazeera observed, that battle also took place on Internet sites, blogs, Facebook pages, and Twitter feeds. International web activists also drew world attention to the DDoS (distributed denial of service) attacks on servers of companies that blocked payments and server access to the whistle-blowing websites. Wikileaks also joined in solidarity with the Tunisian uprising by publicizing documents supportive of its cause. Sofiene Chourabi, a blogger and a journalist for the *Al-Tariq al-Jadid* (The New Way magazine) and known for his unabashed criticism of the Tunisian authorities, was unable to recover his e-mail and Facebook accounts after they were hijacked at the outset of the revolt. He said he believed that the Tunisian Internet Agency was responsible for hijacking his accounts, blocked access to his Facebook and rendered his blogs unreachable from Tunis. Other Internet users also complained that as of a certain date, they were unable to change their passwords for Facebook. Within hours the authorities were able to delete all information from e-mails and blogs. Others received mysterious phone calls that warned them to delete critical posts on their Facebook pages or else face the consequences. These phishing techniques, were carried out by a malware code, and both Google and Facebook denied any complicity. But web activists and journalists alerted others of the hacking by the government via Twitter, which is not susceptible to the same kind of interference. Tunisian activists were able to contact international groups who then came up with a solution to deactivate the government's malicious code, which was much more intelligent than what the Chinese hackers had used a year before to break into the Gmail of dissidents, in that it was the communication with Gmail that was intercepted. The Committee to Protect Journalists confirmed that there was clear evidence that the phishing campaign was organized and coordinated by the Tunisian government.

The web activists in Tunisia found an ally in *Anonymous*, whose international activists' attention was focused on defeating the Tunisian manipulation and censorship of the web. The DDoS counterattack had succeeded in taking down no fewer than eight websites, including those of the offices of the president, the prime minister, the Ministry of Industry, the Ministry of Foreign Affairs, and the stock exchange. The site of the government internet agency, nicknamed Anmar 404 by Tunisian dissidents, was also targeted. The activists coordinated their operations through discussions held in internet relay chat (IRC) networks, a type of Internet forum. It would have been much more dangerous for Tunisians to attack government sites, because they got arrested once they were identified by the authorities. Thus, it was left to activists from the outside to launch the assaults. Nevertheless, some fifty Tunisians participated, and they were provided online security from exposure to their government. But after a few days, the government took steps to protect its websites from attacks by making them inaccessible from overseas, though they remained available within Tunisia. The Tunisian government had for years also blocked popular video-sharing websites, and in 2008 Facebook was completely blocked. But during the Spring, they only identified without much effort pages that needed to be blocked and they blocked them, and Twitter became the bastion of activists, since people could access it via clients rather than going through the web itself, enabling many Tunisians to still communicate online. April 2010 was identified as the time of most web censorship in Tunisia; more than one hundred blogs were blocked, in addition to other websites, to the point that one activist said, "Here we do not have really Internet, we have a national intranet." If that is what happened in Tunisia, one can imagine how much worse the situation was in countries like Syria, Yemen, and Libya, where censorship had always been more intrusive and controlling. Under these conditions, one could better appreciate the courage and ingenuity of the dissidents who braved all the restrictions and maintained their relations with the world.

Tiny Bahrain too, which barely experienced the beginning of a Spring before it was nipped in the bud, was included by Reporters Without Borders on March 13, 2012, in the list of Enemies of Internet (together with Belarus). The list, published on that day to mark what the organization dubbed World Day against Cyber-Censorship, also included China, North Korea, and Saudi Arabia. US Secretary or State Hillary Clinton kept silent on the subject, though on June 4, 2011, she had shared in Washington her "concerns by the reports that Internet service had been shut down across much of Syria, as have been mobile communication networks. We condemn any effort to suppress the Syrian people's exercise of their right to free expression, assembly and association." Two weeks previously, the White House had released the International Strategy for Cyberspace, which noted that "states should not arbitrarily deprive of disrupt individuals' access to the Internet or other networked technologies. We condemn such shutdowns in the strongest terms." In Bahrain, an ally of the United States, which maintains a naval base there, RWB charged that the government had "bolstered its censorship efforts" in reaction to the pro-democracy uprising that broke out on February 14, 2011. The RWB report went on:

> Bahrain offers a perfect example of successful crackdowns, with an information blackout achieved through an impressive arsenal or repressive measures: exclusion of the foreign media, harassment of human rights defenders, arrests of bloggers and netizens, one of whom [in the meantime there was a second] died behind bars, prosecutions and defamation campaigns against free expression activists, and disruption of communications.[4]

Probably due to the prolonging of the Syrian civil war and the inhumane nature of that internal strife—which indiscriminately decimates entire populations in the tens of thousands and sends hundreds of thousands as refugees to neighboring countries—the question of violating freedom of expression looks comparatively minor, and therefore is viewed with much less concern by the world than the questions of life of death or of humanitarian aid. In March 2011 all Internet service in Syria had been cut, as fifty thousand protesters filled the streets in a call for Children's Friday to remember the dozens of children killed in the protests, and to demand the resignation of Assad. Government sources confirmed that all Internet service across the country had been cut, including in government institutions. Internet had always been monitored in Syria, with dozens of websites inaccessible, Facebook and YouTube once banned, and a teenager convicted of espionage and sentenced to five years in prison for political poetry. But March 2011 was the first known instance of total shutdown, an indication of the grave manner in which the crisis was evaluated since its inception. The Syrian protests peaked in March 2011, after erupting in January, when a video of the corpse of a thirteen-year-old boy—Hamza al-Khateeb, who was allegedly tortured by Syrian security—was viewed thousands of time on YouTube and other social networks. The protesters were also angry over the deaths of another seventy-three children (now they number in the thousands) resulting from the shooting and shelling of the Syrian army. At the time, seventy-three constituted some 15 percent of the total civilian losses of 1,100. If that proportion holds through in September 2012, when the total casualties have surpassed 25,000, then the number of children killed would amount to a horrifying 3,750. The casualties figure doubled again by the end of 2012, when the number of victims approached the harrowing 50,000 mark, more than the casualties from all Syrian wars against Israel since the origin of the Arab-Israeli conflict in 1947. By the spring of 2013, the total figure of casualties amounted to close to 100,000, probably 20 percent of them children. And the killing goes on.

Notes

1. www.bbc.co.uk/news/world-middle-east-16511685
2. www.theatlantic.com/technology/archive/2011/01/the-inside-story-of-how-facebook-/responded-to-tunisian-hacks/70044
3. Al-Jazeera editorial, January 15, 2012.
4. Reporters without Borders Report, February 14, 2011.

6

Turkey, Egypt, Tunisia, Pakistan, and the Republican Model

This bloc of countries representing the republican model is made up of the oldest countries in the Islamic world, which have been experimenting for about a century with modernization and democratization, at time advancing valiantly toward becoming a model of it, at other times being held back by Islamic reaction which called for a halt of that process in order to permit their societies to rethink their way. Except for Tunisia, which is a small previous French Mandate, as one of the three Arab countries in North Africa under French tutelage for most of the time spanning the nineteenth and the twentieth centuries, these countries are among the largest in the Islamic world, hence their large impact on the world Islamic population. All of these countries had experienced a traumatic event of some sort that forced them into the modern era but did not permit them to overcome the basic problems of population, standard of living, poverty, and alienation. They sought to enter the modern, Western world, but they remained locked in their local issues, regional conflicts, and questions of legitimacy of power and of world conspiracies against them. But a common trait unites them—that is Islam, a brand of Islam that had been trying to strike a balance between modernity and moderate religion, development and faith, Western liberalism and Islamic puritanism, trying to relegate religion to the domain of the individual while adopting for the state as secular a system as possible.

Turkey

Ever since the Ottoman Empire crumbled at the end of World War I, the likelihood of an Islamic Spring there was constantly at the gate, because the collapse of a four-hundred-year-old empire cannot be summed up by a sudden and cruel transition from an imperial religious regime into an utterly secular and anticlerical one. Certainly, the vast empire had shrunk, the multiethnic and multicultural and multi-linguistic entity had melted into a modern nation-state where one predominant group—the Turks—spoke Turkish, identified itself as Turkish and its country as Turkey. But the imperial culture and the imperial religion that made the Empire glorious and world-renowned could not be wiped out at once as if it had never existed. Indeed, in the countryside, which remained backward, illiterate, and traditional after the Attaturk revolution was imposed on the country, enclaves of puritanical Islam had survived, hidden from Western tourists and from the spoiled bourgeois urbanites who boosted the growth of the civil culture that was to transform modern Turkey and push it to the arms of NATO and the European Union. In all those eight decades between the Republic in 1922 and 2002 when the Islamic government took over the country, the politics, the economy, the culture, modern education, intellectual life, and the opening to the world unfolded in the great cities, which continued to attract a constant flow of countryside migrants, while the rural areas remained backwaters unconcerned with world trends. The elections, which ran regularly unless interrupted by military takeovers, were mainly a business of the urban populations, and the successive civil governments, which were essentially made up of urban intellectuals and politicians and oriented toward the West.

In the atmosphere of aggressive secularism, where the military old guard permanently threatened to intervene if the secular heritage of Attaturk were endangered, the survival of religious tradition was ignored, considered as nonexistent and nonrelevant, though it was still live and kicking, albeit pushed to the sidelines. Even when such a great leader as Turgut Ozal was in charge in the 1990s, his total commitment to civil government and to his American allies obscured the fact that he was himself a religious Muslim. An Islamic party was there most of the time, though it did not pass the threshold of representation in parliament, and when it did under Necmettin Erbakan, Erdogan's mentor, in 1996, it won the plurality for the first time and was entrusted with forming a government. That was a dramatic proof that all the Western experts who had killed and buried Turkish Islam for eternity, and did not believe that Islam was ever likely to gain power in Turkey, had to swallow their hats and adapt to a new reality of an Islamic-led government of a member-state of NATO, a candidate for membership in the European Union, and a close ally of the United States and

Israel. The United States, as has been their wont, might continue to deny that Turkey has any Islamic inclinations, just as they continue to deny that the Muslim Brothers are infiltrating the US government, but the truth will reveal itself ultimately, perhaps after the Americans and their allies will have paid the price of negligence and under-estimation of the new contours of the Middle East and of Islamic penetration into their own ranks.

At the time of successive civilian governments since the 1980s, the Turkish army had reached the conclusion that in matters of armament, security, and strategy Israel was a close ally, and forced the government in place to hold those relations as a high priority. Relations were brought to the highest diplomatic level of embassies, business and trade flourished, arms deals peaked, and training areas were made available to Israel in the vast Anatolian plateau, as well as a water supply from Turkey in case Israel ran into drought. Two difficult problems continued to mar the relationship nonetheless: Turkey's special sensitivity with regard to the Palestinian issue, which the Turks felt somehow responsible for due to their inheritance of the Ottoman heritage. For while all other Arab countries established their own states, the Palestinian problem remained unresolved. The second problem was the slow revival of Islam in the heartland of Turkey, which those in power in the urban areas, and especially foreign observers who were persuaded that the era of Islam that had waned was never suspected to rise in such a dramatic fashion. But already in the 1990s and even before, the anti-Semitic poison was being spread in the countryside, under the chief mentor and ideologue Necmettin Erbakan, and with the help of his dedicated disciples like Erdogan and Gul. Side by side with that quiet and long-term revival, there were other Islamic movements of Turkish inspiration among the Turkish population in Europe and Muslims in the West in general, such as the *Fethullah Gulen* and the *Milli Gorus*, which won a large audience at home and developed a growing one abroad, especially through education. These movements would be the precursors of the Islamic Spring in Turkey one full decade before Tunisia and Egypt, and will have pursued three or four decades of patient and dormant activities, just like the Muslim Brothers in Tunisia, Egypt, and the rest.

Necmettin Erbakan, who was removed from power by the army in 1998, and his Islamic party declared as illegal and banned, had also been the founder of the *Milli Gorus* which was the hotbed for the rise of Erdogan and co., who would attain the highest positions of power after the elections of 2002. Before that, some of them had reached prominence in local government, like Erdogan, who served as mayor of Istanbul until he was tried and incarcerated for incitement. Erbakan's removal by the military was accepted as a matter of course, inter alia because during his rule the daughter of Iranian President Rafsanjani visited Turkey and declared to the press that the ambience in the country reminded her of the prerevolutionary atmosphere in Tehran in the final days of the shah, something that sounded like a threat to civil government in Turkey, though its diagnosis of the situation and the prognosis on the victory of Islam could not be more precise. Erbakan did not hide his bigotry, exclusion of non-Muslims, and anti-Semitic hatred, which he bequeathed to his disciples, and after Erdogan won the elections at the head of a new-old Islamic party in 2002, his mentor increased the pace of his anti-Christian and anti-Semitic propaganda and brought it to levels unknown since the Nazi regime. In the elections of 2007, he was interviewed by various television channels and spoke to them in terms reminiscent of the maddened remarks made by Erdogan himself against Israel when he decided to veer toward Islam and to embrace Iran and Syria as allies instead of Israel, and to send Muslim terrorists aboard the *mavi marmara* to Gaza in order to defy Israel and discredit it. Those interviews with the Turkish media[1] reveal the sources of his hatred toward Christians, Jews, and Israel, whom he dubbed *bacteria* and *disease*, and he repeated that infamy in every city and town where he stopped. A selection from his outrageous remarks will make the point:

1. All Infidel nations are one Zionist entity; Jews want to rule from Morocco to Indonesia. . . . These elections are about whether we will be, or we will cease to be. I'll tell you where this is coming from, and for this we have to first expose the infrastructure. . . . The right path to the happiness of all humanity is our path, the *Milli Gorus* way. Our Prophet was sent with love and compassion, and our goal is the happiness of all six billion people in the world. We are Muslims, and our civilization has brought happiness to the entire world. This is the good, but there also is evil. Our religion says that the infidels are one nation [*Millah*]. That means evil is run by one control center. When we look at the map of the world, we see about two hundred countries painted in colors, and we think that there are many races, religions, and nations. The fact is that for three hundred years, all these [two hundred nations] have been controlled from one center only. This center is racist, imperialist Zionism. Unless you make this correct diagnosis for the illness, you cannot find the cure to it. You will ask, "What is this belief, this racist imperialism that destroys happiness in this world?"

2. This belief began 5,765 years ago, when the children of Israel were living in Egypt, with a book of magic that was written by someone called Kabbala. The author or authors of this book later claimed that they belonged to the tribe of Moses, but this is not true. They distorted the Tevrat [Torah, Bible] of Moses and put in it the Kabbala. If you want to see proof of this, you can look at their Tevrat and then look at the Kabbala. What do these people believe in? Their belief has three principles that say: . . . (1) You [the Jews] are the real people of God; all others are created to be your slaves; you were created as men and others [were created] as monkeys that later turned into men. This is what they believe and what they teach. They believe that they are the superior class. (2) This superiority will be not only in thought, but will be materialized, actually realized. They will be the masters and the others will be their slaves. (3) For all this to come true, they must perform three duties: The first duty will be to gather all the exiled sons of Israel into Quds [Jerusalem]; the second duty is to build Greater Israel between the Nile and the Euphrates, within these determined borders; and the third duty is to provide for the safety of this Greater Israel.

3. Do you know what the safety of Israel means? It means that they will rule the twenty-eight countries from Morocco to Indonesia. Since all the Crusades were organized by the Zionists, and since it was our forefathers the Seljuks who stopped them, according to the Kabbala there should be no sovereign state in Anatolia. This is these people's [the Jews'] religion, their faith. You can't argue or negotiate with them. This is their religion, and it comes from the Kabbala. Why did this man, Kabbala, write this book? Because he wanted to encourage those who were oppressed by the pharaohs, by saying that they were superior and were God's true people. Kabbala says that this people defeated even God—may Allah forgive. The same line is found in the Tevrat as well.

4. They will destroy—Allah forbid—Al-Aqsa mosque and in its place build Solomon's temple. Only then will their messiah come and establish them as the rulers of the world. This is what they believe in. To realize these goals and meet their obligations, they [the Jews] have been working for 5,767 years! Their history begins with this Kabbala. They say that they want to be the rulers of the world. This is a racist religion. If your mother is not a Jew, you cannot be a Jew. That's why they cannot multiply and grow. Among six billion people they are only thirty million. . . . So how will they rule the world? They say, "Wait a minute, we have conquered the power of money within the capitalist order. As one can see in the symbol of the thirteen levels of a pyramid that is depicted on the American dollar, all peoples will serve us at the top. With the power of the dollar, we have established a world order where money and manpower are dependent on us. This is how we rule the world."

5. Now, let's come to us [the Muslims]. Thanks to our beloved Prophet, light and happiness came to the six billion people of the world. We became the masters. We [the Muslims] ruled for eleven centuries. But unfortunately, in the last three centuries the children of Israel have grabbed this material power. Now they control the world that we live in. What kind

of a world did they build? Without understanding this, nothing can be comprehended. Ballots, elections are all details. The essence is this: Let's assume you, as a Muslim, want to go to [Mecca for] the haj [pilgrimage], and you want to fly on a Turkish plane. For an airline to get a permit to fly and land in other airports, it must be a member of the IATA. IATA is an organization of the children of Israel, of Rockefeller. To become a member, airlines must give them [the Jews] 9 percent of the ticket proceeds. You know what this means. It means saying to Israel, "Take this money, buy guns, and kill me tomorrow, [so that you can] occupy Turkey." This is the order that they have built and have implemented for three centuries.

6. Let's say that you, as a Muslim, want to send money to another Muslim country. Say you want to send money to Pakistan. You cannot send it, because you don't have the infrastructure to do that. You are living in their [the Zionists'] world. To send the money, you need to take it to a Turkish bank. Then the Turkish bank will give it to the American bank. The American bank will give an order to its branch [in Pakistan], and that branch will give the money to the Pakistani bank that will pay out the money that you sent. But in all this, you will pay 1 percent. From wherever [and] to wherever the money goes, 1 percent is paid to the Jew. They have taken the world into their hands. That green dollar that you recognize is Zionist money. The owner is not the American central bank. The American central bank only rents this money, paying $500 billion a year for rent. They [the Zionists] print this green money, the paper, and they bring it to our sheikhs in Saudi Arabia and they say, "Here, take this green paper and give us your oil." And they take the oil with these pieces of paper. There are five trillion [of these] dollars outside of America.

7. And look at what else they do. I am telling you all this so we can all recognize this bacteria. What do they [the Zionists] do? They go back to the oil sheikh and tell him to return the green papers, and give him a yellow paper instead. What is this yellow paper? It is an American bond. There are bonds outside the US valued at $5 trillion as well. That means they took back their green papers to use them again. Those bonds go to the central banks. And what does the American central bank do? It gathers all the central banks, to give them a white paper. So where are all the reserves of the countries? Our reserves are not in the safes of our central bank. They are in the safes of Rockefeller. He is using all this money. What do we have? The head of our central bank has a white paper in front of him. On this paper it is written that such and such a number of billions of dollars are in the banks [in the United States]. What we have is only a piece of white paper.

8. They are crooks three times over. They suck [money] from everybody— five trillion with green papers, another five trillion with yellow papers, and they keep trillions with the white paper they give you. Every child born should be told, "Welcome to this house, my dear, but this house has an owner, and there is rent to be paid. The owner of this house—that is, this world—is the Zionist, and you must pay him $1,200 every month." Every one of us has to pay this $1,200, because of those trillions of exploitation

dollars. There's more: Say you go to a supermarket, wherever you are in the world. You [select] some products, and you pay for them. Say the cashier tells you the total is 300 lira. You pay 300, and you walk out with your sack. No matter where you are and where you buy, 100 lira of the 300 is interest. You buy bread. The tractor was purchased with interest. The flour mills, the factories were built with interest. We are made to pay for these interest [charges]. If you read the book we wrote on this, you would see clearly that one-third of the money we pay for a loaf of bread is paid out in interest.

9. My students and disciples [the current rulers of Turkey] must have thought, "Since there is so much money going around, why shouldn't we have a share of it too?" But that money is exploitation money. It is not good money. Our students apparently have not understood what we have been teaching them for thirty years [in *Milli Gorus*]. Let's go back to the [Zionist] bacteria. About $22 trillion out of all the money we spend every year is paid to these racist imperialist Zionists. We, as a country, are paying $200 billion every year to the Zionists so that they can prepare their bombs, so that they can one day come and take our country. This is the world that the Zionists have built. . . . This racist imperialist Zionism organized nineteen Crusades just to reach its goals. To organize the Crusades, it used the Christians. Why is it that the Christians are helping the Jews? A rabbi goes out on the balcony and tells them, "Oh Christians, isn't it the Messiah that you are waiting for? We too are waiting for the same Messiah." What the rabbi is doing is *taqiya*,[2] of course. Then he goes into his synagogue and tells a five-year-old, "What you heard me say outside is not true. Our Messiah is different. Jesus is someone whom we killed. He will not come or go anywhere. I told them that to deceive them." These people tell the Christians: "You are waiting but you have no guidelines as to how to make him come. Our Tevrat tells us what to do. Let's do it together and let's bring the Messiah." And what were those guidelines? To bring the Jews to Jerusalem, to build and secure Greater Israel, and so on.

10. It was Zionism that established the sect of Protestantism. The capitalist order of today is the religious order of Protestantism. It's because the pope rejects the concept of interest, so as not to allow the exploitation of his children. That's why the Jews decided to change the [Christian] religion, and founded Protestantism. This way they can charge interest and make everybody work for them. That's also why they built the Evangelical sect in America, which now numbers ninety million members. Most people you see there [in the United States] belong to this sect. Take [President] Clinton: He said that he did not serve in the military for America, "but for Israel," he said, "I would take up arms, go into a bunker, and fight." You ask him, "Hey, Clinton, are you a Jew? Why is Israel your business?" He says, "Nooo. It is not because I am a Jew that I say this. It is because I am a good Christian that I think that way. It's because I want Jesus to come that I am saying this." All this is because the Evangelical sect was built by the Jews for them to think that way. Bush belongs to that sect.

Clinton belongs to that sect. Anyone you know. . . . Now look, when we look at someone we see his skin only; but behind it are all the muscles, bones, nerves. I am now giving you the anatomy of the world to show you what is behind the skin, behind the surface.

11.   Without knowing all this, you cannot comprehend what is going on in the world. When we learn all this, we will know that there are no two hundred countries in the world. There are only two. One is the world of Islam, and the other is all the others. Who uses these others? Racist imperialism [meaning Zionism]. The Zionists are holding the Christians in the palms of their hands, and using them. China's and India's industrial development is being carried out with Jewish capital. Japan's too. They control them too. Now, only Islam remains against them. The Jews say you will be our slaves. Islam says *la ilaha illa'Allah* [there is no God but Allah]. We won't bow to anyone but Allah. Nobody will be slaves to anybody. So this is the clash between the two—the clash between good and evil.

12.   These Jews started nineteen Crusades. The nineteenth was World War [I]. Why? Only to build Israel. They used the Christians to build Israel. The Canakkale [Gallipoli] victory was only one of our battles. We fought on thirty fronts during the war. Then they had us sign the Treaty of Sèvres. They told us they would eliminate us and build Greater Israel and make us their slaves. No other nation could fight against them on thirty battle-fronts like our nation did. After they made us sign the Treaty of Sèvres, the French came to Kahramanmaras [on the Syrian border], not to keep it but to give it out so as to make it part of Greater Israel. The English went to Palestine, not to keep it for themselves, but to build Israel. They are doing all this just so that Jesus will return. If we do not see these realities, we cannot understand world affairs. What does Bush say? He says that Jesus ordered him to invade Iraq. He says that the most important factor in making his decision on Iraq was his being Christian. [He thought,] "I will take Iraq. I will build Greater Israel, so that Jesus can return." These people work with that kind of belief. If you don't know about these peoples' beliefs, you cannot understand why they do what they do. Our youth must learn all this. [. . .]

One wonders how this ignoramus, inhuman, anti-Christian and anti-Semite, full of hatred and steeped in fantasy, could serve as Turkey's prime minister when his party won the plurality in the 1996 elections and then serve for nearly two years as the head of a coalition government before his party was ousted by the military (and they call that democracy), mainly due to his rapprochement to Iran and the cold shoulder he showed toward the alliance with Israel. He and his party were then outlawed and excluded from politics. His disciple, Erdogan, who was jailed for incitement while serving as the mayor of Istanbul, ended up as the head of the AKP, an Islamist party that won the majority for the first time in 2002, and dwarfed the civilian parties. Erdogan, who did not hesitate to attack Israel's president in a very uncivilized fashion during a debate in Davos, and especially during the flotilla affair (summer 2010), when he sent Muslim terrorists to defy Israel in Gaza, was not far from the statements of his master, mentor, and predecessor, hence his false accusations against Israel that pushed the relations between the parties to the brink. With his allies in Syria and Iran toeing the same line, that entire anti-Semitic alliance found itself reinforced, until Ankara realized that Assad and Ahmadinejad were not exactly the sort of allies it needed to increase its reputation in the world. After he purged his army from the personnel who wished to maintain a good relationship with Israel, and placed his own men in their stead, he embarked on a campaign of hatred and lies, in order to occupy his place of leadership in the Islamic world, in replacement of the position in Europe that his allies in NATO denied him. It stands to reason that as long as Erdogan heads that party, and as religious fanaticism takes the place of rational calculations, that man whose cynicism and hatred know no limits, will continue to manufacture accusations and encourage anti-Israeli hatred to justify his irrational policies.

On December 28, 2002, columnist Y. Bayer of the high circulation Turkish daily *Hurriyet* (Freedom) wrote:

> Did you know that in 1974, when Erdogan was President of the *Beyoglu* Islamic youth Group in Istanbul, which belonged to the Erbakan National Salvation Party, he wrote and directed a theatrical play called *Maskoyama*, and also played the lead role of the bad son. Maskoyama stood for Mas-ko-ya, the acronym for Masons, Kommunists and Yahudi (Jews), which was built on the combination of the evil concepts of these three terms and the hatred towards them, and was staged all over Turkey.[3]

Not only did Erdogan's anti-Semitic virulence match his mentor's, but it turned out that the terrorist organization IHH, which staged the anti-Israeli flotilla in 2010, had acquired the *mavi Marmara* from the AKP-run municipality of Istanbul. IHH was an example of how NGOs are used by the Turkish foreign ministry to execute dirty missions without openly sullying its hands. Indeed the IHH, which originated in the *Milli Gorus*, was also used by the Turkish government to distribute aid to populations in Northern Iraq without seeming to have invaded that foreign land in order to thwart any Kurdish inroads into Anatolian territory.[4] If one adds to that Erdogan's attacks against the secular Turkish constitution while serving as mayor of Istanbul (1994–8)—describing it as a "huge lie" and declaring unequivocally that "Sovereignty belongs unconditionally and always to Allah," and that "one cannot be a Muslim and a secular"[5]—one understands the avenues by which he proposes to lead the Turkish people if his plot to alter the constitution so as to permit himself to reign supreme as an executive president free from the supervision of Parliament succeeds.

The more serious problem with Turkey is that it has been peddling the Turkish model to be emulated by other Islamic countries emerging from the Spring. Egypt seems to be the first to follow it, after Erdogan made sure to visit the Muslim Brothers in Cairo, who won the elections (see next section), and prevailed on them to emulate the same tactic that enabled the Islamic Party of Turkey to emerge from long years of civil government and conquer the necessary votes to win a landslide. The tactic consisted of building silently and patiently a pool of support in the countryside, and using those bases to assault the cities that were the strongholds of the intelligentsia and the bourgeoisie and take them over. Later, Erdogan moved to dismiss the top military brass in order to avoid a repetition of the Erbakan ouster. The assumption that prevails today in the Spring circles and in the West is that the Turkish model marries moderate Islam and democracy, both accompanied by the impressive economic success that moved Turkey forward. Egypt has begun to copy that model, for example as President Mursi has removed the heads of the military and intelligence establishment and several senior military officers, to replace them with his own men, in order to avert any possibility of the military command rising against him when he decides to neutralize military influence over government, as Erdogan had done. In Morocco, where the elections of April 2012 have delivered a great victory to the Muslim parties, there is also talk of following that model. The founding of the Party of Justice and Development there, also a close imitation of successive Islamic Parties in Turkey, has been the first step in that course. But the name is the easy part; it remains to be seen whether the matters of religion and state, secularism and Islam, and personal piety and public service can be addressed in the new mood of revolution that has swept the Islamic world. The AKP example has been considered to be the epitome of moderation, pragmatism, good governance, and the convergence between Islam, democracy, and modernity. But the question is whether that image is justified. For example, the Turkish model has been famously known for its peaceful and gradualist strategy, which respected the red lines of the established order, and by its reduction of the number of the Islamic candidates it fielded in elections, while avoiding revolutionary rhetoric, as long as it was struggling for hegemony. Along these lines, when debate raged about the compatibility between Islam and democracy, the Islamic party sounded more democratic than all the rest, in order to avoid raising suspicions as to its designs.

Things changed radically, however, when the Islamic Party gained power, won a majority that allowed it to take over the government machinery and to remove into retirement the old military brass that alone could threaten its rule. For example, Erdogan's and Gul's wives appear completely veiled in public, on campuses students are again permitted to sit in classes covered, journalists who bluntly criticize the rulers are arrested, the state media go into blunt and bigoted incitement against rivals and enemies, and in general, their style of Islam does not appear to be moderate, but rather following the outrageous wordings of Erbakan and Erdogan cited above. At the same time, democratic procedures are enforced as a choice tactic to win the trust of their constituencies, something that was taken in the Arab countries of the Spring as an example of reinforcing democracy, and they might be assuring their followers of adopting the same means of instituting democracy in their countries. In this regard, Ghannouchi, the head of al-Nahda fundamentalists in Tunisia, praised the Turkish model for promoting human rights and for extending political freedoms to meet European standards, as an example to erect his own democratic state. Similarly, the Egyptian Freedom and Justice Party, the political arm of the Brotherhood, also consulted with the Turkish AKP before the Egyptian elections, in order to make their platform and campaign more palatable to their general electorate. They wished, as they promised, to assure the public that they did not intend to monopolize the political process. But, judging from their repeatedly broken pledges to field less than half the candidates, and then not to present a candidate to the presidency, it is evident that as they gained in self confidence, their expectations and ambitions increased.

The Turkish model can also have international repercussions. At first, when the AKP came to power, and knowing that the army was in favor of a good relationship with Israel, it maintained on the surface the good relations between Ankara and Jerusalem. But after it removed the old guard and replaced it with its own people, it came out openly and totally against Israel and adopted a hostile attitude toward it. Tunisian Ghannouchi referred to that aspect in the shift of the AKP conduct, and presented it as part of the Turkish model worth emulating, because it "strengthened Ankara's Islamic identity." This all-around praise for Turkey by the Islamic parties that have come to power in the Spring countries has indeed endeared it to those parties as the model to be followed, making even the Salafi movement in Egypt, which came in second in Parliament (30 percent) to the Brothers (45 percent), turn to Turkey for guidance on the much-damaged Egyptian tourist industry during the upheaval. They suggest that since the Turks had successfully adopted male beaches that are segregated from female beaches, and still attracted Arab and other foreign tourists, Egypt should act similarly. Morocco too, which has not suffered yet from the ripples of the Spring, but has experienced the rise of the Justice and Development Party in the last elections, has been inspired by the successes of the AKP in Turkey, which have been accompanied by all the amenities of democracy for now. What remains to be verified over time is whether as the AKP rule is perpetuated, the government will not move to Islamize the country even further, first by soft measures of persuasion, then through social pressure to conform, and finally through means of coercion under Shari'a law. One thing is sure, when the West had recommended to other Arab countries that they democratize following the Turkish model, that was in the days of the civil governments of Menderes, Ozal, Ecevit, and Ciller, when indeed Islam was moderate and arguably married well with democracy. But since December 2002, when the AKP came to power, the rule is no longer moderate Islam, neither domestically nor externally, as the embrace of that model by Muslim Brothers affiliates elsewhere well testifies.

The present Spring in which established Islamic nations try to retrieve their identity is also providing an opportunity to ethnic/national/religious/linguistic minorities within them to claim their own separate existence, a sort of spring within spring, which may cause even more turmoil than normally expected. For example, if Syria is dismantled and minorities like the Kurds, the Alawis, the Druze, who are already territory-bound, try to carve out their autonomous areas, like the Kurds in Iraq, this can signal a longer and insoluble conflict while the champions of national integrity, artificial as it may have been initially, strive to maintain unity. Turkey is one of those countries, and as the Erdogan government is seeking to reassert its Islamic identity, minorities like the Alevis and the Kurds may try to vie for their own autonomy, other minorities like the Armenians and the Greeks, the ancient inhabitants of the land, having been already murdered or physically expelled.

Turkey's Islamic Prime Minister Erdogan, before he left for the opening of the London Olympics in August 2012, issued a bellicose warning against the rising of an autonomous Kurdish region in Syria. A *Wall Street Journal* article left the impression that Erdogan was determined to throttle a Syrian Kurdish autonomy by tying it to the presence of the outlawed PKK that the Assad regime had inserted in the Syrian Kurdish heartland over objections of Kurdish groups. In effect, Erodgan was attempting to stifle the alternative of a secular federated Syria as a post-Assad alternative to a Sunni Muslim Brotherhood and Salafist supremacist regime that could devolve into a prolonged period of sectarian violence. Moreover, Turkey warned that it might take action to stop groups it deemed terrorists from forming a Kurdish-run region in Syria, underscoring Ankara's growing concern that such Kurdish rule in Syria's north could provide sanctuary to Kurdish militants from its own territory. "We will not allow a terrorist group to establish camps in northern Syria and threaten Turkey," Prime Minister Recep Tayyip Erdogan said in Ankara ahead of his trip to London. "If there is a step which needs to be taken against the terrorist group, we will definitely take this step." At the same time he would condemn any Israeli step against the Hamas terrorists in Gaza and would even go to their rescue, as he did during the Gaza War of 2008–9. Only Turkey's terrorists in its vast land, who by no stretch of imagination can endanger its existence, are to be eradicated, to his liberal and democratic mind, but those who threaten the very life of tiny Israel on a daily basis are to be encouraged. What counts is not who the terrorists are but against whom they operate, according to his faulty logic.

Mr. Erdogan's remark came after the Turkish media had carried pictures of Kurdish flags flying over installations controlled by the Kurdish Democratic Union Party of Syria, or PYD, which Ankara claims is affiliated with the Kurdistan Worker's Party, or PKK, which has been fighting against Turkey since 1984 to gain its autonomy. But Syria's Kurdish areas have avoided much of the violence that has plagued Syria since the uprising that was launched in March 2011. Like in next door Iraq many Syrian Kurds saw a chance to achieve near-independence through economic prosperity. Turkey's military has been monitoring developments inside Syria's Kurdish regions, and has warned lest the PKK should attempt collaboration with the PYD.[6] The PYD stresses that its only links to the PKK are ideological. But the group's assertion of control over towns near Turkey's border has led to squabbles with the other Kurdish groups in Syria. That includes the main Kurdish political group, the Kurdish National Council, and other Syrian rebel factions, which allege that their members have been intimidated and assassinated by PYD members. The main opposition grouping in Syria, the Syrian National Council, was led by a Kurd, Abdulbasset Sieda. He has reportedly characterized the PYD's growing influence in Syria's Kurdish region as a policy of the Assad government to split the opposition. "The Syrian regime just handed this [Kurdish] region to the PKK and the PYD, and took a step aside," Mr. Sieda was reported to have said in an interview widely quoted by Turkish media outlets.

As the internal strife in Syria has increased, approaching two years of all-out war confronting the various rebel groups now under a unified command against the dwindling power of Assad, and as the flow of refugees continues to Turkey, Jordan, Lebanon, and Iraq, Turkey has stepped up its border control with Syria, where it has positioned American Patriot batteries to shoot down any intentional or stray Syrian army missiles. The Turks have even threatened that they might launch war against the Syrians if more bombardments of their territory are pursued, purposely or accidentally from Syria. To illustrate their dramatically altered attitude toward Israel, they are on record as favoring Hamas's continued shelling for years, with rockets, bombs, and missiles, of Israeli towns around Gaza, and labeling any attempt by Israel to defend themselves, as aggression. Who bombs rather than who are the victims of the bombing, is the criterion that Turkish foreign policy has adopted to distinguish between aggression and self-defense.

Egypt

Of all the Islamic countries affected by the Spring, the most important and most significant is Egypt, not only due to its size and might, and to its centrality in the Arab world, without whom no war or peace can be decided, but principally because of its Muslim fundamentalist forces (the Brothers and the Salafis), which offer the most viable alternative to Mubarak's rule, and also a likely example that other Spring-stricken countries would try to follow. The new Muslim Brother President Muhammed Mursi has pledged that his presidency would maintain a civil and democratic rule, together with equality between the genders and civil freedom, and promised that he would honor all the Egyptian international obligations, including the peace with Israel. His test will be in the practice of his rule, especially when the new regime settles into a normal relationship with the parliament, which is 75 percent Muslim fundamentalist (45 percent the Brothers and 30 percent Salafis). In the meantime, many debates are taking place around the new constitution that is to be adopted by a popular referendum against the background of a deep division of public opinion and vast demonstrations by Mursi's supporters of an Islamized new constitution and their bourgeois-liberal and Westernized-secular opposition. New coalition governments and unprecedented ruling styles are yet to be experimented with, for on the one hand, under the watchful American eye, Mursi will not perhaps be able to strictly enforce the platform of the Muslim Brothers that he has championed all his years, along the tenets of Banna and Qutb, namely a Shari'a state, accompanied by the freezing of the peace with hated Israel; but on the other hand, he will be under tremendous domestic pressures from those who have waited almost a century to seize power, and will have no patience to wait any longer. Pressures will increase especially on the part of fundamentalist clerics, such as Yussuf Qaradawi, and on the part of the Salafis who would demand everything and now, as the price of their participation in the government coalition.

If Mursi is true to his party and its platform, he will have to align according to its aggressive ideology, thus producing violent shake-ups in the domestic and external political lineup of the country. His temporary compromise with General Tantawi, which limited his authority in military affairs, was scrapped shortly thereafter when he moved courageously to dismiss the heads of the military establishment and to take over the powers of the supreme commander of the Armed Forces. But if he remained loyal to his public statements to his people and to the international media, he would have had to produce a new pattern of Islamic government, updated to conform with the spirit of the time, which might not be acceptable to the hard core of the Brothers. Perhaps no less important is the desperate state of the economy, which makes Mursi inevitably dependent on the United States, the EU, and the international financial bodies that alone can rescue Egypt from the state of insolvency it is seriously facing. First loans in the billions of dollars were already granted by all those bodies, on the assumption that Mursi is taking the necessary measures to moderate the alternative government he is trying to build. But judging both from the authoritarian powers that he has appropriated for himself, in the face of internal and external protests, and from the import of the new Islamic constitution, which is bound to rock the country in the months to come, it is hard to see how those expectations can be met.

Perhaps the most seemingly revolutionary statement by Mursi in Tahrir Square the day before he was sworn in, on June 29, 2012, in front of his hypnotized and ebullient crowds of followers, was his assertion, which he uttered again and again, as if he did not believe it came out of his own mouth, regarding the authority and legitimacy that he drew directly from the people. In the popular gatherings that they used to hold in Cairo, Nasser and Sadat before him used to make the same pledge of "the people and the masses as the source of authority and legitimacy," at a time when their rule rested on the 1952 Revolution, not on any semblance of free elections. But in gatherings of Muslim Brothers in Egypt, such a statement was not a matter of course, although as Y. Weissman has demonstrated, Syrian Brothers such as Mubarak (not Hosni or his relative) and Dawalibi had toyed with that idea.[7] As Y. Meital has shown, such ideas or similar ones existed in latter-day Egypt too, at the end of the Hosni Mubarak Era, when the Muslim Brothers were so far from attaining power that they were ready for some compromises and even suggested the idea of a civil government that went hand in hand with a Shari'a state.[8] However, knowing how the Brothers in Egypt can increase their ambitions as their success may warrant, the borderline between civil government and authority of the people on the one hand, and the Shari'a state and Allah's authority on the other, may well come up for revision as the Brothers' rule firms up.

One cannot disregard the fact, however, that these lenient views among the Brothers toward the rule of the people, by the people, for the people were all voiced by Muslim fundamentalists who aspired to power, and in Syria took sometime part in governments. Therefore they do not reflect the mood of victorious parties that are ready to celebrate their electoral triumph by insisting on their core beliefs. For indeed, the doctrine of most fundamentalist movements—as practiced in Saudi Arabia or by the Taliban when they ruled Afghanistan, and as quoted even by Erdogan as cited above—is anchored in the divine law that considered people's claim to sovereignty as heresy and affront. So, if a Muslim state wishes to revert to the Shari'a rule, it cannot recognize the sovereignty of anyone save Allah, sovereignty being the key for determining the source of authority and legitimacy of legislation and government. The rationale is overwhelming in its simplicity: if it is a Shari'a state, then Allah, the sovereign, has already dispensed to humanity the most perfect of laws, making superfluous any need to legislate anything further, especially that human-made laws can never compete with the authority of divine laws. When the Muslim Brothers in Egypt used elections to form a parliament in which they and the Salafis constituted a majority, for the purpose of making laws, some may have regarded that as defiance of divine authority. It is possible that Mursi believes that the will of the people has been expressed through the elections, where the Brothers and the Salafis have obtained three-quarters of the votes, namely that the Islamic parliament merely confirms the people's will, which is Allah's will, thus bringing to bear the saying that *vox populi vox dei*, the two dwelling together without contradiction. Had a non-Islamic parliament been institutionally put in place, it would have been on a collision course with the president, but since the popular vote was reflected by the Muslim majority in parliament, the two are about to work in harmony, although tension will always remain between a fiery Muslim parliament who demands the implementation of the Shari'a, and a pragmatic executive who will have to sacrifice some ideology in order to safeguard national interests.

Observers from the outside of these puzzling phenomena can either try to learn and understand, or based on past experience try to guess what direction the new Egyptian government will take. From the Turkish experience we have learned that the likes of Muslim Brothers take the long-haul view of developments, adopting their measures slowly and cautiously, preferring to get the public used to their reforms toward Islamization, rather than precipitating changes that cannot be accepted wholesale by the public. We saw how Erbakan and Erdogan showed their smiling face to Israel at first, and then they removed their masks and revealed their hatred of Jews and Israel, in spite of all the various commentators and observers who could predict no Turkish interest in reversing the close relations of their country with Israel. As we learned many times in the past, what we view as Arab or Muslim interests from the outside, the Muslims themselves may not see; therefore they may act irrationally from our point of view. This aspect is worth keeping in mind for those who profess that the Brothers have always been pragmatic and rational, and they gauge them and their reactions by their own standards, invariably coming to the conclusion that they would never do anything against what we believe are their interests. Their interests are different from ours, they count in their eyes differently than ours, and they would be prepared to renounce them in situations that would look unlikely to us. For example, when Prime Minister Erdogan coarsely and savagely attacked President Peres personally during a public symposium in Davos, it was not only a violation of international norms of conduct and a show of ignorance and barbarism, which caused other civilized personalities present to question the sanity of the Turk, but it caused humiliation to him and to his country. Nevertheless, faced with the opportunity to pour hatred and a cascade of lies on one of the most respected, civil, and moderate political leaders of Israel, Erdogan could not restrain himself. Haunted as he is by the massacre of the Armenians, which weighs on the conscience of his nation, and the horrible oppression of the Kurds that no civilized nation could tolerate, he opts to act aggressively to preempt those accusations from being hurled in his face.

The elements among the population of Egypt that entertain a fervent hatred of Jews and Israel are found not only in ultra-nationalistic circles, but mainly among the fundamentalist Muslims, including the Brothers, precisely those who have won the majority in parliament. The latter have spectacularly dwarfed all those liberal, traditional, and revolutionary groupings that had pretended to represent the Egyptian voters during the sixty years since the 1952 Revolution. In all those previous elections, which were rigged, 90 percent of the vote went to the president and to his Democratic party, which had nothing democratic about it; and at the first occasion when there were free elections, not much remained from all those voters, since 75 percent of the popular vote went to Muslim radicals. It seems, therefore, that the long-term and patient work of the Muslim Brothers, who were banned for all those years, had more impact on the Egyptian population than the official leaders and their corrupt machinery. Their work began in 1928 in Isma'iliya, where a young Imam Hasan al-Banna, founded the movement, which committed itself externally to expel from the Suez Canal the British occupiers, and domestically to return Egypt to the rule of Shari'a law, as befits the main Arab country. Banna's activities came in reaction to the alienation of the Egyptian people, under the impact of Westernization and modernization instigated by the British, and in recognition that the ancient glory of Islam, as in the times of the Prophet, could not be retrieved unless faith and practice of Islam can be revived as of old. It was clear that Islam had been at its height, expanded its conquests, and extended its victorious rule, only when it was righteous, and that since its abandonment of the path of the Prophet, under the impact of the colonial West, a dangerous process of withering set in, which it was necessary to arrest and to reverse.

To go back to the good old norms of Islam was not a Banna innovation (notice the paradox that innovation is anathema in Islam [bid'a], but the myth is maintained that every century there appears a giant innovator [mujadid], who breaks new pathways, the latest being recognized by some as Ayatullah Khumeini). Before him, great thinkers came about, like Ibn Taymiya in fourteenth-century Mamluk Syria, and ibn 'abd al Wahhab (father of the Wahhabiya) in the Arabian Peninsula in the nineteenth century, who called for a puritanical conservatism to be restored in Islam. The latter even destroyed the tomb of the Prophet in Medina to protest the worship of the stones at that place, instead of just sanctifying the persona of the messenger of Allah. But after a while, people cyclically return to their routine life and tend to become obtuse to the requirements of the faith, which necessitates the arrival of the next innovator (Allah forbid, one could exclaim paradoxically). Al-Banna's sweeping contribution to Islamic revival was not in altering the doctrine, but in operationalizing the tenet of jihad, which was there since the time of the Prophet, but dormant as the expansionist era of Islam is past and then the Muslim world had become the object of European occupation. In fact, since the decline of the Ottoman Empire, the passion and capacity for aggressive jihad had declined, and the term continued in usage mostly metaphorically to designate an intellectual striving to improve personal piety, to do the good and avoid the bad. Jihad had then gained, and been promoted as, a positive and peaceful trend that, far from aspiring to more conquests, was happy to maintain and defend what it had, which had come under attack by the colonial powers. Passionate and visionary Banna rejected that passive interpretation and reverted to the original meaning of jihad, as in the time of the Prophet and of the Islamic *futuh*: in other words, the conquests in the path of Allah and expansion of *dar-al-Islam* for the sake of Islam.

Moreover, even the more passive and quietist brand of Muslims, who saw no use in aggressive attitudes toward the overwhelming might of the powers, agreed that in any case, Muslims must be called upon to launch jihad in defense of their lands and properties. It is nevertheless a bit problematic to first conquer lands, oppress nations, expand and wage aggressive wars, and then claim that in order to defend those conquered lands, Muslims are obliged to wage jihad, but almost all Muslim streams were unanimous that when it was a defensive war, the tenet of jihad was universally applicable and binding. The issue then became only a matter of interpretation, and the discretion remained with the Muslims alone to decide when a war was aggressive and when it became defensive. For example, the establishment of Israel by UN resolution was for the Muslims an aggressive act that required a war of jihad, and since then all the Muslim wars against the aggressive nature of the Zionist state were dubbed jihad. In al-Banna's time the enemy was readily identifiable: first, as the British who occupied the land and exploited the resources of the country for their own needs, and then the Zionist Jews who settled in Mandatory Palestine under British tutelage.

Since the Palestinian Muslims were opposed to Jewish settlement in the land, it has become a duty for all Muslims to assist the Palestinians in their opposition to the twin evils of the British Mandate and Zionism. Banna's further interpretation, which won currency to his leadership and to the Muslim Brothers movement that he founded, was that those killed in that holy battle of jihad were not simply subtracted from the list of the living, but died as martyrs (*shahid*) guaranteeing their place in paradise, near the throne of Allah. He was telling his followers, "Brothers, do not be afraid to die in this Jihad," thus encouraging them not only to die for their turf against the identified enemy, but also to volunteer to assist other Muslims in other lands, like those in India, who were oppressed or threatened by other powers. In other words, he taught that the tenet of jihad was universal and the reward of the *shahid* was eternal. More recently, mujahideen from all over the Islamic world, including the Arab world, Iran, and Chechnya, have been known to volunteer in Afghanistan, Bosnia, Iraq, Kosovo, Palestine, and any number of Muslim countries where war is rife.

World War II created an ideological and practical collaboration between the Brothers and the Nazis against both the British and the Jews, in both Europe and the Middle East, with the aim of defeating the British and creating a German hegemony in Europe and the Mediterranean basin on the one hand, and decimating the Jewish population of Europe and Palestine, on the other. Arab and Nazi war purposes could not be more similar. Thus, the Brothers harnessed their organization, both in Egypt and in Palestine, to serve Nazi propaganda goals and then the war aims of Germany in the Middle East and in Europe, as Britain stood practically alone against the Germans and their allies. The mufti of Jerusalem, Haj Amin al-Husseini, who became al-Banna's deputy in the Brotherhood, was recruited by the Nazis, who were fighting the British and annihilating the Jews in Europe, to expand that enterprise into the Middle East. He spent most of the wartime in Berlin, met with Hitler, and led the Nazi propaganda in the Islamic world. He was flown by the Nazis into Muslim Bosnia, which had become part of the pro-Nazi enlarged Ustasha state of Greater Croatia, and helped recruit the Thirteenth SS Hadjar (dagger) Division to serve in the rapidly thinning ranks of the Germans after the debacle of Stalingrad, convincing them that Muslims shared the same war aims as the Germans: namely, beating the British and exterminating the Jews. Hence, the sharp anti-Jewish turn-about in the Brothers' ideology as a result of the war. While not much love had been lost for the Jews in Muslim societies since the beginning of Islam, the war atmosphere escalated that dislike into outright hatred, the moment it was combined with a useful and purposeful collaboration with the Germans. Since then, a brutal and violent attitude toward the Jews was cultivated by the Brothers to a degree that has no parallel in other nations since the Nazis. It came to its frightening and inhuman paroxysm in the 1950s when Banna's lieutenant and successor as the guide of the Brotherhood, Sayyid Qutb, wrote and published his *Our War against the Jews*"[9] whose venom and degree of hostility was not surpassed even by the Nazis.

It is noteworthy that when the Nazis tried at first, through their offices in the Arab world, to incite Muslims against Jews, they met with failure because a reasonable relationship had existed between the Muslims and their Jewish minority, especially in Egypt, in spite of the occasional outbursts of violent anti-Semitism during the Damascus Blood libel of 1840, and the pogroms that had accompanied Jewish existence from Morocco to Iran over the centuries. However, when the Muslim Brothers harnessed themselves to the Nazi propaganda, attacks against the Jews escalated (the most infamous unfolded in Baghdad, Iraq, Libya, and Morocco in the middle of World War II and its aftermath). This tradition remained stable thereafter: in 1948 the Brothers sent their men to fight for the Palestinians in the 1948 war, and branches of the Brothers were founded in all the Palestinian territories, including Transjordan. It was those Islamic Associations that erected along the years the infrastructure for Hamas in the West Bank and Gaza, and it is these forces that today lead anti-Semitic campaigns in their most heinous manifestations, and scuttle any attempt to conclude peace between Palestinians and Israel. Therefore, even on those rare occasions when there was a peace accord with Israel, it has been the Brothers who led the forces violently opposed to it. Sadat, who was assassinated by extremist elements of the Islamic Jihad, was the one Arab leader who tried to courageously face them, and he paid with his life. For that reason, the prevailing opinion in Israel has been that there is no point in cutting any deal with these Muslim fanatics, because they would not live up to it. Hamas, which is a branch of the Brothers, says expressly in their platform that their problem with Israel is not territorial, because even had Israel been left with a minor piece of land in its possession, that would still not be acceptable to them, due to the fact that the entire land of Palestine was a *waqf* (holy endowment) conferred on the Muslims by Allah to safeguard for all generations to come, with the result that Israel cannot keep any part of it for itself.

101

The moment Mursi could tactically (and temporarily) placate the fears of the military council and assure it of his docility in accepting the limitations imposed on his presidential authority, the road to his rule of the country was paved. The process of recognizing and declaring Mursi as the elected president was long and painful. On the eve of that final declaration, numerous were his supporters who demonstrated on Tahrir Square, holding white shrouds in their hands, to mean that they were prepared to sacrifice themselves as *shahids*, if Mursi were not declared the winner. It is clear that had his opponent Shafiq been declared president, bloody unrest would have broken out, for the Brothers were not prepared to accept any other election result. That, of course, prompted many to fear that the elections were not truly democratic, if only one result could be accepted and all the others rejected under threat of violence. In other words, did the official in charge of announcing the results have any other choice but that Mursi was the winner? That choice seemed logical when in the preceding parliamentary elections, 75 percent of the voters opted for the Brothers and their Salafi allies, meaning that Mursi should have enjoyed a much larger popular vote than the one officially accorded to him, of slightly over the 50 percent mark. In any case, on that day while they were gathering in the Square, a fateful atmosphere reigned in the streets: either Mursi is elected or war was breaking out. For Mursi's followers, his election stood beyond doubt, and anything less would have meant a return to the old rigging practices. Elections under the threat that only one result was acceptable are not exactly a democratic process. More question marks were raised in Egypt and elsewhere about the undemocratic procedures adopted by Muslim fundamentalists, in spite of the façade of liberal democracy that they put up. We recall that at the beginning of the revolution, in order to assuage the fears of the Egyptian public, the Brothers announced that they would not vie for more than 50 percent of the representatives in parliament, but at the end they won 75 percent of the seats together with the Salafis, their allies. At the outset they assured that they would not participate in the presidential elections, but in March 2012, they changed their position and even accused the military council of intending to rig the results. They threatened that if any of the vestiges of Mubarak regimes won, they would respond with mass demonstrations, for as Mursi's campaign manager announced, "The Egyptians have rid themselves of Mubarak, not in order to get another Mubarak, like Shafiq and co." Mursi pledged that if he won the elections, he would see to it that no one of Mubarak's people would continue to hold any position of influence. And that was a pledge he promptly implemented.

The Salafi movement, Mursi's allies in government, was founded by two of the Muslim giant thinkers at the beginning of the twentieth century: Jamal- al-Din al-Afghani and his disciple and follower, Muhammed Abdu, during their exile in Paris. That movement was particularly active in Egypt, where Abdu served as the great mufti, whence it spread to other Arab and Muslim countries, where it took various forms under various names: Aligar in India and Muhammediya in Indonesia. However, while true to its name (the Predecessors) it has aimed at returning to the roots of Islam, just like the Brothers, but in fact it also adopted several modernist movements aiming at modernizing Islam. Keeping all the differences in mind, one may compare the first trend to the Jewish conservative movement in America and the second to the reform movement in Germany prior to World War II and in the United States after the war. This sort of openness toward the world, even when it is necessary to bend the law to accommodate reality, was widely discussed when Abdu was the mufti, as he wanted to dismantle the four archaic schools of law of the sunna, which made for rigidity, and unite their doctrines in a modern legal way. He also tried to provide a rationale for the tenets of Islam, in order to persuade believers through logic to hold on to their practice of the faith: for example, that the Ramadan fast is good for health, as some Jewish authorities had explained the prohibition of pork by the fact that it is repulsively dirty. Thus, Abdu and his disciples, who were trained to disseminate Islam through persuasion rather than belief, could praise their faith and show how much more progressive and modern it was than Christianity and Judaism, its competitors for monotheistic believers.

Surprisingly, the Salafiya has become the first Islamic movement to come close to feminism, by giving high positions and respect to Muslim women, not only due to their function as "a factory to manufacture men fighters for Jihad," as stated in the Hamas charter. They declared their adherence to creationist theories that are otherwise anathema in Islam as in other monotheistic religions, and they heed the findings of science if they seem to run contrary to Shari'a. The organ of the movement al-Manar (the Lighthouse), was edited for many years by Rashid Rida, the third link in the apostolic chain started by Afghani, and turned into the real lighthouse of this movement, until its name was overtaken by Hizbullah in Lebanon, who thus names its media worldwide. One can thus see the long strides made by the Salafiya from the moderation, openness, and modernism of Abdu, through the restorative trend of al-Banna and the Brothers, the closing up to the world and the hatred introduced by Qutb, and down to Shi'ite Nasrallah with his sectarianism, belligerence, and uncompromising aggression. The present-day Salafiya in Egypt has nothing to do with Hizbullah, but it has also distanced itself from the liberal approach of Abdu. It still toys with the scientific base with which it can embellish its faith, whenever it can show a solid scientific base for its system of beliefs, in order to tempt into its circle young and educated people who seek an explanation for and a logic to everything. For example, they are able to show through all kinds of far-fetched explanations and theories that atomic energy is mentioned in the Qur'an, something that lends scientific credibility to the holy book. This also enables the Salafis to claim that all human knowledge originates from the Qur'an, and whenever a contradiction appears between Islam and scientific truth, they can circumvent the Shari'a without being accused of heresy. The paradox persists today in which the most illiterate people have become the most fundamentalist extremists and follow the Brothers, while the Salafis, who are reputed as more extremist, are precisely the more educated, led by Noor, who profess rational approaches to the faith. Exactly as the Brothers keep adapting their ways to reality, so do the Salafis, who keep developing while underlining their emphasis on reviving the way of the ancients.

These ideological commitments notwithstanding, one must follow the first practical steps of the Mursi government in the real world and observe to what extent he is able to harmonize policy making with his Muslim Brother doctrine. He must be stunned not so much by the reaction of the people, who had enough of Mubarak's corruption and were waiting for the change they finally got, but by the hypocrisy of the West, which never raised a voice against the regime's corruption, the rigging of elections, the arrest of dissidents, and the perpetuation of illiteracy, poverty, and disease in Egyptian society. He was also dismayed to face the runaway demographic growth, which brought the country from a population of thirty million sixty years ago, and which used to export food and other goods, to a poor, import-dependent society of eighty-five million souls today. When President Obama decided to appeal from Cairo to the Islamic world, in 2009, he did not say one word criticizing that destructive state of affairs, hoping thereby not to damage the famous stability that was the top priority in his calculations, and did not pay attention to the crying of the political prisoners who were rotting in prisons. All Mubarak could assume then was that America stood firmly at his side without qualification. Then, what incentive would he have had to improve? The Americans were also loath to take any measure against the Mubarak regime, which had turned the American-supported peace treaty with Israel into a bad farce, as Egyptian tourism to Israel was completely discontinued; anti-Semitic attacks on Israel and the Jews—with Sho'ah-denial a major theme—inundated the Egyptian press, including the state controlled one; Sinai was invaded by terror, smuggling, and illegal migrants, and Mubarak, unwilling or unable to do much about it, was hiding behind American support without any incentive to mend his ways, until he was abandoned by his allies and thrown to the dogs.

Already in his first weeks at the helm, Mursi—who was credited, as a Muslim Brother, with long-term planning and patience borne out of experience—precipitated things when he faced the military council that in fact held power since the revolution and allowed him to take over the presidency, and neutralized its overwhelming influence. In early August 2012, merely two months after his swearing-in ceremony, he had to make his first major choice between his Islamic commitment and his national security considerations. The Sinai Peninsula was becoming a base of al-Qa'ida–type terrorists, who thought they could take advantage of the chaos in Egypt to support the nearby Hamas in Gaza, to help smuggle into Israel drugs and illegal Muslim migrants from Ethiopia, Eritrea, and Sudan, and to mount attacks against Israel, while the latter was considered unable and unwilling to retaliate due to the restrictions put on it by the bilateral peace treaty with Egypt. According to straight Islamic calculations, Mursi was supposed to support these Muslim provocations of Israel. Thus, in early August, a group of Bedouin smugglers, reinforced by Hamas and al-Qaida, who sought hideouts in Sinai, penetrated to the proximity of the Israeli border in order to exploit the *inter-regnum* in Cairo and try to precipitate border incidents that might escalate to a full conflict between the two countries, thus putting an end to the Israeli-Egyptian peace arrangement. The gas pipeline through which Egypt supplied gas to Israel under contract was blown up fifteen times within a year and a half after the revolution, and it became evident that the Egyptian army was neither willing nor able to protect it. When Mursi came in and demanded to be sworn in so as to take up his duties, General Tantawi, the minister of defense and the head of the military council that controlled the country, concurred, provided he kept the portfolio of defense so as to safeguard all the privileges the army had enjoyed since the 1952 Revolution. Exactly following the advice he received from Prime Minister Erdogan on his previous visit to Cairo, Mursi accepted the terms on the face of it, until he was in a position to move on his own, purge the army from that old guard, and appoint his own people that would no longer threaten him, so as to enable him to implement his program.

The problem of Sinai immediately climbed to the top of Mursi's activities, not only because it borders the Gazan Palestinians as well as Israel, but it also built up as a threat against Egypt's own national security, a concern that any president must tackle, due to the imminent danger displayed by combatant groups moving to the Sinai Peninsula that is part of Egypt. Since the Sinai was a popular destination for Israeli vacationers, the Netanyahu administration was among those who issued a warning, urging Israelis to leave that area and return to their homes, thus showing that the fear over the safety of visitors to the peninsula was not unfounded. The Sinai bombings of 2004 had targeted tourist hotels and killed 34 and injured 171. The Israeli prime minister previously aired his concerns over what he believed to be the lawlessness situation that the Sinai was descending into, which contrasted greatly with the three decades of peace the country had enjoyed with Egypt. In response to this, Arab critics have said that the current unease and rising tensions acted as a motive for Israel to step into the Sinai region and "achieve its ambitions under the pretext of the deteriorating security conditions." A growing number of sources have claimed indeed that armed groups have made camp in the area, which resulted from the fall of the Mubarak's government, thus caus-ing a lack of adequate security and creating a safe haven for groups with extreme Islamic fundamentalist values. According to informed members of the Egyptian security forces, Sinai's lack of military per-sonnel, embedded in the peace treaty of 1979, allowed such groups to build upon their resources and plan their attacks without fear of being counter-raided by either the Israelis or the Egyptians. Further information has unearthed that if they were not stopped soon, their growing array of nationalities and expertise would propel them to become a frightening threat to Egyptian and Israeli security. That dark prospect appeared to already be underway, if the reports that they were in possession of smuggled weaponry, en route from Libya and Sudan, were held to be true.

Many residents of Rafah, an important Egyptian town located in North Sinai, have also come forth with their accounts. They claim that those groups are attracting young men with the promise of riches and, in some cases, paying for their marriages. Such an appraisal of these young men doesn't concur with the previous notion presented to the world of the young Middle Eastern liberals who set the Spring protests and demands in their countries, which amount to rebellion against the regime. However, the danger felt by the local Sinai community suggests that the tides have turned and those men have found another battle against perceived injustice to fight, which is the anti-Israel cause. On the other hand, reports have suggested that many of these men are escaped prisoners, and the freedom they gained amid the chaos created by the revolution in fact greatly added to their threat. Egyptian political figures have also contributed to the matter, the majority believing that these groups are exploiting the country's current fragile state of chaos to go where they wish and do what they wish. Some of them have been indentified to be Palestinian organizations, whose particular intentions have not been fathomed as yet. Such groups as the Mujahadin Shura Council have recently posted an Internet video horrifically boasting of their targets near the Egyptian border with Israel and claiming that such actions are a gift to their brothers, members of other similar extremist groups. Another jihadist organization took responsibility for the calculated bombing of the main gas pipeline that supplied gas to the Zionist entity.

What these groups hold in common is the view that they must eradicate infidels, in other words non-Muslims. This is further evidenced by the horrendous suicide bombings carried out by the Jihad Group, also believed to be situated in Sinai, against the Israeli and US embassies in the capital city of Uzbekistan. The attacks killed at least nine people and wounded many more. However, some have been questioning the credibility of the danger posed by that medley of incoherent groups. As far as individuals belonging to towns, predominantly inhabited by the desert-dwelling Bedouins, are concerned, these fears are considered exaggerated, because they are merely based on rumors. They have claimed that while they have heard of the presence of militant groups in the deserts of Sinai, they haven't come across them. While they cannot yet confirm the militants' existence in the area, it would appear that the Egyptian security forces are dependent on the Bedouins to attempt restraining the groups' activities. This appears to be their preferred route as opposed to direct armed intervention, so as to avoid straining the tension between the Bedouins and the forces. Furthermore, the security forces believe armed intervention will result in large losses that simply could not be afforded amid the country's new developments. Mursi's ascent to the presidency may have nevertheless introduced a firmer mode of action.

The day of truth arrived on August 7, 2012, in the middle of the searing heat and the reckoning of the Ramadan fast, when everything usually sinks into torpor, and an ambience of fateful solemnity envelops all men and places of Islamdom. Late at night, while one of the Egyptian military bases in Sinai, close to the Israeli border, was busy with its pre-fast meal, a terrorist group of Muslim fundamentalists attacked, killing sixteen soldiers, robbing two vehicles, and heading toward the nearby Israeli border, which it crossed instantly and exploded accidentally in the process, killing all occupants of the armored car. The other vehicle raced toward an Israeli border settlement in order to explode a second car bomb there, until it was intercepted from the air and eliminated. The Egyptians had known for the past few years that Muslim radical terrorists of all sorts were infiltrating into the Sinai, where following the chaos of the Spring they could find hideouts like the ones in Pakistan, Afghanistan, Yemen, and the fringes of the Sahara. All along, the Mubarak administration was either unable or unwilling to quell them. After Mursi was sworn in, and in view of his known Brotherhood background, terrorists must have thought that their era had dawned. They had blown up the gas pipeline to Israel on fifteen occasions since the turmoil began, but they probably miscalculated this time, because the killing of Egyptian soldiers—who are considered national assets, not defenders of the regime like in Mubarak's time and in Syria, Libya, and the rest of the Spring countries—raised strong nationalistic sentiment across Egypt, especially because they were slain on Ramadan while preparing to observe the fast.

In the recent past, whenever Israel was attacked from Sinai, the Egyptians denied, against all evidence. But this time, Mursi, the consummate Muslim, had to align with the hurt national pride and to react. Judging from his later acts and the swiftness with which he acted against the top brass of the military, which had just two months earlier compelled him to accept the curtailment of his authority and to concur to Tantawi's appointment as minister of defense, one can conclude that Mursi jumped on the occasion to settle his accounts with the army and to retrieve the authority he was robbed of. Paradoxically, as was their wont, Egyptians perpetuated the rumor that it was all the work of the Israeli Mossad, at the same time that popular demands were heard for the need to revenge the wanton killing of the sixteen hero *shahids.* Big unfriendly crowds gathered in front of the Israeli Embassy in Cairo, demanding revenge against the perpetrators, and the Muslim Brotherhood site condemned Israel for her infamy in attacking innocent and peaceful Egyptians on their Ramadan day. They were apparently oblivious of the fact that in Ramadan 1973 it was their President Sadat who had launched war against Israel. But President Mursi also swiftly delivered, and he pledged in public that there would be revenge. In other cultures, retaliation is launched for such attacks in order to punish the culprits for their violation of some rule (in our case—the peace with Israel), or to deter further attacks, both rational and strategic reactions. Here, the need for revenge came to satisfy a gut feeling of hurt pride, and the popular demand to act had nothing to do with what Egypt might or might not gain from the operation. After having appropriately received clearance from Israel to introduce into Sinai armored weapons and aircraft—which were otherwise banned under the peace treaty of 1979—in order to finally lead a mopping operation against those terrorist bases, both Mursi and Tantawi showed up in Sinai to direct the troops in their sweep. Who would have thought that Brother Mursi would order and conduct an operation that Mubarak had dodged for years? The worst was yet to come, and Mursi continued to surprise.

In the course of the mopping operation, Mursi and Tantawi were shown in the media leading the troops and discoursing with them, and even eating the *iftar* (end-of-the-fast meal) with the soldiers. And suddenly, out of the clear blue sky, Mursi sent his spokesman to announce the dismissal of Tantawi as minister of defense and Anan as chief of staff, after he had removed the week before the chief of intelligence, and appointed others in their stead. This immediately presented Mursi as a fearless and determined leader, who had a program of action and followed it scrupulously. When some free-spirited Egyptian journalists complained that the authorities had not heeded Israeli intelligence warnings of an impending terrorist attack, he avoided attending the funeral of the sixteen slain soldiers, and it was his Prime Minister Qindil who took most of the popular blame and rage, as he was accused as the murderer. Another reason for popular anger was a great deal of talk about the needed permission from Israel for the Egyptians to operate in Sinai with armor and aircraft. Why should great and glorious Egypt, went the argument, the pride of the Arabs and their defender, need permission from that cowardly Jewish entity? In the meantime, Egypt's obligation to live by the peace treaty and prevent any hostile activity from its territory against Israel was forgotten. During the still-raging debate about why the president and the defense minister joined hands in cleansing the Sinai in a major operation that Mubarak had never dared to undertake came Mursi's sudden dismissal of the top brass, proving his dogged determination to defy the military council, which had tried to curtail his authority and his privileges.

Israelis had all along heeded Mubarak's warnings that the alternative to him were the Brothers, because they understood that waiting in the aisles to inherit him were not some enthusiastic democrats, as it was naively believed in the West—which took at face value the sloganeering of the demonstrators who screamed *democracy!* from the top of their lungs—but multigenerational adepts of the Brotherhood who had been dreaming of this day, and who looked more like the Taliban of Kabul than the members of the American Congress in Washington, or MPs of the British Parliament in London. For that reason, in spite of the sympathy that many Israelis felt for the young demonstrators in Tahrir Square, they did not think that it was time to terminate the relatively quiet and workable relationships they had established with Mubarak in the previous three decades. Moreover, many of them never thought that the Brothers were heading to take over the rule of Egypt, or that if they did, they would behave fanatically. But in fact, if we take for guidance the declarations of Ahmed Badi', the chief spiritual guide of the Brotherhood, repeated on Egyptian media that "the foundation of Israel was the most grievous international disaster that ever happened," and calling the Arab armies to challenge her, there is not much room for optimism. Nonetheless, Mursi keeps repeating that he is obligated to respect all the international obligations of his country, including the peace with Israel, though he usually adds: "but also Egypt's interests." Are we then watching a sophisticated deception campaign of the Brotherhood to mislead the entire world, until its rule takes root and it is self-confident enough to do what it wishes and finally realize its dream of Islamizing Egyptian society, in line with their step-by-step long-haul strategy? Or are we in for a surprise by a visionary president who realizes that leading a complicated and restless society is slightly more difficult than sermonizing about it and criticizing civil and military leaders who had been doing the job before him?

While the military council governed Egypt during the eighteen months that followed the Spring, many candidates ran for elections, and most of those who aspired to the presidency were discarded, including some famous names like Muhammed Barad'i, 'Amr Musa, and Ahmed Shafiq, until finally Mursi was elected. In that protracted process we learned something about Egyptian society that had not much of a democratic nature about it, but was reminiscent of Republican Turkey until Erdogan, where the army became the supreme arbiter of power when the civil system failed. Egypt under the military council had succeeded behind the scene in disqualifying many of the candidates for election, disbanding an elected parliament, curtailing the president's authority and prerogatives before he was elected—as they passed an amendment to the constitution taking away his rights to declare war and to command the army, and even depriving him of some protocolary symbols like being sworn in by parliament, which would have fixated the symbolic link between the executive and the legislative branches of government, both dominated by the Muslim Brothers. As already mentioned, one of the most enthusiastic visitors to Cairo after the Revolution was Erdogan, who certainly warned his host Brothers that for the Spring to succeed, the army had to be dissociated from politics and returned to its barracks, as he had himself done in Turkey. Precisely because of that lingering suspicion did the Egyptian military demand from Mursi guarantees that their prerogatives, political and economic, would be preserved and that they would not be court-martialed for conspiracy against the elected ruler, as Erdogan had done to his top brass.

Fears and suspicions were raised as to what the future held for Egypt, not only in the West and Israel but also in the larger Arab and Islamic worlds. For example, concern was voiced in Egypt, like in other places, lest the Muslim Brothers apply the well-tested strategy of educating the young generations on the vision of returning to the roots of the ancestors (that is the meaning of Salafiya), once their Salafi partners won 30 percent of the vote in parliament, thus bringing the total achievement of the fundamentalists to an overwhelming 75 percent. With such a spectacular success, fundamentalists in power are bound to alter the curricula at school and re-orient them to the past, to emphasize classical Arabic, the language of the holy book, and Islamic studies, including the *Hadith*, Qur'anic exegesis, Shari'a, the Prophet's *Sira* (biography), and everything related to that, like the biographies of the ancients and the heritage of the predecessors. This is usually accompanied by separation between the genders in education, and enforcing the veil for women. These practices are already applied in Saudi Arabia, Iran, Iraq, partly in Turkey, and in Sudan, Afghanistan, and Somalia. In many of those countries, lessons about European history, languages, and thought are cancelled and replaced by Islamic history and by chapters of the Islamic past that have relevance to the contemporary world. For example, during the study of the *Rashidun*, Abu-Bakr's primacy is underlined for the Sunnite students, and Ali's for the Shi'ites.

Not only is the study of foreign languages and history likely to suffer, but also art and dance and anything likely to contradict Shari'a teachings. Those Islamizing educators even wish to teach medicine solely in Arabic, and some even plan to cancel the programs of adult education to eradicate illiteracy. Some say it is because of the mixed audiences in those courses; others cynically claim that it is precisely due to the fact that the fundamentalists came to power thanks to those illiterate social strata that they have to eradicate their further educational programs. Those who fear the impact of fundamentalist education also predict the enforcement of censorship in general, especially on any physical contact between young men and women in public, and on the exposure of anything feminine, be it even a curl of hair that escaped the control of the head scarf. They also talk of appointing a minister to supervise public morality, whose budget would equal that of other highest spending departments like the Ministry of Defense, the rationale being that the latter would "defend the homeland from Zionism, while the former would protect the nation from libertinism." From the discussions one can read and hear in Egypt, this is the price it is feared that society would have to pay for the rise of the Brothers and their allies—unless Mursi is concocting a surprise that no one could have predicted.

If these dreary forecasts do materialize, then Egypt would be slowly edging toward the like of the Taliban regime in Afghanistan (1996–2002), until it was swept away by the American intervention there following September 11, 2001. Under that order, women disappeared from the public square and from the education system, to remain confined in their homes and prohibited from any social interaction with their peers; Muslims who missed prayer time were arrested and lashed, and everything was decided by Mullah 'Umar, who except for religious books on Shari'a had never read anything or known or understood much with regard to the world. Fortunately, Egypt is different, for it encompasses a thick stratum of educated bourgeois urbanites that would not permit such obscurantist clerics to rule them, but one ought not overlook the contrary trends either. For example, the incredibly obscene event of the destruction of the Buddhas of Banyan under the Taliban, despite the entire world's protests, comes to mind again, as there are clerics who demand the elimination of the pyramids in Giza as the only way to uproot the pagan worship of those giant structures of today. For Islam is bound to attribute the ancient Pharaonic civilization to that black hole that preceded Muhammed, called *Jahiliya* (the Era of Ignorance), which the Prophet had labored to uproot and to replace with the Muslim message. That symbol of paganism had been threatened before by Saudi and Salafi scholars who urged to cover it with wax for insulation, or to destroy it totally. A Bahraini scholar, abdul Latif Mahmud, has already applied to President Mursi to order the destruction of the pyramids, arguing that 'Umar ibn al-'As, one of the Prophet's companions, and the conqueror of Egypt for Islam and its first governor (AD 641), had in his time destroyed pre-Islamic sites, including the Great Alexandria Library which included some collections of knowledge not recognized by Islam, and he even tried to destroy the pyramids, but he desisted only in the face of the huge manual labor that it would have involved, for lack of modern means of destruction. Therefore, he argued, it befitted Mursi to do it. Incidentally, it was at the time of the Muslim Mamluks that the Sphinx, the guard of the Pyramids, lost its nose during shooting exercises with the new invention of cannon fire. So, the fear is hovering over Egypt that if the new rulers of Egypt wish to complete the Islamization of their country, they could definitely follow in the footsteps of their Taliban and Mamluk predecessors, or even wish to emulate the Prophet himself, who conquered the pagan temple of the Ka'ba and turned it into a mosque, and all the Muslim conquerors through all generations, who converted Christian and Jewish places of worship into mosques.

In a news item from August 2012,[10] Mursi was said to support the idea of forming a national council to oversee state and private media. During the radio program *The People Ask and the President Answers*, Mursi said that media figures should be more transparent in how they report news, and should also be committed to a higher standard of ethics in journalism. "I know that media figures support what's in the best interests of the nation," Mursi said, adding that he is sure the Egyptian media will attain a higher level of quality in the coming period, while still leaving room for different viewpoints. All this sounds like a straightforward civil reform, but since prominent figures in the Muslim Brotherhood had complained on several occasions about media bias against Muslim fundamentalists, particularly as the Brotherhood became salient in the political arena after the January 2011 revolution, concerns regarding a Brotherhood stranglehold over media have risen after Brotherhood-member Salah Abdel Maqsoud was named the new information and telecommunications minister. The Brotherhood-dominated Shura Council (the upper house of parliament) was also responsible for selecting the new editors-in-chief of state-run newspapers, like the prestigious *al-Ahram*, despite objections from journalists and activists over the potential for bias in the selection process.

While independent papers claimed that the new shuffle is a part of the Muslim Brotherhood's ongoing attempts to Islamize the state, state-owned papers just mentioned the names of the new top editors without commentary. The most prestigious state-run daily, *Al-Ahram* listed the new appointees for the state-run papers:[11] Several of the new editors who were named by the Shura Council have Islamist leanings, which raised concerns over the Muslim Brotherhood's alleged attempt to monopolize state-owned papers. Privately owned daily *Youm7* stated that the Brotherhood was following in the footsteps of the dissolved National Democratic Party by seeking to control the state media's editorial policies. A number of editors and journalists issued a statement calling on columnists to publish blank opinion articles in protest against appointing Brothers' loyalists to key media positions. Almost all the column spaces for independent papers, like *Youm7*, *Al-Watan*, and *Al-Tahrir*, were left unwritten on a given day, but were signed "in protest of the Brotherhood's attempts to control press and media," but unsurprisingly, state-owned columnists did not respond to the call. Independent paper *Al-Shorouk* wrote that the press leaders also agreed on forming a bloc to confront the rigid stance of the Brotherhood with regard to taking the same strong grip over state's publications that Mubarak's old regime once exercised.

Reporting in the same vein, privately owned daily *Al-Dostour* wrote that tens of journalists from both independent and state-run papers staged a protest in front of the Shura Council. They have called for the replacement of the new editors and the resignation of the head of Journalists Syndicate, Mamdouh al-Wali, who is affiliated with the Brotherhood. *Freedom and Justice* newspaper, the mouthpiece of the Muslim Brotherhood's political party, allocated a two-page spread for the biographical information on after reformation the newly appointed editors along with the history of each newspaper. The long feature is published under the headline, "National Papers in a New Dress." The news of the Egyptian army killing Sinai militants in response to the brutal border assault was also highlighted in the papers. The liberal party paper *Al-Wafd* shared identical headlines with *Al-Shorouk*: "The Army Starts the Revenge Battle for Martyrs." However, there were discrepancies in the reported figures. While *Al-Shorouk* stated that military forces killed twenty militants in a series of raids in the Sinai region bordering Israel, *Al-Wafd* wrote that the death toll for the attack rose to one hundred. It was claimed that the Egyptian air raids were a retaliation after gunmen had attacked several security checkpoints in the Sinai Peninsula a week earlier, killing sixteen Egyptian security officers. *Al-Shorouk* quoted an anonymous military source as saying, "The attack succeeded in arresting 15 terrorists, injuring tens and destroying three armored cars belonging to militants." Finally, the independent daily *Al-Tahrir* published a feature on President Mohamed Mursi's order to force the head of intelligence, Murad Muwafi, to retire in the wake of the Egypt-Israel border attack. Abdel Wahed Shehata has been appointed as the interim head of general intelligence instead.

One more reason to worry about freedom of the press (not that under Mubarak it was any better, it is just that the promise of improvement does not seem to materialize), were the reported charges of sedition against the editor of a paper for insulting President Muhammed Mursi. *Al-Dostour's* website reported that early morning one day, security forces came to the paper's offices to confiscate some of its issues. MENA reported that investigations into the newspaper had been opened after people accused the newspaper of "fueling sedition," and "harming the president through phrases and wording punishable by law." Gamal Fahmy, a member of the journalists' syndicate, told *Al-Dostour* that the investigation was part of a Muslim Brotherhood scheme to limit press freedoms. Other press freedom advocates condemned the raid, saying the Brotherhood was moving to silence its critics. "What happened this morning is a new attempt to impose hegemony, domination and exclusion on those in conflict with the group," said Saeed Ziauddin Garhi, legal advisor for the Justice Center for Freedoms. Earlier in August 2012, *Al-Faraeen* satellite TV channel, owned by the famous TV personality and former parliamentary candidate Tawfiq Okasha, was shut down, due to charges that the TV host incited viewers to attempt to assassinate Mursi. *Al-Dostour* had also been controversial under former President Hosni Mubarak, when in 2010 the mogul publisher sacked editor-in-chief Ibrahim Eissa, an outspoken government dissident. Many claimed that the publisher had fired Eissa under direct pressure from the regime.

Qindil was appointed by Mursi as prime minister and was charged with improving security and the livelihoods of Egyptians in the space of several months. For weeks after Mursi took office on June 30, the

Egyptian media had surmised that he would pick a premier from a list of better-known candidates, who would satisfy a mercurial coalition of allies that had reluctantly supported his election. The choice of the technocrat Qindil disappointed Mursi's secular allies, the more so because the new premier may, like Mursi, be a Muslim Brother. On social networking sites, Qindil was said to be so devout that he banned his children from listening to Western music, and that he did not even own a television. Such gossip is impossible to verify, but it is a sign of suspicion toward Mursi, who barely won the election after many voters also supported his rival, former Mubarak premier Ahmed Shafiq, in an attempt to block the Muslim fundamentalists from office.

For years the Egyptians have been trying to erode the Sinai force restrictions set in the peace treaty they signed with Israel. Those force restrictions were a necessary condition for Israel agreeing to restore the Sinai to Egyptian control. But it turns out that many Egyptians, who had accepted the restrictions under duress, for otherwise there would have been no Israeli withdrawal, now see the force restrictions as impinging on their sovereignty, while Israel always considers the restrictions as critical for the Jewish State's national security. Now, with the Muslim Brotherhood leading Egypt, the troop restrictions may be needed even more than ever. But now, after having authorized temporarily the entrance of extra forces in order to battle against terrorism, which now threatens Egypt no less than Israel, the latter finds itself with massive Egyptian forces deployed literally on its border. And as Arab affairs expert Ehud Ya'ari has noted, "We now have no idea if those tanks, attack helicopters, mobile artillery pieces, etc. are going to actually be moved back in a few days." This is the time, then, for the establishment of a very clear timetable for when this equipment is going to be removed from the area, if it is to be removed. One has to specify nonetheless that under the treaty, the Egyptians can put as many cops as they want near the border, and the quality and training of those cops is at the discretion of Egypt. Therefore, Egypt can bring to the border large forces of police (with or without quotation marks) forces, but what is verifiable are the weapons they can bear. This means that after the days of mopping-up operations have elapsed, Israel must insist that those forces be evacuated, lest they confirm the old adage that in the Middle East nothing is more permanent than the provisory. But for now, the Mursi government seems firm and intent in its battle against terrorism, something that has shown some positive results for Israel too; hence the latter's patience with those reinforcements.

When Mursi dismissed the top brass of the defense establishment and appointed both Defense Minister Tanrtawi and COS Anan as his advisers, presumably in order not to alienate them and set them against him, he also appointed Abdel Fattah al-Sisi as defense minister and head of the armed forces. Spokesperson Yasser Ali also announced that Mursi canceled the supplement to the Constitutional Declaration, which was passed by the SCAF on June 17 and limited the president's powers. Ali said that the supplement would be replaced with Article 25 of the original Constitutional Declaration passed by popular referendum in March 2011, which stipulated that once a civilian president was elected, the SCAF's powers would be transferred to the president. Mursi also ruled that if the work of the Constituent Assembly is impeded for any reason, he would form a new Constituent Assembly to prepare a new constitution within three months of the date of its formation. In addition, parliamentary elections are to be held within a few months of the day the new constitution is approved. Ali also announced that SCAF member Mohamed al-Assar was appointed deputy defense minister, and head of naval forces Mohab Mamish, also a SCAF member, was appointed head of the Suez Canal Authority, one of the main sources of foreign currency income for impoverished Egypt. Both Tantawi and Anan, in addition to earning the title of advisers, also got each the Nile Medal, the highest state honor in Egypt. Mursi also appointed Mahmoud Mekky, a judge, as his vice president.

Significant also was Mursi's meeting with Iranian Vice President Hamid Baghaei on August 9, 2012,[12] which was the highest-level official contact between the nations in decades, until the later travel of Mursi to Tehran to attend the Conference of the Non-Aligned, where he harshly criticized Syria, Iran's ally and protégé. This also perhaps signals a new era in Egyptian diplomacy, the like of which Prime Minister Erbakan of Turkey had initiated in the 1990s—and lost his post as he was outlawed as a result—and is also similar to the rapprochement to Iran that Erdogan had attempted in the 2000s after he acceded to power, but was interrupted by the Syrian crisis in which he remains divided from Tehran. This meeting in the midst of the difficulties Mursi has been facing domestically gave Iran diplomatic encouragement amid sharpening international pressure over its nuclear program and its links to Syria. It came as Egypt's new Islamic president tries to revert to the pro-American policies of toppled leader Hosni Mubarak as an expression of the political shifts brought by the Islamic Spring revolts. Though his meeting with the Iranian official failed to produce any immediate results, it was significant that the relations between the two countries had been nonexistent since they had been broken after the Iranian Revolution and Egypt's 1979 peace treaty with Israel. Mubarak had resisted Iran's efforts in recent years to restore full diplomatic ties, although lower-level talks between officials were occurring.

Against this background, it is worth remembering that Israel has suggested it might attack Iran's nuclear program, which it believes is aimed at developing a bomb and which Tehran says is purely for civilian purposes. But Mursi, who as a Sunni leader is not eager to see nuclear power in the hands of the Shi'ites, has also been under Israeli and American pressure to ameliorate security in the Sinai, in view of terrorists' attempts to harass Israeli territory from there. Indeed, Egyptian forces had killed about twenty suspected extremists earlier and had also targeted "terrorist hotbeds" in Al Arish and around the Rafah border crossing. These developments had prompted Mursi to seize the opportunity to fire Egypt's intelligence chief and the governor of North Sinai, namely to dismiss the high command in order to tighten his grip on the armed forces. The reshuffle also included Mursi asking Defense Minister Mohamed Hussein Tantawi, who led the nation during the first year of the revolution, to resign prior to the elections. It seems, therefore, unlikely that Sunni Muslim–dominated Egypt's relationship with Shiite Muslim-controlled Iran will shift in the short term, at a time when Mursi is on record pledging to the Americans to respect his peace treaty with Israel.

Mursi is also cautious not to strain his relations with Saudi Arabia and the Gulf monarchies, which in an emergency would remain as his only linelife in his dire economic situation. The situation is extremely volatile since under Mubarak the Saudis were suspicious of the Muslim Brothers, who undermined the regime, and now Mursi would be hard at work to convince Riyadh of his honest intentions. Egypt, which is in no position to defy its major allies (the United States, Saudi Arabia, and the Gulf monarchies) cannot in this situation lend primacy to its relations with Tehran, in spite of the praise one could hear in Iran of the "Islamic Reawakening" under Mursi. Syrian President Bashar Assad, Iran's reliable proxy, has been weakened by months of protests and bloody insurgency. If Assad is overthrown or relinquishes power, Tehran could lose an ally in its maneuverings in Lebanon and the Gaza Strip, which is governed by the militant group Hamas. The Muslim Brotherhood, which inspired the founding of Hamas, has been urging closer relations with Iran, but many Egyptian Muslim clerics have been opposed to strengthening ties given the historical animosity between Sunnis and Shi'ites. Baghaei's mission in Cairo was to invite Mursi to a meeting of the Non-Aligned Movement in August 2012 in Tehran. The visit was preceded by controversy in June when Iran's *Fars News Agency* reported that Mursi was keen to improve relations with Tehran. Mursi denied that he had ever spoken to the agency, and his office said the president had not committed to the NAM summit. Ultimately he did participate, but it is doubtful whether his firm condemnation of Assad there has contributed anything to improving the Cairo-Tehran relationship.

Mursi faced more pressing problems in August 2012 as the Egyptian military expanded into the Sinai in an offensive dubbed Operation Eagle. The air strikes against the militants, the first by Egyptian forces in the peninsula since the 1970s, indicated that Cairo was moving to restore stability to the lawless desert region, not to please Israel's desire for quiet on its borders or to yield to American pressures, but to avenge the death of its murdered soldiers during Ramadan, and to signal to the terrorist niches that have been built there that they cannot challenge his rule and sovereignty over that peninsula the way they did with Mubarak. The government said a joint police-military operation would regain control over militants who have grown bolder in arms and human traffickers. The trouble in the Sinai has led to new calls for a wider Egyptian military presence, while under the 1979 peace treaty, much of the region was designated as demilitarized. Before Mubarak was toppled in early 2011, Egypt increased the number of lightly armed troops in the region. Now, as Mursi declared war on Palestinian border smuggling tunnels,[13] the military has begun to destroy them systematically under the Sinai-Gaza border, with a view to stopping infiltrators and smuggling. The work started with the tunnels far from the border town of Rafah, most of which are now shut down. The crackdown is part of the military response to the militants' attack on the Egypt-Israeli border in early August, which has spurred violence that continued throughout the succeeding week in Sinai.

Locals in Sinai said there are about 1,200 tunnels between Egypt and the Gaza Strip. Some of these underground corridors have been developed recently for vehicles that run on tracks and are pulled by machinery, including cranes. The tunnels also have ventilation openings and communication devices to link people inside to the outside, facilitating the transfer of goods to Gaza. The tunnels belong to families and individuals on both sides of the border. These people depend on them as a source of income, despite cooperation between Rafah residents and security forces in combating this phenomenon. The tunnel-clearing operation comes at the same time that the military and police are attacking armed militias in the Sinai with the aid of *Apache* helicopters. This campaign continued for a few consecutive days in Sheikh Zuwayed and Rafah, both of which are south of the North Sinai capital of al-Arish. Those tunnels have been there for years, but despite Mubarak's bombast that Egypt would build, with American aid, iron screens going deep into the earth to block any tunneling activity, it went on undisturbed. The rhetoric around it also grew ludicrous: people on both sides of the border, just like drug growers and traffickers, first indulge in illegal activity, and then when the authorities finally awake to deprive them of that, they claim that their livelihoods depend on them, turning themselves from criminal trespassers to helpless and innocent victims. Poor creatures! They deserve as much compassion as the son who kills his father and then claims compassion to his miserable condition as an orphan.

A comprehensive summary of the saga of the ascension of the Brotherhood to Power in Egypt can be found in an article published in July 2012, whose main points are cited here.[14] Most striking was Mursi's inauguration speech, where he seemed to commit himself to international treaties and agreements, declaring himself carrying a message of peace to the world. The authors estimate that it accords neatly with the Brotherhood's sophisticated strategy for dealing with outsiders. They cite Mustafa Mashhur, the Guide of the Brothers from 1996 to 2006, who explained in his *Jihad is the Way* his movement's beliefs and aspirations, especially the role of violent jihad in bringing about a world under a unified Islamic caliphate. These references, which are true to what al-Banna himself had written in the 1930s in the beginning years of the movement, give reason to doubt Mursi's reassurances. For one thing, *Jihad is the Way* defined Israel and Israelis as the criminal, thieving gangs of Zion, and Mashhur stressed that the notion of Israel's foundation on stolen land is not an opening position for negotiations, but a nonnegotiable article of faith and religion. Further, he claimed that the land was stolen not only from Palestinian Arabs but from Islam, in his words: "Know that the problems of the Islamic world, such as Palestine . . . are not issues of territories and nations, but of faith and religion. They are problems of Islam and the Muslims, and they cannot be resolved by negotiation. . . ." These words are echoed by the Hamas charter, which is also an adept and affiliate of the Brotherhood. Mashhur explained that, "Jihad and preparation for jihad are not only for the purpose of fending-off assaults and attacks against Muslims by Allah's enemies, but are also for the purpose of realizing the great task of establishing an Islamic state, strengthening the religion, and spreading it around the world." Like Banna who exalted jihad and martyrdom, and like Hamas, who glorifies them in its charter, Mashhur writes that "Martyrdom for Allah is our most exalted wish," and Mursi never rejected this ideology. So how are these contradictions to be understood? Why does Mursi talk peace when he supposedly adheres to an ideology of jihad war?

Another view, along the same lines by noted columnist Mordechai Kedar,[15] described the history of the Brothers in some very sharp points worth mentioning. It was when the British ruled Egypt after World War I and tried to influence it to Westernize, that local reactions to those endeavors found expression in the public square. One of them viewed the Pharaonic heritage as reflecting the national character of Egypt; others saw the Arab nation (of Muslims, Christians, Jews and others, all of whom spoke Arabic) as the province of affiliation; and there were also those who saw the Greek (Alexander the Great, Ptolemy) and the Roman past as the source of European identity of the Egyptian people. All of these trends were anti-Islamic, and certainly pre-Islamic, and the Brotherhood headed by the founder of the movement, Hassan Al-Banna—saw the occupation by the Christian, wine-drinking and pork-eating British, as the source of all the cultural problems of the Land of the Nile, so they placed the struggle against the foreign occupation at the top of their priorities, and as a secondary task only the purification of Egyptian society from the influence of Western culture, which in their opinion was rotten, corrupt, permissive and not suitable to Islamic society. The struggle over the course the culture ought to follow placed the Brotherhood in conflict with the new sociopolitical theories that debated the source of collective inspiration of the Egyptian people, which ought to be heeded. In answer to all of these trends the Brotherhood claimed that "Islam is the Solution"; for it was forbidden for a Muslim society, whose Guide is on high, to search among other cultures for solutions and arrangements that are the mere work of men.

The third task that the Brotherhood took upon itself was to prove that indeed "Islam is the solution" by imposing Islamic Shari'a in all spheres of life, private, family, political, economic and diplomatic. This task, which aspires to impose the rules of Islam on politics and the state, has created the concept of political Islam in contrast to other religions, which separate between religion and state. The symbol of the organization expresses this ideology well: the color of green represents Paradise and the favorite color of the Prophet, two swords in the center express the two basic avowals of Islam— there is no god but Allah, and Muhammed is his messenger—and one word, which appears in the Qur'an just once, written above: "Wa-aidu"—(and prepare). This word is the beginning of the passage from the Qur'an[16] "and prepare whatever you can of your strength and your harnessed horses in order to impose fear (*irhab*, i.e., terror) in the hearts of Allah's enemy and your enemies." When the Muslim Brotherhood was founded in Egypt, King Fuad the First ruled, and in 1936 his son Farouk succeeded him, and ruled until the Officers' Revolution in July 1952 overturned him. During the monarchy, the Brotherhood acted very freely, because the regime was incredibly ineffective. In December 1948 an activist from the movement assassinated the prime minister, Nukrashi, and two months afterward the movement's founder and leader—Hassan al-Banna—was murdered, apparently by agents of the regime.

The regime of the Officers was much more determined and decisive, and in general, conducted a stubborn battle against the Brotherhood because it saw them and their activities as an attempt to undermine its legitimacy and stability. In 1966 President Gamal Abd al-Nassar hung the ideologue of the movement, Sayyid Qutb, because in his writings he claimed that any regime that does not implement Shari'a is like the heresy (*jahiliyya*) that preceded Islam, or idol worship, and therefore justifies a jihad against it. Because the Brotherhood was marginalized politically during the years of the Officers' Regime, it found its fertile field of activity within the economically and politically marginalized people and turned their energies to charitable activities within the society of the tens of millions of Egyptians living in the poor, chaotic neighborhoods at the margins of the cities, without running water, without sewage, without electricity, without telephone lines, without medical services or educational services, without work, and without hope. It was the Brotherhood who supported these miserable people for years, out of a feeling of commitment, responsibility, and mutual trust rooted in Islamic values, which did not differentiate between the sort of Muslim denomination, society, politics, economics, and culture of the people they took under their wings. The regime allowed them to operate among the weak neighborhoods, since it did not see acts of charity and kindness as a danger to the stability of the regime, and because the burden on the state of caring for the poor population was eased thanks to the Brotherhood's activities.

The common and needy people held the Brotherhood in high regard, because for many years it supported the poor wholeheartedly, and because the Brotherhood did not appear as corrupt and greedy as the fat cats who ruled the state. Moreover, the Brothers related to the people with respect, unlike the officials of the system, who humiliated them and oppressed them cruelly. Those who initiated the street riots that broke out in Egypt on January 25, 2011, which some called the Arab Spring, were throngs of Egyptian secular youth, some of whom were educated, who were sick of the corrupt and cruel regime, which was slated to be passed down to the son of the ruler. The Muslim Brotherhood did not take a meaningful part in the demonstrations at first, but rather sat on the sidelines watching to see which side would win. After the military forced Mubarak to resign on February 11, the Brotherhood went out to al-Tahrir Square in order to take advantage of the opportunities that it had awaited patiently for many years. The Qur'an states that "Allah is with the patient,"[17] and indeed Allah is with them: in the period that preceded the November 2011 elections to parliament, the Brotherhood activated Operation Da'wah' (Islamic outreach), in order to translate their investment of years of community efforts into political support by the public (Just like Obama in the Chicago area prior to his running for elections first in the US Senate and then for the presidency).

Spokesmen of political Islam, headed by Yussuf al-Qaradawi, mobilized themselves in support the Brotherhood, and the result was that almost half of the seats of parliament were won by the Party of Freedom and Justice, the representative of the Brotherhood, and a quarter more of the seats were won by the Party of Light (al-Noor), the representative of the more conservative Salafi groups. This is how the decisive majority of the Egyptian parliament was suffused with the color green, the color of the Islamic Paradise and the favorite color of the Prophet, in a truly democratic way. It is important to note here that one of the most eloquent spokesmen of the Brotherhood, Sheikh Safwat Higazi, gave a speech that was broadcast live for thousands of people to see and to hear on May 1, 2012, and as part of the Brotherhood's preparations for the presidential elections. In his fiery discourse, Higazi announced that the goal of the Brotherhood was the unity of all the Arab states into one giant Islamic caliphate, under Mursi's flag, whose capital will be "Not Mecca and not Medina but al-Quds [Jerusalem]."

His words reflect very well the goal of the movement—to erase the heritage of colonialism, principally the borders marked by colonialist interests, which damaged both the Arab world and Islam; the elimination of Israel; and imposition of Islam on Judaism. It might be that this refers to a far-off hope and not to immediate plans, but the cheers of support from the throats of the masses who crowded into the street expressed the collective energy behind the idea, just waiting for the suitable moment to turn it into reality. Moreover, Israel must take very seriously the hopes of others, because the state of Israel is exactly the realization of such hopes, and its enemies learn from it how to realize hopes as well.

A new turn in the relations between the Islamic world and the West was marked on the eleventh anniversary of September 11, when a large coordinated attack on the American consulate in Benghazi by forces of al-Qa'ida and their affiliates, burned down the entire consulate and its attached property and killed the ambassador who happened to be visiting. The official trigger of that heinous attack was an idiotic film made by a private individual, a Copt in exile in America, that grossly mistreated the figure of the Prophet Muhammed, which is deeply venerated in Islam. Although it is clear that the attack must have been prepared months before that film was made and distributed, it was easy to incite the ready-to-explode Muslim crowds, from Casablanca to Jakarta, with anything that smacked of anti-Americanism in defense of anything that is understood as Islamophobia. Indeed, American (and also British and German) embassies were attacked in several Arab and Muslim countries, from Africa to the far east, and fierce and violent demonstrations have erupted in many Muslim cities, chanting anti-Western slogans and burning foreign flags, notably American and Israeli. It is noteworthy that precisely Cairo, which Obama had chosen to "engage" the Muslims and "open a new page" with them at the beginning of his term, when his ally Mubarak still ruled the place, has been taken over by the Muslim Brothers, who proved unable (and perhaps also unwilling) to prevent the attacks on the American Embassy.

Although all Muslims who commented on this new outburst of maddened fury attribute this string of violent acts to that film, it is worth mentioning that prior to September 11, there was no such film to provoke this new eruption of the 2005–6 drama of the cartoons in Denmark. And since the lessons were not learned there, the same scenario was bound to be repeated, and will happen more and more in the future due to the basic religious, legal, and cultural disagreements between Islam and the West about freedom of expression and creation, tolerance of others and their ideas and religions, the separation between church and state, the self-confidence of the culture and its readiness to compete with others peacefully in the open market, and the extent to which any democratic country can interfere with and be held responsible for the noncriminal acts of its nationals. Muslim countries have been trying to impose universally, via the UN and other international bodies, their own norms of morality and respect for religions, which they themselves do not respect: For example, Muslims in the West raise enormous demonstrations and protests when they are not afforded enough facilities for their prayers, while Saudi Arabia, which finances most Muslim installations in the West, does not permit any non-Muslim house of prayer on its land. If, for example, the West had made the building of new mosques conditional on opening Saudi Arabia to the same freedoms of worship of all religions, the situation might be amended.

Another example is the situation that Israel allowed to develop on Temple Mount. The Muslims laid claim to that holy place while they knew that it is also holy to the Jews. But if they are allowed to claim exclusivity for it, then the rights of others are thereby violated. In the Tomb of the Patriarchs in Hebron, which they have turned into a mosque, thereby making it exclusively Muslim and denying the Jews over the generations their right to worship there, Israel reversed the situation after 1967 and allowed both Jews and Muslims to make provisions for partition of time and space to accommodate both communities. The same could be done for Temple Mount, but by being generous and ready to share with others, Israel in fact forfeited its right to share the place with Muslims, who continue to regard the site as exclusively theirs. Maybe an enforcement of time-sharing, notwithstanding the resentment of the Muslims, would have brought home to them the realization that Islam is only one of many faiths and Muslims certainly have their rights, but not to the exclusion of others. The jealousy and fanaticism of Islam, which was adequate for the Middle Ages, when Christianity behaved similarly, are no longer fit in the multicultural world in which people must learn to accept the other on equal terms, and if the West does not enforce this standard of conduct, we are bound to see more anti-Western eruptions in the future. For instance, if Muslims respond to any insult, apparent or imaginary, to their Prophet and are ready to burn, kill, and destroy for it, but take with total complacency Iran's president's or the Muslim Brothers' repeated insults and threats of annihilation against Israel and the Jews, whom they vow to destroy, one wonders about their scale of values, which prioritizes the memory of a dead prophet over the lives of millions of live people and their state.

The problem indeed lies with a value system in which Islam places lower value on human lives than on religious principles, about which they are apparently so uncertain that they are determined to enforce them by force and violence instead of by persuasion, debate, and goodwill. They claim the right, and also implement it in the West, of propagating their faith, but they do not let Christians, for example, preach or even maintain theirs in lands of Islam. We witness everyday churches (and synagogues, before Jews ran away for their lives) being burned down in Egypt, Nigeria, Iraq, Libya, and elsewhere (none in Saudi Arabia, because they do not exist there). Had the West made Islamic rights in its midst conditional on the respect of rights of its nationals and coreligionists in Islamic lands, or ousted Iran from international forums until it repented for its threats against Israel, which is also a member of the international community, things might have been different. But instead, engagement has been foolishly and disastrously adopted, which only causes those fanatics to persist in their conduct. In no other religion is the individual who has reneged on his faith (*murtadd*), which is a basic human rights issue, condemned to death for *ridda*. In fact, entire populations in the tens of thousands perished during the bloody Ridda Wars of the seventh century, when after the death of the Prophet (AD 632) entire tribes that had sworn allegiance to him and his faith reneged on their oath. If entire tribes can be wiped out for *ridda*, then certainly so can individuals, who expose Islam to mockery, they fear, by renouncing it. Again it is a matter of insult, which they cannot bear due to their complexes rather than to the intrinsic value of the slight—because if the insult had any validity, then Israelis should be entitled every day to burn and destroy anything Iranian on earth.

Would Buddhists, Jews, or Christians have dared to attack, kill, burn, and destroy others because someone insulted Buddha, Moses, or Jesus? If the West does not teach Muslims that while they are free to adulate, adore, and worship their prophet as much as they wish, they cannot force their ideas on others; that each individual creator and artist, in literature, poetry, visual or performing arts is free to create without state interference; and that he is not accountable to anyone for this

126

freedom, nor is his country answerable to anyone for his creation—then science, art, spiritual productivity will be totally stifled, as they have been in the Islamic world, precisely due to these limitations. And even if Muslims decide to enforce these limitations in their own lands, that is their business. But when they threaten Salman Rushdie's life for his blasphemy, or Hirsi Ali for her heresy, or Oriana Falacci (a Christian) for her "hatred of Islam," and force them first to live behind a screen of fear and bodyguards and then to migrate to the land of freedom in America, this is a situation the world cannot countenance, because when it does nothing, it reinforces Muslims in their beliefs that acting violently worldwide is part of their right of defense against the Islamophobia, which they have very deservedly earned.[18]

Two years after the outburst of the Egyptian revolution, the dust is still far from settling. The main obstacles are several:

1. The dire economic situation that has forced Mursi to lobby for new loans from the international monetary institutions, where the United States is the major wheeler and dealer. Some rich Arab regimes have promised him to help if worse came to worse, but none of them is prepared to disburse the billions that are needed to fill in the gap while Egypt is sinking into insolvency and fear persists that in a few months Egyptians might be hungry for bread. Mursi is also under pressure from his party colleagues and from Salafi extremists to revise the peace accords with Israel, but if he embarks on that path he would certainly trigger the wrath of the West, whose funds he needs, and urgently so.

2. Mursi, in spite of his democratic rhetoric, has appropriated for himself near-dictatorial powers. He claims it is temporary until the democratic institutions work and the new constitution is adopted in a referendum. Again, as in the process of his election, his followers threaten that nothing else than the adoption of the Islamic new constitution would be acceptable to them, which puts question marks on the nature of such proceedings when a priori the supporters of the Islamic view announce that nothing else can satisfy them;

3. The new constitution by itself—adopted without amendments by 64 percent of those who voted in December 2012, who were only a minority of all voters—contains the contradictions that can bring its demise, for while the Islamic half of the nation will accept it as the fulfillment of a Shari'a state, the other half cannot accept it wholeheartedly. Thus, instead of being, like the American constitution, a unifying factor, it might turn out to become a divisive element that will tear society apart.

4. Since Americans and Westerners in general have come to accept the Brothers as moderates, nothing can further encourage the latter to desist from in their Islamic platform, assured as they are that the world has reconciled to the idea that it would be faced with Islamic regimes that aspire to a world caliphate and world dominion.

Pakistan

Pakistan is the largest Muslim country tackled here, with some 150 million Muslims, third only to Indonesia (220 million) and India (170 million). Officially, it has not been hit by the Islamic Spring, since from its inception in 1947 it was founded on the notion of an Islamic state in the making that was constantly awakening to coups and counter-coups, with some bouts of democracy in between, and several wars and threats of war between it and neighboring India. In the past decade, the arms race between those two countries having escalated to the nuclear level, Pakistan has come to world attention more than ever before, not only because of the menace to the world per se, but mainly due to the danger that in such a Muslim country in ebullition, with such an abundance of terrorist movements operating there with or without government connivance, and a gigantic manufacture of radically indoctrinated students (Taliban) in its thriving madrassas, where tens of thousands of Muslim students flock from all over the world—if those nuclear devices should fall into the hands of irresponsible terrorists, no positive prospects could be foreseen for the country and the region.

Pakistan is made up of four provinces: Punjab, Sind, Baluchistan, and the Northwest Frontier. It was the first modern state to be set up on grounds of religion. Paradoxically, Pakistan was born in the northwest of the Indian subcontinent where the Muslims were not the majority, but they still lived on the legacy of their former status as rulers of the land under the glorious dynasty of the moghuls (sixteenth to nineteenth centuries). While the diversity of India's Muslims prevented them from uniting under the same banner, at the same time they were encouraged to think of themselves as a separate political category. In 1940, the Muslim League, headed by Muhammed Ali Jinnah, issued its Lahore demand for a separate Muslim state. Jinnah won the support of most Muslim leaders in India, not so much because they wanted a Muslim state, but mainly because they were loath to see the Indian congress, which had become coterminous with Hinduism, rule over them. After the new state was traumatically separated from India in 1947, causing millions of Hindis to move out and millions of Muslims to move in, it failed to establish a working state machinery reflecting the diversity in the country, with democracy, theocracy, martial law, chaos, and military coups (the latest of which occurred in the 2000s under General Pervez Musharraf) alternating, and regional rivalry escalating. Jinnah had envisaged Islam in the new state to be essentially a private affair, but his successor, Ali Khan Liaqat, introduced Islamic elements into the constitution, some of which have remained contentious ever since. But the constitution of 1956 had declared Pakistan to be an Islamic republic. In 1991 the government passed the Shariat Bill, which confirmed the country as an Islamic state.[19]

The war in next-door Afghanistan, since 1979 when the mujahidin battled against the Soviet invaders, and since 2001 in the war against American invaders, has involved Pakistan so deeply in it, in more ways than one, that it does not seem that Pakistan can extricate itself even if it wished to. The country is supposed to be an ally of the United States, which has been pouring in huge sums of money in military and economic assistance. On the other hand it is harboring vast terrorist bases in Waziristan, the inaccessible tribal border mountain area with Afghanistan, which it does not dare to eradicate, even if it were able to. Further, its central intelligence agency is known to subsidize the Taliban, both in Afghanistan, which is fighting the United States and NATO, and in Pakistan, which maintains its own terrorist organization (Tehreek-e-Taliban Pakistan, TTP). Nor is the latter the only antigovernment organization presently operating there. Numerous Islamic currents and groups of fundamentalists are vying to establish the Islamic state they had envisioned with the establishment of Pakistan but never fully realized, like Lashkar-e-Taibah, which stood behind the Mumbai operations and are constantly harassing the Indian troops in Kashmir, and lately also the Haqqani group, a fundamentalist-Salafi movement that has announced anti-Western and anti-American goals. The latter were recently added to the terrorist list of the US State Department. Not a day goes by that tens of Pakistani citizens, of one group or another, do not fall victim to terrorism of all sorts. This atmosphere of unrest, danger, and uncertainty gives the impression that upheaval and change are imminent, that citizens are expecting and preparing for a Spring of sorts, which is bound to come and to be Islamic.

These permanent tensions, which are fed by the indecision of the Afghanistan War and the knowledge that the West will withdraw by 2014 and leave the area to its own devices, prompt the local powers to brace for the day they will have to deal on their own with the residues of that long and inconclusive conflict. For wars do not determine who is right, but who and what is left. And what will be left is the saga of Bin Laden, whom America had to fight with all its might for a decade before they got him, and his al-Qa'ida organization, which although decentralized has now spread to all continents. Pakistan is now more Islamic than ever, and seething with daily terrorist attacks in one part of the country or another, leaving hundreds of casualties. The country is also half-chaotic, where terrorist movements make the rule. (One remembers the cruel murder of Daniel Pearl, the American journalist who was kidnapped for his Judaism and slaughtered like a sheep by one of those groups in February 2002 with an impotent government watching.) Pakistan also has a stake in keeping an eye on nearby impoverished and chaotic Afghanistan, and in maintaining a vigilant stance toward its other mighty Indian neighbor, with whom the issues of boundaries and Kashmir will continue to be inflammatory. Its domestic radicalization of the various Islamic groups who would like to pull their country in the direction of the Shari'a state, and heavy involvement of the military in government, also add to the complexity of Pakistani affairs.

Following an attack in July 2012 by TTP on a Pakistani military camp in the town of Gujrat, Islamic militants of this affiliate movement of the Taliban warned that they would carry out similar attacks against the Pakistani army and other government targets. Intelligence reports say that more attacks of this sort would be forthcoming if NATO supply routes through the country are not shut down. These warnings were found in pamphlets the movement disseminated. In another piece of information, Iqbal Aka Sarit, a key commander of TTP Maulana Fazlullah Group, was arrested by the Pakistani police in the district of Batagram, in the Hazara Division of Pakistan's Khyber Pakhtunkhwa Province, on July 10, 2012. The police also seized weapons and ammunition as well as parts to make suicide vests. These reports, which constantly make the rounds on Pakistani and foreign media, are seconded by daily reports of arms smuggling into the country, which one Pakistani Daily estimates at twenty million illegal weapons, sufficient to arm several armies. The weapons, which according to an investigative report find their way into Karachi and other large cities, are generated by private manufacturers in Afghanistan and Pakistan's border areas, especially in the Khyber Pass area. Anyone who wonders about the unending political violence and targeted killings by members of political parties and Islamic groups has at least to be aware of the free flow of weapons into the country and the inability (or reluctance) of the government to control it. Wherever the control of weapons is so loose, one can only expect security chaos, which is the prerequisite for the unrest leading to a Spring, in this case Islamic.

Only now, four years after the event, are the details of the Mumbai terrorist operation perpetrated by Lashkar-e-Taiba (LeT) on November 2008, beginning to come to light. On June 25, 2012, Indian security officials arrested at the New Delhi Indira Gandhi International Airport Sayed Zabiuddin Andari, who is thought to be a key member of LeT, which planned and carried out that attack. Ansari is the second key man whose arrest could lead to revelations about how the lethal attacks were planned in Pakistan, which denied any connection to the act of terror. The other man was Ajmal Kasab, the lone terrorist captured alive during that chain of attacks where many fatalities were counted. The Indians say that Ansari was present in the control room of LeT in Karachi when the operation was launched, and his conversations with the terrorists in Mumbai were then recorded. In those recordings, Indian investigators claimed, that an "individual with a Mumbai accent" could be heard instructing the terrorists about what list of demands had to be made to the media for the seized hostages. That man was Ansari. In view of the semi-involvement of the Pakistani intelligence in some terrorist activities that it commissioned, it is difficult to sort out the double game played by Pakistani authorities. Things might get clearer after the Americans exit from Afghanistan, and probably from Pakistan too, and expose that double game; but as long as they are involved there and they depend on Pakistani territory for their logistics, they will have to swallow more contradictions of that sort without protesting too loudly.

Another sign of the times is that the number of Taliban jihadi CDs and MP3s has declined in Pakistani towns after the May 2011 elimination of Bin Laden, the unofficial explanation being that the jihadists are busy fighting, so they have no time for composing, recording, or listening to poetry or songs. Officially, the government has bragged that this was due to a government crackdown on shops selling this sort of recording as part of its reported campaign to the Americans about fighting terrorism. However, many such audio materials are still sold clandestinely. Moreover, it should be emphasized that many jihadi recordings that were freely available in Pakistan towns and cities are now increasingly being posted on free US–based websites such as YouTube, Facebook, and Twitter. Amid this battle of confirmations and denials, a top Pakistani al-Qa'ida official lamented in a new video the recent killings of Islamic scholars Maulana Nasseb Khan and Maulana Aslam Sheikhupuri, and vowed to work for the end to the American hegemony in the region. The speaker, Ustad Ahmed Farooq, traced the current jihad back to the jihad waged by Islamic scholars against the British rule in India in the past centuries. Farooq, who is al-Qa'ida's head of media and Da'wa in Pakistan—and who spoke in Urdu, though his speech was also published in an English translation—also asserted that the final goal of the mujahideen was to ensure that the Islamic flag of the Islamic Emirate of Afghanistan, namely the Taliban shadow government, which is bracing to take over again when the Americans leave the scene, flies over the entire region, including Pakistan, Afghanistan, India, and Bangladesh.[20] Could there be any loftier purpose for an Islamic Spring than attaining this ultimate goal?

Concurrently with al-Qa'ida's boasting and propaganda, its collaborators in TTP have been acting on the ground to increase their influence and take control of more territory, in preparation for the takeover of the country by the Taliban when the Americans depart. In fact, in the summer of 2012 the TTP fighters overpowered the anti-Taliban militia in the Tirah Valley of Pakistan's Khyber Agency, forcing over eight hundred families to migrate to the nearby Jamrud region. Those migrants of the Kukikhel Afridi tribe were moved within three days, according to a report in the *News Daily*. A local official confirmed that the migrants were encountered and registered at Lala Kandaw Checkpost in Jamrud while they were fleeing from the Tirah Valley. The report is problematic because usually, when territory is taken over by a victorious faction, it attempts to win the hearts of the population in order to ensure later control. This incident indicates that TTP prioritizes territory over people in the course of its aspiration to take over Pakistan and return to total Islamic rule. Worse, if the inhabitants indeed flee, that says something about the unpopularity of the Islamic movement rather than the open arms with which it claims to be welcomed in areas it redeems from the America-supported government of chaotic Pakistan. In line with the same modus operandi, the TTP of South Waziristan, an area that has been practically outside government control since the beginning of the Afghanistan war in 2001–2, has also warned the local population to evacuate the Mehsud-populated region, saying that the war was still underway there. The move came as the Pakistani military, whose grip in that zone has been rather sporadic, has been seeking to rehabilitate local people who have been displaced as a result of the anti-Taliban operation in southern Waziristan. An Urdu language leaflet was distributed in the Wana bazaar, the main town of southern Waziristan, mentioning the organizations on the hit list of TTP and urging them to stop operating in that war zone.

An interesting appendix to the activities of the Islamic jihadis in Pakistan, as part of the Islamic Spring, has been the interconnectivity between various Islamic movements worldwide, which gives the Islamic Spring a universal, not only a local or regional importance and relevance. In January 2011, Indonesian terror mastermind Umar Patek was captured in the city of Abottabad, the place where Bin Laden was hiding and in the crosshairs of the CIA, which would liquidate him there in May of the same year. Patek was extradited to Indonesia, with or without any known connection to the underground activities of Bin Laden. On June 7, 2012, while the Islamic Spring was unfolding, he called on Muslims to go to the Palestinian territories to wage jihad, as reported on the website of the *Jakarta Globe*. He was cited as saying, "People should go to Palestine to commit Jihad. If you want to do Jihad, do it in another country such as Palestine, where Islamic people need help." At the same time, he urged Muslims not to commit acts of terrorism in Indonesia. He specified, "I hope we can learn from what has happened to me. I was on the police search list with my photo spread everywhere, and they were offering a bounty on me. But I dared to go out of this nation, because I had the good intention to commit Jihad abroad."[21] He was referring to the Bali mega-terrorism that killed over two hundred vacationers, half of them Australians, and implying the nature of his deal with the democratic government of Jakarta: he refrained from operating in his country but was not hindered in his terrorist activities elsewhere.

Paradoxically, we can find an indication to Pakistan's attitude toward the Spring, in the recurring attempts of this Islamic republic to preserve Islamic monarchies that are precisely opposed to the Spring upheaval that seeks to dislodge the kings and princes from their position of absolute power. In the 1950s not only was Pakistan the only Islamic country to recognize Jordan's King Abdullah's annexation of the West Bank, but it also trained his officers and sent troops when his throne was menaced. Now, during the Bahrain crackdown (see below) it was Pakistani troops who were dispatched to rescue that Arab monarchy. In March 2011, as the government crackdown on pro-democracy protestors intensified, curious advertisements appeared in the Pakistani press, such as: "Urgent requirement: manpower for Bahrain national guard; the following categories of people with previous army and police experience are urgently needed. . . ." The categories included former army drill instructors, anti-riot instructors, retired military police, and former army cooks. In the following two months, and following the visit to Islamabad of senior Saudi and Bahraini officials, some 2,500 former servicemen were recruited and brought to Manama, increasing the size of national guard and local police of that tiny kingdom by 50 percent. Al-Jazeera[22] was told by Nabeel Rajab, president of the Bahrain Center of Human Rights, that continued planeloads arrived in Bahrain carrying Pakistani soldiers, around 2,000. The Sunni recruits were tasked with suppressing Shi'ite protesters who demanded equal rights after years of oppression at the hands of the royal rulers who head the Sunnite Bahraini kingdom. Thus, commented Rajab bitterly, "while the Shi'ites cannot be recruited to the local force, the government was importing recruits from abroad." It sounded like a justified and straightforward argument, but one can also understand that arming fifth-column Shi'ites would be like committing suicide for the regime, something the media and the Human Rights president, himself a Shi'ite, certainly wanted.

In Pakistan, the recruitment was handled by the Fauji Foundation, one of the largest conglomerations in the country, with close ties to the Pakistani military. That foundation owns the Overseas Employment Services, tasked with providing job opportunities to retired military personnel, as well as large cereal and gas companies, sugar mills, security firms, hospitals, and universities. In Pakistan, it is the Baluchis who form a large percentage of the new recruits, and when on duty in Bahrain they are so visible that some of the protestors answer the police in Urdu, knowing that they do not speak Arabic, a proof that they were not locally recruited. The entire defense force of Bahrain amounts to 12,000, and another 1,200 for the national guard, protecting a total population of 1,234,571, including 666,172 (about 50 percent) nonnationals as of 2010, mainly Shi'ites. Thus, the new recruitments of Baluchis doubled the national guard, which carries the main burden of standing up to the demonstrators. For Pakistan, this means not only exporting trained forces at a time that it is facing large unrest domestically, but it is forced into balancing its relations between Saudi Arabia (and the United States), its benefactor on the one hand, and Iran, which supports the Shi'ite mutiny and denounced the Bahraini government for the crackdown on the other.

In Bahrain, the Pakistanis have encountered ill feeling because they are seen as the main tool of the crackdown. There is also fear among the Shi'a that the government might offer the recruits to settle and be naturalized in an effort to alter the demographic balance in the country. It has been reported nonetheless that when the uprising in

Bahrain seemed to knock on Saudi Arabia doors, the chairman of the Saudi National Security Council, Prince Bandar Bin Sultan, made two quiet trips to Pakistan to seek its support in case protests also erupted at home. He was told by Prime Minister Gilani that his country supported the Saudi stance in the Gulf and the Middle East, and would stand by Riyadh for "regional peace," whatever that meant, probably due to the Pakistani fear of US aid funds drying up, and their need for alternative cash sources. Bandar also used the trip to gain support for the Gulf Cooperation force that was deployed in Bahrain and was at the root of the reports about Pakistani soldiers that were seen there, in addition to the civilian recruits. But in Pakistan these moves created a backlash, since the six million Baluchis are themselves engaged in a struggle for self-determination; therefore many do not see themselves participating in an oppressive army against other people who seek their rights. Many Pakistanis who are part of the foreign work force and are lumped together with the recruits by the oppressed populations suffer from this reality.

In the latest crisis of "insult of the Prophet" that was triggered in Benghazi in September 2011, and supposedly caused the turmoil throughout the entire Muslim world, demonstrators in Pakistan were shown carrying signs: "Butcher/Behead." This cruel and ruthless culture of death, where Muslims and non-Muslims face death for anything the Muslims care to define as blasphemy, has been the mounting wave of what the media have chosen to call a Spring, and the West has found itself impotent respond to. For when American Secretary of State Clinton expressed "surprise" and dismay at her ambassador's murder in Benghazi by Libyans and other Muslim groups whom the West had assiduously assisted to rid of their former tyrants, she was in fact declaring her and her president's ignorance of what is going on in the Islamic world. The more they expressed apologies, instead of clarifying Western values of freedom and taking to task the Muslim authorities who cannot eradicate terror, the more they displayed a miserable weakness, which Muslims will always seek to punish and avenge, no matter how much money and military efforts the United States pour on the ground. The West has to wake up and realize that the battle of the frustrated Muslims, who are unable to set their systems right, is not waged because their Prophet was mocked, but because if they cannot rise to the level of the West, they need to rise against it and destroy it in order to end the humiliation of feeling inferior and impotent in comparison with it. Mockery of the Prophet is not the reason, just a pretext.

The recurrence of blasphemy cases in the Islamic world, where their own citizens are prosecuted for religious trespassing, something unthinkable in the civilized world, is one of the negative manifestations of the Spring. Take Pakistan, for example, where the American presence and aid have only caused the crowds to hate America more and more and to seek occasions to express their bigotry and rage. There are, in Pakistan's hard-line religious leaders, those who have claimed that some international media and NGOs are using isolated cases of blasphemy to undermine Pakistan's blasphemy laws. Thus, the moment one questions the validity of orthodoxy, one is shunned, because just to criticize these laws, one of which is defaming the Prophet, carries the death sentence, since it is considered equivalent to criticizing Islam itself. While Pakistan's constitution allows freedom of speech, the dominant discourse is still controlled by the extreme right-wing Sunni orthodoxy, though one never writes on the issue of blasphemy in religious terms—as to never say that the laws are based on Islamic teachings. But the media instead base their stories and analyses on arguments that revolve around human rights, minority rights, the law, and the constitution so as to appear following a civil discourse. It is nearly impossible for anybody in Pakistan to give a liberal interpretation of Islam, and anyone who criticizes religion in any way is either threatened or killed. When in early 2011 Governor Salman Taseer was killed for such a criticism of the orthodoxy, many venues, like the Karachi Press Club, refused to allow a memorial reference for the slain governor at its premises, so inflammatory was the atmosphere.

Scholars often argue that since the blasphemy laws were passed by General Zia-ul-Haq, the former military dictator of the 1970s, they cannot be repealed. They argue that one needs to look at the entire educational system, and not just *madrassas*, which would be obvious, but also public schools where children are indoctrinated about jihad. There are, however, some optimistic prospects of future change even though change cannot be expected to happen overnight at a time when the right wing has the streets and the media in their grip, and liberals cannot seem to agree even among themselves or offer each other protection when threatened. Conversely, according to general belief, the forces that can keep a pluralistic society together are not vigorous enough. On the positive side, even if the voices that oppose the prevalent orthodox discourse are few and far between, at least one can sense their existence, for unlike other Muslim countries where uniformity under one orthodoxy is usually the rule, Pakistan can boast an enormous volume of diversified media, where about every shade of opinion can find its place. Even though those who dissent may not agree among themselves, the fact that they dare oppose orthodoxy at all generates hope. To support the repeal of blasphemy laws is seen by many—but not all—Muslim clerics as undermining their authority. The Khatame Nabuwat Movement is a loosely structured conglomerate of orthodox (Sunni) Muslims who have been campaigning for decades to ensure that nothing that is in their view blasphemous is said, preached, or written about Prophet Muhammed. It was their violent campaign in the early 1970s that caused the government of Zulfiqar Ali Bhutto and the parliament to amend the constitution to declare the Ahmadis as non-Muslims. Even today they draw their strength from the success of that campaign. More recently they have expanded their mission and have been opposing the demand by liberal Muslims to repeal or amend the controversial blasphemy law.

Tunisia (See also Chapter 5 for the use of social networks.)

One of the smallest and less pivotal Arab countries, Tunisia, has become nevertheless the symbol of the Islamic Spring, not only because it was ignited there on Christmas Eve, 2010, but it was the first where its ruler left of his own volition, enabling the country to settle the dust, hold elections, and go back to business. It was also the first where the Islamic Spring played its full course, when the Nahda Islamic Party was allowed to emerge from underground, with its veteran founder and leader, Rashid Ghannouchi, returning from exile to run as part of the new democratic experiment, with impressive success. All this was achieved without too many casualties and without the destruction that we saw in Libya and in Syria. It was almost a velvet revolution. That was due to the more Western, moderate, and open character of Tunisian society, even under the autocrat Zine al-Abidin Ben Ali, who nonetheless had nothing of the cruelty of Saddam or Assad or Qaddafi, and everything of his French-educated predecessor, Habid Bourguiba, the legendary founder and leader of modern Tunisia for a few decades, who was also an autocrat. Ben Ali's reign had begun with a bloodless coup in November 1987, about the same date when his authoritarian rule was to be toppled twenty-three years later.

The Tunisian Spring started with street protests in the country's underdeveloped interior region of Sidi Bouzid, where a street vendor set himself aflame, followed by street protests and calls for change, which were soon echoed by civil organizations, notably the country's lone labor union, as befits authoritarian regimes. At the outset, no one could predict where it would all lead. To keen observers, however, it was reminiscent of the Tunisia of 1975 and 1976, a time that marked the beginning of the slide of Habib Bourguiba, Ben Ali's legendary predecessor, who lingered too long in power before he was discredited and removed. Although there is disagreement about the precedence of Facebook or Twitter in spreading the uprising that forced Ben-Ali's removal on January 14, 2011, there is no doubt that it was the social networks that made the difference this time. It is said that back in July 2010, Mark Zuckerberg, the founder and president of Facebook, was shown on his website holding up a sign with a slogan for the freedom of expression campaign. Later, the image of Zuckerberg appeared on a sign outside the Saudi Embassy in Tunis, carried by Tunisian protesters demanding the arrest of Ben Ali. In other words, the young inventor of Facebook had become a freedom symbol so powerful that his picture on signs of protest had become a major mobilizer for the cause of freedom. In that regard one can say that what political, clerical, artistic, academic, scientific, military, or business leaders could not achieve, this young man in his early twenties, with no other record behind him than the huge mobilizing power of a social medium, did attain with flying colors, even if he never intended to do so. One can surmise that thanks to that success, by force of circumstance in that country where it was relatively easy to succeed—for Ben Ali was no Saddam Hussein and no Assad—the barrier of fear was quickly broken, and copying that model by the rest of the Islamic audience became a matter of course. That is the power of precedent that Tunisia firmly set up, and that is its importance as the pioneer in the process.

It would seem like a fascinating paradox that the most relatively Westernized, open, and permissive state of the Islamic world—which also protects its Jews and opens its gates to Israeli tourists, sports the most opulent markets, and maintains the most intimate relationship with the West—should have been where the first spark was kindled that set aflame the entire Islamic world, and also the first that settled into a new social pact signaling a permanent arrangement in the country. Maybe the reason lies in the fact that with all the tyranny of Ben Ali, his was still the regime most lenient toward civil liberties, and much more accepting of social dissent than, say, Libya and Syria, which permitted absolutely no protest and where any sign of social unrest was immediately crushed. Tunisia also remains the first and only regime where the ruler understood his situation immediately and decided to flee with his family and some state funds while he could, rather than stand up and fight a lost war, where bloodletting would have even increased the loathing of the public for his rule, as in Libya, Yemen, and Syria. But this was also the first country where the head of the Islamic opposition, Ghannouchi, was repatriated, and thanks to the underground work that his movement established over the years of illegal activity he also won the first elections after the Spring. It was also the army that took over to prevent chaos, but unlike the Egyptian army which insisted on seeing through the entire constitutional process, it handed over power immediately after the elections and stayed behind the scenes, and is not heard of any longer in the political context.

Tunisia is officially a constitutional republic, exactly as the constitutional monarchies of Morocco and Jordan are; in other words, they control the constitution instead of the constitution controlling them. The president serves as chief of state, the prime minister as head of government, and a bicameral legislature and a court system influenced by French civil law control the judiciary and the legislative processes. While Tunisia was formally a democracy with a multiparty system, the secular Constitutional Democratic Rally (RCD), formerly Neo Destour, had controlled the country as a repressive regime since its independence in 1956. President Ben Ali, previously a minister and a military figure, held office from 1987 to 2011, having acceded to the executive office of his celebrated predecessor, Habib Bourguiba, after a team of medical experts judged Bourguiba unfit to exercise the functions of the office, in accordance with Article 57 of the Tunisian constitution. The anniversary of Ben Ali's accession, November 7, was celebrated as a national holiday. He was consistently re-elected with enormous majorities in every election, the last being October 25, 2009, until he fled the country amid popular unrest in January 2011. The bicameral parliamentary system—including the Chamber of Deputies, which has 214 seats, 25 percent of which are reserved for opposition parties, and the Chamber of Advisors (a modern version of the *shura*) consisting of 112 members and composed of representatives of political parties and professional organizations—was patronized by the president, and by personalities appointed by the president of the Republic. The prime minister and cabinet, appointed by the president, played a strong role in the execution of policy and approval of legislation. Regional governors and local administrators were also appointed by the central government. Largely consultative mayors and municipal councils were elected. This system in itself shows how authoritarian it had been prior to the Spring, and there is no certainty that it will be weaned from that age-old character subsequent to it.

The president's Constitutional Democratic Rally had consistently won large majorities in local and parliamentary elections, which were obviously rigged, judging by the overwhelmingly negative attitude of the voters against the president and his party as a result of the Spring. It was composed of more than two million members (20 percent of the entire population and more than 50 percent of the adult polulation, namely proportionately more than the membership of the Communist Party in the Soviet Union or even China), more than six thousand representations throughout the country, and largely overlapped with all important state institutions. Although the party was renamed (in Bourguiba's days it used to be known as the Socialist Destourian Party), its policies were still considered to be largely secular, though not socialist or liberal. Rare for the Arab world, women held more than 20 percent of seats in both chambers of parliament. Moreover, Tunisia is the only country in the Arab world where polygamy is forbidden by law. This is part of a provision in the country's Code of Personal Status, which was introduced by former President Bourguiba in 1956. The Tunisian legal system is based on the French civil code and on Islamic law; the judiciary is appointed by the Ministry of Justice. The Code of Personal Status remains one of the most progressive civil codes in the Muslim world. Enacted less than five months after Tunisia gained its independence, the code was meant to end gender inequality and update family law, to enable greater social and economic progress and make Tunisia a fully modern society. Among other reforms, the code outlawed the practices of polygamy and repudiation, or a husband's right to unilaterally divorce his wife.

Human rights groups in Tunisia have documented that basic human and political rights were not respected amid the chaos during the initial course of the Spring. All the while, the president's official speeches were full of references to the importance of "democracy and freedom of speech." But abuses by his security forces continued unabated and were committed with impunity. In practice, no public criticism of the regime was tolerated, and all direct protest was severely suppressed and did not get reported in the local media. In January 2010 US Secretary of State Hillary Clinton mentioned Tunisia and China as the two countries with the greatest internet censorship. Hundreds of thousands of young men dodged the draft and lived with the constant fear of arrest, although it appears that the police went after them only in certain times of the year (the "raffle") and often let them go if a sufficient bribe was paid.[23]

Since the revolution of 2011, religious violence has increased in Tunisia, primarily consisting of Muslim attacks on Christians and members of other non-Muslim groups. Tunisian journalists and human rights activists were harassed and faced surveillance and imprisonment under harsh conditions. Others were dismissed from their jobs or denied their right to communicate and move freely. The authorities also prevented the emergence of an independent judiciary, further compounding the problem. Islamic groups have also violently repressed artistic expression that is viewed to be hostile to Islam. But now, the prohibited al-Nahda is in power, and its chief, Ghannouchi, is back from exile and pulling the strings, although he does not hold an official position. It will take much more time to be able to judge whether he or others who head the government, after their victory in the parliamentary elections, truly reform this harsh state of affairs or continue to play the double game of speaking democracy and freedom but in fact suppressing them. For now, and based on the experience gained from other Islamic parties in government and the conduct of Islamic movements within Tunisia itself, one may doubt the consequences of this hopeful Spring.

The great puzzle with regard to Tunisia has been to try to penetrate the thinking of Rashid Ghannouchi, the founder and leader of the Brothers'-affiliated al-Nahda (the Awakening) Party, which operated clandestinely for decades and waited patiently in the wings, with its leader in exile, first in Germany and then in England, for its hour to come. Now that it has come and was played out, so far, with extraordinary moderation and legality, questions are raised about whether the Brothers will likewise act rationally when they are in positions of management and responsibility, or whether this is merely their patient and long-haul tactic that directs them until they are firmly based in power and strong enough to carry out their desires. Tunisia, although a small country in itself, is important to study as a test case that is relatively accessible to the Western media and may serve as the lighthouse for other Islamic countries, since it has also been the first where the dust seems to have settled and order been restored.

In June 2011, Ajmi Lourimi, a member of the Politbureau of al-Nahda, described the Tunisian revolution as a "secular" one, in the sense that it was "neither Islamist nor secularist." This seemed to mean that the so-called Arab Spring had erased the Islamic-secular divide, or to the more astute observer it was another tactic of allaying the fears of secular-liberal-intellectuals that the takeover by the Nahda does not signify the Islamization of the country. This kind of question goes back to the time of independence in 1956, when President Bourguiba, almost following in the footsteps of Attaturk, pursued a staunch policy of secularization. This fit with his pro-Western orientation and his authoritarian style of government, which needed to abolish the force of Islam by marginalizing it. Thus, he abolished the Shari'a courts, closed down the Zaytouna, an important center of Muslim learning, banned scarves, and dethroned the ulema from positions of importance. Even Egypt's tremendously powerful and charismatic Nasser had never dared to take similar drastic steps in Egypt, like closing down al-Azhar or canceling the role of the qadi in adjudicating matters of marriage and divorce. Unlike Nasser, who harnessed Islam to his political vision by including it as one of his circles (the others were the Arab and the African), for Bourguiba, as for Attaturk, Islam represented the past while the West stood for the future. It was only natural that among the many groups opposing the privatization of Islam and Bourguiba's authoritarian style, Ghannouchi founded the Islamic Association, which later became al-Nahda.

It was only from 1979 onward, as a result of government oppression of public demonstrations following the Iranian Revolution, that Ghannouchi also became the leader of the Islamic Association (Jama'ah Islamiyya), at a time when in Egypt an association with similar name became under Sadat and then Mubarak the most extremist Islamic activist and also committed political assassinations. In Tunisia, the group formed a political party mainly concerned with social and cultural issues, but Bourguiba could not countenance it and cracked down on it and had its leader imprisoned. Under Ben Ali also, the crackdown was pursued, until the Spring, when the people acted against the repression and launched free elections where al-Nahda won 40 percent of the vote, like the Freedom and Justice Party in Egypt. But while in the latter the second-largest party was the Salafi al-Noor, and together they made up 75 percent of the vote, in Tunisia the second party, the Centrist CPR, headed by Moncef Marzouki—a civil rights secularist who shows respect for Islam and refused to demonize al-Nahda people during the elections—is prepared to collaborate with them after they won. That means, as Elizabeth Hurd has shown,[24] that the old dichotomy between secularists and Islamists either was never true or has come to collapse during the Spring, which proves that so-called democrats can be counted among Muslim adepts, and sympathizers of Islamic traditions can be counted among the most liberal secularists. Apparently, the latter refer to Islam as a culture shared by most of the public, while they believe that ritualistic Islam should be confined to the mosque and the realm of the individual. Only time will tell whether under a Nahda-majority government such a compromise can persist and for how long.

In mid-December 2012, the government sent troops into Siliana, south of the capital, after four days of violent protests demanding jobs and more government investment. Hundreds of the demonstrators were wounded in clashes with the police. President Marzouki acknowledged on that occasion that the government had not met the expectations of the people, showing that as of old the sources of the frustration have always been the gap between the pledges and the expectations.[25] Once again, even in the softest case of the Tunisian Spring, as in other places, the people who are hardened by experience have learned to heed the authors of Churchillian blood and sweat, like Khumeini of Iran, Yassin of Hamas, rather than the hollow sweet talks that are never fulfilled promises. The reason is that while the popular leaders of the radical Islamic movements speak the truth and themselves live moderately as a good example to their people and show constant care and sensitivity to the needs of their people, the autocratic tyrants are secluded in their palaces and could not care less about the livelihood of their nations. That is also the reason that when the slogan of "Islam is the solution" is proclaimed, it attracts more attention and inspires more hope than rosy pledges that never come true.

Notes

1. TV interview given by previous Prime Minister Erbakan to Flash TV on July 1, 2007, as part of a preelection program http://www.milligorusarsiv.com/videolar/file.php?f=5.
2. *Taqiya* is an Islamic term that means concealing one's true beliefs to avoid repression.
3. MEMRI, Special Dispatch No 916, June 6, 2005.
4. Yaakov Lappin, http://web.archive.org/web/20100428140334/http://eng.akpati.org.tr/english/lifestory.html.
5. MEMRI, Special Dispatch no 1596, May 23, 2007.
6. "Turkey Ramps Up Kurdish Offensive," August, 2, 2012. http://online.wsj.com/article/SB10000872396390443545504577565122536657382.
7. Y Weissman, "Fundamentalism and Democracy in the Discourse of the Muslim Brothers in Syria," Meir Hatina and Uri Kupferschmidt, *The Muslim Brothers: A Religious Vision in a Changing Reality*, Hakibbutz Ha-Meuchad, Tel Aviv, 2012, pp. 125–146.

8. Y. Meital, "The Muslim Brothers in Egypt at the End of the Mubarak Era," in Hatina and Kupferschmidt, op. cit., pp. 147–169.

9. Qut'b, Sayyid, *Ma'rakatuna ma'a al-Yahud* (*Our War against the Jews*), 7th edition, Beirut, 1986.

10. MENA, 09/08/2012.

11. Appointments for state-run papers: Abdel Naser Salama for *Al-Ahram*, Mohamed Hassan al-Bana for *Akhbar Al-Youm*, Suleiman Qenawy for *Al-Akhbar*, Gamal Abdel Raheem for *Al-Gomhurriya*, Shaker Gamal Eddin for the *Middle East News Agency* (MENA), and Essam Abdel Aziz for *Rose al-Youssef* magazine. Several of the new editors named Wednesday by the Shura Council, the upper house of Egypt's Parliament, have Islamist leanings, which raised concerns over the Muslim Brotherhood's alleged attempt to monopolize state-owned papers. Salama, who now heads the state's flagship paper, *Al-Ahram*, wrote a column against Pope Shenouda in 2010, accusing him of provoking sectarian strife between Muslims and Christians. It is also alleged that Mohammed Hassan al-Bana of *Akhbar al-Youm* daily paper is the grandson of the Muslim Brotherhood's founder, Hassan al-Banna.

12. *Egypt Daily News*, August 9, 2012.

13. *Al-Masry Al-Youm*, September 8, 2012.

14. Marcus, Itamar and Nan Jacques Zilberdik, "The Muslim Brotherhood's Patient Jihad," *Jewish Ideas Daily*, July 25, 2012.

15. Kedar Mordechai, "The Brothers and the Muslims," *Israel Against Terror*, June 28, 2012.

16. Chapter 8, p. 59.

17. Chapter 2, verse 152.

18. For a wider discussion of the Cartoon Affair, see this author's *The Spread of ISlamikaze Terrorism in Europe*, Vallentine Mitchell, 2008, Chap. 5, pp. 277–362.

19. Ali Usman Qasmi, "God's Kingdom on Earth? Politics of Islam in Pakistan. 1947–69, *Modern Asian Studies*, 44, 6 (2010), pp. 1197–1253.

20. www.memrijttm.org/content/en/blog personal.htm?id=6098&param=UPP.

21. Ibid.

22. www.aljazeera.com/indepth/features/2011/07/20111725145048574888.html.

23. http://world.silkapp/com /page/Tunisia.

24. Editorial on al-Jazeera, April 11, 2012.

25. *International Herald Tribune*, 3 December 2012.

7

Saudi Arabia, the Gulf States, Morocco, Jordan, and the Monarchical Model

Of all the monarchical systems in the Islamic world, so far tiny Bahrain has been the only one to be directly hit by the Spring. Unlike other countries, which belong to the same category only by their phenomenological resemblance to the others, the monarchical model has much more in common to share, and therefore its members also tend to hang together, knowing that the fall of the one may signal the decline of others. This model is in the minority in the Islamic world, for its members are typified by absolute power of the monarch; therefore any demand for reform is bound to be rejected, and attention is directed elsewhere in order to escape any change. It also so happens that most of these countries are rich in oil, and their immense wealth helps them bribe their way out of trouble. Therefore, they have been able to avoid so far all the demands for change, in spite of the challenges that have come closer to their doorsteps than ever before. These countries are also relatively sparse in population relative to the immense territories and vast wealth that they wield, which for that reason attracts envy and subversion, when hopes to share with others some of that wealth peacefully by way of donations are not requited, and the quest of large countries with demographic surpluses and a scarcity of resources—like Egypt, Pakistan, and Turkey—to sink their teeth into those juicy pears is refuted. Therefore, these monarchies assist each other for their own survival. Their defense pacts, like the one of the Gulf area that began as a regional necessity, were extended to Jordan recently for that very reason, and probably will be extended later to faraway Morocco.

In all those countries there is the problem of legitimacy of power, since no one elected those monarchs, who own their countries, instead of the other way round. So, all of them seek a way to justify their rule by imputing to themselves titles of all sorts: The Saudi king is known as the Curator of the Two Holiest Places of Islam (Mecca and Medina), the king of Morocco as the progeny of the Prophet, the Jordanian king as the Guardian of al-Aqsa Mosque in Jerusalem and, while the princes who rule the Gulf states do not even pretend to be anything else but the proprietors of feudal estates, who have sole discretion in how to dispose of the massive resources they possess. Some of them, like the monarchies of Morocco and Jordan, pretend to be constitutional, but they know very well the difference: they can suspend the parliament and appoint ministers, while in the constitutional monarchies of Denmark and Holland, England and Sweden, the monarch cannot even make a speech without his elected government's approval. In Morocco, where the Islamic parties won the elections of April 2012, the king tries to play the liberal and to solidify his position as one of the three symbolic apexes of power—Allah, the king, the homeland—whereas the king of Jordan pretends that he is democratic and pro-Western, though during the Gulf War of 1991, he (in fact his father) did not hesitate to side with Saddam Hussein the tyrant. This Hashemite king used to lean for his survival on his old alliance with the Transjordanian tribes, but that pillar has begun to shift, and the monarch attempts to find new ground. In both countries, the echoes of the Spring are heard, though it has not hit more directly this far, beyond Tunisia on the one hand, and the Syrian border on the other.

The Saudi monarchy and that of the princes of the Gulf are preoccupied by what is happening nearby, but are also dreading the gathering shadow of the Iranian bomb that is being developed at their doorstep, which when accomplished will drag them into a new arms race they have no desire to embark on. They are also wary of the developing domestic battles in their neighboring countries for democratization of the systems, which will by necessity hit them at some point. All this occurs in the midst of the growing tensions and competition between Sunna and Shi'a, right around the Gulf, where the oil resources of the world are at stake and the Iranian threats to build the bomb and to close the Hormuz passes loom on the horizon. Part of these tensions and competitions have consisted of the struggle over the souls of the population in the Gulf, much of which is Shi'ite, while all the rulers, except in Iran, are Sunnite. This is the background of the unrest in Bahrain, while all the rest of the Gulf countries have collaborated to keep the trouble as far away and as long as possible.

146

The monarchs also have the characteristic of bequeathing their power to their children after them, unless the young generation rebels prematurely and takes over the authority of their fathers, as it was the custom in the Moghul Empire (for example, the celebrated Shah Jehan was imprisoned in his Agra palace by his legendary son Aurangzeb in the seventeenth century while the latter was fighting his brother for inheritance of the throne). That device looked to non-monarchical authoritarian regimes in the Islamic world so much more promising than relying on uncertain elections, or on the hazards of military coups, that many of them adopted it and thereby triggered the Spring in their countries. Mubarak, Qaddafi, Saleh had indeed designated one of their sons to inherit their mantle, thus causing the fury of their masses; in Syria, that was put in practice when in 2000 Bashar Assad replaced his father Hafez. The second attribute of the monarchies is that most oil reserves are in their hands, which make them fabulously rich and capable of dispensing enough money to keep their authoritarianism going, at least for now. Because of all these common grounds, all these kings and princes have a great common interest in maintaining their privileges. They know that the fall of one of them might trigger the departure of the others; therefore they hang together, ready to fight for each other and even bring Morocco and Jordan, the outsiders, into the fold of the Gulf state security arrangements. Standing to lose the most from a revolutionary Spring in their midst, they resist it tooth and nail, and are still the only model of Islamic states that remains almost untouched by its traumatic events. At the same time, the wave of democratization that has overtaken the Spring seems mostly to threaten the monarchical regimes that are the most inimical to it.

The Bahrain Crisis

When the Bahrain Spring broke out right in the beginning of the process, there was a temptation to see it as the expression of the awakening of the majority Shi'ite population against the Sunnite rulers, who are supported by the Saudi military force, which was in fact fending for itself lest trouble knock on its door. That was similar to when it happened in Iraq against Saddam, by the Shi'ites who were deprived of rights and therefore their resentment was seen as legitimate and was encouraged and institutionalized by the Americans. The distance between the Saudi mainland and the island of Bahrain is minimal—barely a few kilometers, with a desert causeway connecting the tiny island with the Saudi coast. The Americans hold an important naval base on the

147

island, so they appeared embarrassed when they supported the Shi'ite demonstrators and advocated their civil rights as they did with Tahrir Square, but they kept quiet when Saudi troops entered the island and put an end to the rebellion. For the Saudis, that was required for their own survival, so the Americans did not protest and were content to see their dilemma resolved by their supposed ally. The Saudi king operated under the Gulf Defense Pact and was intent to protect the ruling king, his monarchic regime, and the ruling Sunni family against a rebellious Shi'ite population, which sees its basic rights trampled upon, as if he had acted in defense of his own country.

The stakes were high this time, because the sweeping winds of the Spring have shown that the discontent was not merely economic and social, but mainly political, as the masses were demanding political participation and a legitimate representative government, both of which were missing in Bahrain, as in the entire area of the Spring. It took time to the actors to realize that they had mistakenly believed that by quelling the unrest they resolved the problem. The thermometer was broken all right, but the fever is far from cured, and the unrest is bound to reawaken. The disaffected demonstrators of Bahrain were not rising against poverty or economic deprivation, as in Egypt, Tunisia, and Libya, but against the rule of the Sunni monarchs, and they wanted their share in the system. Thus, one might say that it was the Sunni rulers who were violently shaken by the uprising when they realized that their sweet dream of living in their small but opulent paradise was coming to an end, by reason of the simple demand of the Shi'ites for equality and human rights.

The awakening of the Sunnites in Bahrain is nothing less than a shake-up. There are talks, hardly ever heard before, of national rally and of the need for unity among the Sunnite population, which excludes the Shi'ite part. A spontaneous organization, Sahwat al-Fatih (the Awakening of the Fatih, after the name of the mosque where these meetings take place), got the attention of the Sunnite public who until then had paid little notice to civil activities. While the original intention of the organizers was to counteract the grave uprising against the government, later political forums were announced, which demanded firmer action against the disturbers of public order. In the fringes, more demands were voiced for the first time to uproot government corruption and to expand the powers of the parliament. To drag the usually indifferent Bahraini public into this sort of involved political activity has been a novelty. But it is still early to estimate whether this truncated Spring will also head in the direction of more reforms to check the absolute powers of the prince, or if it is only an alarm call to the ruling Sunnites lest they lose their privileges, or even their Bahraini state. The organization of Sahwat al-Fatif is linked through some of its leaders with the Muslim Brothers, who already attained the majority in Egypt, Tunisia, and Morocco, and this might indicate the same trend in the island's politics. At any rate, this is a case where from the unrest that was quelled for now a new Islamic Spring has been developing. In the elections to parliament of 2010, the Islamic Party al-Minbar (the Rostrum) and the Salafi party al-Asala (the Source) did not mark any impressive results; therefore the new organizations of the Spring have risen outside the established parties and may make the difference.

Al-Khalifa family of the rulers—and its prime minister (the uncle of the king, who is disliked by the Bahraini public), who has served, like Qaddafi for forty-one years—have also apparently sensed that the time for reforms has come. But the monarch, with strong Saudi backing and American quietist acquiescence lest it lose its Bahraini Mubarak, does not show any appetite for change, which can lead to unforeseen results once it begins. Even the heads of the new civil organizations in Bahrain are wary, exactly like in Saudi Arabia, not to cross the boundary of challenging the legitimacy of the monarchy. And every time they do, they back down for fear of wrecking the ship of fools that they have been riding for half a century. All this does not mean that the ruling house does not negotiate with the Shi'ite opposition behind the scenes. To be sure, the new civil organizations oppose these informal talks, probably because they were not asked to participate in them. The government justifies its foot-dragging by its fear that any concession to the Shi'ites might jeopardize the rest of the population (in other words, the privileged Sunnites) and serve the interests of the feared Iranian neighbor across the Gulf. There is also a widespread feeling of bitterness at the waste of public funds for recruiting foreigners to maintain security while there is a shortage of housing and employment for the permanent residents. In the meantime, due to the new civil organizations' hesitance to criticize the monarchy, they serve as a matter of fact only as an opposition to the opposition. It remains to be seen whether they will be given a seat at the negotiation table so as to be recognized and given the standing to enforce some reforms in the long haul. But one thing is clear: the Spring that has been seemingly quelled has after all had an effect on domestic politics, and things will not return to what they were before. One blogger wrote, "I woke up to politics, and I shall not return to the position of a passenger at the back of the ship. For the consequences of keeping quiet are too great for my country, for me to leave our future in the hands of people who decide upon it by issuing ultimatums or casting dice, as if telling me: either my way or the highway."

Bahrain is one of the few, or possibly the sole, Arab country that does not state a person's religion on passports, certainly to avoid bringing up the fact that the minority religion is controlling the country, though the government tries to present that as a proof of liberalism toward religion. King Hamad wishes to introduce a choice to his people and the world: either a state he governs, in which all religious groups are allowed to build houses of worship, and indeed worship freely without any restrictions; women can work and drive and wear what they want; gays are not persecuted or harassed; private enterprise is encouraged; alcohol is available in the shops. In short, people are free to live as they please—with the red line restricted to antigovernment agitation—or face the turmoil of the Spring with uncertain rule and the hovering danger of seeing a fundamentalist Islam take over and restrict human rights. This is perhaps as good as it can get for an Islamic country. Indeed, one can surmise that should the government be replaced, life would be immeasurably worse—for the Sunnis politically as well as the Shi'ites economically—for Bahrain might then become a smaller version of Iran. As it is now, Bahrain is far from perfect, but the inevitable alternative is too awful to contemplate. Just think what misery other revolutionary changes of government elsewhere have caused their people in the name of freedom, democracy, and human rights, and that might temper a people's revolutionary passion.

The Hashemite Kingdom of Jordan

It can probably be said that Jordan started its Islamic Spring before other Sunnite countries, for King Abdallah II, the son of King Hussein, who ascended the throne upon the death of his father in 1999, was a pioneer of sorts in reforming his inherited system, when he understood that the alliance that his father had concluded with the ruling elites in Transjordan, and which had survived for the forty-five years of his rule, had begun to decay. That alliance was founded on the two pillars that accompanied this artificial state since its inception, torn from Palestine and confirmed by the San Remo Conference in 1920. This recognition was based on the legitimacy that the Versailles Peace Conference of 1919 had conferred on the Four Powers who emerged victorious from World War I (Britain, France, Italy, and Japan) and constituted the basis for the League of Nations granting to the British the Mandate over Palestine in 1922, which adopted the Balfour Declaration of 1917 regarding a homeland for the Jews in Palestine on both banks of the Jordan River. At the time, when the British decided to tear away part of mandatory Palestine in order to grant it to Emir Abdallah in compensation for his father's loss of the Kingdom of Damascus, the Jews protested the shrinking of the territory where their national home was to develop, but the colonial power imposed its decision, and later turned the emirate into a kingdom and the emir into a king under the military and political tutorship of Britain.

King Abdallah I, who should have been grateful for his kingdom, which he received as a political refugee from the Hijaz whence he was expelled, on the contrary opposed the establishment of the Jewish state, for he coveted the entire territory of Palestine for himself, having had the generosity of offering the Jews autonomy if they accepted his annexation of the land and the legitimacy of his rule. That determination of the king did not change consequent to the Partition Resolution of the UN in 1947, in which a second division of Palestine partitioned the land again after Transjordan had been severed at first. Thus, the king, willy-nilly, was dragged into the 1948 war, at the end of which he remained in control of the West Bank and East Jerusalem, which he annexed to his kingdom, much to the displeasure of the international community that refused to acknowledge this annexation, save for Britain and Pakistan. This means that while the new Jewish state of Israel was legitimate, the birth of Jordan, and even more so its annexation of the West Bank and East Jerusalem, remained illegitimate. Thus, King Abdullah's primary task, backed by the British, was to manufacture a Jordanian identity to justify his rule over his kingdom and his conquered territories, something that he failed to achieve by the day he was murdered during a visit to Jerusalem in 1950, and his grandson Hussein acceded to the throne.

Hussein, who was a boy when he was called to reign, succeeded during his long years as king in strengthening the two pillars of the Hashemite rule: the military, based on the Bedouin tribes who had sworn loyalty to his grandfather, and the state bureaucracy that he built painstakingly over the years, and where people became attached to the king through political appointments and jobs, so that in spite of the epithet of constitutional monarchy that he attached to his kingdom, there was nothing in common between it and the constitutional monarchies of Western Europe in terms of the centrality of the monarch in the system. For he retained, to the end of his life, the control of the supreme locus of power, so much so that he suspended the parliament for twenty years in the 1970s and 1980s when he thought that doing so served his purposes, and he did not feel necessary to apologize to anyone for that. The Palestinian element in the kingdom, which was initially made up of the migrants from the West Bank, mainly following the 1948 war and the annexation of the West Bank, and then of the refugees of the 1967 war, was turned into an even greater Palestinian majority when the Palestinian residents of Kuwait, who sided with Saddam during his invasion of the country in 1990, were forced to migrate in the hundreds of thousands and naturally found refuge in Jordan.

During his reign, Hussein turned the Transjordanian element of his kingdom into the predominant one in the military and the bureaucracy, and alienated the Palestinians from important positions of power, though he occasionally threw them a few crumbs in ministerial and diplomatic positions. The Palestinians, who constituted the majority of the population during most of the time, focused on the business sector, which they almost monopolized, and succeeded in turning Amman from a miserable township into a thriving capital of over one million inhabitants, in effect the largest Palestinian city in the world. Thus, a typical division was established between the Jordanians, who became the public servants, and the Palestinians, who dominated business, the private sector, and the property owners. When King Abdallah II acceded to the throne, he inherited a stable and Western-supported kingdom, after his father, Hussein, had succeeded in whitewashing his sin of supporting Saddam Hussein during the Gulf War of 1990–1. But, since Hussein had again miscalculated by aligning with the loser in that war, he lost considerable aid from the West and the rich Gulf states, and was driven into economic straits. Thus, Abdallah, in an attempt to remedy the situation, began to curry favor with Palestinian businessmen and to reduce the wasteful and corrupt public sector. Expectedly, this very much displeased the Jordanians, who saw themselves disinherited from their vested interests, while watching with envy and resentment their traditional privileges being assigned to the Palestinians. The king was thus faced with an acute dilemma: either care for his country and rule, or lose the traditional pillars of power and enter an era of uncertainty as the Islamic Spring began spreading throughout the region.

It is noteworthy that in Jordan too, including within the parliament, Islamic power—under the heading of the Muslim Brothers or other

152

epithets, or in the form of independent lists or individuals—was also trying to erode the monopoly of the king on the reins of power, and the instant and sweeping success of the Brothers in Egypt and Tunisia, with similar advances looming in the horizons of Syria, Libya, and even in Morocco, could not constitute a source of encouragement for him. Therefore, he was called to act cautiously and slowly before he was overtaken by events. For example, the fact that Jordan has become, together with Lebanon and Turkey, the main shelter of hundreds of thousands Syrian refugees fleeing their ruthless ruler can only prompt Jordan's Muslims to seek the Turkish, Egyptian, or Tunisian models to imitate and to demand more reforms that would further reduce the monarch's powers and even jeopardize his rule. Busy as he is weighing the options of rescuing his royal house from extinction, he adopted a lower profile in foreign affairs. Naturally, he was attracted to the other monarchies in the Arab world, with which he shares a common destiny and which can also assist him to overcome his economic woes. Although not belonging to them geographically, he found himself edging toward joining the security alliance of the Gulf states. Even his particular sensitivity with regard to the Palestinians, who constitute the core and backbone of his country, has had to be readapted to reality, since his father declared in August 1988 his detachment from the West Bank, for fear of the intifada seeping into Transjordan and challenging his throne. Now, it turns out that the two intifadas of 1987–92 and 2000–2 were perhaps the precursor of a Palestinian Spring, which might directly affect the Hashemite rule in its wake. Thus, besides paying lip service to Palestinian rights, he has kept his distance from them and leaves them to their devices. He does not need another threat on his quiet border with Israel; therefore he causes no incidents and he controls terrorism, in contrast to the Sinai border between Israel and Egypt, where much trouble has been building since the Spring. It is to be expected that if the Brothers take over in Jordan too, their built-in hostility to Israel might revive that front-line too.

The Hashemite relationship with Israel, which has been more problematic than Israel and the United States like to think, was particularly marked by the three wars of extermination against the Jewish state, which the Hashemite leaders had joined when they thought they were opportune from their point of view, using British and American arms to achieve their goal. Israel fought valiantly and scuttled their plans at great human and material losses, but the Hashemites cannot be exonerated as pro-Western and moderate, because they are neither; if it were left to them, there would be no Israel. The first time was during the 1948 war, when all Arab states conspired to nip the new Jewish state in the bud, and the Jordanians took control of the West Bank and East Jerusalem and cleansed them from Jewish presence. In the second instance, Hussein joined the Nasser bandwagon in 1967, put his army under Egyptian command, and planned to besiege Jerusalem once again and eliminate the corridor that linked it to the coastal plain; only the sweeping victory of Israel rescued it from that fate. The third time was in 1990–1, when Hussein joined Saddam Hussein, who threatened to destroy Israel and tried to do so by launching missiles against it. That time, it was the Americans who defeated Saddam and undid the alliance between the two Husseins. Thus, the legend of Hussein's moderation and peace-loving inclinations still needs to be proved.

Only in 1993, when Hussein realized that foolish Israel had sealed its own demise with his archenemy, Yasser Arafat, by bringing him in and handing him territories and weapons, did he understand, faster and better than Israel, who Arafat was, and who was threatening him too. Hussein then hastened to conclude his own peace with Israel, under which he got legitimacy and recognition from Israel for his Hashemite rule and laid the entire burden of resolving the Palestinian issue on Israel's shoulders. Thus, instead of insisting that Jordan remain part of the solution, due to its being part of Palestine and home to half the Palestinian people, the mindless Israeli negotiators, who gave priority to perpetuating the Hashemites over resolving the Palestinian issue, ended up complicating the problem even further by dividing it into five separate slices and trying to isolate each slice on its own: the Israeli Palestinian Arabs are Israel's problem; Jordan's Palestinians are Jordan's problem; the West Bank and Gaza will get independence, either each separately or both jointly; the refugees in Syria and Lebanon will be addressed by the UN's UNRWA; and the diaspora Palestinians will either settle permanently in the countries that have absorbed them or will be repatriated when a Palestinian entity is ready and able to accept them. The end result is that in its quest to sacrifice the Palestinians in order to strengthen the Hashemites, Israel has weakened the Jordanian crown and rendered the Palestinian issue insoluble. In the entire so-called peace process, which has put Israel on the slippery slope of making concession after concession and in return receiving an increasingly vicious hatred by the Muslim world toward Israel, the latter has irreparably compromised its positions and weakened its standing in the debate. For if the Hashemite regime goes down during the Spring,

154

and Palestinian Muslim fundamentalists gain the upper hand, all the concessions made to both the Jordanians and the Palestinians by a naive and squeezable Israel will have been in vain.

In a learned article, Oded Eran, the previous Israeli ambassador to Jordan, summed up the year and a half of Jordan's mounting difficulties since the civil uprisings had broken out in the Arab world.[1] In early July 2012, the government endorsed an "improved" proposal that increased the number of those to be elected in national lists from seventeen to twenty-seven, but this did not accept the opposition claims that not only does the government's proposal not meet the demand that half the members of the House of Representatives be chosen on a national basis but also that the government has diluted its proposal by increasing the size of the parliament from 140 to 150, thereby maintaining control over its majority. Moreover, the Muslim Brotherhood is not alone in the opposition criticizing the proposal; other movements, such as the Jordanian Democratic Popular Unity Party and the National Reform Front have also announced that they will boycott the elections. Even personalities who in the past were identified as clear supporters of the regime, such as Awn Khasawneh, a jurist with an international reputation who was prime minister until recently, are criticizing the government's attitude on the issue of reforms. It is clear that while the opposition wants to erode the monarchical powers of the king and make the Palestinian majority overbearing, the king still seeks, maybe in vain, to let the Jordanian-Bedouin minority element in his kingdom, predominate.

Khasawneh also stated, obviously under the pressure of the Spring environment, that Muslim nations "long for freedom and justice," and that revolutions could be expected to erupt where poverty and tyranny prevailed, but it is doubtful whether he, or anyone else in the kingdom, has the vision, the authority, and the courage to initiate the necessary changes. Interestingly enough, he referred to Muslim nations, hinting that a Muslim Spring was there, not merely an Arab one. Moreover, new problems were added with the spillover of the Syrian crisis into Jordan, where two hundred thousand (later revised to half a million) Syrian refugees, some with family links to Jordan, have been pouring across the border. The bloody battle in Syria between the Bashar al-Assad regime and the opposition has implications for Jordan and creates immediate and long-term dilemmas. Prime Minister Fayez al-Tarawneh claimed he was misunderstood when he was quoted as calling for military intervention in Syria. According to al-Tarawneh,

"I just said that as the umbrella of international legitimacy, the Security Council can impose a ceasefire as a prelude to finding solutions to the crisis." Either way, his statements reflect increasing concern in Amman that Jordan will perhaps be called on to allow the transfer of aid to the rebels, and perhaps even the use of Jordanian territory for expediting the fall of the Syrian regime. Jordanian government spokesmen vehemently deny this possibility and downplay the importance of the exchanges of fire that occur between Jordanian and Syrian military units positioned along their border.[2]

Abu Dhabi and the Gulf States

Abu Dhabi, the tiny but most enterprising Gulf principality, an important component of the United Arab Emirates, which is immersed in great wealth and a tremendous fervor of development and growth, has been trying, like the rest of the Gulf states, to ride the wave of the Spring without being drowned by it. What remains preponderant for the ruling sheikh is the maintenance of his monarchy, and keeping intact the defensive shield around it that the Gulf Cooperation headed by Saudi Arabia affords it. But Abu Dhabi, like the rest of its allies, is haunted by the long shadow of adjoining Iran on the other side of the Gulf, not only due to the deepening ideological divide between Sunna and Shi'a (they are Sunnite and Iran Shi'ite), the looming menace of Iran's nuclearization, and the large foreign population living there as guest workers without basic civil rights, but also because of its predominating preoccupation with preserving its riches in a shaky and uncertain Gulf area. Therefore, while its security needs are taken care of by its allies and the overarching American security umbrella, it is focusing on how to circumvent the Straits of Hormuz and how to secure its cash flow should the Gulf be blocked, as Iran threatens to do in case of open hostilities. Thus, acting energetically in the name of its allies in the Emirates, it has been promoting grandiose programs to build an oil pipeline that could transport the Gulf oil to its consumers without using the Straits. Abu Dhabi, which holds the largest reserves of oil among the Emirates and is considered the sixth-largest producer of oil in OPEC, has been toiling to complete that mammoth circumventing pipeline with a capacity of transporting 1.5 million barrels a day.

Before Abu Dhabi's initiative, Iraq and Kuwait—numbers four and five, respectively, in the ranking of OPEC producers—said that they too were pondering ways to circumvent Hormuz. In Iraq too there has persisted much resentment between the ruling Shi'ites and the disinherited Sunnites, between the Arabs, who insist on the unity of the land and of its resources, and the Kurds, who insist on autonomy and control of the oil in northern Iraq (Kirkuk area). In Kuwait, tensions exist due the autocratic regime and to the deteriorating balance between the minority citizens and the majority foreign workers, on whom depends the wealth of the principality. Hence the predominant preoccupation of these rulers with keeping the money coming in, without which they could no longer quell the looming Spring. One should also recall that some fourteen supertankers cross the Straits daily in a narrow passage no wider than thirty-four kilometers, and that when these rumors began circulating, the prices of oil shot skyward, before they stabilized again. But in the meantime, the circumventing pipeline went into the implementation stages, and when completed, its initiators brag, it is likely to make the Straits redundant, at least in terms of oil supply to customers of the Gulf states, and turn them into an Iranian sea, without competition for its name (the Arab/Persian Gulf) or for its use any longer. The new Abu Dhabi oil pipeline is expected to transport the oil from Habashan on the Emirate's coast, where the oil from the sea drills will be capped, through 350 kms of deserts and sharp-peaked mountains, to the east coast of the Emirates on the Oman Gulf east of the Straits.

However, it is worth remembering that this pipeline, together with other existing Saudi networks and the Iraq-Turkey line, can hardly transport half the combined production of seventeen million barrels per day that pass through the Straits. Already today, Saudi Arabia is capable of transporting half of its daily production of five million barrels through the pipeline it built in 1982, which stretched from the oil fields in the east part of the kingdom to the Red Sea on the west coast. For a while Iraq has been connected to the Cehan pipeline on the Turkish Mediterranean coast, with 1.5 million barrels per day. On the table are also options for pipelines from Saudi Arabia to the Arabian Sea, in the Indian Ocean, via either Oman or Yemen or both. The Iraqis are also talking about reviving the old and now inoperative pipelines through Syria and Lebanon. The Kuwaitis are envisaging the transportation of their resources by overland tankers to Saudi Arabia or the Emirates for exportation. Qatar, the hyperactive new player in the Arab arena, and the home base of the al-Jazeera network, which lends it an influence and prestige much beyond its tiny size, has become the largest exporter in the world of liquid gas, and it totally depends on the Straits for the seventy-seven million tons of gas it exports annually. This situation

157

shows to what extent the prosperous economies of the Gulf depend on their oil income; therefore none of them would be interested in blocking the Straits, least of all Iran. But we have also seen in the past how ideological motives and gut feelings, religious fanaticism or madness of political leaders can lead any country to behave contrary to political and military logic, or in contradiction to economic interest or pragmatic consideration, and bring disaster upon their nations. In case of closure, not only would the economies of the Gulf face bankruptcy, but the great economies of Asia—Japan, India, China, South Korea and others—unlike the United States and Europe, who educated themselves to reduce their dependence on supplies from the Gulf, have remained totally depended, and will probably suffer dire consequences. Under these circumstances and the constraints of the heavy reduction on income, the rich Gulf countries will find it difficult if not impossible to nip the Spring in the bud and prevent it from spreading into their countries, or contain it if and when it erupts. We can then realize how much the economic prosperity and stability of the world, and the situation of peace in the Middle East and the Gulf, domestic and international, hinges upon whether or not Iran decides to close the passage in Hormuz.

The immediate consequence will be that the prices of oil might double or treble, but that is not the worst scenario. One can imagine what turmoil the world will witness if entire industries come to a standstill, their employees are dismissed, and the unemployed add to the enormous economic disruptions already shaking the world during the current economic crisis. It is also easy to imagine how in the already traumatized Islamic world, under the effects of the Spring, its impoverished and desperate masses will seek to take revenge on their leaders, as the rich monarchies, which usually run to the rescue, will themselves see their purses shrink, as they turn from being the customary money dispensers who can alleviate the turmoil of the Spring, into its first victims. In the meantime, the governments of the Gulf are on the verge of hysteria as they ponder these issues, both from Iran and the impending troubles, and from the Spring, which has so far affected only Bahrain, while all the others in the Gulf area have so far escaped its fury, thanks to their money and the American defense umbrella. At the same time, dozens of horror scenarios are being brought up in the Arabic press and by the worried circles of these flimsy political systems, in the vein of "what if . . . what if . . ."

Qatar

In the Gulf states, it is the emir who determines the policies of his state, because it is considered his property and all the decisions are exclusively his. In Qatar, it was the ruler's ambition and pretense to transcend the provinciality, insignificance, and remoteness of his desert *nowhere*, and to take advantage of his huge natural resources to make a mark on local, regional, and world politics. This prompted him to found the al-Jazeera network. Within ten years, it effected an immense breakthrough in Arab attitudes toward the media; brought in investigative reporting; questioned legitimacy of rulers; criticized suppression of human rights, corruption, and mismanagement; and often aligned with the most fundamentalist brands of Islam in the Islamic world. In so doing, the emir, who is excluded from such criticism, bought for himself some insurance and acquired a license to act more or less at will without incurring domestic rebellion, Arab criticism, or international censure. He also brought into Qatar the exiled chief of Shari'a scholars in the world, Sheikh Yussuf al-Qaradawi, who is internationally known, connected, and respected and has a weekly program on al-Jazeera. Al-Qaradawi's influence around the Muslim world, including the Muslim Brothers everywhere, surpasses even that of the sheikhs of al-Azhar in Egypt. Being a refugee from Egypt for decades, due to his criticism of the tyrants there, added considerably to his prestige and appeal throughout the Muslim world. In that regard, one can say that the venerable octogenarian cleric, through his Shari'a verdicts, internationalized through al-Jazeera sermons, made him and the media outlets that back him the precursor of the Islamic Spring, which he strongly supports, the views of the Islamic monarchical model countries notwithstanding. Paradoxically, then, one of the monarchs who has the most to fear from the Spring has become the patron of those who most support it.

As a result of this mostly successful policy, the emir of Qatar catapulted himself to the center of inter-Arab politics and often posits himself as a brave and rebellious alternative to the established choices of the Arab League. For example, when the League has convened a summit of its members, a process sometimes opposed by some dissident Arab leaders, the emir is known to have sponsored alternative summits, to challenge the Arab consensus; or when the League hesitated on whether and how to intervene in other Arab countries' affairs, as during the Islamic Spring in Libya and Syria, it was Qatar who took the lead in such an initiative, which put it in the forefront of Arab politics. Moreover, through this extensive activity that is backed by large subsidies, the emir has succeeded in thwarting any possibility of seeing the danger of the Spring knocking at his door and jeopardizing his power and successes. In consequence, Qatar has specialized in exploring ways of collaborating with the mounting influence of the Muslim Brothers and their affiliates throughout the Islamic world, who seem to have achieved marked successes in places like Tunisia, Libya, and Egypt, where the dust has begun to settle and permanent arrangements are being worked out. In the eyes of the emir, then, an alliance between Qatar and the Brothers seems a promising avenue to the future of the Middle East, and paradoxically also an insurance against the danger of removing his monarchical rule in Doha. In October 2012, his dramatic visit to Gaza, where he pledged $400 million for the construction of that Hamas-led territory, endeared him to other Muslim radicals and highlighted him as the one who does while others merely talk.

Thus, the relationship between Qatar and the Brothers seems to bear fruits in the eyes of the emir, inasmuch as the Muslim Movement has been involved in the entire Muslim world save for the internal affairs of Qatar. To be on the safe side, the Qataris also permit the Americans to use their bases, as during the American invasion of Iraq, but at the same time the emir is pretending to be the champion and defender of Arab rights. The organization of the Muslim Brothers under this title had dissolved itself in 1999 in Qatar, probably as part of the ruler's policy, since in all Arab countries, perhaps except Sudan, the Brothers opposed all rulers. The heads of the organization in Qatar simply consented (they probably had no choice) to the argument that since their country was fulfilling its Islamic duties, there was no longer any need for a formal organization to exist. It is with this type of thinking that it is possible for the Egyptian prince of the Brothers, Sheikh Qaradawi, who is accepted as the great cleric of his generation in the Sunnite world, to live in Doha for years, and to criticize in his sermons all the leaders of the Muslim world, and support the Islamic Spring, and even be involved in European Islam and head the European Fatwa Council, while at the same time avoiding pronouncing a word of rebuke against his generous benefactor, the emir. This conspiracy of silence allows both sides to go far enough in opposite directions without finding themselves on a collision course.

One of the great Qatari national and Islamic projects was named al-Nahda (the Revival, which is also the name of the Muslim Brother affiliates in Tunisia), undertaken by the emir in order to avoid a clash with the Muslim Brothers Organization. He appointed at its head Mr. Sultan, one of the heads of the dissolved Muslim Brotherhood in Qatar, who is seeking to strengthen the ideological foundations for the Islamic revival that the emir has initiated and at the same time to reinforce the political support of his persona by the leaders of the project. The project has a worldwide reach, with the emir, its benefactor and progenitor, turning to the Muslim Brothers in Egypt prior to the Spring and asking them to convert their style of subverting the state and transforming society though social activity into a new style of partnership with the state, as Qatar itself was trying to do. Sultan himself, the veteran Muslim Brother, is involved in training Egyptian and other Muslim activists in implementing the model of action within democracy. While one could dispute the emir's style of democracy, his intent of subordinating Islam to the state, in which he himself has a stake, has apparently had some effect and has extended its reach elsewhere, based on the personal contacts and commitments created between the Qatari rule which provides the funding, the lodging, the training, and the employment to the Islamic activists flocking to Doha, to enjoy and benefit from the Emir's generosity. One of them, aforementioned Sheikh Qaradawi, whose sermons on al-Jazeera have made him world famous, and who heads the world organization of Muslim *ulama*, is the most prominent example. Some time ago, a picture was published of him in the company of Isma'il Haniyye, the head of Hamas rule in Gaza, who visited Qatar in the footsteps of the many means-less Arab leaders who go there to collect funds, and judging from his sycophancy to the reputed sheikh, one could tell how grateful he was to see his rule in Gaza gaining some recognition.

Another example of the symbiosis between the Brothers and the Qatar ruler is seen in the Academy of Change, which was built in Doha by another Egyptian, Hisham Mursi (no relationship could be ascertained with President Mursi), a physician by training, who is married to Qaradawi's daughter. Though he participated in the Egyptian Spring since its inception, and was arrested and released at the height of the disturbances there, he continued to urge nonviolent demonstrations and wrote leaflets to this effect. He calls for cooperation with Sultan, the head of the Nahda, thus indicating their common interest in collaborating with the Brothers. This international network continues to spread out when one observes Mursi's partnership with Rafiq abd-al-Salam, the new post-Spring Tunisian minister of foreign affairs, and the son-in-law of Rashid Ghannouchi, the head of al-Nahda in Tunisia, which emerged predominant from the Tunisian crisis after the first democratic elections. It is interesting to note that abd-al-Salam was one of the past beneficiaries of Qatar generosity when he was employed as the head of the research department of al-Jazeera. Mr. Salabi, one of the leaders of the Libyan Spring, had also lived several years in Qatar previously. Thus, one can note an increase in Islamic activity, including the founding of al-Jazeera (which affords world resonance), and the training of future revolutionary leaders, all taking place in Qatar under the wings of the emir, and all under the unstated understanding that the ruler and his government must remain outside the frame of ctriticism.

In the course of the Egyptian Spring, Cairo University offered to open a training seminar on democracy, which was initiated and funded by the Qatar Human Rights Organization. At the entrance to the classes, bearded men wearing traditional *galabiyya* sorted out the candidates, who wore traditional clothes, with veils or scarves for women. One can imagine what kind of democracy was taught in those courses, and instructed by a country that had never experienced it itself. It was like asking adepts of the mafia to teach public order. The same spirit of democracy also guided the Libyan Salabi, known for his close partnership with Qaradawi, who asked Qatar to extend aid to Libya in its first steps in reorganizing its post-Spring government.

It is noteworthy that the heavy involvement of Qatar in the Libyan crisis, and now in the events of the Syrian bloodletting, is fed by this very approach that impels the emir to pioneer the effort of reform domestically in other Arab countries and on the inter-Arab level, in order to deserve to be exempted from this dangerous obligation. There were rumors in Hizbullah circles in Lebanon, who were the most devoted to the Syrian cause and active on its behalf, that the acrimonious arguments between Assad and Qatar in the process stemmed from the latter's attempts to pressure Damascus to set up a provisory council to govern the country, which included also representatives of the Muslim Brothers, his most sworn enemies. For they well remember the slaughter of twenty thousand of their people in Hama in 1982 by Hafez al-Assad, a horrifying number that his son has already surpassed in his present Spring massacre. The Qatari policy of launching initiatives and financing them is not only geared to ensure the continuation of the emir's rule at home and his international prestige, but he is also eyeing several economic benefits that may accrue to him after the dust settles. His calculation is that since the Brothers will attain power in several Muslim countries in the coming years, Qatar should expect economic and political privileges from the Islamic leadership it had itself trained and indoctrinated over the years. Qatar expects the new Islamic leadership to recognize its past gratitude, and as Qatar's own advantageous position among them affords it a mediating role with their many rivals and enemies, especially in the West, who following the Afghani war and the hostility they leave behind, elect to do business with open Qatar. Even the Taliban in Afghanistan, who have been fighting the United States and NATO, have recognized that role and opened an office in Doha, something that could further increase Qatar's bargaining position. By all appearances, the emir, who believes that his immunity is guaranteed through those activities, has never learned that those who steal for you will end up stealing from you too; and those who kill for you will end up killing you.

Saudi Arabia

Saudi Arabia is the largest, the most populated, the strongest, and the richest of the Sunnite monarchies along the Gulf. It is struggling to accommodate several contradictions that handicap its policies and conduct among the Arabs, the global blocks, and the Muslim lands. On the one hand, it controls a fabulous income of over $100 billion annually from its oil resources, but on the other hand it does not possess the military might to defend its wealth and vast and exposed territory from the neighboring Arab countries, which are poorer but mightier, who covet Saudi's wealth, which it produces, in oil and dollars, on a mammoth scale. This is the most puritanical and strictly conservative country of the Islamic world, save perhaps for Taliban-ruled Afghanistan (1996–2001), and is governed by the Hanbalite school and Wahhabi doctrine, but at the same time it also must bend and accept American protection over its much vied-for resources. It is the strictest of monarchies and the least open to reform and change, which makes it the most susceptible for the Islamic Spring. However, Saudi Arabia is also the most reluctant to undergo such a transformational change, lest such a metamorphosis curtail the monarch's authority and help bring about his demise—but also knowing that those most likely to press for such a change would not dare to do so. For domestically, Islam—the main factor likely to undergo such changes, since demands are usually advanced in the Spring countries for Islamic legitimation of other regimes—has been, with the Saudi House, the supreme ruler of the country for decades: the Wahhabis provide the ideological underpinnings to the Royal House and the justification of the Saudi rule, while the latter provides, in return, protection of the principles of Islam in the spirit of Ibn Taymiyya and ibn abd-al-Wahhab, a generous funding of all the clerics' needs, and a persisting and guaranteed budgeting of the Wahhabi *da'wa* in the world, which does not attempt to resist it due to the immense financing behind it.

This means that all those who would potentially rise against this most oppressive regime that leaves no crack open for change are, internally, of those social strata and elites that strive for some kind of democratization and power sharing, but are deprived from it by the combined efforts of the monarchy and the clerics, and externally the Western countries, which depend on Saudi oil and fear that wealth might fall into hostile hands. Those who wish to rise against that obtuse regime are women, who cannot to this day walk the streets without a male chaperone from the nuclear family, cannot drive or mix with male audiences, marry or travel without their patrons' permission, and are even threatened with lapidation if they should be caught fornicating outside wedlock. Common citizens, and even some members of the royal family, who studied abroad yearn for participation in the government and for a fuller share in their national resources, since they became disgusted with a system in which public service positions do not depend on skills and education, but on relations with the ruling family who distribute the privileges to their affiliates. The dissatisfaction from this stifling system, which finds the presidents of the United States and of European countries, who play the role of champions of human rights with the rest of world, speechless when they prostrate before those absolute monarchs, instead of calling them to task, cannot but explode one day into open rebellion and produce the removal of this system the way it is happening with the rest of the Muslim world, but in reverse order: instead of rebelling against tyranny and installing Islam, it will occur against Islamic tyranny in favor of a liberating democracy.

So far, due to its wealth and the way it is dispensing it, the country has succeeded in avoiding internal dissent and sidelining the domestic pressures to democratize, in the face of the turmoil of the Islamic Spring. Several women's demonstrations were dispersed, and attempts to start democratization in local government have been foiled, due to the firm grip of the Saudi-Wahhabi rule on all corridors of government. Thus, while in other monarchies there is at least the appearance of elected parliaments, which operate under the constraints of constitutions, in Saudi Arabia such a pretense does not even exist. The ruler is an absolute one, and any attempt to enlarge a crack into a window to let in new winds is promptly blocked and its existence insistently denied. The rulers have understood that the critical moment in every regime is when it starts loosening the leash, at a time when, in the name of the concessions made, the masses demand more concessions, until control is lost and power is lost. The choice that every authoritarian rule faces, as we were reminded at the end of the Soviet era in Eastern Europe, is between total oppression or total withdrawal. To the extent that there were talks of reform in Saudi Arabia, they were all produced under pressures from the outside. For example, when Saddam Hussein invaded Kuwait in 1990, the Saudis were asked, in order to facilitate the operation of the coalition the Americans gathered to counterattack, to pledge reform after the Iraqis were beaten. Under duress, the Saudis conformed, but as soon as the war was over, their clerics demanded that the foreign forces be evacuated from the holy Muslim land of Arabia, and all the promises were forgotten, with all the monarchs of the Gulf hanging together in solidarity, naturally preferring to dance sheikh to sheikh than to hang separately.

Morocco (See also the introduction to this chapter.)

Morocco pretends to be a constitutional monarchy, although far from the type of European monarchies where the king has no powers, but also very far from the other monarchies of Islam, which are closer to absolute rule than to the powerlessness of the queens of England and Denmark. Indeed, the king of Morocco holds vast executive and legislative powers, including the power to dissolve the parliament, though the daily executive power is exercised by the government, but the king's decisions usually override those of the government if there is a contradiction. Legislative power is vested in both the government and the two chambers of parliament, the Assembly of Representatives and the Assembly of Councillors (a sort of *shura*). The king can also issue decrees called *dahirs* that have the force of law. Parliamentary elections are held to be mostly free and fair. Voter turnout in the most recent elections was estimated to be 43 percent of registered voters, but only about 25 percent of Moroccan adult citizens actually voted. The rest either chose not to vote or they were not registered as voters, thus not allowed to vote. In 2011, the UN's Human Development Index ranked Morocco as the 130th most developed country in the world. Almost all Moroccans speak either Berber, Moroccan Arabic, or French as mother tongues. Hassaniya Arabic, sometimes considered as a variety of Moroccan Arabic, is spoken in the southern provinces (Western Sahara) of the country by a small population.

Morocco recovered its political independence from France on March 2, 1956, and on April 7, France officially relinquished its protectorate. Through agreements with Spain in 1956 and 1958, Moroccan control over certain Spanish-ruled areas was restored, though attempts to claim other Spanish colonial possessions through military action were less successful. The internationalized city of Tangier was reintegrated with the signing of the Tangier Protocol on October 29, 1956. Hassan II became king of Morocco on March 3, 1961. His early years of rule were marked by political unrest. The Spanish enclave of Ifni in the south was reintegrated to the country in 1969. Morocco annexed the Western Sahara during the 1970s (Marcha Verde, Green March) after it gained independence from Spain, but the final status of the territory remains unresolved. Political reforms in the 1990s resulted in the establishment of a bicameral legislature in 1997. Morocco was granted major non-NATO ally status by the United States in June 2004 and has signed free trade agreements with the United States and the European Union. Morocco has always been known for its Islamic liberalism and openness toward the Western world. King Mohammed VI of Morocco with his ruling elite are democratically minded, showing tolerance within the limits of territorial integrity and traditional laws and customs, but once a monarch has executive powers that he inherits instead of being elected to exercize, his democracy can be called into question.

Though not directly hit by the Spring, Morocco like the rest of the Islamic world has been influenced by it. The government, which is headed by a prime minister, is made up of many parties, a feature that was not common to the one-party Islamic regimes which allowed elections. On June 17, 2011, during the thick of the Spring, King Mohammed VI announced a series of reforms that would transform Morocco into a constitutional monarchy. Strangely enough, if Morocco were already the constitutional monarchy it claimed to be, then why the reform? The largest party, Justice and Development, the same approximate appellation of the Islamic parties in Turkey and Egypt, rules the coalition government, but it shares its authority with the king, who is not only the secular head of state, but also preserves his awe-inspiring religious title as of old, the commander of the faithful (*amir al-Mu'minin*), which successive generations of caliphs had proudly taken on following the Prophet himself. His participation in the Council of Ministers as its chair; his appointment of the prime minister and the ministers; his power to dissolve the parliament, suspend the constitution, call for new elections, or rule by decree lend him much more power than any constitutional monarch would dare claim. Upon the death of his grand-father, the legendary Mohammed V, who saw his people through the struggle for independence, his father King Hassan II succeeded to the throne in 1961, and after thirty-eight years on the throne he died and his son Muhammed VI inherited the crown in 1999. The dominating feature in the Moroccan system is that traditional opposition parties do participate in governments, or form them altogether, and the monarch has to mainatin the balance between popular will and what he perceives as the interests of the kingdom.

The unrest, though it had not escalated yet into a Spring, had sprung from the very fact that the Islamic Party, an affiliate of the Brothers, which dominates local politics, cannot see eye to eye with the mon-arch on matters of rule and power sharing. Al-Qa'ida in North Africa, which is advancing radical Islamic causes, does not see eye to eye with monarchs in general, who have too much influence on the rule of their countries, and would rather tend to support the Islamic party, which is in opposition to them, but has nevertheless to simulate docility until it is able to overturn them and take their place. For that reason, the Moroccan king tries to operate like the king of Qatar in courting the Muslim Brothers and activating the Jerusalem Committee of the Conference of Islamic countries, which he heads by inheritance from his father. At the same time, during the November 26, 2011, parlia-mentary elections, the Justice and Development Party (PJD), which was projected to win the largest number of seats, saw itself frustrated by the king, who made sure that the electoral rules were structured so that no political party could win more than 20 percent of the seats in parliament. In those elections, the party won less than one-third of the seats, in a stratagem used also by King Abdallah II of Jordan to limit the power of the Muslim Brothers who threatened his rule. The king thinks that with his Islamic titles and record he can afford to limit his Islamic party, but that game cannot be pursued indefinitely and will have to come to a head one day. It is noteworthy that the main national party, the Istiqlal, won only half the seats of the Justice party (60 to 107), perhaps indicating the trend and the direction the country is slipping.

Notes

1.   Eran, Oded, "Jordan's Internal and External Pressure Cooker," *INSS Insight* No. 358, July 31, 2012
     http://www.inss.org.il/publications.php?cat=21&incat=&read=6963.
2.   *Jordan Times*, July 23, 2012.

8

Syria, Libya, Yemen, Afghanistan, Bosnia, Kosovo, and the Tribal Model

In most Islamic countries, tribalism was supposed to be a thing of the past once the modern nation-states, which provide the unifying frame for peoples, tribes, clans, and ethnic groups, came about. But there remain many states where the ethnic/religious/national/linguistic composition is so varied that it has challenged all attempts to assimilate all nationals into one unified identity and create a homogeneous nationality. This difficulty persists in many Islamic countries, whose boundaries were drawn by colonial powers that were not sensitive to the differences and contentions between various groups of people. Most of the countries hit by the Spring found themselves in such a situation in one way or another, even though they were not included in this category because other characteristics were found more prominent to include them in other groupings. Take for example Egypt, where the hostility and hatred is unbridgeable between the Muslim majority, which grew out of the Arab occupiers in the seventh century, and the shrinking Coptic minority, the original people of the land, who feel occupied, displaced, disaffected, disinherited, and made strangers in their own country by the Arab invaders, who imposed their alien culture through Arabization and Islamization. In Morocco and Algeria, the Berbers/Kabyls, who are the original people of the land, underwent the same process, and they still constitute a sizeable share of the population. Many of them still entertain dreams of independence, or at least of some sort of autonomy. The leaders of these secessionist movements, who are not tolerated in their own countries because they are considered subversive to the central rule, often live in exile in France, whence they lead their hopeless struggle.

In the Middle East also this phenomenon is current. This is demonstrated in Iraq, for example, where governability is difficult due to the competition between the Shi'ite majority and Sunnite minority, and on the ethnic level between the Arab majority and the Kurdish minority, and in addition due to the other numerous minorities, some of them Muslim and others Christians, like the Turkemans, the Assyrians, who have shrunk since the Arab occupation and their influence dwindled. In Turkey, though the majority is Turkic, since their occupation of Anatolia in the Middle Ages and then the Ottoman rule, most of the original Christian inhabitants have been expelled or exterminated, but Kurds remain a sizeable minority in east Anatolia, and until recently they were not even allowed to use their ethnic appellation, let alone their culture and language. There are also Alevis who are as numerous as the Kurds (some 20 percent), but unlike the Syrian 'Alawis, they are still considered Muslim, though they differ from the Sunni-Hanafite majority with their mixture of popular Shi'ism and Bektashi Sufism. In Lebanon, where splinter groups of Maronites, Shi'ites, Druze, Sunnites, and others share power in accordance with their ethnic/religious affiliation, the country has known no repose since its inception, due to the constantly changing demographic balance and the perennial pressures to re-establish the quotas of power-sharing in light of the demographic changes, amid recourse to violence and civil war.

The danger inherent in the tribal structure is that every time a crisis emerges in the central government that presumably unifies the country, the union tends to disintegrate and return to its elemental components. Take, for example, Libya, which was immediately gripped by the Spring malaise since the outset, when the tribal federation of Cyrenaica in the east was countered by its western counterpart around the capital, Tripoli, triggering a bloody conflict that could not be terminated without NATO interference. Or consider the permanent dissidence by minority tribes, which sometimes take over the rule of the country, like the Sunnites in Iraq, the 'Alawis in Syria, the Shi'ite Hizbullah in Lebanon; or threaten to break away, like the Maronites in Lebanon, the Kurds in Turkey, Iraq, Iran, and Syria. This process is not unique to the Islamic world, and it was observed in Congo when Katanga seceded, causing a civil war; in Nigeria where the Muslim north is in constant confrontation with the Christian south, and the Boko Haram Muslim group is resorting to massacres of the Christians and destruction of their churches, just like the Muslim Brothers in Egypt against Coptic churches; and now the situation in Northern Mali, where the Muslim revolutionaries based in Gao and Timbuktu on the fringes of the Sahara threaten to establish their own republic; and so it goes with the Kabyls in

Algeria and Christian South Sudan, which detached itself from Muslim North Sudan after a bloody war of fifteen years.

The tribal syndrome is no less acute in Asia, where countries like Pakistan and Afghanistan are torn apart by internal dissent and inter-ethnic competition, and where a kind of Spring has been taking place for the past two decades, which takes different forms from the Middle East, due to the direct interference of foreign powers there. In those two major Islamic countries, which became the arena of international struggles, and where fundamentalist Islam has been playing a major role, the tribal structures are particularly destructive and sectarian, and constantly threaten to break the central governments, which are perennially challenged by radical Muslim movements. In Afghanistan, half the population is Pashtun, who inhabit the southern part of the country and the regions adjacent to the Pakistani border, and provide a great share of the students to the madrassas, the hothouses of the Muslim fighters known as Taliban, who are in permanent confrontation with the Tajiks in the north, and with the Hazara Shi'ites and the Uzbeks and Turkemans. Pakistan, which was itself torn away from India in 1949 when the two independent nations were created, and again in 1972 when Bangladesh rose out of East Pakistan, tribal and regional divisions between Sind, Baluchistan, Punjab, and other tribal areas have been a permanent feature of modern Pakistan. But there perhaps no tribalism created more bloodletting and chaos than in Syria, Libya, Afghanistan, and Yemen, where only a strong tyrannical regime can maintain the order and the unity of the country, an assumption that runs exactly contrary to the goals of the Spring, which has pretended to bring about the elimination of tyranny and the installation of democracy. It is too early to presume to predict what course events will take there. One thing is clear: individualism and the identification of the individual with the state under a new democratic social contract are not the options most likely to be realized any time soon there. Rather, as in other places, the Islamic alternative appears as the most likely course to be followed, for lack of another well-rooted choice in that cultural tradition.

Syria

Of all the Spring countries, perhaps Syria has been the most bleeding and unruly, because on the one hand a strong dynastic regime holds the country together in an iron fist, even though it was illegitimate from the beginning and did not collapse with the first troubles in Der'a in early

2011. But, unlike Tunisia and Egypt, where the leaders understood their hopeless situation in the face of the enraged masses, at a time when their main pillar of power, the army, had moved in support of the people, the strong army that had been strengthened by Assad the father and then his son, and educated for over forty years in loyalty to the leader and to the Alawi sect, has persisted in its support and devotion to the ruler. For the Assads knew that seizing power was a one-time feat, but maintaining it was a permanent struggle, because losing it means their slaughter by the Sunni majority who disliked it quite intensely. They thought that they were secure only as long as they could hold the reins tight on top of the tiger, and as soon as they dismounted they would be swallowed pitilessly. Hence the ruthless nature of the regime of Assad the father, which survived only by terrorizing its citizens, amid the permanent threat that whoever raises his head is susceptible to losing it. That lesson was learned by the Muslim Brothers, who paid for their uprising in Hama in 1982 with twenty thousand dead and the destruction of their old city, which had become the fortress for their last stand against their cruel regime. That number has apparently become iconic in the eyes of the regime, for in the present Spring thirty years later, where Assad the son has launched an all-out attack against his citizens who fear him no more, the toll has doubled that horrific figure. But there is no telling, as the battles intensify and the toll rises, how much more blood will be spilled before that most tenacious of tyrants is toppled.

In his ruthless fight for survival, Assad has used not only the national army, which was supposed to defend his people from its enemies, and in so doing, he lay siege against his own cities and neighborhoods as if they were enemy territory, using artillery, air force, and armor, but also gangs of thugs, the *shabiha* (armed militia loyal to the regime, like the Iranian Basij) who indiscriminately kill hundreds of people, giving the regime the opportunity to claim that its own hands are clean. The regime also uses fighters and advisers, and weapons from Hizbullah and Iranian revolutionary guards, who regard Assad's fall as the collapse of their entire Shi'ite radical front, that was leaning in the past two decades on the axis Tehran-Damascus-Hizbullah-Beirut, whom Turkey joined for a while, until it realized that NATO and the US would not tolerate this alliance for long. And when Assad's evil caused the massive flow of refugees into Turkey (and also neighboring Jordan, Lebanon, and Iraq), Ankara found itself compelled to disengage from Syria totally and stand at the forefront of those in the West who seek Assad's demise. The rebels in Syria were right when they accused Assad of his impotence vis-à-vis Israel, which he knew could react violently and humiliate him, while against his own citizens he behaves completely ruthlessly. Therefore they constantly challenge him to direct his weapons against their common enemy on the Golan, instead of against them. They also ask for Western intervention to rescue them from Assad's massacre, as it did in Libya, or at least to send them enough weapons to enable them to withstand the assaults of the Russian-equipped powerful Syrian military. They did not understand that the West, which cannot stomach casualties, intervenes only in situations of weak resistance like in Libya and Africa, and in ways, like in Libya from the air, that would not cause it such losses as to turn public opinion against their leaders. In Syria, by contrast, the Syrian land army and air defenses are on paper larger than those of the shrunken military of NATO, save the United States, and while America would not dare open another front while its involvement in Afghanistan has been deteriorating, no one else would venture into the Syrian quagmire.

It seems quite surprising that the Syrian army has remained loyal, on the whole, to the leadership, unlike in Egypt and Tunisia, and even more amazing how the regime remains unmoved by the daily sights of children and their families cut down in indiscriminate fire, and their entire city neighborhoods bombed and destroyed and turned into war zones where normal life can no longer be conducted. Refugees in the hundreds of thousands have been streaming to the four adjoining countries of Jordan, Turkey, Iraq, and Lebanon, pursued by fire, bombing, and shelling by Assad's forces into their shelter countries, while the number of casualties has already surpassed anything Syria has known during its bloody history. Nearly all the public institutions of education, health, food supply, housing, and social welfare have come to a standstill, with all the state resources directed to the military only. All this demonstrates, sadly and dramatically, what tribalism can do to a country when central rule devolves, citizens of the same country turn overnight into sworn enemies, the national army becomes a servant of the ruler, the rebels turn into the enemies of the country and the people, and others who operate against the regime turn into "foreign agents, terrorists and subversive elements who deserve death" and are treated accordingly. These destructive elements, which reach an extreme degree of acuity in the tribal model, are present in other types of tyranny too, like some monarchies—for example Hussein's Jordan during Black September 1970, and some republics like Iraq under Saddam and Libya under Qaddafi. It is true that these extreme manifestations of cruelty and disregard for human lives and welfare are fully reflected when the regime is in danger or the tyrant fights for his life, but they are always latent under the surface, always threaten to explode, and there is nothing in the state structure and institutions to prevent them from happening. Under these conditions, the commoners who go about their daily routine and are afraid to trigger this kind of violent eruptions against them usually bend their heads and are ready to absorb in silence many of the abuses of the rule, like killings, torture, arrest, and sudden disappearance of loved ones, with no independent juridical institution to appeal to, as a matter of survival. The very same simple folks who we now see outraged, tormented, and prepared to rebel in Cairo, Aleppo, Tripoli, and San'a during the Spring, had walked the same streets one year earlier full of praise for their leaders and running short of words to laud the freedom, prosperity and good order they were basking in under their generous and benevolent leaders. What happened in the interval? Nothing, except for the incentive to rise and speak up. Thus, not a sudden act of cruelty, mismanagement, or a whim have prompted these people to rebel, to throw their yoke, to overcome their fear and to shout out loud: "Enough is enough! We shall tolerate no more! The barrier of fear has been removed!"

At the outset of the Spring revolt, the Arab and Islamic world tried to tackle it in low profile, to keep it under wraps, within the family, so as not to reveal in public their collective embarrassment at the sight of their regimes collapsing one after the other, with no one surviving as a sign of tenacity and resilience, which could become the model for amendment and reform. For years, during successive civil governments, Turkey seemed to the West to be a model for the rest of the Islamic world, due to its presumed ideal combination of moderate Islam with democracy. But now it has reshuffled the cards when in 2002 the Islamic party came to power, democratically to be sure. Under the new regime, the privileges of the military were curtailed, but the bourgeois and urbanite population that opposed the rural-based Islamic party and cherished the previous freedom of the press, were dismayed to watch the incarceration of journalists, the campaigns of hatred, lies, and incitement against the great and close ally of yesteryear, Israel, who became the favorite enemy of all the Muslim fundamentalists, including the new Turkish ruling party. What has happened to the privileged status of Israel as a close and loyal strategic ally? Has Israel suddenly changed? Certainly not; it was the Turkish government that changed, and its Islamic conviction has altered its political orientation and behavior, as more veiled women were seen in the streets of Turkey than ever before, including the wives of Erdogan and Gul, whereas veils had been banned under the Kemalist regime in all public institutions. The new orientation toward Muslim regimes, including the most virulent enemies of Israel—Iran, Syria, Hizbullah, and Hamas—has by necessity brought about alienation from Israel and the shameless and indecent campaigns of bigotry and lies against it. A similar process had happened in Tehran three decades early, when the extremely friendly relations with Israel had turned overnight into the most venomous vitriol that Jews and Israel have known since the Nazis. One has to recognize the reality that Islamic regimes, of the kind the current Spring seems to be adopting, are almost by definition inimical to Israel and the Jews.

Rebelling Syrians had from the outset no model to follow, despite Turkish efforts to peddle their regime as a worthy one. During Erdogan's visit to Egypt after the Spring broke out, he counseled the Brothers to deprive the military from its inherited prerogatives, as he had himself done. Before that he had turned Assad into his ally and even counseled the Americans to end the Syrian isolation and re-establish diplomatic relations with them, which they foolishly did, a position they had to reverse when the Spring broke out and Erdogan became the leader of the call to remove Assad altogether from power since he "had lost legitimacy"—as if he ever had it—as he and Obama wished to believe. Both of them never recognized their grave mistake in public, nor the tragic damage they had caused to the Syrian people by leading Assad to believe that he had their support and could behave at home as he wished. The Arab League, which was embarrassed to expose in public the massive killings that went on in Arab lands, day after day, saw fit to address the UN and ask for a solution, bearing in mind that in Libya it was foreign bombing that enabled the rebels to overcome Qaddafi and murder him. This Arab initiative was once again, as in the case of Libya, led by the emir of Qatar, who wished the affair to remain within the boundaries of the Muslim family, and who had a personal interest in quieting the situation, lest its permanent brewing transport it to his monarchy and his other monarchical neighbors too.

But this whole enterprise grew into a bad joke, when in order to keep the Spring within its Arab contours, observers from the Arab League were delegated to reach a cease-fire between the forces and put an end to the endless killings throughout the cities and towns of Syria, with the armed forces of Assad taking the lion's share of the killing, in view of the ill-equipped rebel forces who could not match the jets and tanks of the national forces. The farce slowly emerged, the moment a Sudanese general (who had participated in the mass genocide of the Darfur population, and himself belonged to the entourage of General Umar Bashir, who was indicted by the International Court in Hague for genocide and crimes against humanity and considered as a fugitive from justice since his country refused to extradite its president) was appointed as the head of the UN-Arab League mission of observers. That mission was posted on the ground for months and then withdrawn as ineffective, as it could not sanction Assad for his crime on the one hand, nor respond to the rescue cries of the displaced and threatened populations on the other. Kofi Anan, the previous UN secretary general, stepped in, promising to do through diplomacy what the others could not do; and though he was seconded by a new mission of international observers headed by a Norwegian general, they all resigned their posts and avowed their failure after Anan's trips to Damascus, Tehran, and the Western capitals boiled down to nothing. It was declared that the UN observers could not endanger their lives in the war zone, and therefore they had to be withdrawn, like firefighters retreating because of their inability to extinguish the fire, just letting it burn. UN incompetence in solving real conflicts and stopping killings was again dramatically exposed, as was the fact that except for seeking to be reelected and maintaining a mammoth and wasteful bureaucracy, UN secretaries after Dag Hammersjkold were all spineless and ineffective failures.

In the meantime, the massacres by the Syrian army in the service of Assad continued, while the weapons smuggled to the rebels, from Turkey or from Western and Arab countries, which hope to gain something from their ultimate victory, have had little effect and only tended to prolong the conflict, because equally determined allies of Assad, like Russia, China, and Iran, are interested in Assad's survival, and they continuously equip him with the most needed ammunition and other supplies to last through this protracted and exhausting conflict. In the township of Triemse west of Damascus, under the torrid heat of July (2012), 150 civilians were murdered by regular soldiers, and while the ineffective observers were rushing there to report the slaughter instead of preventing it, Assad's troops were on their way to another township on the Turkish border to perpetrate another mass murder. When these were terminated, a squadron of helicopters was sent to Khirbet Ghazaleh, in the Der'a area where the rebellion had started about a year and a half earlier, to bomb it, then assaulted it with tanks and infantry until it was totally conquered, and then they set ablaze the abandoned town whose inhabitants had fled for their lives. These wanton massacres culminated in the Christmas Eve 2012 bombing of hungry citizens lining up for bread at a bakery, some insist with chemical weapons. A hundred citizens, mainly children, perished. Regardless, the killings continue.

These horrible massacres were but links in the long series of crimes committed on a routine basis by all the tyrannical regimes that preceded the Spring. They became such a matter of course that few were surprised by them or dared to protest against them. But the Israeli neighbors of Syria, who are tormented and pained by what they see around them, say to themselves that if this is the way Arabs deal with their kin (and they did the same in Libya, Iraq, Jordan, Lebanon, and among various factions of the Palestinians), one can easily imagine what fate would be reserved for Jews and Israelis, if Arabs had the opportunity. Hence Israeli determination to draw this lesson from the Spring events, and vow to themselves and to the world how one must stand on his own when one is doomed to live in a prosperous and pleasant villa in the heart of a bad neighborhood in the middle of the jungle. In fact, they need hardly to guess or to draw analogies in view of the terrorist war that organizations like Hamas, Hizbullah, al-Qa'ida, and countries like Iran and Syria wage against Israel and world Jewry when they are not busy in their own wars, or the casualties they have inflicted in other major terrorist acts in New York, London, Madrid, Bali, Mumbai, and more, and the many more massive terrorist attacks they concoct against civilians but which are foiled daily. This all shows the bloodthirsty character of these groups, peoples, and regimes, who educate their youth in the same spirit, lest that horrifying heritage be forgotten.

The Turkish prime minister, Erdogan, who within one year shifted from being the defender and ally of Assad to his sworn antagonist, partly due to the large numbers of Syrian refugees who continue to flock to his territory, has been the most severe outsider demanding the ouster of the regime, probably in an attempt to cover up and palliate the resurgence of the Armenian grievances against the massacre committed against their people by the Turks during the first world war, and push to the sidelines the horrors committed by recent Turkish governments against their large Kurdish minority. Erdogan is also worried by the harsh European criticism against continued Turkish occupation since 1974 of northern Cyprus, who is a member of the EU, with no solution in sight. Any visitor to the Turkish-occupied part of the island faces the unpleasant facial expressions of the immigration officers when they recognize the Israeli passport, though one must say that they remained completely correct and courteous, perhaps hoping to make up in Famagusta what they lost in Israeli tourism in Antalya. And suddenly, Assad the righteous, who could do no wrong in the heyday of Erdogan's courtship of that tyrant, became in the eyes of the chameleon-like Turkish prime minister, "coward and cruel, like all the rest of them, and he will have to account for his deeds after he is removed," as if he himself did not have a touch of their authoritarian rule. It would be interesting to speculate what he would have said had the Syrians granted shelter to oppressed Kurds in Turkish territory, as he has permitted Syrian rebels into his land. In fact, such a situation occurred previously, when the Syrians had given refuge to fugitive Turkish Kurdish leader Ocalan, and the Ankara government (that preceded Erdogan) threatened to invade Syrian territory, and even concentrated forces on its border with Syria, which caused Damascus to back down immediately.

The penetration of al-Qa'ida and other terrorist movements into Syria in the expectation of getting their share from the devolving power amid the mounting chaos, is the issue that some responsible powers have been attempting to tackle, especially in view of the concrete danger that such irresponsible organizations, which do not bear any accountability toward the international community, may lay their hand on the mammoth stocks of unconventional weapons under the Syrian regime, especially chemical, said to be the largest in the world. Such weapons, considered the nuclear power of the poor, do not even have to be used in practice to become a menace. It is sufficient for an organization or regime that claims to possess them simply to threaten to use them for blackmail against any country or government; this causes the world order to collapse. It is ironic that it was the same al-Qa'ida that Assad supported when its fighters ran away from the Americans in Iraq to seek refuge in Syria had been the cause for the deterioration of Damascus's relationship with the United States, which also brought about the rupture of diplomacy between the two and even almost a massive retaliation by President Bush against Damascus, and finally to a humiliating Syrian expulsion from Lebanon after three decades of occupation. But with Obama's disastrous policies—engagement, which generated irreparable damage to American interests in the Middle East; his renewed relations with Assad; license to Hizbullah to take over Lebanon; his abandonment of his loyal ally Mubarak; his hypocritical advocacy of human rights while allying with some of the most obscure regimes in the world; and his permitting Iran to edge proudly and defiantly toward nuclear power—he was compelled by reality to swallow his hat. He met very adequately the definition that a neo-con is a liberal who was mugged by reality. He was compelled to sever the relations with Syria again, to step up sanctions and threaten military action against Iran, and he has been trying to create a bridge to the Muslim Brothers, whom his predecessor had shunned so consistently.

But al-Qa'ida, as it proved previously in Somalia and Yemen, and after that in Sudan and Afghanistan, is skilled in penetrating countries and societies, and therefore is certain to position itself, amid the Syrian chaos, in a way that helps determine the succession to Assad. In Iraq, where al-Qa'ida played an important role during the war, its stature was reduced following the first elections and the apparent stabilization of the rule there. But in Yemen, in the Horn of Africa, and possibly in Syria and Libya, it has not yet had the last word, and the more uncontrollable the chaos becomes, the greater its opportunities to leave its mark on the final settlement in those countries. All this assuming Syria emerges unified from the present trauma. But judging from the preparations currently being made by the Kurds, the Druze, and the Alawites to carve their own respective territories in case the country falls apart, there is no guarantee how this might end. The fear of the disintegration of Syria, despite the efforts to the contrary by Russia—its patron in international forums and in arms supply, in order to cultivate it as one unified unit under its aegis and keep its naval base in Tartus, while President Putin is striving to return his country to its original grandeur—is not totally baseless. It is founded on the fact that Syria has historically been more of a geographic than a political unit, and its borders have expanded and shrunk upon the whims of its rulers. Lately, under the Ottoman Empire, Syria also included Palestine, Transjordan, and Lebanon and was known as Greater Syria. Modern Syria has never renounced its ambition to return to its wider boundaries. But as Syria can expand, it can also shrink; in other words, it has no credible social contract between its parts that can hold it together, since they sense that no great love is lost between them, as we observe daily on our screens, and there are enough centrifugal forces in the country that can precipitate such a division.

The Alawis—who constitute 12 percent of the population but have been imposing tyrannical rule on the country for the past forty-two years and who fear, for good reason, the wrath of revenge from the rest of the country—may seek refuge in an enclave in the area of the seaports of Ladakia and Tartus, and dig in for a long stand. The Sunnites, who are most typically represented by the Muslim Brothers and their affiliates, and who are disgusted with the dynastic rule of the Assads for the last four decades, will certainly be happy to rid themselves of the rule of the heretic Alawis and constitute a Muslim state, if they can overcome the many contradictions between the rural and less advanced population of the countryside and the wealthier, more educated and more bourgeois elites of the large cities of Aleppo, Damascus, Hama, Homs, Der'a, Deir al-Zor, and any number of other urban centers whose names appear on our screens daily during the conflict. The Druze, who are already concentrated on the Druze Mountain, would probably wish to link up with their kin in Lebanon, Israel, and the Golan, while the Kurds in the Qamishli far north would certainly watch the fate of their brethren in adjoining Iraq, Iran, and Turkey, where they make up, in the aggregate, a strong and ethnically and culturally committed national group of some thirty million that seeks independence or at least some sort of autonomy. The many Christian denominations, whose survival has always depended on their incorporation into the state machinery (for example, the minister of defense slain by the rebels on July 2012 was Christian), had a priori joined the alliance of minorities with the ruling Alawis, assuming that a minority would respect the rights of another. But this assumption has not been proven beyond doubt under the Assads, because the ruling minorities always live under the fear that when they are toppled, no one would rush to their defense. In any case, if Syria is not kept together, then either new independent units can between them partition the vast Syrian territory, or they will resort to the much more unstable and ineffective rule by quotas of next-door Lebanon.

No less worrisome has been the view from Israel, which during most of the Assad reign has watched quiet prevailing on their common border on the Golan since 1967, save for the short interlude of the 1973 war. The strong regime of the Assads, until its downfall, knew how to read the geopolitical map of the area and to realize that Damascus was only forty kilometers from the ceasefire border and reachable by Israeli artillery. Therefore, it knew how to respect in minute detail the ceasefire with Israel. There is no telling what a new regime—either based on autonomous units or in the hands of Muslim radicals like in Gaza, who embrace a policy not always consistent with logic or interest—might do or what way they might choose to tread, which can evolve into a conflict it did not want or was not prepared for. Many of the rebels against Assad belong to the Brothers or al-Qa'ida, and judging from their war cries, *"Allah akbar"*—heard in almost all demonstrations by almost all groups of rebels, under shelling by the Syrian army, or rallying against the tyrant in massive gatherings in the cities, or urging foreign powers to come to their aid, or supplicating foreign correspondents to report their plight to the world—there can be no doubt where their hearts lie. Auguring ill were the additions to the signs carried by the demonstrators when Assad began to show signs of weakening and tumbling, with the inscriptions: "Forward to Damascus and Jerusalem!" meaning that the rebellion was not only directed against the "cruel, oppressive and murderous tyrant," whose grip on Damascus seemed to loosen up, but also against "Assad the traitor," who instead of directing his guns to Israel, has been using them against his own people. One can conclude from that a pledge, that when they take over the rule, they would correct both wrongs: eliminate tyranny and revive the Golan front.

There will also be far-reaching international consequences to what is happening in Syria. First of all, the revival of the Russian position of old in the Middle East, and the new stature that China has been acquiring thanks to her newly-gained economic power and to her joint UN votings and vetoes which have so far obstructed harsh sanctions against Iran and Syria, will both suffer a setback in case Assad falls. This, however, does not guarantee the rise in American prestige or a gain in her positions, if to replace the departed regime new fundamentalist powers come instead. The second most injured party will be Iran, as Syria under Assad was the main link which connected revolutionary Tehran with Hizbullah and constituted the pillar of the Shi'ite crescent that has been so much feared, suspected, mistrusted and resented by the Sunnite world headed by Saudi Arabia. Syria has been also the bridge and the go-between to transmit Iran's directives to her most loyal and devoted agents of terror in the Middle East and the world—Nasrallah and his Hizbullah. Through Damascus, Hizbullah received his arms, money and instructions, and the movement to and fro from Tehran to Beirut and back. In case this axis is severed, Hizbullah's future is much in doubt, and Tehran's link to Gaza will be much disrupted. Anticipating this, Hamas itself has evacuated its offices from Damascus as the security situation keeps worsening, but the new administration there will hasten to build alternative frameworks and networks of relations to fit the nature of the new regime, and the remaining terrorist movements who will still lodge in the Syrian capital will have to look for better shelters if the new administration decides to abandon the terrorist path. The new rule will also have to build new outreaches to the Arab world, to get out of their country's isolation, and perhaps weave new lines of communication and cooperation with the West, especially the United States.

Next door Lebanon, which will be relieved from the giant shadow of her dominating neighbor, which had directly occupied her for too long, and pulled the strings of her policies, domestic and external, for even longer, will have to work out new patterns of government to liberate herself from the violent grip of Hizbullah, once the latter's Syrian patron and protector has lost its influence and lowered its profile. And, above all, the powerful and concerned neighbor—Israel, which for forty years (the period predicted by former Prime Minister Begin during the Lebanon War of 1982, of which 30 have already elapsed) has enjoyed peace and quiet on its borders on the Golan (though not entirely on the Lebanese border), may find herself suddenly threatened, either by another regime which will embrace a different agenda than its predecessor or be showered by missiles, with conventional or unconventional payloads, which may transform life within her borders and entice her to alter its strategy.

It is noteworthy that when the danger of Assad's collapse became concrete as he approached the end of his fighting stamina, both Iranian and Arab spokesmen threatened an imminent Iranian reaction against Israel in the context of the Syrian crisis, which may have already begun with the terrorist attack in Bulgaria in July 2012, against an Israeli tour bus, which claimed 6 casualties. These spokesmen have underlined the connection between the situation in Syria and the Iranian nuclear debate, therefore Iran regarded herself committed to defend her ally due to her suspicion that Israel and Saudi Arabia collaborated in arming the Syrian opposition, which is dubbed by Assad and Iran as made of "terrorists," who are poised to topple the Syrian regime. Those spokesmen have warned lest those riots spread to the entire Middle East, bring about the rupture of the Iranian-Syrian axis, thus harming Iran's geopolitical posture and irreparably damaging Hizbullah, which has become the joint long executive arm of both Tehran and Damascus, and the agent of both in Lebanon.

These spokesmen tend to believe that any Israeli attack on one of the partners of the axis Iran-Syria-Hizbullah would produce an immediate combined counterattack of the three against Israel. In Nasrallah's speech on July 18, 2012, he reiterated that Israel was preparing a first strike against Lebanon, as it did on two previous occasions (1982 and 2006), but he boasted that Hizbullah was itself busy preparing a "great surprise" in retribution. Whether he referred to the Burgas (Bulgaria) terrorist operation, which was perpetrated on the same day but had been in the making long before, or to the long promised revenge for the killing of 'Imad Mughnia, his legendary chief of operations in Damascus a few years earlier, it remains unclear. One way or another, as the Western siege on Tehran is tightening, and due to Iran's inability to respond by any significant diplomatic countermeasure, and to stop the tumbling process of its Syrian client and ally, it has no option left than to dispatch terrorist attacks against the West and Israel, without however admitting responsibility for them, in spite of the clear footprints that Hizbullah leaves behind as its agent for this kind of activity. This is apparently what happened in Bulgaria, but this does not preclude more attempts of this cowardly type, or of more spectacular import, in the weeks and months to come, in order to prevent or slow down the process of disintegration of the Damascus regime.

This sort of convoluted strategy, which allows Iran to act without admitting it, also deflects world attention from its nuclear program and shifts the burden of proof, and the responsibility for the Syrian events, to the West, which is accused of both persecuting peaceful Iran and aiding the rebels in Syria, to create havoc by arming them, thus prolonging the strife and increasing the bloodletting. This thinking is enthusiastically embraced by China and Russia, which lend to it international prominence by using it in the UN and other diplomatic arenas. This explains the series of terrorist attempts concocted against Israel and the West, which were fortunately scuttled thanks to efficient intelligence gathering and international coordination. The aborted terrorist operations in Azerbaijan, Thailand, India, and even against the Saudi Ambassador in Washington in the recent past; and the "successful" operations in Kenya in June 2012, in Cyprus in July, and in Bulgaria again in July, on which Ahmadinejad commented saying: "we try all the time and sometimes we also succeed," referring to the murder of five Israeli and one Bulgarian innocent citizens as "success," are all cases in point. In all the documentation that was seized after the fact, the implementation was confided to Hizbullah. An authoritative hypothesis has been that the purpose of these acts has been to trigger a strong reaction by Israel against Hizbullah and /or Iran, something that would compel Tehran to launch an all-out war against Israel, amid her accusation of "provocation," thus causing the world to forget about the nuclearization program. Conversely, another estimate contends that Iran would not take the risk of total war, that could cause much destruction and death in the country before it has had the chance to complete the project of the bomb, which could deter any attack against her. But who knows what this irrational regime can do, if it is poised on war for ideological reasons? These pro and con arguments also play out in the Syrian scene, where Iranian positions are increasingly threatened, and their implementation on the ground is seen as contingent upon Assad's longevity, since the red lines that Iran has drawn are connected to her direct involvement there, not only in terms of her strategic involvement but also in terms of her active participation in fighting on the various fronts.

Syrian commentators also emphasize that Iran has been committed to Assad's protection, and that any harm to him can trigger a regional conflagration in the Middle East. Both Iran and Syria have also demanded that Russia should stand against, and constitute a counterweight to the Western insistence on Assad's departure. This sort of expectation has been repeatedly stated by the Russian Foreign Ministry, whose heads have been very actively involved in monitoring and charting the diplomatic struggle on behalf of Damascus and Tehran. Syrian spokesmen, seconded by their Russian allies, have also warned the "new Ottomans," that is the Turks who have "betrayed" the Syrian cause, that they had championed not long before, on the eve of Kofi Anan's visit to Tehran, that they should not seek to apply to Syria their military involvement in Libya, and be drawn to a military intervention in response to Western manipulations against her own interests.

In a press conference in Tehran, where the Syrian Ambassador also took part, Iranian spokesmen warned that an all-out conflict in Syria may turn into a world war and precipitate rebellions in Saudi Arabia and Jordan as well. It is obvious, that being aware of Western sensitivity to those two bastions of its interests, the Iranians have elected to wave them as scarecrows in order to deter and prevent any idea of shipping massive troops into Syria, the way they had done into the Gulf two decades earlier when Iraq invaded Kuwait and threatened the monarchies of the Arabian Peninsula. Not incidentally, Iran pulled its trump card that it uses whenever a threat of hostilities looms in the horizon, that is, "to eliminate the Zionist entity," which they know the West would not let come to pass. They perennially claim that Israel is under a permanent danger to the point of being hostage to the mercy of three regional powers: the Syrian regime, the Lebanese Resistance (Hizbullah) and the Gaza Resistance (Gaza). This means that if the Zionist regime or NATO dare to attack Syria, those three combined operational powers will direct their missiles to Israel and bring destruction upon it. Ali Akbar Velayati, Iran's expert on foreign affairs, appeared before the Council of Experts of the regime on March 7, 2012, and described Syria as the "frontline of the Resistance," and determined that Israel has been the source of the pressures exerted on Syria, due to her concern about the developing changes in the regional balance of power.

None other than Ayatullah Misbah Yazedi proclaimed on February 26, 2012, one year into the Syrian revolt, the importance of Damascus as the bridge between Iran, Hizbullah and the Palestinians, indicating the new direction of the Iranian order of strategic priorities, whereby Iran is seeking to preserve Assad's regime, not only for its own sake, since the collapse of an autocratic regime can seriously crack Iran's own autocracy, but as the essential link with the other members of the alliance who constantly hold Israel in check. Thus, Syria being merely the long arm of Iran in the front line of the Middle East, whoever fights Damascus, either from within or without, *eo ipso* challenges Tehran itself. This explains the direct involvement of Iran in the Syrian fighting and killing, and also in its internal politics, which also affords her the opportunity to deflect world opinion from her nuclearization program, while energetically pursuing that program toward completion. And if in the process twenty thousand or forty thousand Syrians die, the human prize should not justify the abandonment of that strategy. The ayatullah also reminded of the aid of his country to Hizbullah during the second Lebanese War in 2006, praised Syria for being the most loyal Arab country to the Islamic cause as represented by Iran, and dubbed the rest of them as "worse than unbelievers," as they join the latter in order to strike Syria, and thereby also Iran. Already in October 2011, at the height of the Syrian uprising, one of the leaders of Iran, Muhsin Razai, stated to the Manar network that any harm to the triangular thread: Syria-Hizbullah-Hamas constitutes for her a red line, since they form the Islamic front against Israel, that she will not permit anyone to touch. This sounds like *casus belli*, and the only question remains, as in other contexts, whether Iran is capable to carry out its commitments when the chips are down and the hour of crisis comes.

Interesting are also the reactions of other Arabs, led by Qatar, who often stand outside the Arab League consensus. Ahmed Jibril, the head of the Palestinian Popular Front- the General Headquarter, for example, who has been living in Syria under the Assad dynasty, announced to the press that his allies in Syria, namely Iran and Hizbullah, would be ready to coordinate their reaction with him in case of attack. This is not to say that Jibril disposes of any significant forces to bring to bear, but his statement does reflect the thinking of the Syrian leadership, when he declares that he met with Nasrallah and high-level Iranians in order to coordinate a retaliation for any assault on Syria, knowing that Iran would under no circumstance abandon Damascus to its fate, and that Tehran had warned Ankara from "playing with fire" in the Syrian crisis, since it is clear that any external intervention in Syria, constituted a red line for Iran's strategic considerations. In Lebanon, many are the commentators who believe that Hizbullah would not be able to tolerate the dismissal or removal of Assad its benefactor, therefore it would be compelled to act militarily unless this would clearly mean a suicidal measure on its part. It is said that Hizbullah is busy preparing to dig in the Dahiya neighborhood of Beirut, and at the same time it has stepped up the oral defiance of its rivals and the publication of fatwas by its clerics, permitting to fight hostile Lebanese and Syrian troops in case of a civil war, in order to ensure its survival, and/or direct its artillery and missiles against Israel. According to commentators, Hizbullah will also be able to seize the rule in Beirut by launching a coup, either by activating mass demonstrations in its favor, like the one of May 7, 2007, which allowed it to overtake parts of Beirut, or by using its limitless sources of weapons, to create chaos in the country, prompt UNIFIL troops to leave the country, as happened in May 1967, when UN Secretary U Thant thought that exactly when the Sinai Peninsula was about to be set aflame, it was appropriate to withdraw the UN firefighters from the arena, who had preserved the peace for the previous eleven years.

In Jordan, another passive watcher of the massacres happening next-door, and of its own helplessness in the face of the massive waves of refugees which flood her territory daily, has been very sensitive to the reports of changes on her border, since it was in nearby Der'a that the uprising in Syria had broken out. Saleh al-Qilab, her minister of information—a position unique to the Muslim world and other authoritarian states, where the regimes shape public opinion instead of reflecting it—stated in July 2012, when the pangs of the end of the Assad era could be felt in the air, that Iran, in collaboration with Russia, was interested to kindle a regional or even a world war, just in order to rescue their ally, contrary to the Western, Arab and Islamic public opinion. According to the Jordanian Minister's understanding, Russia, Iran and Assad have been pondering this option since the first days of the Syrian uprising, aiming to trigger local border incidents with Israel, in order to create the impression that Assad was busy tackling external threats, in order to free him from internal pressures, by claiming that the unrest was being created by Zionist agents and aggressive Israel. But the members of this axis have been compelled to abandon this idea only due to their fear from fierce and destructive Israeli retaliations that would have certainly come. However, as the siege on Assad by his restive opposition tightened the noose around his neck, this option was again raised, and the Minister saw in the downing of a Turkish jet over Syrian territorial waters, and in the escalation of massive Russian deliveries of weapons to Syria, via the Damascus airport and the naval ports of Ladaqiya and Tartus, an indication of the beginning of the implementation of this plan. To his mind, the Russians stood behind the downing of the Turkish plane, which was aimed to trigger a retaliation by NATO, calculated to create a chain reaction that would kindle war. According to the Minister, Russia and Iran who would have been in favor of starting the war, would have stayed out of it, while all the consequences and damages would have been suffered by the local peoples, and the provoking powers could have even gained something from it. This sounds like a classic conspiracy theory that Arabs are experts in manufacturing, especially in view of the inaccessibility of small and weak Jordan to such a highly classified information, but the desperate situation of the three members of the axis make it more and more plausible by the day.

It is more plausible, however, that the Minister was citing from the Iranian daily *Kayhan*, probably reflecting official views, which published an editorial outlining this sort of convoluted strategy.[1] In the editorial, *Kayhan* which is close to Iranian Supreme Leader Ali Khamenei, called on the regime of Syrian President Bashar Al-Assad to fight Israel, with Tehran's backing, on the grounds that Israel was responsible for the July 18, 2012, suicide bombing in Damascus, in which several of Syria's top security officials were killed. The daily went on to state that Israel's military deployment along the Syrian border prior to the bombing was further evidence of its responsibility for it, and that Israel was also behind the July 18 attack in Bulgaria against what it referred to as Israeli diplomats, with the aim of implicating Iran. *Kayhan* presented two options for a Syrian war against Israel: a "limited war" waged by Syria "to liberate part of the occupied Syrian territories," or a "comprehensive war of no set duration" to be waged by the entire "resistance axis" [including Syria, Hizbullah, and Hamas]. The paper urged the

Assad regime to make open military moves against the uprising at home and also against Israel, which he said was currently unprepared for war. Such a Syrian initiative would, it said, serve both Syria and the resistance axis, as well as harm the Zionist-American front and its allies: Turkey, Saudi Arabia, and Qatar.

Tehran, which is currently under steadily increasing political and economic pressure, contends the paper, is unable to launch a direct military confrontation with the West or Western allies like Saudi Arabia and the Gulf states, and is therefore urging its proxies to take military action against Israel. This modus operandi is typical for it, and serves to draw world attention away from its nuclear crisis, as well as to indirectly retaliate against the West for its harsh sanctions against it. It would be worthwhile to bring a few citations from that important mouthpiece of the Ayatullahs:

> A few days prior to the [July 18 bombing in Damascus], the Zionist regime deployed militarily in the occupied territories in the Golan Heights and on Mount Hermon, and went on maximum alert. On Thursday [July 19], it was even claimed that Israel's opponents were firing on these areas. These measures in themselves indicate advanced planning of the Damascus bombing by the oppressive [Israeli] regime, and by the same token, it can be assessed that [Israel] itself [staged the attack] against the Israeli diplomats in Bulgaria, blaming it on Iran on the very day of the bombing.

> An important point regarding the changes [occurring] in Syria is that [the regime's] atmosphere of preserving security is gradually changing to a military atmosphere. The recent developments in Damascus—namely the bombing at the [National] Security Council [building] and the elimination of terrorist forces in the Al-Midan neighborhood—underscore the role of the military in [conflict] resolution. By purging the [Al-Midan] neighborhood in a single day, the Syrian army showed that although it has been embroiled in this crisis for 16 months, it is absolutely capable of [taking on this role]. The shift from a security atmosphere to a military atmosphere is undoubtedly dangerous for the Zionist regime as well as for Turkey, because it means the beginning of a war between Syria and Israel. On a larger scale, it undoubtedly means a joint war by Syria, Iran, Hizbullah and others against the Zionist regime. Such a confrontation can take the form of a comprehensive war of no set duration, or a limited war to liberate part of the occupied Syrian territories.

> In any case, Syria's entrance into military confrontation, whether comprehensive or limited, would definitely change the atmosphere

[in the region]. It is patently clear that Israel is currently totally unprepared for military confrontation—on the contrary, the worst possible scenario for it right now would be a confrontation with Syria. Such a confrontation would turn the atmosphere in the region against the Zionist regime, Turkey, Saudi Arabia and Qatar, and against the entire American-Zionist front—thus unifying the resistance front and making it operational.

Syria's shift from a security atmosphere to a military one will free it to deal resolutely with the armed elements operating on behalf of other parties, as in the past few days. There are at most 5,000 armed terrorists in Syria, who operate in one place, disappear, and move to another. When Syria was operating in a security atmosphere, it was difficult for it to act against this number [of terrorists]—but in a military atmosphere, the task will be simple; Syria has more experience in this area. Shifting to a military atmosphere will [also] force Turkey and Israel to pay dearly for every action against Syria, and for their part in [creating] an atmosphere of instability in Syria.

Syria's entrance into the military realm means entrance into a realm of unforeseeable consequences. In a military atmosphere, the defending country [i.e., Syria] has the advantage, whereas the attacking countries are very vulnerable. The creation of security [instability] in Syria warrants the transfer of this [instability] to the countries that fomented it—which will make it easier for Syria to manage the arena [of the conflict].[2]

Whatever the speculations about whether and when the Syrian Spring would enter its critical phase, and even before the Spring across the board throughout the Islamic world was pushed one notch up due to the silly episode of the anti-Muhammed movie which when released in the United States in September 2012, was taken as a declaration of war by America/ Christianity against Islam, plans for the post-Spring period in Syria have been revealed by all sorts of parties. For example, according to one source,[3] Syria's rebels distributed on July 30, 2012, a "national salvation draft" proposal for a political transition in the country, bringing together military and civilian figures for a post-Bashar Al-Assad phase. The draft by the joint command of the Free Syrian Army (FSA) proposes the establishment of a higher defense council charged with creating a presidential council, which in turn would bring together a total of six military and civilian figures to lead a future transition. The proposal "meets all the revolution's demands," said the umbrella Military Council Joint Command, based in the flashpoint city of Homs.

At the same time, another source revealed[4] that Arab Islamic fighters were eager to join Syria rebels, as the expression of a small but growing influx of militant Arab Islamic fighters, joining the fight against President Bashar Assad, a trend that seems to indicate the possible direction of Islam that post Assad Syria might take, just like Egypt, Tunisia, and more recently Libya. A case in point is Abdullah Ben Shamar, a Saudi student, who put a small copy of the Qur'an among his few belongings packed neatly in a holdall, as he prepared to set off with a Libyan friend across the hilly terrain separating southern Turkey from Syria. "It is our duty to go to the great *Bilad Al Shams* [Syria] and defend it against the Alawite tyrants massacring its people," said Shamar, 22, a lightly bearded engineering major, who spoke to Reuters in Reyhanli, a Turkish town whose Arab inhabitants have historic links with Syria. He and his friend are part of a small but growing influx of militant Arab Islamists determined to join the eighteen-month-old rebellion against President Bashar Assad. Their presence will alarm those in the West who have warned against al-Qa'ida style militancy in Syria, whose conflict has the potential to spread sectarian strife far beyond its borders. Ben Shamar and his Libyan friend Salloum say they are following the footsteps of their ancestors who fought in legions sent by the Prophet Muhammad at the dawn of Islam to liberate Greater Syria from those they regarded as Byzantine heathens. Syria's twenty-first-century heathens, they say, are Assad and his cohorts in the ruling elite from the minority Alawite sect, a remote offshoot of Shi'ite Islam, no longer considered Muslim by the Sunnites, that has dominated the power structure of Syria for the last five decades.

Sunni militants, such as the foreign fighters now making their way to Syria, cultivate hatred for Assad's Alawites, whom they regard as infidels, as well as for Shi'ite Iran, which backs the Syrian leader. "Syria's Muslim population has finally risen, after Assad and the Alawites pillaged Syria with the support of Iran and Hizbullah. Muslims everywhere cannot stand aside and do nothing to help the revolt," Shamar said. The two young middle-class Arab youths, who first met in the British town of Brighton several years ago while attending a language course, arrived in Turkey in July 2012. They sensed a landmark change in the course of the revolt after the assassination of four of Assad's top lieutenants in Damascus on July 18, an event that encouraged bolder rebel attacks in Damascus and Aleppo, the country's commercial hub.

In the last few months, a steady flow of Arab men, including Libyans, Kuwaitis, Saudis as well as Muslims from Britain, Belgium and the

United States, have joined Free Syrian Army forces, several rebel commanders in the northwest of Syria said. They are forming what opposition sources describe as an accelerated, but still small, inflow of foreign fighters into the country. They include young Syrians who were born in the West and whose families fled persecution under Assad's rule. Most have headed to the province of Hama, in central Syria, where a few jihadists, or Muslim religious fighters, with experience in Afghanistan, have been giving them rudimentary training in handling assault rifles and guerrilla warfare.

Hundreds of foreign jihadists, opposition sources say, now operate in the city of Hama, a major center of the anti-Assad rebellion and a veteran of the previous anti-Hafez Assad uprising in 1982 which had cost, just like now, over twenty thousand dead. Some have gone to fight in Damascus, but their numbers are too small to alter the balance of power overwhelmingly against Assad's forces, rebel sources said. Several reported massacres of Sunni villagers and the bombardment of mosques are fuelling hatred of the Alawites that has prompted some Sunni scholars to start preaching in support of jihad, or holy struggle, in Syria. A Western diplomat following the movement of foreign fighters to Syria likened them to the European idealists who headed to Spain in 1936 to help fight against General Francisco Franco, but were ultimately no match for the dictator's forces. Salloum said he fought with Libyan rebels in the battle of Zawiya, near Tripoli, before the fall of Muammar Qaddafi a year earlier. He declined to disclose where he was going in Syria, but said it was his religious duty to help Syrians in need. "Our Syrian brothers need any help they can get, because unlike in Libya, the international community has abandoned them. "They welcome us and are eagerly waiting for us. We want to tell them: "you are not alone in this fight to liberate this land from the tyranny of the minority," said Salloum, 24, who claimed he had dropped out of Libya's Tripoli University, where he was studying chemistry. Salloum, who planned to join a unit called the *Ahrar Al Sham* (Syria Freedom Fighters) brigades, said participating in jihad was one of his highest aspirations as a Muslim. Rebel sources said most of the foreign fighters had joined this unit, including Mohammad Salem Al Harbi, a young Saudi cleric who is believed to have been killed in the battles in July, and had triumphantly cried out: "Victory comes from Allah!"

The helpless international and inter-Arab forums, which have now been preoccupied by the new eruption of anti-Western hatred triggered (but not caused) by that silly film against the Prophet, which should have been dismissed and not given so much attention in the first place, have apparently raised their hands in despair from the Syrian situation, and once again left it to individual and organized jihadis to deliver the coup de grâce to Assad. The UN, following the withdrawal of Kofi Anan, and the Arab League and UN observers' failure to produce a cease-fire, has appointed a new mediator, veteran official Lakhdar Ibrahimi, to try his land. But after a meeting with Assad he declared that he could not see a way to resolve the conflict which posed a threat to the entire area and the world, in view of the many and various Arab, Muslim and international actors meddling in it. The choice of Ibrahimi, as of Anan, made by a secretary general who himself grew up in a background of authoritarian regimes, are not perhaps the best choices, because if they wish to democratize the system and to replace the tyrannical rule of Assad, they need someone who was nourished on a democratic tradition: a Swede, a Briton or a Dutch. Failing that, any mediator has to understand, that unlike homogeneous Tunisia and Egypt, where the departure of the ruler constituted the beginning of a solution, in Syria the removal of the dictator would only signal the beginning of a long and bloody civil war.

Libya

In September 1969 a junior anonymous officer in the Libyan army, Mu'ammar Qaddafi, took over by a coup that dismissed the Sanusi king, the ruler of Libya. His own dictatorship lasted forty-two years, until that proud and unbalanced tyrant was killed in the battles of the Spring in 2011 on the Libyan coast. He had led his country via a series of delusions, envisaging a "republic of the masses" (*jamahiriyya*) led by "popular committees," never seen before, except during the "killing fields experience" under another mad leadership of Pol Pot in Campuchea. Qaddafi also pretended to be a political thinker, who put together his childish "green revolution" booklet, which he peddled as a parallel of Mao's Red Book, that was then in great vogue during the Chinese Cultural Revolution (1966–76), though he himself had nothing of the stature of Mao Zedong. His ideas of a Green revolution were more connected to the Islamic green than to the environmental one, and he used his gigantic income from his oil resources to buy weapons from European manufacturers who competed between themselves for the honors they accorded him and for meeting all his eccentric demands, including erecting and lodging in his show-case luxurious tents in the heart of European capitals.

Qaddafi's eccentricity, including his long, tiring and boring addresses to the UN General Assembly, in which he distinguished himself more as a clown than a statesman, he made outrageous remarks against the West and Israel, supported revolutionaries like the Palestinians against Israel, and the IRA against Britain, and also encouraged and financed international terrorism, though he also undertook a gigantic irrigation project to develop desert areas of his vast and sparsely populated arid country. The peak of his mischief was attained when his intelligence apparatus blew up a Pan Am airliner over Lockerbie, Scotland, killing all its 240 unsuspecting innocent passengers. During the 42 years of his tyrannical rule, during which he aged but never wised up, he prepared his sons for the succession of his rule, and finally yielded to American pressure, via boycott and economic restrictions, to abandon his nuclear program that he had bought from the Pakistanis. He even was talked into surrendering to Britain the mastermind of the Lockerbie horror, apparently after he concluded a secret deal with London that the man, who was dying from terminal cancer, would be released shortly thereafter for humanitarian reasons, a strange and ironic pretext for a human beast who had no compunction to blow out of existence 240 innocent civilian passengers.

But exactly as his relations and fences with the West were being mended and he was being accepted once again as the permanent ruler of Libya, who deserved a forgiving smile for his strange conduct, the Spring broke out in neighboring Tunisia to the West, the eve of Christmas 2010, and then in his other neighbor to the East, Egypt, soon after New Year, 2011. Possessing no strong army or police, he had no means to quell the unrest when it erupted at home, because he could never imagine that his popularity would ever be questioned or that his "popular committees" would ever mount a revolt against his leadership. One wonders what he did with the huge stockpiles of weapons he bought from the West, in addition to shipping some of them to revolutionaries from the Moro Muslims in Mindanao, the Philippines, to Palestinians in Jordan and then Lebanon, to IRA Catholics in Northern Ireland. The partition of that vast country between two polar groups of rival tribes: Cyrenaica in the East centered around Benghazi, and Tripolitania in the West focused on the Capital Tripoli, did not help the integration of the country into one nation-state either, and the eruption of unrest and violence did not find stupefied Qaddafi, by the intensity of the hostility to him, and by the widespread extent of the rebellion, prepared to respond effectively to extinguish the fire, except for some temperamental and pathetic explosions of public rage and pitiful disarray. The fighting soon seeped into the coastal cities and the oil fields, generating the intervention of NATO air forces, until Tripoli the capital fell to the rebels, and Qaddaifi himself was killed in a humiliating fashion during one of the battles, when he was found hiding under a bridge and he was assaulted by rebels who did not particularly sympathize with him.

Following many tribal differences and a huge diversity of political opinions in a country that had never seen a democratic exchange of ideas in a peaceful and amenable atmosphere, and a long period of chaos, insecurity and uncertainty, seemingly democratic elections were held in July 2012, which aroused many hopes in the West regarding the "victory of democratic and liberal forces," in a country that had never known any of those, naively believing that any of those lofty ideas can emerge without a long-term education, organization and preparation. These beliefs and hopes were held especially in the West, to justify, *post factum*, NATO intervention in the conflict, and prove to its own constituencies that it was not in vain. Is was also hoped and believed that such a new democratic wave would necessarily overcome Islamic tendencies that are so much more deeply rooted in the tradition of the country, that even lunatic Qaddafi had been constrained to respect. However, too early as it may be to speak about the realization of these dreams before the dust settles, their very discussion is revolutionary and immensely innovative, inasmuch as they were taboo and anathema during the long years of tyranny that had reigned in the country.

In the elections of July 7, 2012, candidates representing the Brothers, or other independent tendencies, did not do very well, leading certain Western observers to conclude that "democracy" has come on top. However, it is too early to judge, because there, the Western dichotomies of religious versus secular, or conservative versus liberal, do not apply, in their Western sense, in view of the fact that if we look at the platforms of the various parties which ran to the elections, none of which has had any previous experience of that sort, none of them responds exactly to these characteristics as we understand them. Take for example the Alliance of National Forces, headed by Ahmed Jibril, the temporary prime minister, which encompassed many diverse elements but assembled essentially under the banner of removing Qaddafi from power, and then on applying democracy that no one of them really understood, did not mean it would be able to produce a ruling coalition. Unlike Tunisia and Egypt, where the predominant and well-organized Muslim Brothers were able to immediately come forward with plans of governance, even if not exactly pleasing to Western tastes, it seems that in Libya the largest political organization (one dares not call it *party* as yet), has a long way to go in internal parleys and agreed compromises, in order to tackle the difficult issues that the long months of fighting, death, destruction and chaos have impacted on the country, society and the economy, not to speak on the much longer decades of the stifling tyranny of Qaddafi. There too, like in Egypt, an effort will be made to create a consensus around a new constitution, as if it were the most important issue, though it is known that previous versions of many constitutions were not worth the paper they were written on, and it was solely the incumbent tyrant who made the great decisions that counted.

Another major issue that will have to be tackled urgently, which afflicts other countries of the Spring as well, like Syria, Lebanon, Iraq, Somalia, Afghanistan, Yemen, and the Palestinians, is the self reckoning by any new prospective rule, that "one gun," that is one sole armed force under one government should be enforced, lest the country be afflicted by armed private militias which make governability impossible, as the example of those countries demonstrates, which protect tribalism against the prevalence of central governments. Even in countries which ban unauthorized weapons, like Syria and Libya, the long months of uprising and civil war, where weapons were traded domestically or shipped from the outside to help topple the rule, generated enough widespread distribution of weapons as to cause uncontrollable disorder and a real threat to the rule. The problem with such a tribal society as Libya, as in other Arab and Islamic societies, are the suspicions, fears and hatreds between their components, which lead the different groups to arm themselves for self-defense, as happens among the Kurds of Turkey, Iran, Syria, and Iraq; among the Druze in Syria and Lebanon; Hizbullah in Lebanon, the Shi'ites in Yemen, and Hamas among the Palestinians in Gaza. Any attempt to collect those illegal weapons will necessarily be met with armed resistance, because the concerned parties find it difficult to trust other groups which in the past had massacred them. Thus, like Hizbullah in Lebanon, Hamas in Gaza, the Kurds in Iraq, the Taliban in Afghanistan and Pakistan, al-Qa'ida in Yemen, the Shabiba in Somalia, and the new rebels in Mali, they refuse to submit their arms, and even often go out to fight for their own survival. In Libya, like in other places, the collection of arms is the key to putting an end to the fighting between the tribes in the vast uncontrolled deserts of the country, and to the infiltration through the thousands of kms-long borders between Libya and its neighbors: Egypt in the east, Tunisia and Algeria in the West, and the rest of Saharan and sub-Saharan countries (Sudan, Chad, Niger, Mali) in the south, where the Spring has already begun to brew on the fringes.

Many experts who are familiar with Libya have questioned the surprising results of the first elections in Libya, at a time when they expected that like in Tunisia and Egypt, the Brotherhood was poised to seize the rule as a result of the Spring, due to the overarching legitimacy under which only Islam could unite the tribal divisions. According to Jawad Tamimi, a scholar from Oxford University, who was himself convinced of the Islamic victory in the elections, the results are due to the fact that the success of the Brothers in Egypt was understood in provincial and suspicious Libya from two generations of Qaddafi rule and self-isolation, as alien and given to foreign influences, especially of Qatar, whose alliance with the Brothers we have discussed above. Therefore, he believes that since the Brothers in Libya, like in Tunisia and Egypt, Yemen, and Syria, understood belatedly the opportunities that the rebellion opened for them, they were late in joining the bandwagon, which they did only when the rulers in place seemed to stumble, thus pushing themselves as alternative rule, something they did not envisage at the very outset of the rebellion. But in the meantime, new leaderships had arisen which took command of the revolt, and it is not easy now to remove them and replace them by the free riders who sacrificed little and were now ready to reap the fruits. It remains to be seen whether the victorious "Alliance," which assembles together in Tripoli the representatives of the main participants in the uprising, will be able to surmount the intertribal rivalries and the interregional competitions when time comes to divide the spoils of power among them all.

The new two-hundred-member legislative Council, which was elected for the first time in Libyan history, in what seems a free and democratic process, does not guarantee, of course, that an iron-clad precedent and permanent pattern was set for the future election of legitimate government, for a smooth transition of power to the winners of the election, or for the free and legitimate activity of opposition, instead of being arrested as was the practice to date. One hundred twenty of the delegates represent tribes, cities, and townships, that is, local interests, as expected in a tribal regime, while the remaining eighty were elected by national lists of political parties. The surprising results, compared to the expected victory of the Islamic party, stem from the popularity of Abdul Hakim Belhaj at the head of the jihadist movement since Qaddafi was removed, and the general estimate that he would ride that wave of success as had happened in Tunisia and Egypt. However, what is now described as "democratization of Libya" will not depend on those elected delegates seating in Tripoli, but on the suspicious desert dwellers, who had become accustomed to alienation from remote Qaddafi, and regard their local tribal framework as their shelter from oppression of the central government. What has changed is not the tribal identity of the desert population, but the identity of the perceived oppression of the central authorities. Therefore, great doubt exists whether the representatives gathered in Tripoli to speak for their constituencies, are capable of creating the requisite trust, and the necessary novel pattern of free government, which had never been experienced before, as well as the new ways of communication between the new authorities and the villages and tribes of this vast country, in order for this democracy to operate effectively.

A democratic system is not a one-time declaration, and not only an intention to treat the people fairly, equally and justly, but an organic state of mind which must grow naturally into the public over many years of education and practice, and would take many more years to maintain and reinforce. It would be too simplistic and naive to assume, that a society where violence was rife and the number of illegal weapons double the figure of the population, in a situation of illegitimacy and injustice throughout the vast country, with the *lex talionis* still prevalent, that a democratic society could develop instantly, like a deus ex-machina, only because one-time supposedly free elections were held, immune to reversal as they may be. Democracy takes time and an adequate social milieu, and a spiritual and educational ambience to grow and develop into. Libya is hardly in the beginning of that process.

One has to assume that those who helped to organize the first elections, like foreign advisers, have also learned some lessons from the process. For example, that the Tunisian victory, in comparison to tabula rasa Libya, of al-Nahda, had involved a veteran party which had operated clandestinely during the Ben-Ali rule with its exiled head, Rashid Ghanouchi, who acted in secrecy among his constituency, and only when the despot was toppled, he returned to Tunisia, ran an ideological party for elections, deeply committed to a Muslim Brother- affiliated movement. In Egypt too, the Brothers were banned from activity during the Mubarak era, and they were compelled to run as independents, which compelled them to act socially among their constituents along the tradition established by Hassan al-Banna the founder and great master. Even though their greatest guides, like Sayyid Qutb who was executed by Nasser, sheikh abdul Rahman who was persecuted and ran away to the United States, or Sheikh Qaradawi, who exiled himself to Qatar to escape Mubarak's persecution, had to act underground until Mubarak was toppled, but when he was removed, they were ready to advance their candidates for parliament and for the presidency, and made palliating statements to assure that they had no intention to take over the rule of the country. And when Qaradawi was allowed to return to the Tahrir Square, he could gather a million followers who raveled in his address to the enthusiastic public. The elections were won by the Brothers in this sort of victorious atmosphere, where they won 45 percent of the vote while another 30 percent was won by their Salafi allies. For the presidency, the Brothers were determined enough to advance their candidates after others were disqualified, until Mursi was elected, by the huge support of his followers, who were ready to erupt in mayhem had they been deprived from their triumph. It was their sense of organization and their firm ideological commitment to run and win any free competition, by reason of the thorough work they had invested in society, which in due course rewarded them for their consistent effort in the times of Mubarak's regime.

All these preparatory features that made the takeover by the Brothers possible in Egypt and Tunisia had no trace in Libya which, due to Qaddafi's absolute rule, did not allow any extragovernmental and antiestablishment organization to exist and then take the relief when time came. Moreover, even during the rebellion, no unified leadership emerged that could take matters into its own hand when the rebellion succeeded and Qaddafi was removed. From the outset, it was tribal and local or regional groups which entered the fray, for want of national leadership that could unite them all under its umbrella, something that could not have grown under the Qaddafi regime had it appeared during his rule. Therefore, the leadership which grew from the beginning of the upsurge understood that it could not launch elections, when the time came, based on competing ideological parties (for example religious versus civil, or conservative versus liberal, or right versus left) which did not exist in any case, but had to rely on existing tribal and local or regional groups, in spite of the deep divisions and the competition and tensions between them. For this reason, the first elections were planned to rely only for 40 percent of the seats on the new ideological parties which were hurriedly organized for the occasion, like in Iraq and Afghanistan which faced similar situations, where they had no roots in local tradition, while 60 percent of the seats, namely 120 out of 200, were allotted to tribal and local representatives who stood for clearly local or regional interests. Thus, if and when democracy is to be installed in post-Spring Libya as a permanent solution, it will have by necessity a different character, and it is doubtful whether it will be able, by the composition of its institutions, to enforce the all-national theme which today seems to guide the leadership of the country. A few years will be needed, with trial and error, theory and practice, experiment and amendment, enforcement and reform, to reach a model of government that suits Libya's conditions. For now, the new leadership, who had no experience in operating a democratic system, and no government experience at all for that matter, must side by side with its democratization dreams, even supposing they are sincere and aiming for change, take into account the real forces on the ground, whose representatives are supposed to reflect their wills and ambitions in the parliament in Tripoli as "independents," a term that in itself does not hold high promise for the success of democratization and effective central government in the new era. Thus, the new Islamic parties, like all the other ideological parties, who for the first time are facing new experiences of rule, have received a more limited and shrunken representation in parliament that they had hoped or expected. Only when the new parliament convenes and the new regime starts working, will the new array of forces make itself clear, with the "independents" joining new political blocs or forming their own, and then, it might dawn on us that the "liberals" did not necessarily win the majority in conjunction with the tribal representatives, whose political orientations have not yet been crystallized.

Only when the dust settles, and the new elected parliament will discuss the new constitution, appointing the new foundational commission that is to write it and agree on it, will the negotiations begin on the division of labor and powers between the various elements, which under Qaddafi were all concentrated in his hands. The question will also stand whether it will be a president or a prime minister, that are elected by the people or appointed by parliament, would head the governmental pyramid, what is the role of the judiciary and the status of the military. Turkish Erdogan, who had gone to Egypt during the Spring to give advice regarding the neutralization of the army from political affairs, as he had done in Turkey, has certainly reinforced the new Libyan leadership, which did not like the lingering

199

role that the Egyptian Military Council had ascribed to itself for more than a year after the revolution, including curtailing the authority of the elected president to command the army and to declare war, until it was removed by President Mursi. General Tantawi had also taken the liberty to disperse the parliament, though with the backing of the Constitutional Court, and on the other hand he dragged his feet on the drafting of the new constitution. In Libya, these struggles are still to come and the decision will be debated in a parliament where the tribal representation is strong, though not dominant for now. The new rapport of forces will have also to determine the source of legislation: will it rely on Shari'a alone, or with a mixture of civil law? In Qaddafi's Libya a high lip service was paid to Islam, with the son of the ruler and heir-apparent, Saif-al-Islam (the Sword of Islam, which sounded threatening). But despite the ascetic-for-show style of life of the leader, he allowed outrageous extravaganzas around him that ulema would not have approved of. At the same time, he did not allow any political or religious organization as long as he was in power. With him gone, and in view of the declarations of human and civil rights by the new regime, it is natural for new organizations and groupings to emerge, political, religious, social and ideological, with among them also a demand to base the new constitution on Islam. That sort of intention has already been declared by some new leaders, and it will certainly find resonance in Libyan politics in years to come.

The massive participation in the elections in Libya (62 percent), as in Iraq, Tunisia and Egypt due to a first experience, after being deprived of free elections for generations, and their rush to experience the thrilling novelty of participatory democracy, demonstrates a very high inter-est in the process of democratization that the Spring countries have been tasting and testing for a first time in their lives. It is evident that the citizenry which has had enough of killings, chaos and anarchy, which have paralyzed its life for the long months of unrest, wishes to put an end to them. Every one of the 58 parties which took part in the elections in Libya as partners in the "National Alliance," headed by Mahmud Jibril, understands that it will not necessarily bend in the long haul to one unified political platform, once the common goal of removing Qaddafi was achieved. So, based on the assumption that they do not all subscribe to the heading of "liberals" that well-intended foreign media assigned to them, rifts and differences, jealousies and debates, will emerge sooner or later that will differentiate between the various components of this alliance. Muslim fundamentalists, who have achieved less that their Egyptian neighbors, due to the structural and historical differences between the two, have learned from their Egyptian mentors to call their party Justice and Construction, whose many members have voted for the local tribal parties. The more radical party of Belhaj, which dubbed itself al-Watan (the Homeland), who had personally headed one of the armed groups of Algerian inspiration during the rebellion, has coalesced with another Muslim group for the elections. In the final analysis, the two groups might find in the new parliament enough tribal allies to make their mark on national political and social affairs. The National Congress, as the new parliament has dubbed itself, will have to determine a procedure to choose the sixty members of the Foundational Council that is to write the constitution, on a regional base, like the American Senate, not on the base of numbers of voters in each region.

Three areas are to send their representatives: Tripolitania in the West, Cyrenaica in the East and the Fezzan in the Saharan south, twenty seats for each. The new Congress is also supposed to vote confidence in the new temporary government that will manage the affairs of the state until the general elections of 2013, to give the various forces time to organize. This time table will be valid, of course, only if these rosy predictions do take place and run their course. But in the meantime, the events in Benghazi on the eleventh anniversary of September 11, when the American ambassador and some of his colleagues were murdered under the assault of radical Muslim groups, who used the flimsy pretext of the movie *The Innocence of Muslims*, produced by a Coptic émigré in the United States and insulting the Prophet Muhammed, may have shuffled the cards. For, this assault, which triggered a worldwide fury against the West throughout the Islamic world, from Casablanca to Jakarta and from Pakistan to Nigeria, including a direct onslaught on the American Embassy in Cairo, has demonstrated, first of all, that the transitory government of Libya is far from controlling the security of the country, and that radical Muslim groups are still capable of sowing terror, fear, disorder and uncertainty throughout the land. This vicious attack may also signal that the real battle for the fate of Libya and the soul of the Libyans will not be decided only in the ballots of Tripoli and the other urban centers, but no less by the bullets of the medley of local and tribal forces which are not about to submit to any central authority.

Zvi Mazel, a former Israeli Ambassador to Cairo and a noted commentator in the Israeli media, wrote a remarkable piece in the *Jerusalem Post* of September 16 analyzing the new situation. He emphasized that

201

the war on Islamic terror that was declared by President Bush in 2011, is still going on by President Obama who is approaching the end of his first term of office. He remarked that:

> while operations continued on the ground, an ideological sea change was taking place in the White House. Obama appeared determined to woo Arab and Islamic nations—witness his Ankara and Cairo speeches. He went as far as to distort American history to praise what he called the contribution of Islam to the development and progress of the United States—and went a step further when he asserted that there was no Islamic terrorism and that the United States was fighting "criminals" of an unspecified nature. US Army manuals no longer mentioned Islamic terrorism; neither did those of the CIA and other security organizations. This at a time when terrorists and terrorist organizations were proclaiming daily that they were working in the name of Islam and that their objective was to topple democracy, their principal enemy. Now, isn't America the standard bearer of democracy today? Which begs the question: How can you fight a determined and fanatic enemy such as Islamic terrorism while ignoring its nature and its aims? On the one hand, fighting "anonymous" terrorists in Arab and Islamic countries, on the other, making an all out effort to appease the proponents of the very Islamic ideology which gave birth to this murderous terrorism.[5]

What made the Benghazi drama all the more poignant and American reaction pathetic, was the incredibly naive and apologetic stance of Secretary of State Clinton, who instead of protecting freedom of expression in the West and throwing the blame on the Muslim violent rioters, she followed in the footsteps of her president and adopted a *dhimmi* attitude, which a priori accepts the volatility and whims of Muslims instead of taking them to task, in response to which the terrorists smile under their moustaches and promise to hit harder. Obama and Clinton had apparently believed that through dialogue with the Muslim Brothers, their support of the move to topple Hosni Mubarak, and NATO's contribution to the downfall of Muammar Qaddafi, they were protecting America against terrorist attacks. Hence Hillary's supplication to the media: "how could they do that to us? We have helped them in their revolutions," and she admitted that she could not understand that kind of behavior. Another politician who followed blindly his leader, remarked nevertheless that he opened his eyes from time to time just to make sure that his leader had his eyes open. Had she done her homework better, or called to task her president instead of following him blindly, she would have understood that the attacks in Benghazi and Cairo did not come out of the blue. There had been warnings. On September 10, the Egyptian daily *Al-Fajr* published a communiqué signed by several jihadist organizations such as the Egyptian Islamic Jihad, Gamaa Islamiya, and others, announcing that they were going to set fire to the American Embassy in Cairo and to capture whoever remained alive, if the United States did not release all the jihadists jailed in Guantanamo as well as the blind Sheikh Abdel Rahman, spiritual leader of the *Gama'a Islamiya* and the man who gave his blessing to the Anwar Sadat assassination in 1981 as well as to the first attack on the Twin Towers in 1993, who is serving a life sentence in the States. If that information appeared in the press, the intelligence services of Egypt and of the United States must have known more details.

That is not all. On the morning of September 11, claims Mazel, further communiqués received by public institutions indicated that after 5 p.m. that day there would be a demonstration against the American Embassy to protest against that hitherto unknown film insulting the prophet. Yet even this new communiqué did not bring about a tightening of security round the place. In any case, Obama could have called President Mursy to ask for added protection, and Mursy could have done that of his own initiative, knowing the sensitivity of the matter. Then, when the demonstration started, security forces did not put much of a fight and let protesters scale the walls and take down the Stars and Stripes, which they defiled and burned (together with the Israeli flag) and in its stead raised the Salafis' black flag. It was not so long before, that the young Egyptian who had done the same to the flag of Israel during the infamous assault on the Israeli Embassy (on September 9, 2011) had been made into a hero and covered with praise by Egyptian media and his fellow Egyptians. But Benghazi was worse. The consulate burned to the ground and four Americans were murdered, among them the Ambassador, a dedicated friend of the Libyan people, who was visiting Libya's second city. It since became clear that this had been a well-prepared attack not necessarily connected to the film. Heavy weapons, including rocket-propelled grenades, were used. It is difficult to believe that Libyan authorities and their informants—and American intelligence services, were unaware of what was going on.

In fact, the Libyan vice minister of the interior, when reporting on the attack and the murder of the Ambassador, blamed the Americans, somewhat disingenuously, for not having taken the necessary steps to protect the building and to provide for an escape route. The American Embassy in Cairo, which knew of the planned demonstration, hastened to condemn "those who had made the film which was the apparent reason for that demonstration." Obama too berated the filmmakers at length, after condemning the murder of the Ambassador and swearing that he would cooperate with Libyan authorities to catch "the criminals." (Not a word about Islamic terrorism). But criminals commit crimes for gain of some sort, while terrorists on the contrary put their lives on the line in the process of fulfilling their ideological (Islamic this time) commitments. It seemed as if there were more condemnations by the White House for the film than for the attackers, though it is far from clear that it was the real reason behind the attack. Freedom of expression is enshrined in the American constitution, yet American leaders were apologizing to terrorists who had attacked them, as if they were acknowledging that America itself was guilty of the creation of the film! America's apologies did not help. The fire spread all over the Arab/Muslim world. American embassies, institutions and even shops were attacked in many countries. This was also a show of force by the Salafi and jihadist organizations to embarrass the new regimes of the Muslim Brothers which need more time to strike root, and indeed the security forces in Cairo, Benghazi and Tunis were slow to react.

It soon became clear, however, that the attacks in Cairo and Benghazi were part of a new wave of anti-American hatred. It very much looks like a worldwide pogrom intended to instill fear in the hearts of the infidels of the West and to tell them bluntly, "Don't mess with us." It is indeed a sad day for all those who believed that an Arab Spring would bring Arab nations closer to first steps toward democracy and progress. The opposite happened as it transpires that liberal and democratic values are still foreign to Islamic and Arab traditions. Instead, the Arab world is turning to religious dictatorships, under the Muslim Brothers and their other Muslim variants, while Islamic trends such as the Salafis are dragging it toward extremism and instability. What remains to be seen is how the West will react—and more importantly, what America will do. Obama said that Egypt was no longer America's ally, though also not an enemy—perhaps the beginning of a painful awakening, concluded Mazel. But to awaken from the torpor that Western leaders have fallen into when releasing the Lockerbie culprits, or when refusing to call a spade a spade by dubbing Islamic terrorism by name, it will not help them if they sink deeper in the mental *dhimmitude* where they are today and dare, on the contrary, to rise jointly against the terrorizing atmosphere that has been imposed on them by the Islamic world, the hopeful signs of the Spring notwithstanding.

There were particularly noticeable reactions in Africa to Qaddafi's fall, since in his lifetime he was treated alternately there as an iconic hero, who spent aid money to help his neighbors and restore the pride of Africans by occasionally defying the West, or as an erratic lunatic who could not be counted on. African countries accordingly mourned or celebrated his passing away. It has become an accepted norm in Africa that the longer the leader stays in power the more he tends to personalize his rule in his country (see Mugabe, for example), thus the long rule of Qaddafi has eroded the institutional basis of the state. African countries, just like Libya, are marked by growing internal/tribal divisions, and bear little ressemblance to more homogeneous Egypt and Tunisia, which are also in Africa. Hence the more direct grievance caused to Africa by Qaddafi's fall than by Mubarak's or Ben Ali's disappearance. Moreover, Qaddafi's removal has brought a new equation to the forefront, namely the connection between the internal opposition and external governments, for even those who mourn Qaddafi's departure while they cheered Mubarak's and Ben-Ali's removal, emphasize that the change in Tripoli would have been unlikely without foreign intervention. This preoccupies many African leaders lest intervention by outside powers in the continent become more likely, especially by the new challengers like China, whose role in Africa has increased dramatically, as in Sudan, Zimbabwe, Ethiopia, Kenya and Nigeria. That role has been primarily economic for now, in the domains of building infrastructure, while India has been developing a policy of supporting its own big corporations there. The Libyan precedent preoccupies them all, especially in view of the crisis in Mali which will be tackled below.

Yemen

Yemen is perhaps the most unfortunate and miserable Spring country. Its location in the Arabian Peninsula, its proximity to Saudi Arabia, and its position on the strategic straits which lead from the Indian Ocean and the Arabian Sea in the East to the Red Sea in the West, facing Somalia and Djibouti on the Horn of Africa, and dominating the vital Bab al-Mandab and the Socotra island, turn it into a coveted base both by the Powers on the one hand, and their nemesis—al-Qa'ida and other Muslim terrorists and jihad fighters—on the other. Yemen has been the only country in the Peninsula so far which has altered its monarchic system into a republican one. That is perhaps the reason that it has been the only one that was deeply hit by the Spring so far. Her change of political system, which was effected half a century ago, did not produce, however, any liberalization, an argument used by the monarchies in the Gulf to claim that toppling the monarchies does not necessarily produce democracies. In fact one may claim with some merit that some of those monarchies, like Qatar, Bahrain and Oman, are in fact more benevolent than the Yemenite tribal autocracy, on the one hand, and on the other hand the autocratic republics of Iraq, Syria, Libya and the rest did not bring salvation to their peoples either.

After half a century of various experiments in all these regimes, the Spring appears as a new promise. But in Yemen, which has been plagued by dictatorship, poverty, backwardness, tribalism and religious division, the prolonged conflicts between the various components of the country, like for instance the Sunnite majority with the Zaidi (a branch of the Shi'a) Houtis, the entrenchment in place of various radical groups and fundamentalist Muslim leaders, and the direct involvement of local and regional powers in the affairs of the state, like Saudi Arabia and Egypt, opposing each other in the 1960s, and Iran currently, tear the country apart. Moreover, al-Qa'ida, which has been seeking strategic but remote areas to shelter itself since its expulsion from Afghanistan by the Americans, in order to hit its enemies but escape retaliation, has been seeking new bases all the time, like East Africa where it previously blew up the American embassies in Nairobi and Dar al Salam, and now in Sinai where it has constituted a terrorist threat for both Israelis and Egyptians. We recall that in 2000, al-Qa'ida in Yemen caused a heavy damage to the American Warship *Cole* in Aden seaport and caused it high casualties and great damage. Aden was the capital of South Yemen, which had received its independence from Britain in 1967, and united in 1990 with the north based on its capital San'a, which had become independent from the Ottomans in 1918, under the aegis of dictator Abdallah Ali Saleh who was supported, like Mubarak, by the United States and Saudi Arabia until removed by the Spring.

The eruption of the Spring in Tunisia and then in Egypt, did not have to wait too long before it appeared in San'a too, and then in the rest of Yemen, where the most pressing demand was the removal of the three-decade dictator, who had also started grooming his son for the job after him. But the other most immediate themes of the demonstrations were the elimination of corruption and unemployment in the face of the increasing population, the shrinking economy, and the decreasing supply of water after the long years of drought and the poor development of alternative water sources. There were also talks of a new constitution, as though new words would change any reality. In the outset, Saleh tried to quell the uprising by force as has been his and other dictators' wont, but after he was bombed and wounded within his own presidential palace, he was compelled to resign, after more than three decades of rule, and his vice president al-Hadi took up the post in February 2012. The recurrent pattern was there also, of a pledge of a new constitution, new elections and a provisional government to prepare and supervise them in 2014, new presidential elections, and the completion of the new constitution. As in other places, the transition period will be the most problematic, because one cannot predict what parts of, and for how long would the old elements of the revolved Saleh regime hold on, nor by whom, how and when they would be removed, as Mursi has courageously and firmly done in Egypt. It is also hard to predict who among them will continue to influence the new regime from the outside, nor what would be entered into the new constitution.

An impression has been created in all these places where the Spring has raged, that the main rage has been channeled to the old regimes who are required to depart, as if it were a personal, not a systemic or structural shortcoming that the demonstrators wished to mend. Thus have departed Mubarak, Ben Ai, Saleh, to be followed by Assad, while not much had changed there until the advent of Mursi in Egypt. In Yemen too, due to the old structures of the tribal society, much time will elapse before a generally accepted rule rises in San'a. In the meantime, a Shi'ite Houti uprising, supported by Iran, has been raging in the north, with Saudi Arabia doing its best to aid Yemenites in quelling it lest it spreads to its territory. Into these widening cracks, al-Qa'ida who has specialized in subversion, and maintains its Arabian branch in the country (AQAP) has no difficulty to penetrate, after it had decentralized into separate regional commands in North Africa, sub-Saharan Africa, Europe, America and Asia following the American invasion of Afghanistan in 2001. But it is also true that even in its Yemenite hideouts, the American long arm, with its drones and secret operations, reaches it and is able to eliminate its chief operatives, like Yemenite-American Sheikh al- Awlaki.

Saudi Arabia, the most susceptible to be impacted by the Spring in neighboring Yemen, has been cultivating its direct links with the various tribal groupings there, over the head of the official government, inter alia by providing employment to thousands of impoverished Yemenites to its south. Already in 1989, Yemen had established, together with Iraq, Jordan and Egypt the Arab Council for Cooperation (ACC), which was to counter the Saudi-led Gulf Cooperation Council (GCC), in order to speed up economic exchange between the member countries; but the days were still Saddam's days, when he still licked his wounds from the eight-year devastating war with Iran (1980–8), and this new flimsy organization, like so many unions in the Arab world that had come and gone, was geared to help him maintain the Arab front which had supported him for the duration of the war, and was dismantled as soon as he invaded Kuwait in 1990. But one has to recall that due to Aden's independence in 1967, and the creation in its territory of the Popular Democratic Republic of South Yemen, it became a client of the Soviet Union in the height of the Cold War, something which triggered tensions and clashes with neighboring Saudi Arabia; supported the rebels of Dhufar against the sultan of Oman; and even voted in the UN and the Arab League against admitting in both the new Gulf monarchies that had just been released from British rule. Only when South Yemen united with the North in 1990, which happened with the collapse of the Soviet Union, did there occur a sea change in the alienation of that region from the rest of the Arabs and the West.

But Ali Abdallah Saleh, who ruled united Yemen, had become an ally of Saddam Hussein, and was alone in supporting Iraq's invasion to Kuwait in 1990, which provoked the cooling of his relations with the West, and generated a reduction of their aid programs to him, and even caused the expulsion of one million Yemenites (and Palestinians, for the same reason) workers from Saudi Arabia and the Gulf states, which were the providers of much of both economies. The deterioration of the relationship was so bad, that Saudi Arabia began erecting a real wall to prevent the penetration of Yemenite people and goods to her territory. Even after liberating Kuwait by the Americans, Saleh persisted in his close relations with Saddam, which blocked him from returning to the Arab mainstream. Only from 1994 on, did Saleh's efforts to return to the rich Arab countries' lap reap fruit, and his border with the Saudis was recognized and marked. This process of repentance, that is characteristic of inter-Arab relations which keep shifting here and there like desert sands, according to changing whims or needs or necessity, reached its climax in Summer 2000, when San'a and Riyad signed a border agreement, which finally settled the half-century old disagreements between them.

One of the major problems in this chaotic and ungovernable country, has been the kidnapping of foreign tourists by tribal groups who make a living on levied ransom, as they probably learned from their neighbors in Somalia who do the same with maritime piracy. In June 2009, for example, nine foreign nationals were kidnapped near the town of Sa'da, seven of whom were killed and only two rescued. Due to the proximity in religion, customs, and commercial relations, the two countries have developed much cooperation in their illicit occupation. The Somalis, who brought many Somali refugees to impoverished Yemen, and have reluctantly elected to find some sort of shelter there rather than to go overland to neighboring Ethiopia or Eritrea where the situation is even hungrier and worse. In 2007, there were already one hundred thousand Somali refugees in Yemen, in addition to the more than seven hundred thousand Somalis who reside there permanently, and many of them married local Yemenites, something which has complicated even further the tribal system reigning there, through deteriorating impoverishment and involvement in international terrorism.

The domestic war among the various Yemenite forces, who find it impossible to control a vast area larger than France, but not nearly as developed, which has been going on between Sunnites and Shi'ites since 2004, has seeped also into Saudi territory and dragged in its wake not only Saudi Arabia, but also Iran, Jordan and Egypt. Thousands of civilians who are caught in the crossfire flee, while the others are equipped, as in other tribal countries, with millions of illegal weapons, more than even in Libya, and suffer from the same tribal syndrome of the need to defend themselves, in a country where security, national and personal, leaves much to be desired. No wonder then that in this situation, individuals, families and clans wish to seek survival on its most elemental level, even if we leave apart the national and philosophical level of public debates, as is done in Egypt, on the nature of the regime, the state relations with religion, military and civilian rule, the state budget, the people's needs and the like. The unrest and frequent uprisings in South Yemen, in the mountains and deserts which surround Aden, where the Americans show interest in holding on to their naval base, add additional significance and urgency to the general will for change which has been manifested with the Spring elsewhere. The current American antiterrorist activity too, especially through their deadly drones, and sometimes via their cruise missiles, against positions and individuals involved in international terrorism, especially in the San'a and Abyan areas, instead of being welcomed by the population who seeks security and tranquility, is on the contrary loathingly rejected by the Muslim fundamentalists and their supporters. The latter, like in Afghanistan and Pakistan, are much more inclined to expel the foreign invaders and aggressors from their land, than to enjoy the little security that they can provide in exchange, to be sure, for the heavy price of sustaining civilian "collateral casualties" by populations that are usually not part to the conflict.

Until the new constitution has been written and the new elections held, as promised, in 2014, the new provisional government, like its predecessor which was just removed, hardly controls the cities, while the countryside all lies beyond its reach and is ruled by tribal/armed groups whose area of "jurisdiction" has been widened during the Spring, when its main concern has been not to render its rule more efficient and to bring remedy to the people, but just like everybody else, to survive together with one's kin and entourage. Two unruly groups of this kind emerged on the ground, and they are sure to demand their share should matters settle down permanently. The one is Ansar al-Shari'a (the Supporters of Shari'a), whose very name indicates the Islamic tendencies of its followers. It is considered a branch of al-Qa'ida of AQAP, and the second are the Houti Shi'ites, who have been up in rebellion in the northern mountains. Already during their Spring uprising, and especially after it, these groups and their peers have announced the establishment of several Islamic Emirates in the southern provinces of Abyan and Shabwa, and the northern province of Sa'da, respectively, which as in Afghanistan, have escaped official control and intend to make that situation permanent. In the north, the Houtis have conducted their rebellion against the Sunni authorities since 2004, without any force, including Saudi intervention, being able to quell it. In Afghanistan, the same has been unfolding since the American incursion in 2001, where the Taliban, defeated militarily but not in spirit, declared an Islamic Emirate headed by their own affiliates, managed by their own fighters in the battle zones, who held a concrete and firm grip on vast parts of the land to which the Americans have no real access. In Yemen, as in Afghanistan, the moment the Americans depart and the local government troops are no longer subordinated to them, it stands to reason that all the infrastructures erected by these groups in the areas of the Emirates will become the nuclei of the new post-Spring alternative rule. It is hard to envisage how democratic elections or a new constitution can be implemented in these regions, even if they are achieved and agreed upon, because under the scenario of the Emirates, they will by then be popular and recognized enough on the ground, and will have extended their rule on a wide enough area of the country as to become the actual power. The enmity is well established between the Sunnite al-Qa'ida, the product of puritanical and Wahhabi Saudi Arabia, which now rejects it since it turned its terrorist arms against it, and the Shi'a, which is often dubbed by critical Sunnite clerics as "heretics, worse than Jews."

If one assumes that any change in Yemen will have to use as a launching pad the current institutional structure, which has never been popular, effective, or clear of corruption, and has never assembled around it any kind of consensus, the planners of the alternative regime, if it could be brought about, will have to take into account what had been in place until the insurrection. One has the impression that though the revolutionary passion elsewhere wanted first to get rid of the tyrants before anything else could be done, without a priori thinking about alternatives or planning them until the process of the revolt had succeeded, in Yemen things have been so decentralized and large tracts of the country in rebellion, and tribal interests so different and even contradictory to each other, that beyond throwing out the loathed tyrant, no one dared think about new options of a centralized government beyond the local Emirates that were there already in the process of emerging when the Spring was launched. They did not ponder the issue of creating a new regime based on a new vision for the country, but wished to rid themselves of the ruler and his American sponsors in order to eliminate the authorities that had fought against them, with American aid, thereby reinforcing their private emirates without outside disturbance. It is doubtful whether any of them shows any humanitarian or political concern for the people of Yemen, except perhaps some intellectuals and urban political leaders who know the ancient Yemenite tradition and wish to revive it in a tranquil and civil ambience.

What there is now is a corrupt and flimsy republican regime that replaced the obscurantist rule of the imam in the 1960s. The republic rests on a bicameral house of a parliament with 301 members, accompanied by a *shura* (upper house) of 111 members. In theory, the rule is partitioned between the president, who heads the state, and the prime minister, but in practice authoritarian rule of the president has taken over the affairs of the state, and the rest obey and rubber-stamp his fiat. Its constitution, updated in 1991, determined that the president was to be elected by popular vote out of at least two candidates, each supported by at least fifteen MPs. This is on paper a great advance compared to Egypt, for example, when it was prohibited from submitting more than one candidate, lest differences and arguments come to cloud the happy event of a unanimous vote of 90 percent or more, which was expected to be cast in his favor. In view of the appointment of the prime minister by the president, as in Egypt, the entire executive branch was built into the authority of the president so as to make him a dictator that so many during the Islamic Spring, throughout the Islamic world, wished to remove from power, even if nothing else followed. The main party in power in Yemen, the General Popular Congress—the party of the president, again as in Mubarak's case—always saw to it that a majority in parliament was concocted, so as to assure the passing of all the president's orders as law, in order to lend legitimacy to the dictatorship of Saleh. This is precisely what the rebels wish to prevent from recurring, if the system is ever amended. This is the claim of all rebels of the Spring who wish to put an end to the unlimited powers of the tyrant, to be replaced by democracy.

Prima facie, as in the other Spring countries, all the components of dictatorship were there and all the elements of a needed reform are here. But, unlike countries with high governability—like Egypt or one of the monarchies, where institutional experience has been accumulated to serve as a base for amendments, reform, additions, and innovations—in chaotic Yemen tranquility never reigned, and the dictator never controlled all elements of power in the entire country, and when and where government worked—this has been only partially, only in select places, like the capital and a few urban centers, that are open and accessible to all. In this situation, no legal precedent, no exemplary rule, and no pattern to learn from were established to guide the generations of past rulers. Take for examples the standards set by the existing constitution regarding the unification of the two codes of law existing in the two parts of the country (north and south) into one system. The system includes in theory also commercial courts and a supreme court seated in San'a, the capital. But unlike the Egyptian legal system, where cases of violations against the regime were dealt with and perpetrators convicted—although judges were not usually courageous enough to confront the supreme ruler of the country in questions of human rights—there were no such legal cases in Yemen worth noticing. The constitution said that the source of law is rooted in the Shari'a, and qadi's (religious judges) often sat in courts of law, and dealt with many cases according to religious law, but civil lawyers could have as well treated the issue at hand based on civil law. Thus, if in Yemen, as in other places, Muslim fundamentalists take over the rule, the legal system would have to adapt to the religious one, for dearth of precedents and an established legal tradition, whereas in Egypt, despite the many deficiencies, a long tradition is there, at least in theory, that cannot be dismissed out of hand. For a long (though incomplete and not tightproof) experience is there that prevented the religious courts from encroaching upon the authority of the civil courts, until the advent of the Mursi regime, which will reshuffle the cards.

Afghanistan

Afghanistan's tragedy has been that it is so divided tribally that only aggression from the outside can unify its intrepid fighters and lead them to victory against any outsider. But the problem is that they have been eaten up by so much internal conflict for years that it is hard to see how this unfortunate country, which is the land of the brave, can emerge into modernity, peace, and reconciliation. Strictly speaking, there has been no Spring in this ill-fated land of scorched earth and snowy mountain crests, but if we are talking of an Islamic Spring, it is evident that in the past decades, since the Soviet invasion of Afghanistan on Christmas 1979, and up until now, the most successful fighters for their cause have been the Muslim jihadists, who first fought against the Soviets and defeated them, then unified the country under the Taliban after years of civil war. But that rough and cruel regime, which wanted to enforce Islamic law without regard to any other legal or moral code, ended up allying with al-Qa'ida, which challenged the United States in its home, and precipitated a costly American retaliation whose outcome it is still hard to imagine. Taliban-style Muslim triumph will certainly entitle the courageous Afghanis to their full share in the Islamic Spring, indeed will enable them to claim a pioneering role in it, together with Iran, where Islamic revolution broke out simultaneously.

Afghanistan has a long history of foreign intervention due to the centrality of its position in Central Asia, between China and India, and during the Cold War between the Soviet superpower and the vast Muslim hinterland, part of which was under direct Soviet tutorship in the six Muslim republics of Central Asia (Kazakhstan, Uzbekistan, Turkmenistan, Kirgizstan, and Tajikistan) and the Caucasus (Azerbaijan), and into her Arab allies of the Middle East. The watershed in the affairs of the Islamic world and the international arena was the Khumeini Islamic Revolution in Iran in February 1979, just a few months prior to the Soviet invasion, which was patently intended for exportation. This means that beyond all the Shi'ite-Sunnite controversies, doctrinal and political, the deep divide between tyrannical monarchies, one of which Khumeini had toppled, and revolutionary regimes like his, and the inter-superpower differences and tensions, Khumeini was

213

determined to bring the revolution to the doorstep of the rest of the Islamic world. The Soviets, justifiably worried lest their Central Asian Muslim states be contaminated by the fabulously popular Khumeini's revolution, decided to preempt by invading next-door Afghanistan and adding it to the scope of the Brezhnev Doctrine, which had automatically triggered a Soviet intervention in any east-bloc country that faced either internal or external aggression. The decade-long bloody history of the Soviets in the quagmire of Afghanistan, which turned into their Vietnam, was brought to an end when they could no longer sustain their losses in the battlefield, and that instead of preempting an Islamic revolution coming from the outside, they in fact precipitated an Islamic revolution from within their Muslim republics, which turned into an all-out Soviet collapse in 1989–90, of which the dishonorable retreat from Kabul was only part.

The resilient unity toward foreign invaders among the tribal and ethnic groups of Afghanistan (Pashtun, Tadjik, Uzbek, Hazara), each of which was supported by another outside power, finally produced victory for the Afghans, and was remarkably facilitated by the stinger shoulder-held antiaircraft missiles, provided by the CIA, which downed such a huge quantity of Soviet airplanes and helicopters that the loss could no longer be sustained by the Soviets. This caused a huge euphoria among the fighters and forced the Soviets out. Though it seems incredible nowadays, the mujahideen were full of praise then for America, which had engineered their victory. But as soon as the Soviets left, the battle for hegemony between the various tribes and factions began raging, turning Kabul, the capital, into rubble, with increasing numbers of intrepid fighters shooting and destroying each other madly. Among the fighters who began to be evacuated after the anti-Soviet battle was terminated were the tens of thousands of volunteers who came from all over the Muslim world, with CIA and Saudi financing, to participate in the blessings of jihad. Battle-hardened, and sensing that they were fulfilling a holy duty of indefinite duration, they had now to return abruptly to their countries of origin (mainly Saudi Arabia, Pakistan, Egypt, Jordan, and even Chechnya), where they were dubbed the Afghanis. One of them was Osama Bin Laden, who left behind his riches and went to dip his hands, soul, and body in the harsh but thrilling world of jihad. When at home he tried to turn his jihad energies against his own corrupt government, he was evicted from his country, then deprived of the Saudi nationality, and he was then condemned to exile, first in Sudan and finally in Afghanistan.

It was in the killing fields of Afghanistan that Bin Laden encountered the two men who would change his life and much of world history: Abdallah Azzam, his Palestinian spiritual and religious mentor, and Mullah 'Umar, the head of the Taliban faction, who gave him shelter in his country, after he conquered it from all the fighting factions in order to establish in it a religious-Islamic state to his taste, based on the Taliban. Taliban, which means literally *students*, grew in the hothouses of the thousands of madrassas of Pakistan, from which hundreds of thousands of students from all over the Islamic world graduate every year, all indoctrinated in jihad war and the rewards that await them in the hereafter after they are killed (*shahid*) in battle, much in the vein of what Hassan al-Banna had taught in Egypt at the beginning to the twentieth century. When their leader saw that jihad had become, in the hands of the Afghani ethnic factions, a ruthless battle to the end for power and dominion, he realized that his student supporters, the Taliban, who were young, fresh, enthusiastic, devoted, and impartial, would be the best suitable to unify the country behind them and rescue it from total ruin. From his base in Qandahar he launched battle at the end of 1995, and in September 1996 he entered Kabul and installed his Taliban regime.

Almost united under the Taliban, except for a northern enclave, the theocratic regime of the Taliban in Kabul enforced perhaps the most rigid and puritanical Islamic regime ever seen in the modern Islamic world, even more so than the Saudi or the Iranian systems which inspire fear, disgust, and contempt in the West. With Mullah 'Umar at the head of the system as some sort of spiritual leader, like that of Iran, they imposed obscurantist politics such as: forcing people to attend prayers and lashing out at latecomers or foot-draggers, as during the times of 'Umar ibn-al-Khattab, the second Righteous Caliph (634–44), who used to prod passerby with his whip to join public prayers; banning women totally from the public square, including places of education, and when in public they were forced to wear those mobile tents that covered them from head to toe, including their faces; enforcing Islamic morality in the streets, banning music altogether; overhauling the educational system to eradicate non-Islamic studies and expanding the Qur'anic ones; and finally, eliminating all the manifestations of non-Islamic art, which culminated in the abominable blowing-up of the giant Buddha statues at Bamyan, despite the protestations of world leaders, including some civilized and enlightened Muslims. Many guesses circulated in the market of ideas as to the possible longevity of such a regime, where visibly many people, certainly the women, who had been enthused by and supportive of the Taliban while they were liberating the country and uniting it with a view of bringing peace and tranquility to it, gradually turned to resentment and bitterness when they realized the harshness and inapplicability in the twenty-first century of those outdated medieval concepts.

Backward Afghanistan, which had begun during the five years of Taliban rule to re-Islamize society, which was in effect its early version of the Islamic Spring, did not abstain from meddling also in international, especially Islamic, affairs. Inter alia, it gave shelter and a base of action to Osama Bin Laden and his entourage, and permitted him to build training camps in its territory, when it recognized the value of his doings for the cause of Islam and against the West. Bin Laden, who had been evicted from his native Saudi Arabia for his subversive activities against the monarchy, found refuge in Omar Bashir and Hassan Turabi's Sudan, where he based his terrorist activities, trained terrorists, and spent large parts of his personal fortune on both world terrorism and local development. When hounded by the United States there, and following several American retaliatory acts that Khartoum could not sustain, he was compelled to depart, and his choice fell, naturally, on newly constituted Taliban Afghanistan, where he found a very supportive leadership to his cause and ideal ground conditions (mountains and deserts for hideouts and inaccessibility). One has to admit that Bin Laden made great use of the terrain for his purposes, launching world terrorist activities that had such resonance, like the bombings of the two American embassies in East Africa in 1998 and the attack against the USS *Cole* in 2000, that the United States and the world were in for a new era of facing terror, which the Clinton Administration had underestimated and in any case proved inadequate to resist and to counterattack.

Encouraged by his invincibility and the cover he was given by Mullah 'Umar, Bin Laden had the daring to plan leisurely from his base in Afghanistan the September 11 attacks against New York and Washington, as President Bush was still a novice in world affairs. The disastrous consequences prompted Bush to prepare for a large-scale retaliation, but not before he attempted to persuade the Taliban government to extradite the chief perpetrator to American justice. 'Umar's loyalty and obstinacy as he defied the United States and stood by his protégé were truly remarkable and could only be the fruit of deep religious faith in the cause, whereupon America reacted massively and with determination, so that in a matter of weeks almost all Afghanistan, including 'Umar's stronghold in Qandahar, were in American hands, and the Taliban regime was toppled. It was relatively easy to conquer the country and to install the illegitimate, unpopular, and corrupt government of Hamid Karzai, hand-picked by the Americans to rule the country, but he was not any more highly regarded or more accepted by his people than Mubarak in Egypt or the shah of Iran.

Contemporary Afghani history is marked by the Americans, with a symbolic and reluctant participation of NATO, attempting for a dozen years to reinforce Karzai's regime, strengthen the national forces of the country to stand on their own, and help build, as in Iraq, a civil society base that can sustain some sort of stability and participatory order, if not a total democracy when the Americans leave in 2014. However, since the date of Western withdrawal was announced, the Taliban are back to controlling much of the countryside, in the face of the weakening Western grip on the land, both ideological and physical. Sometimes, Karzai seems to control not much beyond Kabul, and often even the capital is shaken by explosions of terror triggered by his many enemies and rivals. It seems that, like elsewhere, the Islamic fundamentalist alternative is building confidently and patiently for the long haul, and that the West, which is tired of more than a decade of unpopular war that goes nowhere, might be the first to blink. In the eyes of the Islamic fighters, after they inflicted defeat on the Communist superpower twenty years earlier, it was now the turn of the capitalist power to be routed, thus demonstrating the ultimate superiority of Islam to both rival Western doctrines.

Worse, as we learn from some experts, the economic prospects for Afghanistan, on which hinge the entire plan for the country's rehabilitation after the war (if it ever ends after a few consecutive decades), were not very bright either. Ahmed Rashid and Alexis Crow[6] have claimed on the Internet that the projected foreign aid, designed to help the country and its economy, will simply not be sufficient. They say that as of July 2012, 70 nations and institutions pledged $16 billion for Afghanistan's development over the next four years, but sadly, the money is likely to be wasted, exactly as the vast sums invested since the US-led intervention in 2001 has made little progress in creating a self-sustaining Afghan economy. During what the Afghans term the "occupation" of their country, development agencies have been short of investing enough in local people to enable them to earn their livings. The result is that dependence on foreign aid has increased. Demographically, two-thirds of the population are under 25, and there will be no jobs for most of them when foreign troops are gone, for the government has never had the capacity to produce jobs, while the private sector has not been encouraged sufficiently to do so. Yet, only by enabling local people to share in their own profit can stability and growth last, contend the authors. But Western institutional aid has such difficult monitoring and accounting rules that most Afghans cannot benefit from it. Western state-driven development agencies are ill equipped for encouraging the local private sector.

The authors claim[7] that only greater involvement by the West's private sector could likely help bridge the gap. However, the private sector will only invest more and more readily once security improves, and that is not likely to happen anytime soon if after the departure of the West, it is the Taliban who will take over. They contend that a new model for economic development is needed that gives Afghans profit-based incentives to build their own economy. They suggest that big Chinese and Indian mining companies should now encourage bold private equity groups with a long-term, high-risk investment strategy. They believe that a new model will be hampered not so much by Taliban intransigence as by infighting in Washington and addiction to old style diplomacy. They contend that

> Western institutions still act like 19th-century imperial behemoths, ignoring their opponents' cultures and values. The US military expects the Taliban to accept that they have lost the war and surrender as the Japanese did in 1945. Yet the Taliban demand negotiations between equals. Accepting this will be the only way to end the war. Only when the west stops imposing its will and vision of governance on the Afghan people, they argue, will a permissible environment be created for peace. The Taliban have repeatedly said that once the Americans leave, Afghans will determine their own future. This is said not as a threat but an assertion of the natural order.[8]

The UN diplomat Lakhdar Brahimi, who later got involved in Syria and failed again, had tried to forge a new way of negotiating in Afghanistan during the creation of a new government after the US invasion in 2001. He had assembled a group of civilian scholars and journalists who knew the region far better than diplomats. They had formed a core advisory group that declined to treat any side as loser or victor and approached peacemaking as locals would. The group worked with Afghans from all social sectors to create both political and economic incentives for all groups to back peace negotiations. Mr. Brahimi regretted at the time being unable to include the Taliban in the process, but even if he were able, it is hard to understand how a UN messenger who himself grew up in an authoritarian regime and a large state-owned public sector could advise others on their political and economic regime. To negotiate with the Taliban now, the United States needs a similar team of civilian experts, perhaps led by a US official. Peace will come only, argue the authors, by mobilizing all sectors of society for national reconciliation. They believe that stability and growth will follow only by enabling local people to share the profits and encouraging private sector solutions. In 2012, two years prior to NATO's planned withdrawal from Afghanistan, they thought that the United States could still change strategy—but throwing billions of dollars of aid at the problem was not the answer, they argue.[9] In the meantime, the Taliban are taking the necessary measures to fill the gap when the time comes by establishing a mission in Doha, Qatar, planning to rely on that wealthy monarchy as an engine for development.

Another interesting indication of the directions that the Afghan economy might take to build avenues of enjoyment amid the war was published in the *Guardian* claiming that the biggest hurdle for Herat Ice Cream company is not the Taliban or rife Afghan corruption but an Iranian competitor. In fact, Ahmad Faizy's trucks travel the risky roads of Afghanistan without problems, and his agents are welcomed almost everywhere in a country torn by war and suspicion. The Herat Ice Cream factory was founded a few years ago with money Faizy had made from a business of imports from China and France. He decided that his hometown's reputation for making the best traditional ice cream in Afghanistan, and very little domestic competition, provided him with a welcome opportunity. He developed thirty-seven flavors of ice cream coated with chocolate and almonds. Other flavors included coffee-chocolate, vanilla with sour cherry and pistachio, and a mango and pineapple Popsicle. Faizy needed guts to defy the odds and succeed in business in a country ranked the fourth most corrupt in the world. He says this is an area where his biggest rivals are companies in Iran. Overall though, "Herat Ice-Cream appears to have set themselves high standards in a country where one could possibly argue they don't need to bother, given the limited market particularly, as nothing they make costs more than about 30p."[10] This is a delightful example of a successful entrepreneur and of the kind of small business initiatives that Rashid and Crow were talking about above. The thought that someone pays attention to the small comforts of life like ice cream in the midst of war, and that multitudes of customers throughout the entire war-torn land can access these comforts, is indicative, perhaps better than anything else, of the hope for a well-deserved Spring of revival that the battered population has been vying for.

Bosnia and Kosovo

Modern Bosnia, which was one of the six federal members of post–World War II Yugoslavia, has been populated for centuries by the mixture of two ethnic groups, Serbs and Croats, part of whom had been converted by the Ottoman *devshirme* process, in which young Christian boys were seized and raised as Muslim elite forces, with total devotion to the sultan, in denial of their ethnic, religious, and cultural group. Those who converted, and their families, raised their status by Islamizing and became the most devoted subjects of the Empire and representatives of the Emperor in the occupied Balkans. In time, though they could not differentiate themselves ethnically and linguistically, they grew different from their compatriots through their religious conviction, so much so that more than half the population was Muslim, one-third Serbian, and the rest Croatian. It was in 1966 that the Tito government recognized Bosnia as a "religio-ethnic" division of the Federation, parallel and equivalent to Serbia, Croatia, Montenegro, Macedonia, and Slovenia, although it was based on the faith of the Muslim majority, not on ethnic origin. The moment that was accomplished and the nationality of Bosniak was recognized and accepted, the major minorities who were there, namely the Serbs and the Croats, started to feel alienation, friction, and hostility, along with alignment by necessity with their ethnic motherlands: Serbia, which dominated the federation, and Croatia, which was not accepting of and submissive to the Serbians' preponderant role. When the federation fell apart after Tito's death, every one of its components fought for its independence from Serbian domination and obtained it. In Bosnia, liberation was from the two major minorities, who represented almost 40 percent of the population and who were also attached to parts of the territory of Bosnia, usually adjacent to their respective ethnic homelands, thus facilitating irridenta.

The Bosnian War (1992–5), in which the minorities wished to detach themselves and be annexed to the home ethnicity groups, raged three years and levied a very heavy toll, with all parties adamant about sustaining their casualties and pursuing the war until victory. It was not until UN and NATO interference, and the US–mediated Dayton Agreement, that a settlement was in fact forced on the parties, under which Bosnia remained one unit, as the Muslims desired, but was divided into three units, later amalgamated into two: a Bosnian-Croatian part, with about half the territory and two-thirds of the population, with a capital in Sarajevo, as of old; and a Serbian part consisting of the rest of the territory, with one-third of the population, centered around Banja Luka. The management of the state remained shared by all three components. It was only natural that the Bosniak-Muslim population should emphasize its Muslim characteristics and that an Islamic Spring of sorts should be felt in the air for the first time since the end of the Ottoman rule. A marked emphasis was put on Islamic revival, and a noticeable fundamentalist trend has been rising there, contradictory to the generally secular atmosphere that had reigned there during the Federation. Thus, the federal idea, which could only be enforced under an authoritarian regime such as the Communists, gave way after the death of the dictator to the tribalism that divided Yugoslavia back into seven ethnicities, and Bosnia (one of the seven) into three tribal subdivisions.

The Muslim part of Bosnia, as mostly expressed in Sarajevo, its beautiful and history-laden capital, has known a true revival, to judge by the number of new mosques in the city and the almost total departure of Serbs, who used to constitute an important part of culture prior to the war. The spread of the houses of prayer, pencil shaped and of extraordinary elegance and simplicity and also located in the countryside, is encouraged by Saudi money. It is said that great Muslim militancy is being fomented there, behind the facade of openness and tolerance of variety. A summons by Saudi scholar Ahmed ibn Nafi' of Mecca, which was circulated to all by the Pan-Islamic Salvation Committee at the outset of the Bosnia War, in effect states in no uncertain terms:

> Let it be known, brothers, that life in this ephemeral world differs immensely from the life lived in keeping with the principles of Jihad. . . . Fortunate is he whom Allah enlightens in this life . . . by waging a jihad for him. Following Allah's instructions, the Pan-Islamic Salvation Committee has devised a holy plan to cleanse the world of unbelievers. We trust you to see to the imminent establishment of the Caliphate in the Balkans, because the Balkans are the path to the conquest of Europe. . . .

> Every individual Imam in our states, and especially Turkey [once the ruler of Bosnia under the Ottomans], is ready to help. Know, therefore, Brothers, that time is working for us. Let us help our brothers who are fighting for the cause of Allah, by sending them as much weapons and money as we can, by sending them new *mujahideen*. Furthermore, in keeping with this holy plan, all women and children and some men must immediately be given refuge in Europe. And you, Muslim brothers, must care for them as for your own, so they will spread everywhere and preach our religion, for our sake and for the sake of Allah. Brothers, give women and children refuge in each center, collect money and weapons and send them to Bosnia. Gather *Mujahideen* and send them to Bosnia. This is your obligation. Help them so that Islam will spread as soon as possible. . . . With all your heart and soul and everywhere, fight the unbelievers! This is your duty! The Caliphate is at hand! May Allah reward you![11]

This appeal was by no mans an isolated case. In the same month, August 1992, a poster was plastered on walls in Sarajevo, signed by the spiritual head of the Iranian Revolution, Khamena'i, which accused the Western nations of not preventing genocide against the Muslims of Bosnia due to "their innate hostility to Islam," and urged them to clear the way for Iranian mujahideen and other young Muslims to wage war and "drive the Serbs from this Islamic country."[12] In Zagreb at the same time, the rally of Muslims against the Serbs echoed that call:

> The Muslim nation in Iran began its revolution with "*Allahu Akbar!*" and succeeded. On the territory of Yugoslavia, the Serbs could not tolerate a Muslim [Izetbegovic] as the President of Bosnia-Herzegovina. Their only rival is Islam and they fear it. The time is approaching when Islam will be victorious.

After the war, radical Islam of the Wahhabi-Salafi type, though far from yet predominating on the Bosnian street, has nonetheless found numerous outlets of expression in several mosques that are said to be financed by Saudi Arabia and its Iranian competitor. Salafi preacher Bilal Bosnic, for example, sings jihadi songs, which were put on the Internet during the thick of the Islamic Spring, on July 21, 2011. He vows: "with explosives on our chests we pave the way to paradise," praising the "beautiful Jihad that has risen over Bosnia," and wishing that "God willing, America will be destroyed to its foundations."[13]

After the Bosnian War was diplomatically settled (1995), the territory of Kosovo, one of the two areas that constituted part of Serbia (the other is Voivodina in the north), an area populated mainly by

Albanian Muslims—raised their own banner of rebellion, learning from Bosnia's experience, and obtained their independence in practice, though Serbia and other countries have not recognized it. There also, though the tradition of secularism remained predominant, the new nationalism is tinged with Islam, and there are some elements of fundamentalism that may follow the examples of nearby Albania and Bosnia. So, not only is a profusion of new mosques noticeable in Sarajevo and the countryside, but also the sight of traditionally garbed people and headscarved old ladies walking side by side with their hot pants–clad daughters and granddaughters, as if they were an organic and harmonic whole. That ambience of folk-religiosity in the midst of secularism is probably the heritage of the Bosnian War, where so many Muslim jihadists—Arabs, Iranians, Chechens, and others—went to fight jihad for Islam, just as in Afghanistan, and they left behind their influence. Even if limited, uncertain, and not yet fully crystallized, this measure of Islamic revival can qualify as an Islamic Spring, won in blood and death, that started to rock the Balkans.

There are far-reaching international consequences for the Islamic upheaval in the Balkans, insofar as when the Americans supported it, and foolishly stood to the side of the Muslims who fought the West in general, they were counting on a moderate Turkey, which would stand at the center of a Muslim pro-Western continuity from Central Asia to Anatolia and on into the Balkans. But, when the Islamic party took over in Ankara, and the anti-Western orientation took precedence there, moderation evaporated, and instead of a moderate Islamic continuity, they got a series of Islamic radical entities that have severed the Christian continuity between central Europe throughout Greece and the Mediterranean, and installed instead an Islamic wedge. The West, especially the United States, will have to tackle this problematic imbalance of its own past doings, in the years to come.

Notes

1. *Kayhan*, July 21, 2012. Excerpts of it translated and published by MEMRI, and commented in an article by A. Savyon and Y. Mansharof.
2. Ibid.
3. *Saudi Gazette*, July 31, 2012.
4. *Jordan Times*, July 31, 2012.
5. *Jerusalem Post*, September 16, 2012. Much of this passage is based on this article.
6. http://www.ft.com/intl/cms/s/0/f5508056-da2f-11e00144feab49a.html#axzz228uvUSU6, July 30, 2012.
7. Ibid.

8. Ibid.
9. Ibid.
10. Ibid.
11. The handwritten Arabic text of this epistle of August 17, 1992, appears in Hadzivokovic, Vesna et al. (eds.) *Chronicle of Announced Death*, 1993, Belgrade, p. 52.
12. The text of the summons, with Khamena'i's picture, appears in Croatian, ibid. p. 54.
13. See MEMRI Daily, June 14, 2012, pp. 1–2.

9

Iran, Iraq, Lebanon, and the Shi'ite Model

The Shi'a, the minority most persecuted and loathed by Sunni Islam, has also constituted a separate and independent model of Spring, which stems from its messianic and ever-expecting salvation and change, upon the impending return to earth of the Hidden Imam (see details in Chapter 4 about the caliphate). Namely, in contrast with the four prevailing schools of law in the sunna, which are fixed and immutable since their *salvador* was the Prophet Muhammed, the Seal of the Prophets—meaning that the ideal utopia happened in the past, from which we can only keep distancing ourselves—the Shi'ite hope is placed in the return of the Hidden Imam in some indefinite future, in order to produce prosperity, justice, and happiness for all humanity. The great luminaries of the sunna, which constitutes about 90 percent of all the 1.5 billion Muslims in the world, usually counsel their followers to submit to the rule under which they live, even if it is not satisfactory to their religious taste, for a bad ruler is always superior to chaos, since in disorder no Islam at all can function. The Shi'ite scholars, on the contrary, have always been rebellious, especially when they were not in power. This restlessness, which has always been tinged with messianic and utopian elements, has lent to the Shi'a the characteristics that we today identify in the Islamic Spring. Therefore, the Islamic Revolution that we witnessed in 1978–9 in Iran, which was intended for exportation—indicating its universal and messianic import—must be seen as the precursor of the Islamic Spring, because it professed the exact goal that the current Spring proclaims today: to remove the present illegitimate tyrant and establish in his stead a just Islamic order (the Islamic parties in Turkey, Egypt, Morocco all have this element of justice in their very names), which will precipitate the coming of the Imam Mahdi (the Guiding Imam, coterminus with the Hidden Imam). The fact that this dream did not yet come to fruition in

Tehran does not reflect negatively on the missed and unfulfilled utopia; this is the nature of what Max Weber called the "routinization of the charisma," or what others usually name "the deed that distorts and corrupts the ideal," or what revolutionaries have elected to express in the dichotomies of "theory and practice," "doctrine and praxis," "ideology and organization," or the "wings of vision vs. the feet of reality."

There were many attempts made by Sunnite doctors of the holy law to invite the Sh'ia to join the Islamic consensus by turning it into a fifth school of law, with the intent of unifying all currents of Islam and putting an end to its internal debates, but Shi'a always rejected the conditions of the union, for had the latter joined the consensus, they would have had to renounce during the Friday prayer the denunciation of the first three caliphs for having usurped the caliphate from Ali, the sole heir of the Prophet who deserved it. It is evident that the Shi'ites would not accept that position, since Ali and his descendants were the central figures in their narrative of Islamic history, and their acceptance of Ali as fourth in the apostolic succession of the Prophet would mean admission and recognition that Ali was not wronged, and therefore there was nothing to redress. Conversely, the entire Shi'ite martyrology is founded on the suffering inflicted upon Ali and his children by two people: the first Umayyad caliph, Mu'awiya, and his successors, who have become in Iran the symbol of oppression and injustice; and Yazid, the son of Mu'awiya, the paradigm of murderer for having assassinated Ali's sons. The sunna, on the contrary, will not accept the concept that while it recognized Ali as the fourth in the line of caliphs, and agrees to honor him accordingly, other parts of Islam continue to despise and loathe the three first righteous caliphs as usurpers, disrespecting and cursing them accordingly. The Shi'ites would not renounce the special status of Ali in Islam as the cousin of the Prophet and his son-in-law, while in the eyes of the Sunnites all four first caliphs deserve the title of *righteous*, are equal in status, and are all second only to the Prophet, who is the most perfect of all humans, designated by Allah as his last messenger.

When Ayatullah Khumeini declared his Islamic Revolution in Tehran in 1979, he tried to group the Sunnite-Shi'ite rift under the umbrella of the world Islamic revolution that he was professing as he intended to spread to the entire world and sweep in its path all Muslim peoples. He thought that his revolution, his early version of the Spring, would overshadow all the theological differences that looked insignificant in his eyes, compared with the great unifying themes in Islam. He indeed had some success, when he harnessed non-Shi'ite Syria and Hizbullah for his purposes and turned Tehran into an international center of terror that attracted other fanatics, including Sunnites like Hamas and Islamic Jihad. That hub of international Muslim terrorism fed, organized, financed, and dispatched many Islamic terrorists around the world. Iran also succeeded in strengthening its relations with Sunnite Sudan when Sudan's famous spiritual leader, Hassan Turabi, was at his peak in the 1990s. During those years Sudan turned into the client of fundamentalist Shi'ite Iran, militarily and economically. This collaboration generated a closer-than-ever relationship between Iran and Sunnite radical movements, in spite of the fact that, doctrinally, not much love was lost between them. For instance, the great doctors of the *shari'a*, like Yussuf Qaradawi and others, so despised Shi'ites as to call them "worse than Zionists." Moreover, sometimes Sunnite terrorists, like al-Qa'ida, who acted in Iraq against the Americans, were asked to direct their weapons against the heretic Shi'ites. Also noticeable was the tension that reigned in the relations between Iran and the Taliban rule in Afghanistan (1996–2001), in spite of their joint revolutionary and anti-American penchant, especially after the American incursion into Afghanistan and Iraq (2001 and 2003, respectively), on both sides of Iran and holding it in a strangulating grip.

It appears that even had Iran found a way to collaborate with other Muslims against the Americans, the instinctive hatred toward that country by Saudi Arabia and Bin Laden is/was so intense, that it would have been a classic case of ideology overriding political interest. On the other hand, this deep dislike does not deter other Sunnite movements, like Hamas and Islamic Jihad, from leaning on Iran and collaborating with it in world terrorism. Along the years of observing the Shi'ite revolution, which was feared by such Sunni states as Saudi Arabia and the Gulf monarchies, lest it became a permanent feature of the Middle East, there developed a new division between the Shi'ite Crescent, consisting of Iran, Iraq, Syria (the ally, not Shi'ite but ruled by the Alawi minority), and Lebanon (especially the Shi'ites Amal and Hizbullah, who calls the shots), countered by the traditional Sunnite front consisting of Saudi Arabia and the Gulf, one of whose cornerstones was pre-Spring Egypt.

The Shi'a has always been embroiled in rifts and differences, not only with its enemies but also within itself. Classical Shi'a, which was usually persecuted within its Sunnite environment, learned to bear its suffering quietly and passively, and carried out its rituals within its mosques or in public without provoking the rulers or the general Muslim population, especially before there was a Shi'ite state after the dissolution of the Fatimid Empire in Egypt in the twelfth century. In Safavid Iran (sixteenth to eighteenth century), Twelver Shi'a was finally established as the official faith of the Empire, and in new Iran, where the Empire was revived under the shah, the Shi'ite clergy, in contrast with the Sunnite which has no clerical hierarchy, was hierarchical all right, but as an institutional religion,[1] meaning it did not depend on the state for existence and did not fill any official role in the government. The rationale was overwhelming in its simplicity: In view of the belief that it was the Hidden Imam who managed the affairs of the world from his hiding place, the proper functioning of society would be impossible without some sort of spiritual contact with him in order to receive his guidance. Not every mullah (cleric) is capable of maintaining such supreme contact with the Hidden Imam; therefore this status is deserved by only the most senior among them, not to exceed two dozen in each generation, people who earned the title of ayatullah (the sign of Allah) thanks to their scholarship, knowledge, and spiritual state. A handful of them, the most path breaking and imposing by their leadership, like Khumeini himself, were titled ayatullah 'uzma (super-ayatullah), and they led this select group and dominated it without challenge. Other senior clerics, with the titles of hujat al Islam (militant for Islam, like the second President Rafsanjani), and lower mullahs, aspire all their lives to advance up the ladder of the hierarchy, as in the Catholic Church. The higher the clerical rank, the more imposing the spiritual impact on society. Even after the Islamic Revolution, President Ahmadinejad is more influential than his predecessor President Hatami, in spite of the latter being one of the few ayatullahs, while the former has no rank in the clergy. Conversely, Supreme Leader Khamena'i, who is not among the top clerics, is the man whose decisions count the most. In both Iran and Iraq, where the status of the ayatullahs was not dominant until recently, the mullahs were influential spiritual leaders who had no effect on state affairs, because they were often executed by Saddam Hussein, or incarcerated, or exiled by the shah.

Ayatullah Khumeini changed this, at least on the doctrinal level. He had begun to develop his revolutionary ideas under the shah—and had they not preceded the Spring by one generation or more, they could have served as its precursor, if one considers their audacious élan, their out-of-the-box thinking, and their far-reaching political consequences. The first thoughts that Khumeini started to develop cost him, inter alia, fifteen years (1963–78) of exile in Najaf, Iraq, one of the holy places of the Shi'a. It is the site where Ali, the first imam, is buried, where he brought to completion and published his *Islamic Revolution*, where he outlined his positions and plan of action. He was then compelled to leave by Saddam, who had sealed with the shah an agreement on the border between the two countries in the middle of the mighty Shatt al-Arab, where the Tigris and the Euphrates converge before they pour into the Arab/Persian Gulf. The main thought, which would have appealed to the Muslim crowds today, was the need to eradicate the tyrant rulers and to install in their stead Islamic regimes under *shari'a* law. Khumeini's Iran was the first to do that, by an Islamic revolution in which the clergy played a part, followed by Iraq, which, under American tutelage, applied that same principle through a Western-style democracy, at least for now.

Khumeini's doctrine is revolutionary from yet other aspects, because it provided the ideological infrastructure and underpinnings for a new model of rule where the clergy are actively involved. For him, in light of the fact that the ayatullahs are the supreme sources of knowledge, wisdom, and inspiration, it is only natural that they should also be the rulers, something similar to the prince in the Western tradition, who is also a philosopher. Khumeini developed two concepts that anchored the suggested revolutionary change. The first is *marja' taqlid* (the reference for emulation); in other words, that the supreme head of the clergy (ayatullah 'uzma) being also the supreme spiritual power, ought to be the role model everyone should aspire to emulate, a modern manifestation of the supreme model of the Prophet that we saw in the sunna. The second concept is *wilayat al-faqih* (the rule of the jurist). These two principles turned the passive state of expectation of the return of the Imam Mahdi in order to bring salvation into an aggressive initiative to precipitate such a momentous event. To those familiar with modern Jewish history, this could be comparable to the revolutionary doctrine developed in the 1920s and 1930s by Rabbi Kook in Palestine, whereby it was not enough for Jewry to sit and wait in the diaspora for the coming of the Messiah to provide salvation, but it had become necessary to rise and practice Zionism by settlement, development, and social and political action as an avenue for redemption. Khumeini probably viewed those two concepts as personified in him, as a result of his scholarship, lifelong struggle against the tyranny of the shah, and spiritual qualities, which made him into a *mujtahid* who is thus qualified to continue his innovative *ijtihad* and express the will of the

Hidden Imam pending his return. Unlike the sunna, where the gates of *ijtihad* had been closed since the passing of the great luminaries, the founders of the four schools of law, by the tenth century, the Shi'ite *mujtahid* undertakes the task of innovative legislation, and his verdicts ought to be the law. Hence it is only natural that membership in parliament was to be assigned to mullahs, who understand the matter of religious legislation and the will of the imam. Khumeini wrote that only the mullahs are able to get people out into the streets and motivate them to die for Islam, and even to beg that they should be allowed to sacrifice themselves for Islam.

Khumeini, like Muslim Brother Sayyid Qutb, was full of hatred toward the Jews and turned his bigotry into doctrine by dubbing them enemies of Allah. These anti-Semitic libels and hoaxes, coming from two such great luminaries of modern Islam from whom one could expect a higher measure of humanity, civility, and good judgment, render anti-Semitism part of radical Islam.[2] No wonder, then, that Ahmadinejad, who considers himself their disciple and the devoted executor of their anti-Semitic doctrine, should feel as compelled as Hitler to repeat on every occasion his nonsense about the extermination of the Jews and their state. Khumeini also included in his political activism a novel interpretation of the murder of Hussein bin Ali and his entourage in Karbala, which is celebrated as the central rite in Shi'ite liturgy (the *ta'zia* on Ashura Day). It was no longer only a memorial day for the greatest martyr of all generations, who was despicably murdered, a man with whom every Shi'ite ought to identify by reliving his suffering through self-inflicted pain and torture, but a war hero whom it became incumbent on all Shi'ites to emulate as the supreme martyr in the path of Allah, on his way to paradise, who will also recommend his followers for admission into the high heavens. When Iraq invaded Iran in October 1980, Khumeini, who was adored as if he were the imam himself, called his people to the defense of the land and produced more recruits than needed, thanks to his reference to Hussein's model.

Iran and the Sunnite-Shi'ite Rift

"The Middle-East map is marked these days by two colors, reflecting the sectarian division between Sunnite majority countries and Shi'ite minority ones," writes Amin Aflah in an article in *al-Quds al-Arabi.*[3] He explains that this is an ancient conflict dating from the seventh century, whose roots were anchored in a bloody war for political rule of the Islamic world. This old contention is augmented these days by the competition over oil resources and arms trade, and a possible reversal in the Arab-Israeli conflict, due on the one hand to the Israeli-Egyptian and the Jordanian-Israeli peace treaties and on the other hand to the Spring upheaval that is far from settling down. He argues, perhaps a little excessively, that the Arab-Israeli conflict, which has dominated the Middle East for the past two or three generations, has been replaced by the dominance of the Sunnite-Shi'ite controversy which he posits as opposing Iran on the one hand and the Gulf states on the other, with the news media becoming the stage where this rift is being played out—so much so that the intensity of the statements on both sides has surpassed the volume of pronouncements in the Arab-Israeli conflict. According to Aflah, the acuity of this conflict releases Israel and the United States from launching an attack on Iran, because the rich Gulf states are prepared to do it in their stead, and have been acquiring weapons from the United States to do just that. He thinks that the claim that Iran is planning to launch war on Israel has no leg to stand on, because Iran faces a more dangerous enemy in the Gulf states, hence replacing the Arab-Israeli war, or the Islamic-Jewish war by the sectarian one between Sunnites and Shi'ites.

Whether the main focus of the Middle East unrest has remained between Israel and the Muslim world, as Hizbullah, Hamas, and some other fundamentalists wish it, or has shifted to the Sunni-Shi'ite dichotomy, it is evident that since the accession to power of Ahmadinejad in the 2000s, focus has become centered on the issue of nuclearization of Iran, a matter equally feared by Israel and the Gulf states, who loathe that idea. The difference is that Israel, having learned to count on no one for its fundamental security, has been doing something about it and preparing at least to damage the Iranian effort, if not to destroy it, while the Gulf states' regimes, precisely those who are opposing the Muslim Spring lest it sweep them away in its wake, are helplessly watching and waiting. In the meantime, they are arming themselves to the teeth, to the full extent of what their wealth affords them, hoping that either the United States will interfere to destroy that nuclear capability, the US being the only one with the military to do so, or at least Israel will attempt to damage that ability by a limited strike within its means. Iran, on its part, being undeterred by economic sanctions and military threats, has been pursuing its course frantically, aiming at getting to the point of no return of possessing the bomb so as to make itself immune to any attack, which it could threaten to retaliate against with its nuclear devices.

231

During the Cold War, MAD (mutually assured destruction) was the key to deterrence between the nuclear powers, who understood that since each had the capacity to destroy the others many times over, none of them would dare to initiate an attack. The assumption was that the actors in both parts of the equation were rational and out of fear bringing disaster upon their peoples and countries would certainly refrain from precipitating a nuclear conflict. For that reason, paradoxically, it was the presence of the ultimate weapons that assured they would not be used. But in Iran, the situation may be totally different. We know from Ahmadinejad's past in the *Basij* militia that he is a fanatic believer of the imminent return of the imam to earth, something that he had prepared for as a mayor of Tehran, when he ordered the widening of the main avenues of the city to absorb all the millions who would flock to the streets to watch the return of the Hidden One. He also said that, when speaking to the UN General Assembly as president of Iran, he could feel the aura of the imam hovering over him and inspiring his speech. Since in Shi'ite eschatology the imam would choose to return, after a millennium of hiding, at precisely the worst moment of misery, injustice and oppression—what in other eschatologies are called the "pangs of the Messiah"—precipitating his return by an extreme and desperate tour de force, like using nuclear arms, could be thought the best and most feasible avenue by mad rulers who do not subscribe to the MAD theory. In other words, in the minds of irrational leaders, whose considerations and reasoning are obscured by religious fanaticism, mutual deterrence would not simply work.

Why would the Iranians wish to attack, and whom? Usually, when leaders concoct a plan of attack, they keep mute about it for the sake of the surprise effect, and they even try to create a reverse impression that they harbor no aggressive intent toward their victim. Ahmadinejad, since his advent to power, did not stop proclaiming his ambition to destroy Israel; to put an end to Zionism, which is another wording for the same; to deny the Holocaust; to instigate and dispatch terrorists against Israel and Jewish targets; to convene international conferences about Holocaust denial; to address the United Nations about his mad plan; to finance and instigate Hamas and Hizbullah against Israel; and to convene and host annual meetings of Islamic terrorism international in his capital and quite the contrary. Is anything else needed to prove his intentions, and to see to it that the lunatic man who was put at the helm of Iran must not possess nuclear arms? His intent against another member state of the UN is clearly aggressive. Instead of the

nations and the secretary general initiating harsh reprisals by ejecting Iran from the UN until it repents, they on the contrary attend the
conferences convened by UN bodies or under their auspices and listen
courteously to Ahmadinejad's convoluted speeches of nonsense and
incitement at the UN headquarters. An attack of the sort threatened
against Israel would be one of indiscriminate extermination and genocide, motivated by hate and fanaticism, while a preventive Israeli attack
geared to preempt such a disaster would be directed only against the
threatening nuclear installations of Iran, though collateral damage will
unfortunately remain inevitable.

IDF chief of staff, Lieutenant General Benny Gantz, declared in an
interview broadcast on Israel's sixty-fourth Independence Day (May
2012) that "The IDF is ready to move against Iran the minute it receives
the green light." "The Iranians are determined to build a nuclear weapon
while they continue to dupe the international community," Minister
of Defense Ehud Barak added the following day. These very fateful
declarations were not gratuitous, for Israel's leaders have been facing
a series of existential questions: should Israel attack Iran or pursue the
diplomatic track? When, if ever, is the right time to launch an attack?
How should it be executed? How will Iran's leaders react to an onslaught
on their nuclear facilities? The most likely day-after scenario, as the
international media sees it, is a devastating Iranian response based
mainly, though not entirely, on its long-range missile arsenal. This
attack would be coupled with terrorist strikes against Jewish and Israeli
targets abroad, and backed by Hizbllah, Iran's proxy in Lebanon, and
perhaps Hamas, its agent in Gaza.

If Israel initiates a military strike, something that is not likely to pass
without response, it will face an unprecedented security challenge.
Similarly, the Iranians will be confronting Israel and the West for the
first time. An attack against Iran would be far different than the bombing of the nuclear reactor in Iraq or the air strike against the reactor in
Syria because for Israel, the element of surprise is already gone with
the Iranians putting their nation in a virtual state of preparedness.
We should assume that the regime in Tehran will make every effort
to cause Israel such severe damage as to impute to itself the status of
a regional power, for Iran cannot allow the campaign to end with it
appearing ruined and humiliated. Iran will also seek to safeguard its
nuclear project so that it can quickly resume operations if damaged.
Those that believe Iran's geographical distance from Israel will limit
the Iranian response, and that it will consist mainly of long-range

counterfire, fail to take into account the Iran-Syria-Hizbullah axis that enables Iran to bridge great distances, despite the current Syrian turmoil that has curtailed that capacity. The Syrian situation allowing, the Iranian Republican Guard ground forces could be deployed along Israel's northern border and even engage the IDF in a protracted guerilla campaign on the frontlines.[4]

In such a scenario, for the first time, Hizbullah would be completely subordinate to Tehran's leadership and to the Iranian military command, even though it is a Lebanese organization supported by the country's Shi'ite population. In an Israeli-Iranian war, and provided the Syrian arena is still operative, Hizbullah would take orders from Iran in its first and perhaps only real opportunity to repay the enormous debt that it owes to Iran for building up its military strength. More options could open up if Iran could launch a preemptive strike and place responsibility on Hizbullah, since Tehran has no interest in becoming entangled in hostilities prior to an Israeli attack. After an Israeli strike, the scope of Hizbullah's rocket fire into Israel's depth could parallel the developments in the fighting between Israel and Iran, and it would take time for Israel before it could completely silence that fire, either from the air or by land attacks. Israel should not be surprised if this time the rocket and missile fire is entirely different from the past. Instead of gradual escalation at the outset, Hizbullah could unleash a massive missile barrage into the heart of Tel Aviv, forcing Israel to proceed with great caution in light of Iran's policy and culture. A long and bitter guerilla struggle may ensue, one that could last for a year or a number of years against Iranian combat units on Israel's northern border, if the Syrian situation allows their deployment.[5] The missile exchange between Israel and Gaza in October 2012, which was initiated by Hamas, may in fact have been an Iranian rehearsal to test the soft belly of Israel in terms of missile defense and the reaction of the Israeli public when exposed to massive missile attacks.

Nevertheless, and despite Israel's warnings, the West was relishing being duped. There had been ten years of negotiations, warnings, sweet talk by Iran, promises that the nuclear plan was only for peaceful ends; ten years of counterthreats of the West, accompanied by sanctions that have not had much effect so far, and after all this the program, if anything, has been accelerated in an effort by Tehran to get the bomb and thus constrain its rivals of all sorts to deal with containing the bomb instead of preventing it. Some US think tanks strongly argued against meeting Iran's demand during the negotiations that its right to enrich uranium should be acknowledged. The text of the Nuclear Non-Proliferation Treaty does not grant such a right, and moreover, Iran has violated the conditions the treaty sets out in order to receive "the right to peaceful use of nuclear energy." Some American strategists go on to argue that Iran was using the demand for acknowledgement of the supposed right to enrich uranium because it places its P5+1 (the five Security Council permanent members and Germany) interlocutors in a lose-lose situation. Therefore the negotiating world powers should challenge this false claim more directly.[6]

Others exposed alleged Iranian nuclear intentions based on what appeared to be the Iranian position papers for its negotiators from the talks in Istanbul in July 2012. The document—whose authenticity is not independently verified—indicates that rather than being prepared to curtail its uranium enrichment activities, Iran was actually planning to expand them, calling for four additional research reactors and new programs to sell nuclear fuel to other countries. The document also indicated that Iran was unwilling to consider closing the heavily forti-fied Fordow nuclear plant, as the international community has been demanding, and insistent on an unlimited right to enrich uranium to 3.5 percent—though perhaps showing some room for flexibility on the 20 percent enrichment (technically very close level to weapons grade) taking place at Fordow. Still others argued that it was probably a bad bet to hope that increasingly tight sanctions would soon bring greater Iranian flexibility at the negotiating table. Current and historical evidence was adduced to suggest that while the sanctions are affect-ing Tehran's oil exports and therefore very important regime revenue streams, this effect is more likely to decrease rather than increase over time, therefore the way forward is to find other means to target the regime's vulnerabilities, including stepping up pressure on Tehran's allies in Damascus, as if they were not pressured enough by their own turmoil, increasing the regime's isolation and bolstering the credibility of military threats against it, bearing in mind that the longer the threat remains a mere threat, Iran is more and more tempted to call the bluff.[7]

Iraq

Iraq was founded following the defeat of the Ottomans in World War I, from the artificial merger of three former provinces (*vilayet*) as an Arab kingdom under a British mandate. It has known an uninterrupted series of violent acts, coups, civil disruptions, rebellions, frictions, and inter-ethnic and inter-religious clashes, mainly due to the forced combination into one state of various ethnic groups (Arabs, Kurds, Turkmen) and religious communities (Shi'ite majority and Sunnite minority), together with an entire gamut of ancient Christian churches like the Assyrians, many of whom were forced under the pressure of violence to migrate to the West. In the modern era, in the wake of the violent coup against the monarchy in 1958, in contrast with the relatively tame nature of the 1952 Revolution of the Free Officers in Egypt, a series of military takeovers followed until in the last of them, in 1975, by Saddam Hussein, the vice head of the Revolutionary Council, was set on the trajectory to become the dictator and head of that most cruel of tyrannies, under the cover of the Ba'ath Party (the revival), which had been founded in Syria in the 1940s and dominated the two countries since the 1970s under Saddam and Hafez Assad, respectively. However, contrary to the Tunisian al-Nahda, which aspired for Islamic revival, the Ba'ath professed nationalism and socialism. All Iraqi upheavals were accompanied by extensive killings, cruelty, and the exploitation of the country's rich oil reserves to afford a heavy rearmament of the country and satisfy the corrupt rulers. But, no tyrant in that sad history had come even remotely close to Saddam, who established new records for murder and cruelty toward his own people, and had a reign of terror that even the Assads in Syria did not attain. He especially annihilated Shi'ites and Kurds, including using chemical warfare to slaughter them by the thousands. Externally, he waged an eight-year war with Iran (1980–88) which cost one million casualties; he invaded Kuwait until Iraq was expelled by the Americans in 1991; and only after America's incursion once again in 2003, on the merit of seizing nonconventional weapons and ejecting the tyrant, did the first normal election take place, under American guidance, an election that put the Shi'ite majority in command of the state destiny.

Thus, in contrast with Iran—which is also predominantly Shi'ite and which initiated its Spring (the Islamic Revolution) thirty years before all the rest, with the same goal of toppling the tyrant and establishing in his stead a legitimate Islamic government—Iraq under Saddam looked so fatally trapped in the dictatorship of the Sunni minority (based on Tikrit in the northwest, in the heart of the Sunni Triangle) and so frightened by the impending ruthless retaliation that would descend irrevocably on whoever resisted, that liberation seemed all but impossible. Indeed, as he expressed his grandiose aspirations by building several palaces and by investing foolishly in the military—for no one was threatening him—he determined that he needed a million-man army to attain his goals and boasted that he could "burn half of Israel" and develop unconventional weapons in order to lend himself credibility as the leader of the Arab world. He was for many of his fellow Arabs the new Saladin, following the death of his great predecessor in that role model—abdul-Nasser of Egypt, who was to resolve all Arabs' problems and bring them salvation and greatness. Saddam pledged to destroy Israel and was the only Arab leader who promised and paid every family of Palestinians who fell in battle a pension of $25,000. Above all, he craved an opportunity to take over most of the oil resources of the Gulf so as to bring the world to its knees and to become the sole arbiter of power and wealth in the world. For that, he planned and executed his invasion of Iran, hoping to take advantage of the chaotic state of revolutionary Iran and seize its Gulf coast Arab-inhabited Khuzistan, centered on Khurramshar, which would allow him to expand his oil resources and his narrow coastline on the Gulf for his growing navy. But his bloody war of eight years and a million casualties ended inconclusively, in spite of the massive support he got from the Arab countries in the fateful "jihad against the Iranian idolaters," as Saddam put it. Two years later, after he had slightly recovered from the Iranian fiasco, he tried again, this time on the other side of the Gulf in Kuwait, which once again would afford him oil riches and coastline of which he had only a trifle. Had he pursued his invasion into Saudi Arabia and not allowed the United States the time to gather a coalition to defeat him, he may have pulled a tremendous victory out of his hazardous gamble, but he did not; he was forced out of Kuwait, and the rest is history.

On the occasion of Saddam's defeat and being forced out of Kuwait, the Shi'ites rebelled, and this could have been their finest hour, had the Americans not betrayed them and left them to be massacred by Saddam after they had encouraged them to rise. They could have launched their Spring thirty years earlier than the rest of the Arabs and achieved it with less bloodshed and less suffering, and with less cost to the Americans. In reality, their liberation from Saddam did not come until twenty-two years after Iran's Spring, but ten years before Tunisia, Egypt, and Libya. They were ready for it then, but unlike 2011, when the Americans supported the rebels of the Spring and abandoned the tyrants, in 1991 they were shortsighted and not prepared to do so, and let the murderer of Tikrit slaughter the Shi'ite rebels at will and quell the rebellion with blood, something that would cost them much when in their 2003 incursion they found that the Shi'ites had lost their trust in them. But the Shi'ites knew how to renew their stamina for a new

Spring, when after the capture of the dictator and his execution, they exploited the American-imposed elections to set up successive elected Shi'ite governments to manage the affairs of the country, even though terrorism and insecurity, instigated by supporters of the *ancien regime*, continued unwavering.

The Kurds too had their own Spring as they had never experienced before, as their formal autonomy was reinforced constitutionally by being recognized as one of the three constituents of the state, and their representative was made the president (though only protocolary) of the federated state. When the Americans departed in 2011, the security problems were bound to escalate, and the low level of concern for human life in the entire country seems to persist, given the nonexistence of an efficient law enforcement agency and the unresolved problems of food supply and electricity manufacturing. The political system is still fragile, and there is no certainty that, unlike in Japan after the world war, the American-imposed constitution and political system will endure. Conversely, neighboring Iran, has had a great influence on the Iraqi upheaval and, thereafter, due to the commonality with Iraq of a Shi'ite background, and Iran's opposition to some of those American reforms as contradicting Shi'ite doctrine. Here too, much time will be required before stability is achieved and clear boundaries are set to the Iranian interference in the affairs of her junior Shi'ite sister in Iraq. Also, the fact that the most important Shi'ite holy places, like Najaf and Karbala and more, are located in Iraq necessitates open borders for the free flow of people on holidays of pilgrimage, a situation that can pose many scenarios of Iranian meddling in the affairs of the country. All in all, it should be remembered that the achievements of this early spring in Iraq were only made possible thanks to American help, for had they not cleared the way by eliminating Saddam and his regime, it is doubtful whether his terrifying conduct would have left Shi'ite rebels any chance of succeeding.

There is another doctrinal aspect that may complicate things in Iraq even further: the Iraqi doctors of the holy law react to politics differently than their Iranian neighbors, though close relationships tie them together; they share common holy sites, holidays, and religious customs with the Iranians; and they also regard Qom, the holy city of Iranian Shi'a and its main center of religious thinking and study, as theirs too, a kind of al-Azhar for the Shi'a. To all those places millions of believers flock from both Iran and Iraq on days of *Ashura*, for the bloody and frightening rituals of the *ta'zya*, the identification with the suffering and death as martyr of Hussein and his retinue. But the Iraqi Shi'a, although it also gave rise to some celebrated ayatullahs whose authority was widely recognized, like Kho'i and Sadr, always lived by the passive model of old, being unable to shake the yoke of Saddam's oppression. Therefore, they never converted to the active model of Khumeini that made the mullahs part of the state political hierarchy, not only spiritual guides. Whether Iranian sponsorship over Iraq will, after the departure of the Americans, continue to impact the Iraqi order by the twin innovations of Khumeini (*Wilayat al-Faqih* and *Marja' Taqlid*), it will take a long time before the newly set political parties in Iraq will relinquish their newly acquired powers, and the revered Iraqi ayatullahs, chief among them Sistani, will reconsider their reluctance to get involved in politics.

Lebanon and Hizbullah

Lebanon has seemingly been the most difficult of all Arab countries to define, as the trend of Spring that was identifiable in all twenty-five Islamic countries (about half of the total) surveyed above in the context of the Spring, is left very much hinging on what will happen in Syria, its sponsor and lifeline. Some commentators believe that Hizbullah will not be able to bear Assad's disappearance and therefore will have to respond militarily and take over the rule in Beirut, unless it will consider that the array of forces against it might cause its total destruction. Others emphasize that Hizbullah has been strengthening its fortifications in southern Beirut's Dahiya neighborhood, at a time when Hassan Nasrallah its leader has increased his verbal attacks in all directions, which are usually a sign or panic and weakness. More-over, clerics who support the party have been issuing a series of fatwas (religious verdicts), allowing their party to fight against the Lebanese troops when the chips are down, and the moment of showdown will come against either the Lebanese or the Syrian forces, or both, if and when an inevitable civil war again breaks out in the country, or orders are received from Iran, or a surviving Assad, to direct the guns and missiles toward Israel. The view prevails that Hizbullah will be able to take over the government in Beirut through a military coup, whether amid a massive civil demonstration, the scope of which had allowed it in May 2007 to take over parts of Beirut, or using its abundance of weapons to create chaos in the country, and then pose as the savior of its sovereignty, something that is surely to be opposed by the rival factions.

Many things have changed since that day of 2007, when as a result of Assad's humiliation by the United States as he was constrained to evacuate his occupation troops from Lebanon, Hizbullah intervened by force to take its predominant part in Lebanon's politics. First, one has to recall that the quota system that had been the base of Lebanese politics since the 1940s, where the presidency went to the Maronite-Christian community, the prime ministership to the Sunnites, the speakership of Parliament to the Shi'ites, etc., had been altered by the Ta'if Accords of the 1980s, mediated by Saudi Arabia, who had accepted Syria's role in Lebanon due to what she thought was the "stabilizing effect it had on the country." Little did she envisage how destructive would Syria become to the equilibrium in Lebanon due to its alliance with Hizbullah and with Iran. In fact, the new arrangement not only recognized Syria's advantageous position, but although it did not nominally change the quota communal system of dividing power, it made sure that nothing could be done or decided domestically in the country without Damascus's approval. Syria ensured that prerogative through its agent, Hizbullah, which gained the veto power in government, although it constituted a minority in the cabinet. Hizbullah, which was until then a military movement, constituted by Iran among the Shi'ites, who had been downtrodden and exploited for generations, took a turn after the Israeli incursion into Lebanon in 1982 and acquired the aspects of a political movement with representation in Parliament and in the Cabinet so as to gain legitimacy as a political force in the country.

Hizbullah, which is armed to the teeth, especially with missiles and rockets from Iran and Syria as their proxy, became an important player in Lebanese politics and imposed its will, backed by its sponsors, to maintain its private militia and armament, which made it a powerful military actor, for whom the weak and spineless Lebanese Forces have become no match. Thus, while the president has remained Maronite and the prime minister Sunnite, etc., none of them could be elected unless agreed upon by Hizbullah/Syria/Iran. This made the top Lebanese politicians in government the stooges of this unholy triangle, and they could maintain their positions only through their assiduous commute between Beirut and Damascus, and their total submission to the Syrian representatives in Lebanon, military or civil, who called the shots. Even Walid Junblatt, the son of the legendary Druze leader Kamal Junblatt, who was in opposition to Syria and one of its major critics, had to repent and made the pilgrimage to Damascus to prostrate before Assad. Little did he know that briefly thereafter, Assad's legitimacy itself would be shaken by the uprising against him from the onset of 2011, and that this humiliating measure of sycophancy would have been taken in vain.

Hizbullah's claim to legitimacy does not only stem from its military power, which is in fact the only real military force in Lebanon, and the only massively armed power that can maintain some equilibrium of fear with Israel, but also the fact that it has a political, financial, and military backing from outside the country. There has been a strong, mainly Christian, opposition as well as Sunni rivalry to the subversive power of Hizbullah in its service of foreign interests, especially in the times of Rafiq Hariri, the Saudi-supported millionaire builder who was prime minister and put in some of his resources to rebuild the country after the civil war; but he was assassinated by the Hizbullah-Syrians-Iranians, and his son Sa'd was appointed instead, in line with the tradition of son often succeeding father in the destructive quota system that was gradually falling apart. The key was the changing demographic proportions between the various communities, with everyone sensing that it grew more than others and demanding a new census to determine the new distribution of power. But the new census never took place, though everyone knew that Christians were no longer the largest community and therefore no longer deserved the presidency. Conversely, as the Shi'ites grew in numbers, they claimed the primacy in the new power configuration. Both communities were satisfied by the Christians keeping the top political post, but provided they followed the Syrian *diktat*. The Shi'ites have been watching with pride their Hizbullah militia occupying a prime and independent position in government beyond their numbers (a few thousands only), while the much larger Shi'ite population, comprised in the Amal Movement and Shi'ite commoners in the south, are kept in their marginality.

The political balance until the Spring often broke down and disturbed the Arab and Islamic scene, essentially maintaining Hizbullah as the real power broker in Lebanon, not by the power of legitimacy but by the legitimacy of power. The Lebanese public remains divided: on the one hand, parts of the Christians, like the Christian militias of Samir Geagea, previously loyal to the Jumayyel family, the founders of the Phalangs who oppose Islamic rule, the Sunnites who support the Hariri family, and some minorities like the Druze who were aligned on this side until their leader submitted to Syria just before the Spring; this faction was in power with Sa'd Hariri, the prime minister, enjoying American and Saudi support, and clamoring for the publication of the investigation results of the Hariri murder, commissioned by the UN. On the other hand, the March 8 forces, part of the Sunnis now in government who obey Syria, in collaboration with some Christians who perversely support Hizbullah, like Michel Aoun, one of those turncoats who make Lebanese politics so hazardous, unreliable, and unpredictable; most of the Shi'ites who relish the power wielded by their community; and other indecisive and undecided elements in the shifting sands of Lebanese politics. In view of the fragility of the Lebanese army, which is ostensibly made up of members of all communities, and can break up at the first sign of a renewed civil war, Hizbullah stands as the pillar of defense of the country, paradoxically as its head, Hassan Nasrallah, has been hiding in a bunker since 2006 when his forces were crushed by Israel.

Al-Asir, the Shi'ite cleric who opposes Syrian and Iranian influence in Lebanon, accused Hizbullah of using its weapons not to promote the Palestinian cause but rather to control Lebanon and subjugate it to Iran. In a July 6, 2012, speech he called Nasrallah and Berri (the Shi'ite Speaker of Parliament) "war criminals," and blamed them for all the assassinations and assassination attempts in Lebanon since the murder of Rafiq Al-Hariri in 2005. Al-Asir and hundreds of his followers—men, women and children—on June 27, 2012, launched a strike at the northern entrance to the city demanding to disarm Hizbullah, and even blocked traffic on the main highway to Beirut. He declared publicly that Hizbullah's weapons "have lost their honor in the eyes of most Lebanese," because, since Israel's withdrawal from South Lebanon in 2000, they have served the organization as a tool for taking over Lebanon.[8]

Notes

1. For this distinction between institutional and diffused religion, see C. K. Yang, *Religion in Chinese Society*, UC Berkeley Press, 1967, chap. XII, pp. 294–340.
2. Khumeini, Ayatullah, *The Islamic Republic*, op. cit.; Sayyid Qutb, *Our War against the Jews*, op. cit.
3. *al-Quds al-Arabi*, London, June 18, 2012.
4. This passage is based on an article published in *Israel Defense*, Issue #8, 2012.
5. Ibid.
6. Michael Makovsky and Blaise Misztal, *Wall Street Journal*, July 8, 2012.
7. David Horovitz, *Times of Israel*, July 9, 2012.
8. Summary of a speech carried by Lebanese media on July 6, 2012.

10

Algeria, Mali, Sudan, Somalia, the Palestinians, and the Revolutionary Model

Although characteristics of every model can be found in each of the five others, there is nevertheless one brand of Islamic countries and entities that does not accord with all others. It is the revolutionary kind, which is always restless and unsettled and does not seem to find any satisfactory base to found a permanent arrangement for a stable future. It is in constant search, in which it finds its real interest, for it yearns not for a set goal but for the way to get there. Mali, that remote, isolated, and scorched land at the edge of the Sahara, which had known glorious days when Timbuktu was a famous commercial and study center on the fringes of the world of Islam, is once again shaken by the Islamic Spring in rather odd ways. In previous years it was the Algerians, the Sudanese, the Palestinians, and the Somalis who provided the paradigms for this model, but this keeps shifting, since none of those has finally settled down in contentment to enjoy the fruit of its revolution. Mali, this vast desert country, following a few decades of independence and cultivation of modern nationalism has reverted to a civil war about its identity, very reminiscent of the one between the national movement of the Palestinians and Hamas, which challenges it from the very heart of the Palestinian people; between the FLN governments since the days of Ben Bella and Boumedienne, until the days when the Islamic armed groups attempted via military action and bullets to obtain power once their victory in the ballots was denied them; in Sudan, it was the breakdown in the alliance between Umar Bashir, the military arm, and Hassan Turabi, the spiritual head, that caused the unrest, in contrast with the seeming harmony between those branches of power that has been exhibited in the Saudi monarchy; and finally in Somalia, where a working government seemed to function after the emancipation of

243

the country from colonial rule, but fell to the gangs of robbers, pirates, and fundamentalist Muslims who have thrown the country into chaos.

Algeria

The Algerians, who had been occupied by France since 1830, erupted in their revolution in the 1960s, and fought, via their revolutionary arm the FLN (Front de Liberation Nationale) to achieve independence, via a bloody and brutal war until they evicted the French colonizer, which had considered that colony as part of France and encouraged settlement in it. But like in other Arab and Muslim cases, dictators took over after liberation, turning the liberators into oppressors. That was the single-party rule of the FLN, copied from the centralist Soviets and from neighboring Egypt under Nasser. That style of rule was brought to its apogee by Houari Boumedienne who ruled with an iron fist most of those postrevolution years until his death. In 1991, after his death, a first Spring dawned on Algeria, when free and democratic elections were announced. For the first time, the Muslim fundamentalists ran, challenging the monopoly on power of the FLN. An extraordinary replica of another revolutionary model under Mao Tse-tung in China, known as the Hundred Flowers, unfolded then in Algeria, and no one expected it to erupt, least of all to succeed, and it put an end to that early Spring.

To explain that example, in 1956, when Mao felt comfortable that his 1949 revolution in China had taken root due to its mass-line, which addressed itself to the concerns of the poor peasants, he announced over the limited media of the time: "Let 100 flowers bloom!" This was taken by the public to mean, based on an ancient historical allusion, that open criticism should be given to more than the one-flower culture of the Communist Revolution. He probably believed that in order to get some kind of half-muted feedback about the achievements of the Revolution, so as to give the feeling to the masses that their voice was heard, he could loosen the leashes of control and let people release their criticism, trusting that they would not go too far. Little did he know that after some hesitation, and seeing that nothing unpleasant was happening, the trickle of different opinions grew into a cascade of criticism that threatened the very fundaments of the Revolution and the state. The backlash was violent, in the form of the Great Leap Forward, which was probably the darkest event in modern Chinese history, when the citizens were asked to double their efforts to catch up with the hated West, Party controls were tightened, and major campaigns for ideological purity and devotion to society and state work—together with the gathering pace of collectivization—made China go backward economically instead of taking the great leap it was trying to achieve. Perhaps no greater disruption of China's economy and social order was registered in China until the Cultural Revolution ten years later (1966–76).

In Algeria, the announcement of the democratic and free elections caused a similar jolt in society, and little by little the excitement brought out the unsatisfied victims of the Revolution who followed the passionate sermons of the Islamic Movement, which seemed to win the elections when they got a majority in every first-round polling, something similar to what happened with the Brothers at Tahrir twenty years later. But unlike the Egyptians, who accepted the results of the elections and had a constitutional court to arbitrate in case of disagreement, the military who backed the FLN regime in Algeria thought that the exercise of democracy had gone too far. When they realized that in the first round the Islamic parties were gathering enough momentum to win the elections handily in the second round, they entered the fray, took over the rule, canceled the results of the elections, and imprisoned the heads of the fundamentalist who dared to win, thus trespassing and abusing the goodwill of the authorities who had hoped that no one could or would challenge the popularity of the FLN. The Islamic parties, which transformed themselves into the GIA (Groupes Islamiques Armes), then launched an unprecedented era of terror against the military government and its supporters, producing casualties in the hundreds of thousands and provoking retaliatory campaigns that some estimate were more violent than even the war of independence in the 1960s. As the slaughter receded and civilian rule was restored, dictatorial all the same, headed by veteran foreign minister under the military rule, abd-al-Aziz Bouteflika, discontent and unrest lingered and erupted again, provoked by what was happening on both sides of the country's borders: Egypt, Tunisia, and Libya in the east, Morocco in the West, and the rest of the Islamic world.

Already on Saturday, February 12, 2011, thousands in Algiers had violated the ban on demonstrations when they confronted policemen and shouted down President Bouteflika and his ban, demanding a democratic regime in the country and wishing the Egyptian people well in aiming at the same goal. According to estimates, the crowds of demonstrators amounted to ten thousand, their way to the city streets blocked by police. They protested against the president, who had been

245

ruling the country since 1999, and demanded plain democracy. Though the state has been ruled by emergency laws in the past twenty years, and gatherings for demonstrations have been banned, the demonstrators, encouraged by the Spring around them, defied all that in the face of the many arrests made by police. This event was seen as auguring ill for the government, due to the success of the Egyptian demonstrations to topple Mubarak in Egypt after thirty years of rule, and less than one month after the removal of Ben Ali from neighboring Tunisia. The Algerian government announced that emergency rule would be abolished soon, but that the ban on demonstrations would remain valid. As a safety precaution, the authorities who knew that this was coming reinforced police presence in strategic parts of the city of Algiers, positioning roadblocks to prevent assembly of large audiences. Like their peers in the Arab world, the young in Algeria suffer from unemployment, poverty, and lack of human rights. But many also remember that in the 1990s an attempt to take over the regime by Muslim parties caused hundreds of thousands of casualties.

Does this mean that the Algerian Spring has been nipped in the bud, as some commentators claim, or that the Algerian people, exhausted by the many years of revolution and unrest, have not so far exhibited the determination and stamina of the Syrians and the Libyans to carry on until the tyrant is toppled? There were extensive street demonstrations, as in Egypt and Tunisia, but no revolution was accomplished. It is true that Bouteflika promised at the outset of the troubles some modest reforms, and he succeeded in holding on to power. True also that in early May 2012 parliamentary elections were held, in which the FLN, like Mubarak's Democratic Party, won a sweeping majority of the votes, but the same suspicion of rigging is inevitably raised, notwithstanding the outrageous and sycophantic declarations of the USA and Europe that they were "a step toward democracy." Despite the fact that al-Jazeera has been banned by the government since 2004 due to its sympathies to the opposition, *People and Power* (May 17, 2012) investigated and released many details of their findings. It found Algiers freer and more lively than its researchers expected, with the open shops and cafes not giving the impression of a place on the cusp of revolution. Only when they began meeting human rights activists did they get a sense of what common Algerians were up against.

One of the most prevalent features that is omnipresent is the DRS, which is the security and intelligence apparatus, compelling the investigators to arrange all meetings discreetly, and only then would the informants speak freely of the economic problems, the housing crisis, unemployment, and out-of-control food prices. They reported many young people (by their own count 130 in 2011 alone) who burned themselves in despair, probably following the Tunisian example. Some young Algerians agreed that their Spring spark had been kindled twenty years earlier when in 1988 their demonstrations in the streets had forced the government of the FLN to hold free and fair elections. But when the islamique Party (FIS is the Front islamique du Salut, the islamique Front of Salvation) was seen as set to win, the military intervened and abrogated those elections. The dark decade that followed saw two hundred thousand Algerians killed in the civil war. That sinister memory assists the DRS in maintaining its stranglehold on a frightened population. In addition, the families of the twenty thousand disappeared people during the decade of the massive slaughters, who still hope to see them back, do not dare to wreck the boat of their hopes by a premature eruption of violence. But many are still certain that Algeria is not an exception and the revolution will come sooner rather than later.

In another article published in June 2012, Anna Mahjar-Barducci[1] made the point that Algeria was one of the rare countries of indecision, where the unrest was neither totally suppressed nor carried its revolution to success. That permitted the May 10 elections to end victoriously for the FLN (208 out of 462 seats), due to the fraud, but even then they won only some 40 percent of the vote, which was enough for the ruling party to lead the government. If anything, unlike the 60–80 percent enthusiastic participation in the free votes of the Spring in those countries where it succeeded, in Algeria it remained only 43 percent, in itself an indication of the lack of enthusiasm that emanated, at least partly, from the call of the Kabyls and some civil organizations to boycott voting so as to delegitimize the fraudulent government which tried to put up the face, with great success, of Western-democratic-liberal free elections. The darker side was expressed in the arrest of bloggers when they posted clips on YouTube urging Algerians not to vote. The bloggers signed their announcement: "Independent Youth for a Genuine Change." Some thought that the low turnout symbolized a rupture with the regime, which represented only itself. It is true that the emergency rules that had been in place for the past twenty years were lifted in February 2011, but this did not translate into greater rights and freedom of association and expression. Instead, the military-dominated government used the opportunity to tighten its grip on society. Instead of the promised reforms, new laws increasing the controls by the army were enacted, for example on the judiciary. The interior ministry gained new authority to oversee political parties and civil society associations. The rule of the DRS over the country, where it is rumored that they also have links to the Islamic groups—including al-Qa'ida, which they are supposed to fight—makes Algeria very similar to Pakistan. Both fight terrorism and collaborate with the West on the surface, but in secret they promote and support the troublemaking Muslim radicals, the fight against whom alone can justify the ruling juntas' continued hold on power.

Mali-Azwad

The characteristic that has accompanied Muslim fundamentalist movements and is now shaking, as part of the Islamic Spring, what was heretofore a quiet and stable country like Mali has been their hostility to folk and popular religion, notably the worship of saints, as if they feared that simple folk beliefs, which do not require any high-flung philosophical dissertations, threaten the exclusive grip that doctors of the holy law have upon the shari'a and its interpretation. The worship of saints is quite current in Islam, especially in Africa, and its persecution is founded on the Wahhabi precedent of eighteenth-century Arabia that stands at the base of present-day puritanical Saudi Arabia. The founders of the movement then, like today in north Mali, condemned the worship of anyone but Allah for fear of the grave sin of *shirk*, namely the association of man with the worship of Allah, who alone is entitled to undivided adulation, which is the obverse of *tawhid*, the exclusive unity of Allah.

It was this fanatic belief that had brought the Wahhabis in their time to the blind extreme of destroying even the tomb of the Prophet in Medina, lest anyone should conclude that if the worship of the Prophet is permitted, so must be that of other humans. Today's fundamentalists of northern Mali not only demand the establishment of a Muslim state in Northern Mali, but they also aspire to turn Timbuktu, the one-millennium-old Muslim city—which became famous for its mosques, the thousands of manuscripts of its libraries, and the international cross-Saharan trade routes that crossed it—into a purely Muslim city, cleansed from all the intrusive foreign innovations that had come to contaminate it. Naturally, the destruction of historical buildings and the elimination of such a long heritage in the name of religion have prompted champions of world culture like UNESCO to their feet, exactly as in the time of the Taliban in Afghanistan in the 1990s when the puritanical regime there decided to blow up the giant Buddhas of Bamyan in spite of the outrage they caused across the world and the supplications from many world leaders, including Saudis, who begged that those cultural sites be spared. It was the international echoes to this development that reverberated around the world and escalated this rather local and parochial event into an international happening of major importance that attracted much interest in the media.

The new state that its initiators wish to detach from Mali and dub Azwad was proclaimed on April 6, 2012, one full year into the Islamic Spring, which had swept across a much wider swath of Islamic land than the minimalist advocates of the Arab Spring initially suggested. The National Movement for the Liberation of Azwad announced on that day its detachment from Mali and the establishment of an independent and secular state comprising all resident ethnic groups: Touareg, Arabs, Mauris, Mandika, and others. For the time being, the exact plans and aims of the movement are not very clear, due to its own self-characterization as secular and pro-Western, which might be just a way to improve public opinion in the West. Conversely, precisely in order to discredit it in the eyes of the West, it was said that it was fundamentalist Islamic and tied to the North Africa branch of al-Qa'ida (AQIM), which is active in the Sahara. In any case, constituting 60 percent of the vast territory of Mali, which is larger than France, it has already raised opposition in its environment. What has triggered fears in the West is the agreement that it signed on May 26, 2012, at the height of the Spring, in the town of Gao, the provisional capital of the provisional state, between one of the heads of the movement, Bilal al-Sharif, and a leader of the radical Islamic Ansar al-Din (Supporters of the Religion) Movement, which is recognized as a fundamentalist trend in the region. It was precisely the fact that the accord was not published immediately after its signature that led to suspicions that some elements in it deserved concealment. Guesses that have not been verified claim that a military alliance has been concluded between the two movements and that the new state will be managed under shari'a law. Other members in the leadership of the movement were reported to say that they opposed the tendencies of Arabization and Islamization of the new state. All in all, it seems as if the struggles regarding the inauguration of Azwad are at their initial stages and that the nature of the new state, if its establishment were to be confirmed, is far from revealing itself. Be that it as may, it is clear that placid and marginal Mali has been swept up in the Spring tsunami of the Middle East.

How Mali can connect to the Islamic Spring has already been exemplified by reported large-scale reprisals that were led by Libya against perceived supporters of Qaddafi's regime, namely the Touareg, who have consequently fled south into Mali.

West African leaders, sensing the malaise of the Spring seeping into their countries from across the Sahara, and wary not to let any foreign forces interfere as they did in Libya, have been consulting on how to deal with the crisis on their own before it spreads into their countries, under the instigation of the former colonizing powers, notably France. On Sep 17, 2012, the leaders of ECOWAS (the Economic Community of West African States) met in Abidjan, the capital of the Ivory Coast, to approve the mission of their organization to Azawad, known as MICEM, with a view to restore stability to Mali after the previous March coup. The organization has had 3,300 regional troops on standby for months, awaiting a formal Security Council resolution for a military deployment. On October 12, 2012, the council approved Resolution 2071, which pressed ECOWAS to speed up preparations for military intervention in Azawad. The secretary general appointed his representative to the Sahel, and military preparations were under way, helped by France, which ultimately took charge of the operation and sent its troops to quell the rebels. But in view of the UN impotence in Bosnia and Syria, and its constant search for soft spots where it may succeed, instead of imposing staunch rules on difficult area where success is difficult and costly, one may doubt the forthcoming speedy solution of this novel issue.

The Palestinians

Like the Mali-Azawad upheaval, which is unfolding within a movement without a state, the Palestinians have been experiencing their Spring since the rise of Hamas in the 1980s, but have not much improved their fate by achieving the independence for their own people that they have been vying for, and for which they were founded in the first place. But unlike Azawad, which most common people cannot even identify on any map, the Palestinians have achieved world recognition and have been regular guests on the TV screens of all Western households. Their leaders have also become household names, and every incident involving Palestinians receives such coverage in the Western press that very often Europeans know more about Palestinians than they know about their own country and political affairs. This trend of Palestinism, which in France even generated a political party that ran for elections on a Palestinian platform, did not differentiate between those Palestinians who were allegedly prepared to negotiate and make peace with Israel, who signed the Oslo Accords (1993) and set up the Palestinian Authority (PA) in conjunction with Israel, and the Hamas members who remain committed to terror and to the destruction of Israel. Both were the wronged underdogs in the eyes of Europeans, regardless of what they did, and by definition Israel then came up as the culprit, no matter what it did not do. This European attitude of forgiveness toward the Palestinians naturally encouraged Hamas to celebrate its early Spring beyond any reproach or criticism, and to push forward with its one-sided subversion of both the Palestinian Authority and Israel, as to precipitate violent Israeli reactions which culminated in the Gaza War of 2008–9, that focused the blame on Israel and stepped up the Hamas Spring, which ultimately came to full fruition when a similar process broke out in next-door Egypt in January 2011, and the two sister-organizations of the Muslim Brothers and Hamas became united in action, not only in theory.

During the forty years of Yasser Arafat's leadership of the Palestinian movement, since his rise in the 1960s until his death in 2004, with few firm achievements on the ground and after having missed many opportunities to settle with Israel and to obtain a state for his unfortunate people, the Palestinians had occupied the frontline of the revolutionary model, which had been led by the Algerians before that. It appears today, after the failure of the Oslo experiment, that all Arafat was interested in was not setting up a peaceful state and dealing with the routine and boring affairs of management and daily life, but more in creating chaos and conflict, undermining others' rule and attracting international attention. Indeed, under his leadership, the Palestinians concocted their national charter in 1964 and amended it in 1968, making it the expression not of the legitimate rights of the Palestinian people for nationhood, or of the dream for national reconstruction in peace, but the nightmare of his neighbors, the Israelis, whom he pledged to destroy and replace. He was given shelter by Jordan, and instead of gratitude, he demonstrated his ambition to reverse the rule of the king in Black September (1970), until he was defeated and expelled. He was exiled into Lebanon, which he robbed from its sovereignty and turned into a base (*Fatahland*) to attack and harass Israel, until Israel felt constrained to mop up that territory and cleanse him out of there, upon which he was evacuated to Tunisia. Mindless Israeli officials tried to coax Arafat by offering him negotiations and a Palestinian state, which he accepted only in order to find a new base to undermine the naive Zionist state from within. Only his death brought his machinations to an end and left his people bereft of any major achievement, except for the division of the Palestinians between those who still sought a settlement with Israel but did not command the majority of public opinion to execute it (the PA), and those who followed dreams of a Spring that might rid them of Israel totally, and therefore refused to negotiate, much less to compromise.

Immediately after the Arab fiasco in the 1967 war, Arafat's proximity in Jordan to the newly Israeli-occupied West Bank put him in a novel revolutionary situation of his own: he had the distinction, he believed, of remaining the only Arab leader fighting Israel after all the others had been routed, something that would enhance his prestige as the chief of all Palestinians, half of whom were in Jordan, one-third in the West Bank (and Gaza), and the rest within Israel and the refugee camps in Lebanon and Syria. The Palestinians could not contain their pride at standing firm as the avant-garde of Arab nationalism, even though defeated and humiliated Nasser still retained his crown of leadership. For want of social networks (Facebook and Internet) and of al-Jazeera at the time—which two generations later were to make the world aware of the common people, thereby reinforcing its power—it was revolutionary leaders like Arafat, and diminished Nasser, who aroused the masses and raised hope among them, hence the tremendous attraction that the chairman had among his people and the Arab masses in the world. His charisma was also reinforced by the near uniqueness of his position as a leader-fighter, which made him known and famous, popular and attractive, able to trigger a spring of hope and promise, unlike the other Arab leaders of the current Spring, who were dismissed and humiliated as stale, condemned, blamed, and rejected by their peoples, if not worse. From this perspective, the Palestinian pre-Spring of the aftermath of 1967 not only preceded the current Spring by half a century, but it also was genuine, because it instilled optimism, high spirits, and a sense of revival among the Palestinian masses, unlike the melancholy, depression, pessimism, despair, uncertainty, and fear of the future that have swept the Islamic world during the current Spring as a result of the unrest, instability, and nebulousness of the future.

Arafat went out of his way to obtain rapid results to his revolution and to take the rule in Jordan in his own hands, by removing King Hussein and replacing him. In its mindlessness, Israel, instead of supporting him with a view of eliminating the anomalous and illegitimate

Hijazi monarchy which established itself in Amman upon a majority of Palestinians, and thus generate a Palestinian state that only border conflicts would continue to separate from Israel, stuck to the non-starter insoluble solution of preserving the Hashemite monarchy. The fallacy was then implanted in the minds of the West and in Israel that because Hussein was moderate and pro-Western, he was preferable to revolutionary Arafat, but that concept was reversed when Arafat signed the Oslo Accords in 1993, and his demands were suddenly recognized and backed by the West, which prevailed on Israel to pay the price and disburse the cost of its naivete. For when Israel agreed, again foolishly, to accept Arafat at the expense of its security positions in the West Bank, it gave up the alternative of basing him in East Jordan whence he would have endangered Israel much less. The false promises of Oslo, that the eliminatory clauses of the PLO charter vis-à-vis Israel would be amended, were never fulfilled, and the Palestinian principles of harassing Israel until its total elimination remained valid.

When Arafat abused the permission he was given by the king after 1967 to act against Israel from his territory, lest he be viewed as a coward while Arafat was regarded as the hero, the intensification of Arafat's activities against Israel, in what was dubbed as the War of Attrition (1968–70) along the Jordan Valley, resulted in Arafat's taking the glory and Hussein the beating from the Israeli air strikes that devastated the entire valley that he had developed at great pain and cost. Thereupon, he decided to move: he demanded from Arafat that he desist from his transborder attacks against Israel, and when he encountered a refusal, based on the PLO's calculation that Hussein would not dare to put an end to the very popular acts of resistance, the Jordanian army moved in, once the king realized that only with one gun, wielded by one authority, can order be maintained in one country. So within a few days of bloody combat known as Black September in 1970, Jordan massacred enough of the Palestinian forces as to compel their survivors to flee to Syria and to Israel and then to Lebanon. There, they constructed new bases, taking advantage of the weakness of the country and its inability to stop the influx of the Palestinian armed forces. Due to the inner divisions within Lebanon, it would have been unpopular for any government to seem to obstruct the heroes of the Arab world from pursuing their battle against the Zionist enemy and to avenge the humiliation of all Arabs in 1967.

After the West Bank and Jordan, which Arafat utilized to fight Israel, Lebanon was the next closest to Israel, since Assad the father would not allow anyone to act from his territory on the Golan and expose Damascus, which was within artillery range of Israel's retaliation. Even when evicted by Israel from Lebanon in 1982, the PLO retained influence that subsisted ideologically in the West Bank and Gaza, and operationally as a base of escalating terrorist action against Israel. One year after their exile to Tunisia, on the eve of Passover, 1983, a hoax was spread by pro-PLO Palestinians in the West Bank that Israel had unleashed a massive poisoning attack against Palestinian schoolgirls with a view to hurt their reproductive organs just as they were ready to wed and raise Palestinian fighters. Despite an international investigation that revealed the nature of the hoax, the belief persisted among the Palestinians, supported by other Arabs, Muslims, and many international institutions, that Israel was out to commit genocide against them. This pattern of repeatedly lying in public and to the public in order to rationalize their deepening hatred of Israel would become a routine means of battling Israel among the Arabs and Muslims in general, with a view of discrediting it internationally. More on that campaign of libel and hatred, which raises questions about Palestinian readiness to accept Israel, any Israel, as a permanent neighbor, was tackled by the author in some of his previous works[2] and will be updated below. In any case, all those manifestations of Palestinian activity clearly point out that their main concern is not to establish a state and enter into a peaceful state of mind, but to spread hatred against Jews and Israel, even at the expense of realizing their dreams.

Loyal to the Maoist principle of permanent revolution lest it settle and become routinized, and committed to the passion of the revolutionary Spring and to keeping it alive, a first intifada (shake-up) erupted in Gaza in December 1987. It soon spread to the West Bank and lasted, with interruptions, until the Oslo Accords in 1993, causing considerable casualties and damage and disrupting the normal course of life in Israel. But in spite of the fact that the chief item in those accords demanded the cessation of all violence pending the negotiations between the parties,[3] and despite the foolish invitation of Arafat and his arms by Israel, from Tunisia to the West Bank and Gaza, naively believing that he would honor what he had pledged in the accords, terrorism never stopped. Arafat simply became accustomed to rebelling and disturbing the order, not to managing civil affairs; to mounting military operations and subverting the state machinery of his hosts, not to enforcing law in his own territory that he never had before. In short, it was like confining the management of public order to the mafia, which has an interest in disturbing it, thus profiting from the chaos. In fact, if that most important of clauses had been honored, Arafat would have thereby eliminated his own revolutionary Spring, something that he patently could not do. It would be only his successor, Abu Mazen, who understood that in the exercise of violence the Palestinians could not win, since they were not the stronger party, and that they could, on the contrary, bring to its end the Palestinian dream, without eliminating Israel, if they did not control violence. He also understood that without cessation of terrorism, the Palestinians would lose Western support, economic and political, which they desperately needed to survive. Especially in view of the challenge that Hamas posed to him internally, Abu Mazen realized that only one gun in one entity would ensure peace and order in the PA, unlike Arafat, who manipulated eleven separate security apparatuses in an attempt to maintain his personal control; therefore he opted for security coordination with Israel, and put an end to terrorism, without ideologically abandoning any major Palestinian goal.

Arafat had refused to extradite to Israel the Palestinian terrorists who acted against Israel and then found refuge in the cities that Israel had stupidly submitted to Palestinian rule. For him it was unthinkable that he would surrender his heroes to Israel. Abu Mazen after him, who was to prove as deep a commitment to the heroes of the revolution, simply avoided that dilemma by preventing terrorism. The Rabin government in Israel was prepared to absorb those acts of terror as sacrifices for peace, in order not to allow the enemies of peace to put an end to it, although the numbers of Israeli casualties after Oslo clearly surpassed the numbers of the pre-Oslo era, which brought many Israelis to doubt the benefits of Oslo if it cost more than without accords. The failure of Camp David II and the quelling of the second intifada in its aftermath (2000), together with the rebellion of Israeli Arabs that same year, when they thought that it was the opportune moment to launch their own Spring, triggered the change of government in Israel and the advent of the Sharon era, which prompted a widespread mop-up operation in 2001 that eradicated terror in the territories, confined Arafat to his Muqata'a offices in Ramallah, and ultimately allowed him to leave for medical treatment in France, where he died in 2004, with Israel predictably accused of his death. The Palestinians, headed by Abu Mazen, then understood that the bells of their peaceful Spring had not tolled yet. Abu Mazen, not a partisan of the revolutionary Spring, due to the suffering it caused his people, which was graver than the strikes that they delivered to Israel, desisted from terrorism in order to collect the benefits of the Palestinian revolution. The Hamas organization, in essence the Palestinians who were members or followers of the Muslim associations in the territories, were crystallized during the first intifada by charismatic cleric Ahmed Yassin in Gaza, into Hamas (acronym for the Islamic Resistance Movement), as a militant group to supplement the young Palestinian rebels in the territories. But when Arafat died and his successor seemed to embrace the more quietist way of negotiations and security coordination, they rose to fill the gap that was left, and they stepped up their acts of terror. They signaled thereby to the Palestinian people and to the world that they had taken up the arms that the PA had abandoned, and that henceforth the Palestinian Spring would be Islamic.

The PLO was ready to negotiate with Israel and was naively brought *bona fide* into the territories to take control of them, was armed to enforce security, and was given control of part of the territories, with a view of arriving to a territorial compromise with Israel. But Hamas radicals published their own platform at the outset of 1988, where they committed to a generational conflict with Israel over the entire territory of Palestine/the land of Israel, which they considered a *waqf* land; therefore they were unable and unwilling to negotiate over it, let alone compromise on it. The maximum they were ready to concede was a temporary *hudna* (truce) that could be reached indirectly, echoing the truce the Prophet had reached in Hudaibiya with his Meccan compatriots, pending the capacity of the Muslims to overwhelm their enemies and take them over. Thus, the rules of the game had changed, and since Israel had mindlessly fallen into the Oslo trap, it realized that its security situation not only had not improved, but had much worsened. The general elections of the Palestinians under Abu Mazen constituted a great victory to Hamas, the new revolutionary alternative for the Palestinians once the PA had abandoned the field of combat. Hamas also formed a new combative government headed by Hamas, which stood in opposition to President Abu Mazen, a situation known in France as *co-habitation*, where the two opposing executive branches of government (the president and the prime minister) share the impossible task of making policy and executing it. In the United States this happens when one or both houses of Congress are from the opposite party to that of the president. The impossibility of such a rule was reinforced by Israel's hurried unilateral withdrawal from Gaza in 2005 without any agreement or understanding regarding security arrangements. The Hamas government, which found itself paralyzed by a PLO president who was prepared to negotiate with Israel, decided to take things in its own hands, as do revolutionaries, and declared its own government in Gaza, in clear and open defiance of the president's authority, but nevertheless drawing their legitimacy from the majority they had obtained in the elections. The Gaza Strip became then the Islamic territory from which Israel could be harassed, and where the flame of revolution could be rekindled, which preceded the Islamic Spring by six years and then merged into it.

The Hamas takeover of Gaza, which can be post-factum understood as an early and pioneering outburst of the Islamic Spring, not only will be able to create a new continuity and harmony with Mursi's Egypt, instead of the Mubarak era's hostility, suspicion, and tension, but it also signals to the Palestinians in general the position of Palestinian Islam as part of the wave of the future. For Hamas will be one of the most Islam-experienced working government in the Arab world (except for Sudan), a sort of pioneer and early-reconnaissance patrol to examine the terrain and ascertain the hazards of such a venture. The Hamas government in Gaza will also serve as a warning to Israel not to commit once again the imprudent step of evacuating vital positions without guarantees for the improvement of security, especially that now Hamas has become an agent of Tehran, causing Israel's security situation to worsen immeasurably. Maybe the West will also awaken to the reality that when radical Islam takes over the rule, security and peace, stability and good neighborliness are not necessarily improved. The Islamic victory in Gaza, which was disputed and doubted by all supporters of the PA hitherto, will see itself recognized and approved by the Islamic world, and gradually also by the West, and it will be the status of the PA that will be in question. In Israel, the growing strength of the Islamic movement that supports the Gaza regime will encompass larger sectors of the Arabs in Israel, turning them into a dangerous and subversive fifth column that future governments will have to deal with. It also stands to reason that the Hamas people will dare more to provoke the Israeli towns and settlements around Gaza, knowing that the Muslim world stands united with them in case of Israeli retaliation. They will probably initiate more border clashes with Israel, in an attempt to create enough tensions and casualties as to drag more Islamic countries to tighten the noose around Israel. It has always been the Palestinian strategy to exhaust Israel by a continuous friction on its borders, except that now more Islamic countries, in addition to Iran, may be drawn into the circle of conflict.

Either as a result of reading the regional map in this vein, or due to its competition with Hamas for the souls of the Palestinians who are still hesitating, the leadership of the PA has also embraced a rather negative attitude toward Israel and insists on boycotting the talks with it unless its unconditional conditions for a jump-start are met. The PA has also intensified its propaganda campaign against Israel in central issues such as: the iconization of past terrorists who murdered Israeli innocent civilians indiscriminately; the negation of any historical link between Israel and its land in order to delegitimize it, by rewriting history, erasing archaeological evidence of Israel's roots in the land, educating its children to reject the existence of Israel; adamantly refusing to recognize Israel as a Jewish state; and more. In the official PA broadcasts of June–July 2012, for example, a hatred poem was repeatedly read, by a young and innocent girl to increase the effect, that described Jews (and Christians) as "inferior and shrunken, cowards and disgusting." In the preceding month of April, another girl read out passionately a poem on "Zion, our enemy, the like of Satan with a tail," amid the mention that the same girl had read the very same educational poem at the opening of a Palestinian exhibition of educational tools previously. Putting this libelous poem in the mouth of an innocent and innocuous girl certainly adds to its credibility, and goes to show the depravity of those who made her play their ugly propaganda game. Their hatred of Israel goes so deep that they do not hesitate to use educational themes for their propaganda purposes, and do not seem to mind the devastation they wreak on the minds and souls of children who are constantly sprayed with these jets of a poison we are asked to believe is the fruit of their own "spontaneous and virgin instincts under the impact of occupation." The complete wording of the poem is repulsive and revolting, and as the moderator was instructing the girl to read it in order to build up a "sense of responsibility and belonging" among her schoolmates, she read without, one should hope, understanding the effect of what she read:

> The usurper robbed my land and the land of my ancestors
> Where is your sword, oh Khaled [the name of a warrior]
> Where is your audacity, oh Salah-a Din [Saladin, the famous Jihad
>   warrior]
> But no one responded to me,
> Where is my weapon?
> Oh, I have just found it! It is the stone,

I have found it and pelted it towards the enemy of Fate,
I have taught the world that the Muslim set on the path of Allah is
    invincible
They use the White House to challenge us
But we challenge them with the Islamic awakening,
And with the Holy Rock of Mecca.
They are not stronger than the Emperors of Persia and Byzantium,
For they are diminished and cowards, inferior and disgusting
They are the descendants of Crusaders [Christians] and of Khaybar
    [Jews],
Oh, Muslims of the world! Wake up! You have slumbered long enough!
Your parents and sons are being slaughtered, and
Your al-Aqsa Mosque is being desecrated![4]

The PA TV moderator, who was encouraging the girl with applause and urgings—"Bravo!"—knew that slaughters were happening daily in the countries of the Spring, not in Israel, and that mosques were being destroyed in Homs and Aleppo, not in Jerusalem. Never mind the destruction of the minds of young children with lies and injections of poison and hatred, and never mind the distortion of the intellect of young people with the confusion between reality and myth, so that they can never grow up thinking freely and recognizing fact from fiction. But the official Palestinian television could not afford to lag behind the surrounding violence of Islamic and anti-Islamic rhetoric that is setting aflame peoples and countries, destroying cities, and killing thousands of innocent people all over the Islamic world. And whom can the Palestinians accuse of all that, without losing the support of their own people, if not neighboring Israel, and its inevitable companion for blame, the USA, both of which have remained the lone islands of security, tranquility, freedom, and sanity in the middle of all that madness? Is one to conclude that in its moderate and roundabout way, which avoids conflict with other Palestinians and other Arabs and Muslims, the PA has been also partaking of the unfolding Islamic Spring, including the distortions and lies that this involves, without incurring too many risks?

One of the most overt ways for some Palestinians to express their reluctant identification with the Spring, of which their Hamas rivals have become the champions, is their novel audacity of rewriting history in a fashion that, on the one hand, lays solid foundations for their claim on the territory of Palestine, while on the other hand completely rejecting and refuting all Israeli claims to the same. This brings them into a common denominator with Hamas and general Islamic arguments to the effect that the Jews are not a nation, therefore they do not deserve a state, and in any case there has never been any factual or historical attachment between the Jewish people and the land, hence the Islamic rejection of any notion of a Jewish state. Never mind history, archaeology, the findings on Temple Mount of ancient Jewish vestiges, and generous Israeli acceptance of the claims of the Muslims on the Mount and Israeli readiness to share with them the holy premises like the Tomb of the Patriarchs in Hebron. What counts for Muslims is only Muslim tradition and legend, which for them amount to history and fact, while all the rest have to be dismissed, destroyed, denied, and refuted. The Palestinians, who on occasion look moderate and reasonable, have definitely and inexorably joined the chorus of deniers that convenes in Tehran all the Jewish haters of the world.

On August 26, 2010, a violent clash developed between the inhabitants of the Silwan village in southeast Jerusalem and Jewish settlers who have been living there since right after the 1967 war. Prima facie, the conflict erupted because of a gate erected illegally by a local Arab, but since in Jerusalem nothing happens just by chance, every simple real estate issue can be linked to an endless string of conspiracies and intentions to impact the future of the city, which can reflect contradictory policies of either Arabizing and Islamizing the city or, on the contrary, Judaizing it. The approach of rewriting history in order to reinforce what is Islamic and reject everything that is not has been part of the Islamic Spring tendency to influence events by ignoring the environment and the world, and striving for victory and acclamation, not for compromise and accommodation; for kindling fires, not for extinguishing them. We saw the followers of Mursi waiting at Tahrir for the announcement of the results of the elections, and ready to erupt in violence if their candidate was not proclaimed the victor. No other result was possible for them. For this purpose, only narratives that encourage the Islamic Spring are championed, not the research of facts and the analysis of findings. Typical to this approach is the recurrent Palestinian claim what the Talmud says, with a totally trumped up charge, without, understandably, any precise reference to back it up. How can they hope to bring up a new generation of scientists that way, if intellectual honesty is thus dismissed for the sake of propaganda? And if they mean peace, how can that be made possible if the next generation is already trained to perpetuate war and hatred?

The manufacturing of lies that has intensified as the Spring unfolded has been aimed at finding all the requisite explanations, justifications, and rationalizations for the newfound rejectionism among the PA leadership, to match the Hamas one, which has been aligned with the Muslim Brothers and their opponents alike, who find it convenient to dump on Israel all their shortcomings, frustrations, and problems. These heaps of lies rely on the ancient tribal *Jahili* tradition of aggrandizing the self's tribe and diminishing the rival or enemy tribes, with the governments of Egypt, Jordan, and the PA, who have supposedly signed peace accords with Israel, reverting to dub Israel the enemy. These trends have to be watched and studied closely because they are likely to persist as long as the Spring unfolds in uncertain directions. Indoctrination by lies, as an educational system to replace human values and historical truth, is not an innovation of recent times, but after the launching of the Spring, more Palestinian and Arab intellectuals than before have harnessed their training to mobilize politically in the service of their nation, with a view of fabricating knowledge and implanting it in the minds of young Palestinians, so as to ensure the continuation of the conflict in the next generation, and to guarantee its longevity in general. We may take for example, once again, the holy places on Temple Mount, where the two Jewish Temples had existed for some eight hundred years, on which the Aqsa Mosque and the Dome of the Rock were built knowing that they were Jewish holy sites. In 1925, and again in 1950, the Palestinian High Islamic Council had recognized the link of the Jews to the place, as if they were attesting that the sun rises at dawn. Even the publicity booklet put out by the council for tourists mentioned that the place was the site where King Solomon had erected his temple, and also the site of the altar built by King David to the Almighty before there was a temple.

But as the struggle of the Arabs against Israel escalated, this recognition was gradually eroded, and with the mounting of radical Hamas-style Islam, it was completely eradicated to the point that the total rejection of the idea of the Jewish state, even in the most moderate circles of the PA, has been nourished by this denial of the previous recognition, for otherwise the Jewish state would be a logical consequence of it. The champion of this denial had been Ikrama Sabri, the mufti of Jerusalem appointed by Arafat, who firmly and uncompromisingly rejected any link between Jews and Temple Mount, and even refuted any spiritual and historical relationship between the Jewish people and the land of their two ancient commonwealths. He also declared that the

Temple Mount was seven floors over ground and seven underground a holy Islamic site, including the Jewish Wailing Wall, which was nothing more or less than the outer wall of al-Aqsa and the place where the Prophet Muhammed had tied his mythical horse al Burak (hence the name of the wall by Muslims). He insistently emphasized that the site belonged for 1,500 years to the Muslims, and to them alone, and he was reinforced in his verdict by generous Israelis who were prepared to compromise with the Muslims, or to even renounce their rights for the sake of settling with the Palestinians at any price. Little did they know that their concession was not greeted by the Palestinians as a sacrifice for the sake of peace, but was viewed with contempt as proof of relenting from their false claim in the first place.

Rachel's Tomb, which had been recognized as a Jewish site on the Bethlehem road for centuries, including by Arab sources, and was confirmed by the Muslim Ottoman sultan, was turned—amid the PA's struggle to delegitimize Israel, since the Spring erupted and even slightly before—into the Tomb of Bilal Ben Rabbah, one of the Prophet's servants who was purportedly buried there, and this historical distortion, both of denying Rachel's (one of the matriarchs) heritage and imposing a freshly invented identity that was never proved, and relating to a person whose standing never inspired any imperative to preserve his remains, was approved by UNESCO's automatic vote, which can rally enough votes for anything anti-Israel that is suggested by the Muslim bloc. This travesty of justice, which is repeated daily under the eyes of the secretary general and his inflated staff, of course encourages the Arabs to invent at will any topic that comes to their mind to harm Israel and the Jews, a trend that has been escalating since the Islamic Spring broke out. For it has transpired that their concern is no longer accusing Israel in the international bodies of occupation and killing, domains where the Muslim Spring countries excel more than any other UN member, but focuses now on the injustice of its very existence. Therefore, the idea is no longer only to weaken it and to punish it, but to eliminate it and replace it by Palestine. The idea of totally refuting the existence of a Jewish state, which had been most dramatically and venomously advocated by Sayyid Qutb in the 1950s on behalf of the Muslim Brothers, upheld by Khumeini in the 1970s and 1980s, who dubbed them the "enemies of Allah," has been taken up by Ahmadinejad and by Hamas and Hizbullah. All those sworn enemies of Israel refuse to accept it or to negotiate with it, and that position was adopted by the PA, which refuses to recognize a Jewish state and is working for its delegitimation. Their rationalization is that Palestine is Arab and Muslim, and the Jews have no part in it.

Therefore, if no written history depicting Palestinian rights in the land exists, it has to be written, taught, and propagated, and if there are extant sources proving ancient Jewish existence in the land, they must be erased, distorted, altered, denied, and refuted, for history in their minds is not the science of investigating the past and writing it, but the task of constructing and reconstituting a past based on myth, national narratives, ambitions, and wishful thinking. And if credible volumes of history or of ancestral tradition stand in the way, they must be eliminated. Once the Islamic movements have embraced this trend, and as the Arab Spring has become Islamic and is being led by the Islamic movement, delegitimation of Israel has become one of their main themes. But in order to lend academic respectability to this long-term effort, committed Palestinian academics were recruited, for whom defending national theses dipped in fallacy is much more important than investigating historical truth, something that does not attest to their outstanding academic standards. Abu Mazen had repealed the use of violence against Israel due to the great damages Israeli retaliation caused him and his people, but the campaign of delegitimation that he is encouraging against Israel, inter alia in the UN and via his academics, being an academic himself, who wrote his dissertation in Moscow on the collaboration between Zionism and Nazism and denying the full extent of the Sho'ah, bring him very close to Ahmadinejad's positions. His own convictions and the venue of his doctorate, in which indoctrination was more important than history, are at play once again, but the circle of actors is growing at Abu Mazen's own instigation. Thus, his strategy of delegitimation is becoming part of the Islamic Spring, and the Palestinian president is one of its actors and agents.

This Palestinian strategy is carried out through school textbooks and the state mass media—as we have seen in the poems above—through speeches of leaders and state-guided sermons of clerics, literature and poetry readings to the public, processions and public exhibitions, public ceremonies, memorial services to the departed terrorist heroes, and welcoming ceremonies to freed prisoners. The recurrent themes on these occasions are the denial of the right of a Jewish state to exist, the false accusation of Jews and Israel of systematic massacres of Palestinian children, even their cremation in crematoria, Nazi-style. These theses are so recurrent, so omnipresent, and so blunt and unfounded that it becomes pointless to start to deny them on a one-to one basis, lest they acquire credibility, as there was never a point for Jews trying to deny every accusation the *Sturmer* concocted against them. But they have become so deeply entrenched in the Palestinian psyche and narrative, and they are so convenient to hang onto them in order to accuse Israel and Jews of all Palestinian problems and misfortunes, that they have been taking over the thinking of the Palestinians so overwhelmingly that even if the leadership should decide to change course, it would find itself trapped by the stereotypes, distortions, and deprecations that it itself invented regarding Israel. In fact, the Palestinians are the first victims of their own propaganda when they realize that the medical help they receive in Israel that saves many of their lives does not accord with the image of the killers of children instilled by their leadership; the peaceful and massive participation of Muslim worshippers in Ramadan in the great mosques in Jerusalem does not accord with the accusations of Hamas that Israel is destroying al-Aqsa, oppressing Muslim worship; the Palestinians flocking to West Jerusalem and shopping and relaxing in its hotels and entertainment centers does not reflect Palestinian propaganda about curfews, oppression, sieges, and roadblocks in the territories. And the hundreds of heavy trucks loaded with food provisions, fuel, and building materials, which cross daily into Gaza, simply belie the propaganda about the Israeli siege and starvation of the poor besieged Gazans.

The Palestinian propaganda also denigrates the Jews as a whole—not only Zionists or Israelis—dubbing them as satanic people whose conduct is treacherous, based on forgery, deceit, and fake inventions. This mobilizes so-called scholars to prove that those qualities cannot be changed or mended, and to distribute their learned conclusions through their media to the masses, so as to turn them into the preponderant public discourse, summed up in a few easily memorized mantras that later can be heard everywhere or cited in all media. In 1998 the Palestinian historians convened a conference in which they voiced a few revisionist views—not as the fruit of their original thinking and research, or the reflection of their opinions, or their professional conscience, or new sources that they discovered, or new ideas that their scholarship created in them—but under PA guidance, as was the practice in the Communist countries where the Palestinian leadership had been educated, or the Arab authoritarian regimes under which they were groomed and now under the impact of the Spring where the rise of Islam has been predominating.

Dr. Yussuf al-Zamili, the head of the history department at the Beit Hanun College of Education, presented at that 1998 gathering the new approach being shaped in the Palestinian educational system, an approach that advocated not teaching history to students, but training them to adopt a political narrative that totally negated the right of Israel to exist in the land of Israel/Palestine. At the conference he urged all universities and colleges to express their creative activity by writing Palestinian history and to not "allow the enemies and the impure to distort it." He knew very well that some of the most scientifically tested, credible, and comprehensive histories of Palestine, from antiquity through the Ottoman era to moderns times, were written by Israeli historians who made their reputation in the West, well before the warnings of distortion were issued by the PA. But those political guidelines will make sure that those reliable writings too will be distorted by the new Palestinian standard-bearers of distortion. Some Palestinian scholars, being unable to deny outright the evidence of Jewish presence in the land from antiquity, simply appropriated that history for themselves and wrote it anew. Without any regard for chronology, like the Qur'an itself, or for the absurdity of their arguments, they claim, for example, that the Hebrew tribes who had inherited the land in biblical times were in fact Arab and Muslim, some two millennia before there was any Islam and at least one millennium before any Arabness was identified in history.

One of those academics, Jirar al-Qidwa, who was appointed by Arafat as his chief librarian, has been the main thinker of this new replacement theology, which Palestinian television frequently broadcasts as scientific. He converted biblical Jews into Arabs, two thousands years before the Arabs invaded the land from Arabia and conquered it, and wrote with his scholarly authority, "As regards the Israelites, they were the sons of the purest Arab tribes . . . and believe me that, by Allah, more Israelite and ancient Hebrew blood flows in my veins than in Sharon's and Netanyahu's blood." After all the faults and deficiencies heaped upon Jews and Israelis in the official Palestinian media, one wonders why a Palestinian scholar would wish to attribute those qualities to himself. To make those points, the Palestinian daily *al-Quds* published a series of articles in July and August 1996, chronicling the history of the Cana'anite-Palestinian people. In these articles, various academics from Palestinian universities explained how the Israeli archaeological findings "confirmed the Palestinian claims of their deep-rooted Cana'anite roots in Palestine."[5] All those revisionist publications led at the end of that summer to the Sebastya Fesrival of the Palestinian Ministry of Education, where young Palestinians wearing Cana'anite robes and waving torches danced in the village's central square, with the chanting and merry-making of PA personnel.

Since then, much water has trickled through the semidry riverbed of the Jordan, but the passion to demonize and disinherit Israel has only increased. Dr. Mustafa Najem, a lecturer on Qur'an exegesis at Gaza's al-Azhar University, wrote that "Jews are characterized by arrogance, pride, deception, wildness, crookery, treachery and cunning." Some time thereafter, this academic confirmed in a TV broadcast that "Jews remained Jews, and we are called upon not to forget those characteristics even for one moment." Those sensational revelations on the Jews—which were emphasized by that cleric, who also pretended he had academic clout, and which were presented on the official channel of the PA at the same time as it was negotiating peace with Israel—showed that more than an expression of negative hyperbole by an individual lunatic anti-Semite, there was a consistent line of guided propaganda. Rather than an attempt to teach the eager audiences the history and anthropology of their enemy, the lecturers were politically manipulating false data to indoctrinate hatred in their youth, again in defiance of the cumulative damage that it would do to the minds and souls of ignorant people who had no way to criticize the sayings of an authoritative source on their national TV. Those listeners and watchers would be doomed to grow up on lies, hatred, hostility, demonization, and conflict, instead of being conditioned to peace, knowledge, good neighborliness, and truth. The fact that successive Israeli governments allowed this destructive process to play out, instead of arresting the Oslo process until this was rectified and the incitement and indoctrination of hatred completely halted, allowed it to grow out of proportion, to become larger than what the leaders had wished it to become, so that it has become irreversible. This also sent signals to the Palestinian leadership that it could pursue its incitement and indoctrination, so as to deflect public opinion from their own shortcomings, as long as they were not made to pay a high price for their violation of this vital aspect of the Oslo Accords. There was no courageous enough Israeli government to stop the negotiations and the process of concessions to the Palestinians, lest the sanctified peace process be hurt, with the result, as Winston Churchill had described the Munich Agreement of 1938, that they sacrificed their honor in order to rescue peace, and ended up losing both.

Dr. Riyad al-Astal, another historian from al-Azhar University in Gaza, like others of his colleagues who became pen-mercenaries of the PA, quotes liberally from the *Protocols of the Elders of Zion* as a historical document, as has done the Hamas charter, and injects that fallacious and poisonous document of hatred, lies, and bigotry into his students, the future generation of Palestinian leaders, through the textbooks that he and his peers are employed to write. In one case, due to international protests—mainly by those Europeans who financed the new textbooks for Palestinian schools—the PA authorities were compelled to excise certain fallacious and inflaming data. But when the lever of outside financing is not present, who can guarantee that the next editions will have the same corrections? Yes, this thermometer was broken and removed, but the fever did not elapse, and other false citations and information are still current in other textbooks.

Dr. Nizami Amin al-Ju'ba, the head of archaeology at Bir Zeit University, is specializing in turning Israeli archaeological findings into Canaanite and Muslim exhibits. He is apparently of the opinion that if he merely states that he opposes the biblical version of the events of Jewish history (something that he is perfectly entitled to do if his opinion is based on evidence and analysis), a history that recounts the momentous happenings of the First and Second Temples, and recounts that the Jews stayed only for a short period in Jerusalem in the first century BC, he is thereby establishing a credible alternative version of history. While this interpretation is a great concession to Jews, for it recognizes some connection, fleeting as it may be, between the Jews and Jerusalem, it nevertheless denies any Jewish presence during the one-millennium history of the two Jewish commonwealths on the land, which were amply documented by serious Western scholarship over many centuries. Yunus 'Amr, the president of the Jerusalem Open University, is one of the propagators of the hoax that the Canaanites are the ancestors of the Palestinians, hence they have rights in Palestine. By resorting to that thesis connecting them to the remote past, which cannot be proven either way, it indicates that they are not aiming for a serious and pragmatic settlement with Israel, based on present realities and a permanent partition of the land, but they prefer to create legends of their ancient links to the land in order to circumvent Jewish relations to the kingdoms of David and the Hasmoneans, by showing their even more ancient link to the Cana'anites. It is interesting that the biblical narration of events, which in their eyes does not establish credible evidence of the existence of the Jewish Temples, becomes suddenly a firm and reliable base for the story of the Cana'anites in the land.

Just to show that these absurd claims are merely something of Palestinian imagination, it is noteworthy that during Camp David II (2000), Arafat attempted to argue, with President Clinton smiling forgivingly, that the Jewish Temple had never been located on Temple Mount. The determining proof, he said, was the Qur'an, which for Muslims is the word of Allah and therefore the ultimate and undebatable truth. They do not realize that non-Muslims do not accept the Qur'an as the truth, and therefore that argument cannot be valid. This sort of argument, which Clinton tactfully dismissed, becomes all the more valid for Muslims today under the Islamic Spring, in light of the prevalent tendency to abandon the frustrating Arab nationalism that has brought only failures, and to rally back to the more promising Islam as the source of rule and legitimacy, where the Qur'an would again be an incontrovertible and immutable truth. Going back to the Silwan event with which we opened this section, it is true that since the Arab/Muslim conquest in the seventh century, that village lay outside the city wall and was expanded, though it kept its ancient name derived from the original Hebrew: Kfar Ha-Shiloah. At the end of the nineteenth century, new Jewish immigrants came from Yemen and settled down in the village. But in the disturbances of 1921 and 1929 Jews were attacked by the surrounding Muslim population, and during the 1936–9 Arab revolt that was led by the Jerusalem mufti Haj Amin al-Husseini—as a precursor of Palestinian nationalism—the rest of those Jews were evacuated by the mandatory British power in order to avoid their extermination. Their houses were taken over by local Arabs, until their owners showed up after the 1967 war and claimed them back. So, to claim, as the Arabs do with regard to all Jews in all of Palestine, that Jews had no roots in the village and on the land is a hoax without a leg to stand on, but it is being reiterated and reinforced by the Islamic Spring.

The most absurd claim against Israel, raised by the Palestinians, vehemently supported by the Islamic Spring, and enjoying some political support in Europe, is the complaint that Israel has been Judaizing Jerusalem, which would be as if someone accused the French of Francizing or Christianizing Paris, or the Egyptians of Arabizing or Islamizing Cairo. In December 1995 the General Assembly of the UN adopted a resolution with an overwhelming majority, abrogating all the Israeli laws regarding Jerusalem. The resolution also condemned Israel's Judaization of Jerusalem, as if anyone would dare to condemn Saudi Arabia for Islamizing Mecca. When the Arabs occupied and ruled East Jerusalem, which was never their capital, they not only Arabized and Islamized it, but they did that at the expense of the Jewish sites that had existed there for generations before, like Temple Mount, the Mount of Olives, and the Jewish Quarter, and no one complained, save the Israelis, whose voice was not given audience anywhere. But the moment Jews dared to recuperate their own ancient sites, without even touching al-Aqsa and the Muslim sites that had been purposely built on the ruins of the Jewish holy places, and while honoring all the existing Islamic and Christian sites in place, cries of Judaization began, warning of the danger to world peace, as if this was not the first time that free access to all holy places had been instituted for members of all religions.

The world hypocritically also disregarded the fact that united Jerusalem has grown, developed, and beautified more than any period in its history, to the benefit of all its inhabitants, with unprecedented social and administrative services that no Arab or Muslim (and Jewish) population has ever had. The absurdity lies in the resolution calling on Israel to abrogate all its measures in Jerusalem; is Israel expected to destroy all the buildings, roads, clinics, social services, houses of prayer it built, or undo the rehabilitation of ancient places, destroy the schools and hospitals and housing projects that were developed for the growing populations? For example, the Jewish Quarter in the old city was totally destroyed by the occupying Jordanians, its population exiled, and it was turned into latrines and heaps of ruins. Does the UN want it to revert to that miserable state and its inhabitants be expelled again? Or perhaps the Jewish tombstones that once were torn from the Mount of Olives and used by the Jordanians to pave roads but are now restored to their place—should these be returned to the state of desecration from which they were rescued by Judaization? Or the archaeological digs completed by Israel with professionalism and sensitivity to reveal the ancient Jewish past of the city—ought they be filled in and that chapter of Jewish history erased? Even the UN cannot countenance such absurdities. And yet, on the agenda of the Islamic Spring countries, this issue is more salient than the killing, the destruction, the bigotry, the chaos, and the oppression that their societies are suffering, and from which it is precisely Judaized Jerusalem that is excepted.

In October 1996 the EU adopted a resolution calling upon Israel to repeal all its rehabilitation and restorations projects in Jerusalem and "return them to their previous state." Does that mean that the enormous Hadassah hospital on Mount Scopus, which serves the entire Arab population of Jerusalem, should be closed down or taken apart?

Will those European countries take responsibility for the health of a quarter-million Arabs? Of course not; they would rather adopt another resolution blaming Israel for the state of health of the poor occupied population and watch it die. Do they want the restored Hebrew University on Mount Scopus, which had been evicted during the Arab siege in 1948, to close its doors and ruin one of the most prominent universities in the world, which is unequaled in the Arab world and one of only a few in Europe? Or perhaps they mean that the latrines that were put in place by the occupying Arabs in 1948–9 on the former places of the destroyed Jewish synagogues should be restored after the rebuilt synagogues are ruined again? Of course, the Arabs and Muslims are elated by the European endorsement of their policy of total destruction that they have practiced under the Spring. As part of their struggle to disinherit Jews completely from Jerusalem and the land of Israel, they have declared Silwan, the village in southern Jerusalem which is under dispute, as a *waqf* land, claiming that any measure of development the municipality adopts there is another phase of Judaization of the city. They are afraid that the ancient garden in the valley, which had been devastated by seven hundred Arab families in order to settle on its land, will be restored to its past splendor, bringing the Jews closer to undermining the foundations of nearby al-Aqsa. Since they are sure of European support for their program of preventing any development of Jerusalem, they also conclude that Europe is supportive of the Spring in general.

These have been the problems in the background of Palestinian discontent and internal divisions. Talks of a coming third intifada have been rife for a few months, conflicts in which Palestinian rage was to explode as an expression of the worsening economic situation of the Palestinians in the West Bank. This crisis would mimic the permanent explosions of their brethren in the Gaza Strip, where occasional shelling of Israeli towns and villages has been sporadically breaking the peace, with Israel responding with precise surgical bombings that either destroy fundamentalist Muslim targets or preempt missile attacks when they are detected on time. Usually, these missile attacks are supposedly initiated by more extremist groups than the ruling Hamas, which despite its bombast is not interested in seeing itself devastated by another Israeli Cast Lead operation if Israel should feel too threatened by attacks so continuous they do not give respite to the Israeli population around the Strip. However, Hamas is not always able to control those groups of Islamic Jihad or other popular organizations, who could not care less about the *hudna* unofficially installed by Hamas. The latter have been trying to draw support from the rule of the Muslim Brothers in Egypt, and are wary of aggravating their situation on their border with Egypt in the Sinai, especially after their long-hailed reconciliation efforts with the PA ended in failure. In despair, Abu Mazen has once again turned to the diplomatic front by placing a renewed request to the UN to be recognized as a non-state member in order to gain access into UN organizations, to divert internal attention to some outside success and placate the internal mood of frustration.

But in September 2012, the crowds in the West Bank, who could no longer bear the cost of living and were looking for someone to blame (as they learned from the ongoing upheaval of the Spring elsewhere), turned first against Salam Fayyad, the economist prime minister, who was supposed to turn the Palestinian economy around and make it more independent of Israel. However, in view of the mounting prices and the inability of most Palestinians to make a living and get Arab and European donors to continue covering the huge deficits of the PA, Fayyad was disappointing as a savior, and became the letdown that must be ousted. Protestors have channeled their rage through slogans and street gatherings against Fayyad, very much reminiscent of what happened in the rest of the Arab world, except for the use of violence, which has remained for now at low level. The protestors demanded his immediate departure and the revision of the economic agreement with Israel that governs much of the PA economy, as if Fayyad were the sole culprit. President Abu Mazen, who tried at first to defend his prime minister, saw the rage turn against him, as the crowds started demanding his resignation as well, as if he were one of the monarchs or tyrants who were made to quit in the course of the Spring. He, like others, will learn that those who incite their people in their own service against others will ultimately see their people turning against them.

Palestinians have been living within a great paradox: they declare their national ambition as the replacement of Israel on its land, but at the same time they are the least able of all the Arab and Islamic countries to make that aspiration come true. Therefore, having tried without much success through revolution, violence, murder, and war, as they had pledged in their national charter, to gnaw at Israel's strength and bring it down, they launched the path of diplomacy of Oslo, counting on the naive policies of some Israeli governments who were willing to compromise, in order to attain that goal without compromising much on their part. That also failed. Now, during this last stage, which coincides and accords ideologically with the Islamic Spring, though it preceded it by several years, they have been attempting to reach their goals via Hamas, which has been practicing Spring policies of "ridding themselves of tyrants and instituting a Muslim state." Their problem is that as a revolutionary movement, they have never settled on one unitary and consensual aim, half their people being Jordanians, 10 percent Israelis, 30 percent residents of the West Bank and Gaza, and the rest residents of refugee camps in Syria and Lebanon. Even those in the Palestinian territories are divided between the West Bank under the Palestinian Authority and Gaza under Hamas.

On the table today, after twenty years of protracted negotiations between Palestinians and Israel, there is still no united Palestinian leadership that would wish to negotiate a settlement with Israel, each one of their components pulling in another direction. To be sure, the PLO has been claiming for years that it represented all Palestinians, and successive Israeli governments—as well as most world governments—have foolishly recognized that claim, while in fact every one of those sections has lived a separate existence. Thus, the Spring the Palestinians dreamt about is far from realizing itself, the main struggle being directed against outside powers, in order to first gain statehood before they can embark on a domestic Spring. This is unlike the rest of the Islamic world, where the struggle is mainly domestic, against tyrants, and for the restoration of some sort of Islamic state. So, even if that illusory solution of two states could materialize, that would only mark the beginning of the Spring, not its end. For even if it were possible, a solution for 30 percent of the Palestinian people in the territories would resolve nothing, and the remaining 70 percent would continue to knock on Israel's doors, crying for a spring of their own so they could fully attain their national and Islamic goals.

For some fifty years now, the Palestinians have occupied the front arena of revolution in the Arab world, including the forty years of Arafat's turbulent but sterile leadership. All those years, Arafat's leadership produced upheavals in all places where he sought refuge (the West Bank, Jordan, Lebanon, Tunisia, and back to the West Bank and Gaza), and drew international attention to his revolution and its victims. Under his leadership, the Palestinians drew up their national charter, which they adopted in 1964 and amended in 1968, each spelling out not the dream of their own state-building, but the nightmare of eliminating all the military, political, economic, social, and cultural manifestations of Zionism in Palestine, meaning the elimination of Israel, and triggering the impasse that would make any settlement with Israel impossible. Compromise had never been Arafat's goal, but since Israel foolishly agreed to negotiate with him, it ipso facto changed the terms of its own elimination when it agreed to that destructive process, which was encouraged by the West. To the Israeli hopes that Israel could be accepted as a Jewish state at least on part of the land, Arafat and his ilk have responded in the negative. Justice, in his eye, as in the eye of the rest of the Arabs and Muslims, meant absolute justice to them, on their terms, where the idea of compromise could never be incorporated.

After the 1967 war and the eviction of Arafat from the West Bank, his main objective was to obtain a more or less firm base in another Arab country. This would enable him to continue his attacks against Israel but also seek shelter from its retaliation. The War of Attrition along the Jordan Valley—which pitted Arafat, who was based in defeated Jordan's territory, against Israel, who launched major destructive assaults against those bases, in 1968–70—left Jordan in such ruin that King Hussein belatedly rose against his guest, and clashes during the Black September of 1970 between his forces and the PLO troops forced him out of the country. In such a revolutionary situation, Arafat received all the credit, while Hussein suffered all the loss and destruction. The king also feared that while Arafat took the praise as the only relentless fighter against Israel and all other Arabs licked their wounds and honored the cease-fire, he could in the long run unwittingly facilitate the PLO takeover of the rule in Jordan, exploiting the Palestinian majority there to gain legitimacy. At the time this seemed a bonanza for his continuing revolutionary Spring, forty years before anyone else in the Arab world had changed, with one difference: instead of ridding himself of the yoke of a tyrant, he was himself the tyrant, and instead of toppling a dictator, he was fighting in vain against Israel, whom he could not eliminate. However, since he was the only Arab leader waving the banner of struggle and war, his claim as sole representative of all Palestinians was upheld by the Arabs and most of the rest of the world. But the Spring has shuffled the Palestinian cards too, as Hamas is becoming more important to Egypt and other Muslim states than the PLO, a trend that might reverse the entire situation, when the inefficient and purposeless PLO is pushed aside as irrelevant and Hamas comes to dominate the Palestinian scene in its independent territory as Israel's new interlocutor, backed by world bodies. Hamas's resignation, under Mursi's sponsorship, to engage itself in a long-term temporary *hudna* with Israel (not a permanent peace), following the missile battle between the two in November–December 2012, may indicate a new trend, where pragmatism may bend ideology, but not change it.

Somalia

Thanks to the work of Nancy Kobrin, an American psychologist who worked with the émigré Somali community in the Twin Cities (Minneapolis and St. Paul), which has grown into the largest Somali community outside Somalia, we can reconstruct some of the links between fundamentalist Muslim trends in Somalia. Above, we discussed some of these in the Yemenite context, and in the previous section on the Palestinians. In a specialized article in *Family Security Matters*[6] Kobrin describes several cases that she dealt with that are instructive to our theme here. Somalia, a poor and chaotic Muslim country that did not settle into any pattern of rule after the end of its colonial period—which did not turn out to be its worst period—has been the home of tribal lawlessness and international piracy, a practically nonexistent central government, and the dominance through the barrels of their guns of Muslim fundamentalist groups who naturally identify with Arab and Islamic causes and find common ground with the Palestinians who, like them, engage in revolution as a way of life and appear to have elected Islam as their solution. One of those groups that vie for power in the midst of the chaos is the Shabab (Youth), believed to be an affiliate of al-Qa'ida in East Africa. Al-Qa'ida first acquired infamy when it blew up the American embassies in Dar al-Salam and Nairobi in 1998, resulting in hundreds of casualties, some Americans and mostly locals. President Clinton thought about a swift retaliation in Somalia, where the perpetrators had found asylum. But in view of a botched operation and the many casualties, he renounced the whole affair, and it was not until September 11 (2001) and President Bush that the Americans would begin to consistently take the battle against world terrorism seriously. It was with some of those al-Qa'ida affiliates that Nancy Kobrin has worked and collected data.

A young man of twenty-four, a member of al-Shabab, was re-arrested in London after having violated his ban not to trespass on the Olympic Park there while wearing his court-ordered electronic tracking device. He was reportedly doing reconnaissance as a suicide bomber against the Olympic Games. He had tried to carry out a suicide bombing, (which this author has elected to dub *islamikaze*, the combination of Islam and kamikaze) against British troops in Afghanistan. He reportedly returned to Somalia after that. He comes from a large family, suggesting emotional deprivation. Two more Swiss Jordanians also joined the foreign fighter wing of al-Shabab, but when charged with terrorism in Kenya they were denied the right of extradition to Switzerland. The ability to move between nationalities and countries is what gives these terrorist mercenaries the international aspect of their activity, just like Zarqawi in Iraq, who was Jordanian by nationality, Palestinian by birth and identity, but leader of al-Qa'ida in Iraq, fighting the Shi'a and the Americans; he had as mentor the Palestinian arch-terrorist Abdallah Azzam, the spiritual guide of Bin Laden. Another member, a nineteen-year-old also of Jordanian origin, grew up in Biel, Switzerland, and disappeared in February 2011. He was apprehended in Kenya, thus showing that neutral Switzerland has a similar problem concerning radicalization of Islam as the rest of European countries, as well as Britain and America. Just as the Somali families of Minnesota were shocked to find out that their youth were being recruited to Shabab, so were the families in Biel. The Swiss authorities fear a Mohammed Merah–type incident (in Toulouse, where a Muslim terrorist attacked Jewish worshippers in 2012, killing some of them). In Somalia, a Portuguese man was arrested with ties to Al Shabab. This was the first time that an Al Shabab terrorist had been apprehended by the Somaliland authorities. The country has endured more than twenty years of chaos, famine, and bloodshed and has little functioning infrastructure. While it is true that Al Shabab has been ousted from Adgoye, a town en route to Mogadishu, Somalia still remains the number one failed state worldwide. There continue to occur acts of piracy and kidnapping of aid workers, with the criminality flowing into neighboring Kenya. Both types of criminal acts bring in significant revenue as well as a warped prestige to shame-riddled Al Shabab.

The UN reported in 2006 during the Lebanon War that there were 720 Al Shabab fighting there. While the report has been disputed, former Israeli ambassador to the UN Dan Gillerman confirmed that he knew of the Somali jihadis. One wonders now how many Somalis have been able to infiltrate Israel, hiding among the Sudanese and Eritreans making their way to Eilat, South Tel Aviv, and other destinations, where their total numbers have already amounted to tens of thousands. We hear nothing about this from the press or government. Fewer know too that the Somali extremists identify themselves as the poor Palestinians and the Ethiopians as the cruel Israeli occupiers. This was communicated by the last young Somali Jew born and raised in Mogadishu, who was forced to flee the country along with his mother in 2010. Somalia is now *Judenrein*. It once had a thriving Jewish community of about six thousand. The Somali Jewish community traced many of its ancestors to Yemen. In Minneapolis, which has the largest diaspora of Somalis outside of Mogadishu, it was common to see bumper stickers saying "Ethiopia get out of Somalia"—reminiscent of the Palestinian part of the Arab-Israeli conflict.

Why is it important to understand this group identification with the Palestinians? First and foremost, Israel and Jews will continue to be targeted. Second, such hatred and relentless attacks cause identification with the aggressor, while Al Shabab encourage the underestimation of what this terrorist organization is capable of doing. Third, the West continues failing to factor in Somali clan dynamics, the level of rage of their male youth, the hatred of their females, and the lack of capacity for empathy for others. Nothing will change, estimates Kobrin, until there is a reconsideration of such naïveté as symbolized by placing an electronic monitor tag on such a hardened criminal as the case cited above. Why was that suspect not in prison in the first place? The Terrorism Prevention and Investigation Measures undertaken by the British, while well intended, prove to be inadequate and naive. There remain many more unanswered questions as the Somali saga continues.

Sudan

The story of Islamic fundamentalism in Sudan is inexorably connected with the dominant figure of Hassan Turabi, who was credited during the New York trial of blind Egyptian Sheikh 'abd al-Rahman (who was convicted and incarcerated in America for concocting the first Twin Tower conspiracy in 1993), as "one of the two Muslim thinkers that have contributed most to their respective countries and to Islam" (the other was Ayatullah Khumeini). Others have compared him to the great luminaries of modern radical Islam: the Egyptian Muslim Brother Sayyid Qut'b, and the Pakistani Abu-'ala' al-Mawdudi.[7] He is a man of extraordinary learning who graduated from law school in Khartoum, then got a masters degree in law from London University (1957) and a doctorate in law from the Sorbonne in 1964. His importance lies in his fluency in both Islamic and Western cultures and their legal systems, and his prolific writings reflect vast knowledge of both. Back at home, he quickly rose to become the dean of the faculty of law and launched himself into political activity, becoming the unchallenged leader of the Muslim Brothers in Sudan since 1964. When the military rule of Ibrahim Abbud was toppled in 1965, he founded a larger organization around the Brothers, the Islamic Pact Front, which acted to get an Islamic constitution for Sudan, until it was dismantled, together with all other political parties when the military coup led by Ja'far Numeiry took over in 1969. He was then incarcerated for a few years and wrote his first acclaimed books in prison. But in 1977, the Brothers reconciled with Numeiry and joined his government, with Turabi filling several legal functions until that alliance was taken apart by the ruler in 1985.

When Numeiri himself was toppled later in 1985, Turabi founded his Islamic National Front, entered the coalition government of Sadeq al-Mahdi, and served as minister of justice and then as foreign minister before he temporarily retired from official duties to remain the strong man behind the scene, returning in 1996 when he was elected speaker of parliament. In 1991 he founded the Muslim International in the form of the Popular Arab and Islamic Congress. He wrote many books on matters like women, democracy, state, and society, and based his arguments much more on rationality than on citations from the Qur'an, which culminated in his recognized masterpieces, *The Revival of Islamic Thought* (1985) and *The Islamic Movement in Sudan*. His combination of religious thinker and political activist made him a model in the eye of many fundamentalist Muslims who understood, like the Muslim Brothers in Egypt and Tunisia, that only this combination can bring them to power. Even though he acquired the image of a liberal innovator, based on such things as striving for the rights of women, he hardly effected any doctrinal revolution, even if one recognizes that he was somewhat more advanced than others on the matter—for example in support of their integration into society and state, not as a breakthrough in doctrine but as a means to gain their support politically. Mawdudi had preceded him in matters of state, and in any case there was nothing, according to Weissbrod, to justify the title of *mujaddid* (reformer or renewer, as the Muslims claim emerges once every century), which was imputed to him by many of his adulators. In state institutions, he borrowed from Qaddafi the model of popular democracy, and on the women issue he learned from the Syrian and Iraqi Ba'ath example, where women were allowed to participate as fighters in social struggles. As for the organizational model, he learned from the tightly controlled example of the Communists.

In spite of this lackluster doctrinal image, Turabi is very much admired in the Islamic world due to his brilliant leadership qualities, which many in the radical Islamic movement have tried to emulate. His modus operandi, especially his way of participating in political life in order to Islamize it from within (a strategy with which the Muslim Brothers achieved brilliant success decades later, by assiduously participating in parliament despite the rigging of the elections to their detriment under Mubarak), has in fact led them to their ultimate triumph. In this regard, Turabi, together with Ghannouchi of the Tunisian Nahda (but not Qutb, who also spent time in America, and maybe Mursi, who was also educated in the United States), both of whom were educated in the West, are credited as the pioneers of a new tendency in political Islam of replacing the old educational system of the Brothers. In this they led Banna and Qutb, with a more pragmatic orientation that takes much more account of reality and wishes to achieve widespread political support first and foremost. This is also the direction Mursi seems to have taken, judging from his first speeches and actions. But only time will reveal the pattern on which he will settle after a few months in governmental reality and dealing with all the contradictory constraints that every new government encounters.

Turabi projected in the West the image of moderation, democracy, and tolerance, as Mursi does today. But examining the system he enforced in Sudan when he was in power, and also some of his writings, a different picture emerges: an extremist man who holds basically the same positions as fanatic Mawdudi and Qutb. As some scholars like Martin Kramer and Gabriel Warburg have insightfully discerned, Turabi is in fact a wolf in sheep's clothing, and very far in reality from the moderate image he is trying to project. When he was in power, he cleansed ethnic minorities of Christians and animists, imposed various limitations on women, and harshly oppressed political opponents. His popular democracy, which was inspired by Qaddafi but also brought to his end, met the predictions of all those who foresaw that after their accession to power, sometimes using democratic means to soothe and mislead their audiences, Islamic movements tend to enforce totalitarian rule and to trample over women's and minorities' rights. The big question now is whether Mursi and Ghannouchi, and other Muslims radicals who may gain power as the Islamic Spring unfolds, will have learned the lessons of Turabi and other major proponents of Islamic rule, and have the courage to impose their own more moderate and human face of Islam, or if they will be swept up by the Islamic milieus in which they were raised and carry their countries toward radicalism, and their societies toward backwardness, dictatorship, poverty, and war, as the Iranian regime did after the initially promising Khumeini Islamic Revolution.

In Sudan, too, demonstrations have swept the streets, and discontent has been expressed, while its president, 'Umar Bashir (who has been convicted as a world criminal for his mass murders in Darfur but still moves around almost freely and is hosted with great pomp in other Islamic countries, including Mursi's Egypt), insists that there is no Spring in his country. For one thing, this part of the Spring has been almost ignored by world media, though the armed forces calling the shots have banned some newspapers and arrested journalists and activists, who are now confined to the social networks to gain information. Bashir has characterized the antigovernment protests against the high prices as "the work of a few agitators." But in fact, protests were sparked across Khartoum and other cities by the austerity measures the government adopted in view of the worsening economic situation, with a hard core of students hoping to turn the discontent into a local expression of the Spring. But Bashir argues that his country has already had "an Arab Spring a number of times" and that when his people revolts, they all participate in it, while for now it is only the work of a few agitators. At the same time, there were reports from the Red Sea Port Sudan that the security forces beat demonstrators who were about to protest, in order to dissuade them, and that the main opposition party the *umma* was ordered not to hold public gatherings.

In al-Obeid, the capital of North Kordofan Province, a group of one hundred university students called for the downfall of Bashir, while other demonstrators gathered in the town's market square. Police responded with tear gas and batons, which became the standard responses when demonstrations began in Khartum on June 16. Reporters saw crowds pelting rocks at policemen. But Bashir, who had seized power in 1989, had become accustomed to such protests. Though the demonstrations were admittedly on a smaller scale than the core lands of the Spring, they went on for more than a week, with citizens blockading streets. Like in other places, the protests were triggered by the government's announcement of austerity measures in view of the secession of oil-producing South Sudan a year earlier. Eliminating a main source of foreign currency revenue, the secession has deprived the Sudanese of two-thirds of their income. Thus, demonstrators have been trying to use rising gas and food prices to build a broader movement to end Bashir's twenty-three-year-old tyranny. But so far, the protests have not gathered enough momentum nor have they ever exceeded a few hundred people at a time, and thus there has been no county-wide upheaval.

Notes

1. *Ha'aretz*, June 8, 2012.
2. R. Israeli, *Poison: Modern Manifestations of a Blood Libel*, Lexington Books, 2002; and R. Israeli, *Blood Libel and Its Derivatives*, Transaction Publishers, Piscataway, NJ, 2012.
3. See Raphael Israeli, *The Oslo Idea: The Euphoria of Failure*, Transaction Publishers, Piscataway, NJ, 2012.
4. PA Television, May 11, and again June 2, 2012.
5. PA TV, June 5, 1997, cited by Itamar Marcus and Baraba Crook, "Anti-semitism among Palestinian Authority Academics," in *Post-Holocaust and Antisemitism*, no 69., June 1, 2008, The Jerusalem Center of Public Affairs.
6. Nancy Kobrin is also the author of *The Banality of Suicide Terrorism: The Naked Truth About the Psychology of Islamic Suicide Bombing*.
7. Amir Weissbrod, *Turabi: Spokesman of Radical Islam*, Dayan Center, Tel-Aviv, 1999, p. 7. Much of this passage on Sudan is based on that book.

Summary: The Islamic Spring and Israel, and What Lies Ahead

Like all other nations and cultures, and even slightly more so due to its proximity to the arena of events and the momentous effects that these developments may have on its future, Israel too is extremely interested in how these events evolve day by day, weighing their consequences and implications. One thing is certain: following the present Islamic Spring, the stature of Islam will be higher in regional and international politics than it ever was in the modern era, and this signifies for Israel harsher, possibly more hostile, and probably more aggressive and belligerent attitudes and policies toward the Jewish state, which the Islamic world has never really accepted, at least in its political manifestations. Even those who have accepted Israel and signed peace with it, like Egypt and Jordan and in part the Palestinians, will see their policies revised by the new rulers who emerge from the Islamic Spring. The countries of the Gulf and Morocco, who have not yet undergone the upheaval of the Spring, were and probably remain the most open and accessible to Israel, insofar as they maintained unofficial relations with Israel throughout the Oslo process and continue to allow unofficial Israeli delegations and individual scholars and sportsmen to participate in international events that they host.

Evidently, the young people who triggered the Spring did not intend it to go the way it is going, given that the Muslim movements that stood on the sidelines in the beginning later joined the bandwagon of success, and being better organized and experienced, they soon took matters in their own hands when they were sure that the dictator had gone and no further harm could be expected from his machinery of evil. But did those young people who initiated the whole process find satisfaction? How will the new regimes address their frustrated hopes and unrealized dreams? Will their economic, social, and cultural situation, for the sake of which they rebelled, improve even a trifle, or after the dust settles will they sink again into a grey and grinding life of despair and poverty, with no horizon in the distance? Were the democratic dreams and slogans they voiced, which they probably did not fully understand, totally evaporate into thin air, or will they erupt again when they realize that their revolution, for which they made many sacrifices, was in vain? But unlike the republican models wherein the Spring has replaced the dictators with legitimately elected leaders, in the monarchies nothing has changed, for they seem impervious to democratic change, which will continue to knock on their doors until either they give way or the democratic forces give up. The success of the Spring in some parts of the Islamic world will certainly be a powerful incentive in the hands of the democrats to keep hammering at the monarchies. In places where the Islamic Spring began prematurely—like Iran, Pakistan, Afghanistan, Turkey; or within tribal or revolutionary societies like Mali, Palestine, and Bosnia, the Spring has simply confirmed the tendencies of unrest that existed previously (Hamas in Palestine, Taliban in Pakistan and Afghanistan, and Izetbegovic's Islamic republic in Bosnia) but it never, or only temporarily, came to fruition. This signals to them that they were heading in the right direction and had better pursue that road.

The Food Problem

But beyond the concerns about immediate political developments in the Islamic Spring countries, there are four major issues looming on the horizon as likely tests of the success or failure of the new governments likely to take over once the dictators are gone: food and water supply, the inherent instability and fragility of the new systems, the effects of the Spring on Israel, and the question of sustainability of democratization of the systems. On the food front, an important article by Nadim Kawach analyzed the hazards of food shortages in the Arab and Islamic world and their impact on those regimes. The author claims that Arab countries have reeled under a cumulative food gap of more than $180 billion over the past ten years, to emerge as the largest single farm products importer despite their massive arable land potential, according to official figures. Except for fish, vegetables, and other minor crops, Arab nations are suffering from a persistent shortage in all types of farm products, and the gap has steadily worsened over the past two decades, as shown by the Khartoum-based Arab Organisation for Agricultural Development (AOAD). Wheat accounted for more than half the shortage, and a decision by Saudi Arabia, the largest Arab economy, to stop costly cultivation of wheat and rely solely on imports, is expected to further upset that balance. Besides wheat, the Arab food gap is underscored in cereal, barley, sugar, cooking oil, corn, rice, and poultry, as the Arab World's self-sufficiency in some of these products does not exceed 50 percent.[1]

According to the findings of this survey, the farm gap, peaked at around $29.8bn in 2008 due to a surge in global food prices before it edged down to nearly $27.5bn. This widened the total Arab food gap to a staggering $182bn during 2000–2009, AOAD's staggering figures showed:

This level is nearly quadruple the cumulative gap of around $45bn during the preceding nine years, when the region's population did not exceed 240 million in early 1990s compared with around 334 million in mid-2008. At the end of 2009, the Arab population was projected at around 351 million. "Since 1990, it has grown by nearly 2.34 per cent annually compared with global growth of about 1.16 per cent," AOAD said and added that "The high population growth in the region is one of the major factors for the persistent deficit in the Arab food balance. Another result of the high growth is that it boosts demand for food, which, in turn, pushes up prices. This means a large number of people will find it difficult to get their food needs." The report of AOAD showed total Arab food exports stood at only about $11.5bn in 2009, while imports were as high as $39.04bn, one of their highest levels. It also blamed poor water resources in the region, low land utilisation and investments, and what it described as "defective Arab farm policies." Nearly three years after they approved a fifteen-year common farm strategy in 2005, the Arab countries have become more reliant on farm imports, as such a strategy remains inefficient in the absence of right policies and sufficient funds, it said. What complicates the problem is that the most wealthy Arab nations are still reluctant to invest heavily in farming projects in fertile member states, for political and security reasons, while only around 12 per cent of the total available arable land in the region is exploited, said AOAD, a key Arab League organisation.[2]

The author found that there were several obstacles and challenges facing development of the Arab farming sector. They included "invest-ments, defective government policies, poor water policies, inefficient use of available land and water and water reserves, and the low level uti-lization of available arable areas," the report said. "The biggest obstacle has been and will remain the relatively small water resources available in the region. This obstacle has blocked investment in the farming sector and will hinder any programme aimed at exploiting those areas." The report said the Arab World "is one of the poorest areas in the world in terms of water wealth, with the quantities of available renewable water resources standing at only around 1.3 per cent of the world's total renewable water wealth, although the Arab region accounts for more than 10 per cent of the total world land area." It also says that the low water resources have sharply depressed the per capita share of water in the Arab World because of a steady population growth of more than two percent. "The Arab region is considered one of the most arid areas in the world and the per capita share of the water wealth is among the lowest as it has remained much below the global water poverty level of 1,000 cubic metres per year. In some countries, this level is even below 500 cubic metres," the report said. "As for arable land, it is estimated at nearly 550 million hectares but only around 12 per cent is exploited. Even in that 12 per cent part, the farming efficiency does not exceed 60 per cent of the world level. This means the Arab World is facing a real problem of not only low exploitation of arable areas but low efficiency in the cultivated land and its productivity."[3]

The absurdity in all this is that the Arabs' immediate neighbor, Israel, is among the world's top experts in water development and water conservation, land development and conservation, irrigation, and high productivity in agriculture. Of course, the AOAD's Arab League report makes no mention of this; and would rather see its compatriots sink in poverty and hunger than ask its neighbor for help. This mental obstacle is much more difficult for the Arabs to surmount than the physical ones, as Israel has learned from its experience. After the Israel-Egypt peace treaty in the 1980s, the former sent, almost secretly, its experts to develop two model farms in the delta of the Nile. These farms have achieved some stunning results. But even President Sadat, who initiated the peace, never dared to publicize this fact, lest he contradict himself when he was boasting of his oldest farming nation of the world since Pharaonic times, implying that Egyptians stood to learn from no one. To admit that despicable Jews could teach the noble Egyptians anything was a blasphemy that even Sadat could not utter. The end result was that the Egyptian press was only willing to publish this fact, in order to blame Israel and the Jews of vile conspiracies to poison Egyptian lands. This is precisely where the Spring can raise new hopes in the Arab and Muslim lands: to use the extended hand and the unique expertise of their neighbor to dramatically increase their farming development (and

284

also other aspects of economic development like high tech). Israel has already done much of that in China, India, and many countries of Asia and Africa, and only narrow-mindedess and bigotry remain a major obstacle in the way of what can become a major channel to communicate peace between Israel and its neighbors.

"One of the solutions to this problem is the need to increase investments in the farming sector and adopt more active agricultural policies," AOAD said. But it omitted the simple and straightforward recommendation of collaborating with Israel, apparently following the approach of the Arab League, which prefers to starve the people it purports to protect and defend, rather than to accommodate, even symbolically, a relationship with Israel that will benefit it first of all. The Arab League economists who wrote that report know of Israel's excellence in many economic and scientific fields, and of the fact that the GNP per capita is tenfold in Israel what it is on average in Arab countries, except for the oil-rich ones. The problem is clearly psychological, and the only hope of changing minds and shifting attitudes is through audacious leaders who might emerge as a result of the Spring.

The surge in food prices in 2008 prompted plans by the UAE, Saudi Arabia, and other arid Gulf countries to fund agricultural projects in Sudan and other fertile areas in the region. But such projects are expected to take time, and they are not large enough to slash the Arab farm import bill, according to experts. The surge in food prices in 2008 was one of the main reasons for a sharp rise in inflation in the UAE and other members of the Gulf Co-operation Council (GCC) given their heavy reliance on farm products. The GCC states, which control nearly 45 percent of the world's proven oil deposits, are among the largest food importers in the world, given their poor farm potential due to their desert nature. The bulk of their food imports come from outside the Arab region and include the United States and other Western countries. Official figures showed that the GCC's combined farm imports exceeded $75 billion during 2005–2009. They accounted for about 41 percent of the total Arab food import value of $180 billion, although the population of the six members, which hovers around 36 million, constituted only about 10 percent of the total Arab population. Arab officials have repeatedly voiced concern about the agricultural gap and growing reliance on food imports, mainly from the United States and other Western countries. Some officials considered such reliance as a risk to their security.

According to AOAD and the Kuwaiti-based Arab Fund for Economic and Social Development, another key Arab League institution, most regional nations are suffering from slackening farm exports and rapid growth in the population, leading to a steady increase in their imports of food products. The shortage persisted despite an expansion in the cultivated areas in some Arab countries as a result of reforms aimed at increasing crops. From around sixty-seven million hectares in 1999, the combined Arab cultivated area widened by nearly 4.3 percent to seventy million hectares in 2002 and continued to expand to reach around seventy-five million hectares in 2009. But the report showed that the cultivated areas remained a fraction of the total arable land in the region, estimated at nearly fifty-five million hectares. "Arab nations have sought to improve farming policies and such moves have resulted in some positive developments," AOAD said. But they have also produced negative results, including the private sector's malpractices, which have hurt the interests of the farmers. New policies are needed to regulate these activities and encourage farmers. The report urged Arab governments to take urgent measures to encounter the food price increases in the future, cut food imports from foreign countries, and achieve self-sufficiency in most farm products. The study said that the creation of a farm fund is crucial for the success of Arab agriculture projects aimed at achieving self-sufficiency, on the grounds that most fertile countries in the region lack sufficient investments in this sector. "This should prompt Arab nations to seriously consider the creation of a large joint fund to invest in farming projects in the region," the report said. "At the same time, Arab governments should take the proposal of setting up a strategic cereal stockpile into consideration, given its significance in ensuring the food needs of citizens and curbing sharp price increases. It could be a pan-Arab stockpile or regional silos. This stockpile should be sufficient for at least one year and should help Arab countries in collective purchasing agreements that will give them a better bargaining position."

Saudi Arabia's decision to halt local wheat production and rely on imports from foreign markets is final, as the world's oil superpower struggles to preserve its dwindling water resources, according to officials. The desert kingdom, which sits atop more than a fifth of the world's proven oil wealth, had produced nearly three million tons of wheat per year to meet domestic needs but output is expected to plunge to one million tons in 2012 following the government's decision to stop subsidizing local production. In the next two years, output could dip further, and the country will become almost totally reliant on imports, mainly from the West. "The decision we took two years ago to halt local wheat output is final and clear. There is no going back," said Fahd

Balghaneem, Saudi minister of agriculture and head of the Grain Silos and Flour Mills Organisation. "The country is now giving priority to water security over food security. . . . [T]his was a cabinet decision, which also directed us to stop producing wheat locally." Balghaneem said Saudi Arabia, one of the poorest nations in water resources, imported in excess of one million tons of wheat last year, and the imports are projected to surge this year as local output is steadily declining.

The Weakness of the State

The second issue the Islamic world will have to address in the post-Spring era is that of instability and weakness, especially within the failed states, as suggested by Yoel Guzansky and Benedetta Berti. The authors claim that the uprisings across the Muslim world that began in December 2010 signaled an era of change in a region that desperately needed to be shaken up. However, while the heterogeneous protest movements in the various Arab states were generally of one mind in demanding the end of authoritarian rule, in most cases they failed to produce a cohesive plan for the postrevolutionary transition. Apart from the partial exception of Tunisia (where the spark for the uprisings was first lit), the divisions within the protest movements, along with the absence of a functioning and developed civil society, have inhibited the process of political change. Further complicating efforts to establish a new political order has been the legitimacy deficit of existing political institutions and the resilience of networks of power and patronage. As a result, the postrevolutionary period in countries where leaders have been toppled has been replete with challenges, including the exacerbation of preexisting divisions, rendering extremely difficult the creation of strong and functioning states. They claim that in general, state weakness is not a new phenomenon in the Middle East and North Africa (MENA) region, but has been significantly exacerbated during the last two years of the Spring since the end of 2010. State weakness can be measured by the degree of the regime's legitimacy, its capacity to deliver social and political goods, and its ability to guarantee a basic level of security. While states that fulfill these functions are considered strong and stable, a state that is utterly unable to meet any of these criteria is perceived as "failed."[4]

The authors emphasize that "lawlessness" may come to dominate the Middle East. They point to Yemen, Libya, Iraq, and the Sinai Peninsula as examples of this "cascade of state failure." There seems to be truth that in the postrevolutionary stabilization period in most Spring countries we are witnessing the exacerbation of preexisting cleavages that weaken central authority. Already prior to the Spring events, half of the twenty-two Arab League member states were defined as weak states, varying between highly dysfunctional states like Yemen or Sudan, and weak but far from collapsing countries like Lebanon. However, if taken from the definition base of Islamic Spring, and including in the sample Muslim countries other than the members of the Arab League, one identifies many more, and much more deeply, failed states than in the Arab sample (e.g., Afghanistan, Somalia). Indeed, since the beginning of the uprisings, there has been a general deterioration in the level of internal stability of MENA states. For example, the new Libyan authorities have been confronting monumental difficulties in their effort to reassert control, to overbridge the regional gaps and accumulate sufficient legitimacy following their overthrow of the Qaddafi regime. The country is indeed highly fragmented—with competing tribal loyalties having always taken precedence over a common national identity—and lacking strong central political institutions. The proliferation of centrifugal forces is especially a problem given the fact that the Libyan security sector, already weak during the Qaddafi regime, has been in a nearly total state of disarray following Qaddafi's overthrow. Although security sectors reforms are being implemented and a large-scale DDR (disarm, demobilize, reintegrate) program does exist, the establishment of a cohesive and well-functioning Libyan state seems to be a remote possibility for now. The events in Benghazi on the eleventh anniversary of the September 11 attacks, where violent eruptions of Muslim radicals against the American Consulate there produced many casualties, including the American ambassador, and their aftermath provide an ample example of the current disarray.[5]

Syria, of course, provides the most stunning example of the volatility of these regimes, as an undone state structure that was held together by an authoritarian regime cannot be welded again together, and has fallen prey to sectarianism and tribalism. The initial clashes between the Syrian regime and the anti-Assad opposition forces have escalated exponentially throughout the months of fighting, leaving the country in a state of full civil war. The depth of the cleavage between the pro-regime forces and the opposition groups suggests that Syria's high degree of state weakness and instability will extend even to the postconflict stage and will postpone indefinitely the permanent settlement. For, paradoxically, while only by force was any regime able thus far to maintain the state structure together, the democratization efforts deployed today can only make the debate between the factions and the ethnic groups more bitter and more acute. There is simply no platform that can be acceptable to all factions as a base for a new agreed social contract. The case of Yemen, currently ranked as the eighth most unstable and weak state in the world, is even more extreme. This challenge is especially daunting, as Yemen is also among the poorest and least-developed states in the region, with the central government lacking internal legitimacy and the capacity to deliver social and political goods. The authors provide a few examples:

> Firstly, failing states represent a challenge to regional stability. This is especially the case because of the large involvement of external actors in the domestic affairs of weak and failing states. The weakness of the central government and the proliferation of groups competing with the state, represent an excellent opportunity for external third parties seeking to expand their influence on the region. The Lebanese civil war between 1975–1990 serves as a reminder of the dangers of protagonists becoming surrogates for regional and international conflicts. Currently, both Iraq and Yemen are increasingly looking like potential arenas for similar struggles between the different regional and global powers invested in the region. Similarly, the conflict in Syria is becoming increasingly more regionalized.
>
> Secondly, failing states are problematic from a human security and humanitarian perspective. Such states are often unable to provide security as well as basic social and political goods, contributing to heightened precariousness of the living conditions of the population. The recent example of famines in both Somalia and Yemen tragically highlight the human cost of prolonged internal instability and endemic state failure. Similarly, apart from the 80,000 or more casualties, and many more maimed and bereaved and displaced persons, the ongoing war in Syria is resulting in a humanitarian crisis, with large numbers of both internally displaced persons within Syria and refugees seeking safety in neighboring states—Turkey, Jordan, Lebanon and Northern Iraq. A third challenge stemming from failing states is the terrorist challenge. Failing states present international and regional terrorist organizations with a convenient base of operations, and are more likely than other states to host such groups on their soil. Fourth is the crime challenge. Similar to terrorist organizations, criminal organizations take advantage of governments' loose control in failing states to advance their interests. A final security challenge is the increased threat of proliferation of non-conventional arms. As Syria implodes, the concern that Syria's chemical and biological weapons may not be secured, or may be transferred by the regime to its Hizbullah ally, has heightened.[6]

The Spring, according to the authors, has accelerated a preexisting trend within the MENA region (if this Spring is considered Arab and not Islamic), one characterized by state weakness and instability. This widespread weakness seems to stem from a number of factors, including the ruling political institutions, and the difficulties in preventing the proliferation of local militias and alternative pockets of authority within the country's territory. But given the problems faced by Spring states, it is unlikely that the regime changes induced by the Spring uprisings will lead to a rapid improvement of the situation, and it is fair to expect continued instability and state weakness, with all the regional instability implied, even given that evil stability is no better than a temporary instability that leads to a stable situation. What's more, the longer and deeper the crisis, the greater the likelihood that other regional actors will become more involved in the various flash points by supporting one or another of the warring protagonists.[7] Based on this analysis of these two sober and insightful authors, the prospects for seeing the Spring as a positive watershed in the fortunes of these countries do not seem extremely bright. But maybe some other additional elements will introduce some balancing points of variety, if not of optimism.

Effects of the Spring on Israel

Few people realize how, in the long run, the current upheaval in the Muslim world will affect Israel in the most direct fashion. This is connected to the fact that Israel's 18 percent Muslim population (more than one million), which has seen its two icons, nationalism and then Communism, collapsing one after the other, has growingly become so attached to the Muslim alternative that the Muslim Spring is its best occasion to see the wind blow in its sails and push it forward to new, though unforeseeable directions. Already that current of Muslims in Israel has been on record as undermining state authority by acting in favor of Hamas, and their head, Sheikh Ra'id Salah, has been convicted for fundraising for terrorist Islam. For example, in their fixation on the Judaization of Jerusalem, Salah and his movement have been inspiring Islamic causes of the Palestinians as echoed by Hamas. In one instance, pamphleteers wrote a 2006 piece in *Sawt al-Haq wa-l-Hurriya* (Voice of Truth and Freedom), the journal of the Islamic Movement centered in Umm al-Fahm in northern Israel and led by Ra'id Salah, where the "plan to Judaize Silwan" is discussed in great detail. The Islamic Movement, a local branch of the Muslim Brotherhood, brought to bear its standing at the forefront of organizing Israeli Arabs to identify themselves strictly as Palestinians, with Salah leading the campaign to defend Jerusalem from destruction by Israel and liberate it from Israeli occupation, while the country in general, and Jerusalem in particular, had never known such an enormous development élan and growth of its Muslim community and its prosperity and welfare, in all its history.[8]

Another unfounded claim of the Muslim Movement against Israel, which is and will be further enhanced as the Muslim Spring unfolds, is the alleged Israeli plot to replace the al-Aqsa Mosque with a Third Jewish Temple—despite the fact that the Israeli authorities have consistently restricted the movement of non-Muslims on the Temple Mount to the point where they have been accused of discrimination against Jews and Christians to favor Muslims. A pamphlet from the Islamic group *Jihad-Beit al-Makdas* (the Jihad for Jerusalem), that is circulated in public, uses melodramatic language to further illustrate the "evil intents of the Jews," accusing Zionists of attacking Jerusalem and Silwan—"the gateway to al-Aqsa Mosque"—and al-Aqsa Mosque itself, which is "the rock of grace of Jerusalem and the crown of the whole Islamic nation." According to this line of thought, Silwan becomes the doorway through which the settlers are trying to pass to Judaize Jerusalem and at the same time, enter the Temple Mount in order to dismantle al-Aqsa and rebuild the Temple. The steps that are being carried out, according to Islamic spokespersons, will lead to a third intifada. As Shaul Bartal, a prominent researcher on Palestinian affairs, has often noted[9]

> the Palestinian Arab assault on the Jewish connection to Jerusalem continues apace aided and abetted not only by radical Muslims or angry Silwanites, but by fellow travelers in the media and in academia, including Israeli Jews. Consider the tours carried out by Emek Shaveh, an Israeli nonprofit organization, and Palestinian residents of Silwan with a view to rebuffing the "political archaeology of the Jews" and to prove the area's "true" archaeological significance. *Emek Shaveh's* founder Yonathan Mizrachi, who has voluntarily left his job at Israel's Antiquity Authority, spares no effort to downplay the Jewish biblical history of the area. As he put it: "After three hours on [an Israeli-organized] tour, you are convinced that you are at a totally Jewish site where evidence of Canaanite, Byzantine, and Muslim, and, of course, Palestinian [civilizations] are pushed aside. Jerusalem has 4,000 years of history. They only focus on the marvelous stories of King Solomon, David, and Hezekiyah, of which, by the way, they haven't found any archaeological evidence that ties them to the place." Mizrachi's website contains an essay of over 5,000 words—"Archaeology in Silwan"—which transforms archaeology into a handmaiden of social

science pieties and criticizes even the use of the phrase City of David as a manifestation of settler objectives. In doing so, he also manages to rewrite history, claiming falsely that "during the main periods of prosperity under the kingdom of Judah . . . the cultural identity of the town and its inhabitants was contested."

Bartal concludes that "sadly, the battle over Silwan (and for that matter the wider Palestinian-Israeli conflict) is likely to continue as long as Palestinian Arabs and their brethren refuse to recognize that another people, the Jews, have a claim to the Land of Israel." Nothing has given more momentum to these anti-Israeli claims than the present Islamic Spring, hence the vitality for Israel's future of the turn it might take.

Sensing the fatefulness of that trend, even the non-Hamas Palestinian leaders who negotiated and signed the Oslo Accords seized upon the nineteenth anniversary of that event (September 13, 2012), which coincided with the successes of the Islamic Spring in Tunisia, Egypt, and Libya, with more promise to come, to signal their desire to withdraw from the Accords. For, under the Spring if they stand to win it all after the Jews are disinherited from the land, why should they hold on to their compromises? They say that the Accords, which were signed September 13, 1993, were meant to be an interim agreement leading to a final peace agreement and an independent Palestinian state within five years. Palestinian National Initiative leader Mustafa Barghouti said that the accords turned out to be "a transition to nothing," and had been used as a cover by Israel "to consolidate a system of apartheid." "We as Palestinians need to liberate ourselves from the terrible conditions of the agreement, through popular resistance, national unity and boycott, divestment and sanctions," Barghouti told Ma'an News Agency.[10] He charged that the Palestinian side has committed to the agreement while Israel selectively implemented the accords to its benefit, adding that nineteen years on the concept of the two-state solution was at risk due to Israeli settlement building. He just forgot to mention that Oslo was signed to commit all the Palestinians, while half the Palestinian people (Hamas') elected to reject it, and that the first clause of Oslo was the end to violence, while Israel has suffered more casualties from Palestinian terror after Oslo than before it.

Together with some Fatah leaders like Mahmoud al-Aloul, who urged the PA to abolish the Oslo Accords, the Popular Front for the Liberation of Palestine also called on the PA to disengage from all agreements with Israel, and be free of political and economic restrictions imposed by the Oslo Accords. It also urged the Ramallah government of the PA to end security coordination with Israel and implement national unity. Chief Palestinian negotiator, Sa'eb Erekat, blamed the international community for failing to hold Israel accountable for its violations. "Our hope for peace and justice has been destroyed by Israeli bulldozers and a culture of racism and hatred espoused within Israeli society. This horrific reality has been facilitated by the immunity which Israel has been granted by the international community."[11] He just forgot to mention that the final results of negotiations cannot be predetermined before negotiations begin; that the issue of the West Bank as a disputed territory is something only negotiations and compromise can settle; and that the Palestinians have signed Oslo II, which divides the West Bank into three zones (A, B, C) between the parties until a new agreement supplants that arrangement. No new agreement is known to have emerged in all those years, and therefore those existing agreements are the rule, and Israel cannot be accused of violating them.

Now, since the beginning of the upheaval in the West Bank in September 2012, it is evident that the Islamic Spring (no longer a Palestinian intifada) is unfolding within the walls, and that at some point not only will the Palestinians get rid of the wimpy Abu Mazen and Fayyad, if they do not resign of their own volition, but Islam will come to sweep the scene and Hamas renown will rocket sky-high, with the support of the successful Muslim Brothers wherever they have already established themselves, notably President Mursi, who has negotiated for them the latest *hudna* with Israel. The Oslo Accords have been the focus of demonstrations across the West Bank in September. Protesters angry at rising prices complained that the economic sections of the treaty have been implemented by Israel selectively and mostly to its benefit, a position shared by UN agencies and economists. Israeli Muslims, led by Rai'd, will soon follow in open rebellion against Israel as part of the Islamic Spring, and their confrontation with Israel will become inevitable. Only then might the Islamic threat against Israel, the only county in the Middle East not participating in Spring, be replaced by some sort of permanent arrangement.

Is the Democratic Alternative Applicable to Islam?

Just because the demonstrators of the Spring have been screaming "Democracy!" without understanding what it involves, and without ever experiencing what it means, many Western media came to the conclusion that democracy was upon us, and that with the fall of the tyrants— some of whom were convinced that their system was democratic to start with—tyranny would come to its end. However, it turns out that those who believe that words have a specific universal meaning often find themselves frustrated when other people from different cultural backgrounds use the same words in different ways, words that carry very different significances than the ordinary Western speaker comprehends. These differences can stem from words that are innocently used to express one thing but are understood differently or, vice versa, that can be said purposefully to make others believe something that was not meant in the first place. One can shout, for example, "Peace!" (meaning cease-fire), only to gain time to reorganize his troops for fighting. Another example: when fundamentalist Muslim ideologues would write or speak at their ease without having to produce instant responses, they would for the most part refute the concept of Western democracy and explain why it cannot stand in opposition to Shari'a. For some of them, the words that are synonymous with, or that approximate Western democracy are the *shura* and *Ijma'*, not anything that is reminiscent of freedom of expression and conduct, clean elections, and equality of women, human rights, tolerance toward non-Muslim minorities, and the rights of expression and assembly for all.

When President Muhammed Mursi of Egypt was elected, he made some moderate statements that raised hopes that he would force other Muslim fundamentalists of his kind to bend the doctrine by opening up to nonreligious people and to democratic fashion of speech as the Muslim Party in Turkey did after it won the elections in 2002, and then again in 2006 and 2010. At least when it comes to elections and recruiting a majority to their side in Parliament, the Turkish Islamic party is playing the democratic game, though it still has a long way to go in matters of freedom of expression, persecution of journalists, incitement of fanatics, dissemination of false information by the state, encouragement of terror, and expression of hatred to political rivals. (Erdogan himself sat in prison for incitement.) In Turkey, as in Egypt, there is a part of the public favoring the application of *Shari*'a there without delay, but in both countries a trend prevails that pledges to lead their respective countries the democratic way, at least on the surface. During Erdogan's visit to Cairo after the Spring broke out, he tried to convince his hosts to follow the Turkish model. On the other hand, the unlimited support that both countries evince for Hamas, which forcibly took over the rule of Gaza from the Palestinian Authority, does not indicate the prevalence of a democratic spirit among them. The coming days will show whether Egypt will go the Turkish path following the Spring and whether the Turks, seeing the success of Islam in the rest of the Arab world, will elect to continue that peaceful trend in order to gain Western favor, or on the contrary will orient themselves toward Iran and Central Asia and try to rally around themselves a bloc of Muslim radicals that would gradually adopt Islamic reform—tinged with democratic conduct to be sure—in order not to alienate the wide popular support that the urbanite, educated, and Westernized Turks sense toward democracy.

What is the Turkish model? Are there models in democracy? When we speak about democracy, we have in mind the model developed over the years in liberal countries of the West, where democracy does not need any qualification, much as its ideal form had been developed by Giuselmo Ferrero back in the 1940s and became a classic model since. That concept of democracy leaves a vast gulf between itself and what Islam conceptualizes as democracy. That difference is expressed also in different words, but even when the same words are used they mean different things, and every time we hear the words that are familiar to us, we must inquire what exactly they mean in their cultural context. Both sides of the aisle resort to that same formula: democracy, although they do not mean exactly the same thing, out of a belief that since that Western word is positive, respectable, and has become an object of universal emulation, better stick to it than invoke some other terminology that would arouse suspicion and require definition. Democracy, everyone knows, will always be associated with positive thinking, with liberal politics, with human rights in mind. Therefore, in the eyes of many uninitiated Western people, anyone who proclaims democracy must be credited with good intentions and cannot be accused of any wrongdoing, much as Muslim radicals in Europe declare in their demonstrations that they hate democracy. Therefore, any novice in Islamic politics and any demonstrator in the Spring has learned very quickly that screaming that word in the street immediately draws sympathy from the West. Few are the Westerners who would care to inquire any deeper into what is meant by that—whether the people who proclaim the word understand what it means, whether they had ever seen it, experienced it, or have just heard about it.

What we hear about "Islamic democracy" indeed varies widely from the democracy we know, both on the conceptual as well as the functional levels. Simply defined, democracy means the rule of the people by the people. But who is "the people"? What is rule? How do we connect between people and its rule? In the West, our need to define these terms stems from the necessity to determine the sovereign, who is also the source of legitimacy, the wellspring and fountainhead from which legislation is generated. The idea is that since the people cannot themselves legislate, as had been the case in the ancient Greek polis, they must elect their representatives, whom they entrust with the mandate, over a set period of time, to make the laws of the country. At the end of that mandate, the power of decision returns to the sovereign—the people—in order for it to determine the sort of laws and the kind of administration that would administer it for the next term. This mechanism is founded either on an unwritten social pact, or on a written constitution, or a basic law, where the people, the authority, the source of legitimacy, and the way to express it are spelled out. When the elected representatives and officials do not fulfill their mandate, they are removed and others replace them according to the will of the sovereign. This is a matter of course that we have become accustomed to in liberal democracies, while Islamic countries have never heard of such arrangements. There are rosy and bombastic constitutions, like those of the Soviet Bloc and of Saddam and of modern Egypt in their time, but what happened in reality had nothing to do with them. The constitutions are customarily ignored there, until the next ruler comes about and imposes his new rules, takes over power, and determines the law, and no one can move him out of office because his term is limitless, and he draws legitimacy from his illegitimacy. Nonetheless, Assad the father and Mubarak, like the dictators of Sudan and Libya, Algeria, and Yemen, were convinced that their system was democratic.

The masses of demonstrators in all countries of the Spring were incensed that the issue of legitimacy did not much concern their leaders of twenty, thirty, or forty years, leaders who were not elected by anyone in the first place, and then automatically succeeded themselves without asking anyone's opinion or permission. It seemed a natural process to the leaders that they should be leaders in perpetuity, that they were not held accountable by anyone for anything, and that they ruled by the legitimacy of their force rather than by the force of legitimacy, which they did not have. Until the outburst of the Spring, their publics too were made to believe that proper elections had been held in their countries, that the presidents were reelected by the public or by the parliament, and will be again and again, and that the rubber-stamp parliaments were not representatives of the people but agents of the tyrants. And suddenly their minds opened up, by force of the open media that transmitted proper elections in other places, where governments alternated, where prime ministers and presidents were sanctioned, dismissed, and even incarcerated for wrongdoing—something never heard of in those countries. The crowds wanted the corrupt leaders just to go so that something new should start, but they knew not whom and what to install instead. And when the dictators refused to go, they were fought with weapons, and as the fighting escalated, the stakes of the revolution went higher; and the heavier the sacrifices of the rebels, the more pressing and insistent their demands, and the larger the gamut of foreign powers who were brought into the conflict, the more clearly they took sides with the tyrants or with the rebellious elements pitted against them. The leaders, who did not understand at first what the rebellions were all about took those outbursts of violence personally, and either tried to quell them, or ran for their lives, or offered reforms too little and too late, or continued to fight to the bitter end.

One can then conclude that the main reason for the bitterness that accumulated in the Arab street and caused the explosion of the Spring was due not only to the chronic problems of poverty, illiteracy, disease, unemployment, hopelessness, corruption, and disparity between the haves and have-nots but also mainly to their despair as, instead of seeing their leaders legitimately elected to sort out their problems and to be accountable for their solution, they were faced with immutable dictators who ruled for life and did not have to account for any misdeed or mismanagement. That was the reason why in all those uprisings, the most strident call of the demonstrators was on their rulers to go. For in almost the entire Islamic world no one has elected the rulers who are either monarchs who need not be elected, and who regard their countries as their own property, or military juntas who took over power and hold it by force, or ideologues of tyrannical rule like Arab Socialism or the Ba'ath, or maniacs like Qaddafi and Saddam, whose only ambition in life was to rule and to count their subjects as dust. Never were there any social contracts developed between rulers and ruled, and rulers persisted in their rule as long as their military might sustained them or outside powers supported them. The young people of the Islamic Spring countries, and certainly their elders, had watched twenty years earlier the Eastern European regimes collapse live on television and power transferred to elected systems, and they began to ask themselves, "why not ours?" And when the Internet allowed the young people to cover the gaps in time and space, as the spark that was kindled in Tunisia started to spread, the snowball effect began, rolling from one country to another until the fire caught everywhere in the

Islamic world. As the hurdle of fear was removed, simultaneously with the rapid passage of the rebellion from one country to the next, one tyrant followed another into oblivion.

It is always easier and faster to destroy the existing structure than to erect a new one. No wonder then that only in two of those countries, Tunisia and Egypt, is there any semblance of a permanent settlement, where institutional and personal issues are being sorted out and new modalities of rule are being explored, to depart from the old tyrannical patterns and rework the relationships between the military and the civil, and the fate of the old regime is to be decided. For example, the military brass, which had a say in politics, as used to be the case in Turkey and Egypt and still is in Pakistan, will have to be sent to the barracks, since they cannot possibly aspire to any sort of working democracy. The problem is that some of the competing new regimes of the Muslim fundamentalist sort posit a challenge to the Western concept of democracy by claiming, for example, that sovereignty belongs only to Allah, and that to pretend that someone else can possess sovereignty or share in it with divinity amounts to heresy, for all creation is the feat of the creator, and to attribute to someone else sovereignty or part of it is also blasphemy. Any Islamic ideologue or thinker can try to circumvent this delicate issue by arguing that people, as part of creation, can participate in divine acts such as sovereignty, and go into hair-splitting arguments on how people can become the source of legitimacy for power. This was done by the new president of Egypt, a Muslim Brotherhood adept, who assured his Egyptian audience that he was founding a civil government, not a religious one. But it is doubtful whether any serious Muslim scholar could risk his reputation by letting any human being cross the red line of divine sovereignty over Muslim lands that is imposed by Shari'a Law.

The crucial significance of these definitions is their reverberation over the vital issue of legislation. If sovereignty belongs to Allah, and he had already dispensed to humanity the most perfect of codes of law, as incorporated in the Qur'an and the sunna, then who would dare to try to improve on it without provoking a blasphemy? If not, would parliaments be needed to legislate laws? Defining divine law as final and unalterable means recognizing that legislation has disappeared from the human world and that all matters of this universe must be arbitrated not by legislators but by jurists who understand and can interpret the laws of Allah. Moreover, while humans legislate over years piecemeal, and then alter, amend, abrogate, and change laws according to their needs, and therefore constantly resort to their legislative bodies, Islam had accomplished that process since the times of the Prophet, and the entire body of Shari'a was dispensed to humanity in one stroke, or at most, by the tenth century, when the gates of *Ijtihad* were closed. All that needs to be done, Islam says, is to study and comprehend the will and intentions of the creator and his messenger, and the interpretive power of the founders of the Four Schools of Law. And who better to do that than the jurists of the Holy Law? In Sunnite Islam, the ulema are only required to counsel the ruler, but in Shi'ite Islam as interpreted by Khumeini, they should be the rulers or the supreme guides to the rulers. The presumption to improve upon divine legislation by ameliorating it through parliamentary committees appears in this light as an affront to Allah, and therefore it is ruled out of the question.

On the functional level also, Western democracy challenges the Arab/Islamic practice in at least three aspects: the smooth transfer of government from one leader who lost legitimacy to a newly legitimized one; the ultimate focus of power; and the place of the opposition in the system. It is characteristic in Western democracy for those who lost legitimacy in free elections to admit their defeat, congratulate the winners, and transfer power in a gracious way, bowing to the rules of democracy. After that, they can ponder the reasons for their defeat and pledge to try again next time around. All these gestures are admission and recognition that such are the rules of the game that are accepted without question. And if the results of the elections remain nebulous, such as razor-thin margins that can be interpreted one way or the other, then a court of law or the central elections committee, which is usually headed by a judge, are invited to decide, and if all that remains divisive and in doubt, then new elections are called for. Nothing of all these smooth and civilized habits was recognized in the Arab/Islamic world prior to the Spring. As the leader was replaced only after he died or was murdered, then of course no one was there to help usher in the new ruler or to transfer the affairs of the state smoothly to him. It is significant that in Egypt, Libya, and Tunisia new parliaments were freely elected, the first time in many decades or ever, and they seem on their way to attaining constitutional legitimacy and to usher in new democratic rules and habits.

Customarily, the new ruler after a coup took over the broadcasting stations, the first tool of control of the crowds, in order to announce the change of rule and the execution of the previous ruler, both of whom shared illegitimacy, but that was considered the normal course of things.

And immediately upon the arrival of the new ruler, he would announce a new constitution—as if old or new had any effect—full of promising plans and rosy visions, but without any built-in guarantees except for pledges from the dictator that some of them might be fulfilled. The only assurance was that the next dictator would bring another constitution when the time came. Against this background one can look with respect and awe upon the process of transition in Egypt, Tunisia, and possibly also Libya, where elections were held, election campaigns were launched with many candidates participating, and the winners were declared by seemingly independent elections commissions, to the applause of large crowds who campaigned for one candidate or the other and went to the polls to determine the results. A totally new sight in these countries indeed came into being. True, this process was watched over by the military, the only remaining organized force in the country in the midst of this chaos, but this is probably inevitable as part of the transition. We do not see yet an orderly transition of power with the former office holder amicably shaking hands with the newly elected, even when not much love is lost between them. But we did see the newcomers welcomed, which is an immense innovation, and if this scene repeats itself in the next term, we can then say that there was a Spring.

We have been accustomed to seeing parliaments, presidents, and governments "elected" in most of these countries, but the ultimate power is always in the hands of the dictator, be he a monarch or a military tyrant or a religious or political figure or a prince who holds power. The elections, whose results were preprogrammed, were always held for a show of participatory democracy, but their rules are at variance from what is known in the West and more like the one-party regimes of the Soviet Bloc, where the list of candidates was decided by the single party and no one else could run against them. In personal elections, like for the president and the mayors, the party announced the lonely candidate, who was sure to be elected and reelected, so as to preclude divisions and rifts within the ruling elite, and to advance a sole and agreed-upon candidate for the position, as befits the dictatorship of the proletariat, except that those elites had forgotten long before what being a member of the working class meant. But the supreme position remained vested in one persona: the secretary of the party, the president, the head of the military commission, the chairman of the revolutionary council, and the like, all intended to point constantly to the supreme location where decisions are made. While in the West the elected representatives vote confidence in the government, and the head of state often commands the army and can dissolve the parliament under certain stipulations, it was the pre-Spring omnipotent dictator in the Islamic world who possessed the undivided authority to do it all: to act as the supreme commander of the forces, to suspend the parliament at will, to decide upon war and peace, to manage domestic and foreign affairs, while the parliament could only formally rubber-stamp what was decided by the leader, not debate him or try to impose control on the executive by parliament. And in Iran, above the elected president and parliament there is a spiritual leader who can override them all.

In those regimes, Egypt for example, the military always stood in the background as part of the power game in the country, since not only did it guarantee continuity of the regime but also took part in the economic and social life of the country. The first slice of the national budget was always assigned to the army, and the commanders of the army always held the controls of power, industry, and many economic sectors, including bread manufacturing and marketing, arms and ammunition factories, restaurants, clubs and entertainment centers for officers, and everything needed for the army to serve loyally the regime that provided all those amenities. The key to stability of the regime was always the tyrant who, as long as he was credible and long lasting, the army supported him, because in his longevity lay the continued prerogatives of the army. But when question marks began to be appended to his policy, conduct, determination to stay in power, or the support he elicited domestically and externally, the army would always be the first to sense in what direction the winds blew. In Tunisia, from the beginning the army aligned with the rebels; therefore it preserved its position as the guardian of the people in time of crisis. In Syria, on the contrary, since it was/is a communal army, whose command was founded basically on the Alawite sect in partnership with other minorities like the Druze and Christians, the army got its fate linked to the regime, and was bound to fall with it. In other intermediate situations like in Yemen and Libya, the army supported the tyrant as long as it could, and deserted when the ruler stood no more chance to succeed. In all instances, the national army was called upon by the rebels to defend the boundaries of the country, that is, to refrain from interfering in domestic affairs, where they remained the only power able to decide the fate of the revolution.

In Turkey, where the army took over on four occasions—from its position of strength as the curator of Ataturk's heritage, and most recently it dismissed the elected government of Necmettin Erbakan in 1998 and outlawed his Islamic party by reason of its far-reaching rapprochement with Iran—a turnaround came about when Tayyip Erdogan's party took over power in 2002. That was the inauguration of the Islamic Spring in Ankara, which has become a general model to be followed by other Muslim countries and an example to be marketed by Turkey, with Western encouragement. Slowly, cautiously, lest he fall victim to the army like his mentor Erbakan who preceded him, but with farsighted vision and firm determination to see his quiet revolution succeed, he started appointing his people to the top echelons of the military—army, navy, and air force. Then he sent to retirement many others, arrested others for conspiring against the elected government, and effected a total change that sent the military back to their barracks and neutralized their capacity to seize power. Erdogan could do that only after he won a landslide in three successive elections, which made him and his party so popular that the army could not move against him without provoking popular resentment. Europe and the United States certainly could not censure Erdogan for that measure, since they too considered putting an end to military meddling in government affairs as a sure sign of the democratization that Turkey was required to adopt on its way to candidacy for the EU. For Erdogan it was a totally different strategy that he was pursuing, in order to achieve Islamization, not democratization of his country, exploiting the usual European and American naïveté (see below) to execute his plans.

The third yardstick for comparing Western democracy to the Islamic style of rule is the status and position of the opposition. In democracies, opposition is the next government, inasmuch as it forms a shadow government that hunts down the incumbent government, pursues it, and criticizes every step of its doings; its views are heard, and its head has an official standing. Opposition in this view is not made of enemies but of apprentices of statecraft who stand ready to replace the government when it fails. In other words, there is an expectation that a failing government would not last and others would inherit that power legitimately after they had learned from the mistakes of their predecessors. In the pre-Spring Islamic countries, this thinking was considered heresy, for the government's success was measured by its ability to overwhelm its rivals and subjugate them. Conversely, the opposition, that negative element that seeks to divide the people and incite them against their government, would by definition be the enemy who tries to scuttle all measures adopted by the government in order to replace it. Thus, opposition is nothing better than an opponent that one would be better off eliminating. The result was that while the Western opposition sits in parliament and its presence is respectably acknowledged, in the Islamic world it was either liquidated or sent to prison. There, it not only could not constitute an alternative government, but since it posed a danger to the ruler and his gang, measures had to be taken against it to protect the public from the enemy within the walls. Only time will tell whether Egypt, Tunisia, Libya, and the rest are able to build vital and aggressive oppositions to act in the face of mounting Islamic regimes. If they do, there is hope that the foundations of democracy can be erected and strengthened, and strong oppositions would act without running the risk of retaliation. But if they fail, the entire democratic experiment will have to be questioned.

All experiments of democratization will not necessarily follow the Western model but rather are likely to maintain authoritarianism of some sort, as in Turkey, even when other ornamental trappings of democracy are adopted. Because during the chaotic situation of the Spring only a strong-handed government can restore law and order and calm the moods after the year or two of upheaval, the question will be what sort of democracy will be installed, if any at all will be pursued. There is the Iraqi model, where reasonably fair elections were held on two occasions so far (2012), but public and personal security are far from restored, and the Sunni portion of the population is not satisfied with the new dominance of the Shi'ites, who were previously downtrodden under Saddam. Similarly, the oil riches of the country have not yet been brought to bear in view of the electricity cuts, and the political arena is not yet serene in the struggle between the autonomy that the Kurds yearn for and the strong federal tendencies that have led the country so far. And then there is the Turkish model, which though more prosperous and modernized has also been plagued with the question of the Kurds, the Islamization that is resented by the bourgeois urbanites, and other problems of domestic and external affairs. And finally there is the Islamic model, where the Muslim Brothers champion a clear ideology of a Shari'a state, but their ability to enforce it in its totality remains very doubtful.

Notes

1. Nadim Kawach, "Arab food gap crosses $180bn over past decade," *Emirates 24/7*, June 27, 2010. http://www.emirates247.com/eb247/ economy/uae-economy/arab-food-gap-crosses-180bn-over-past-decade-2010-06-27-1.259717.

2. Ibid.
3. Ibid.
4. Moshe Dayan Center publishes *Tel Aviv Notes*, an analytical update on current affairs in the Middle East, on the tenth and twenty-sixth of every month, as well as occasional special edition, "Instability and State Weakness": http://www.dayan.tau.ac.il. "The 'Post-Revolutionary' Challenge in the Arab World," by Yoel Guzansky and Benedetta Berti.
5. Ibid.
6. Ibid.
7. Ibid.
8. See Raphael Israeli, "The Islamic Movement in Israel," *Jerusalem Letter*, Jerusalem Center for Public Affairs, Oct. 15, 1999; L. Barkan, "The Islamic Movement in Israel: Switching Focus from Jerusalem to the Palestinian Cause," Inquiry & Analysis Series, report no. 628, Middle East Media Research Institute, Washington, DC, July 30, 2010.
9. Bartal is a lecturer on Palestinian affairs at Bar Ilan University and author of *The Fedayeen Emerge, The Palestine-Israel Conflict, 1949–1956* (Bloomington, IN: Authorhouse, 2011).
10. Ibid.
11. Ibid.

Bibliography

By the nature of this theme, not much has been written to encompass this two-year-old process, which is still going on, except for field and eyewitness reports from both professional writers and reporters as well as common people who used their smartphones or social media to feed the world with what they saw, thought, or heard in the various countries where this Spring has been unfolding. This book is one of the first attempts to encompass that worldwide process that has been unfolding in a wide array of Islamic countries into one coherent account that draws from the same religiopolitical sources.

Documents

The Qur'an
Reporters without Borders Report, February 14, 2011.

Media: Print and Electronic

Akhbar al-Youm (Cairo)
Al-Ahram (Cairo)
Al-Akhbar (Cairo)
Al-Jazeera (Qatar)
Al-Masry Al-Youm, (Cairo)
al-Quds al-Arabi, (London), June 18, 2012.
Emirates, July 2012.
Ha'aretz, June 8, 2012.
Inquiry & Analysis Series (Washington)
International Herald Tribune, December 3, 2012.
Israel Against Terror, June 28, 2012.
Israel Defense, Issue #8, 2012.
Jerusalem Letter
Jerusalem Post, September 16, 2012.
Jordan Times, July 31, 2012.
Jewish Ideas Daily
Jordan Times, July 23, 2012.
Kayhan (Tehran), July 21, 2012.
MEMRI, Special Dispatch no. 916, June 6, 2005.

305

MEMRI, Special Dispatch no. 1596, May 23, 2007.
MENA (Cairo)
PA Television, May 11, and again June 2.
Post-Holocaust and Antisemitism (Jerusalem)
Saudi Gazette, July 31, 2012.
Tel Aviv Notes (TA University)
Times of Israel, July 9, 2012.
Wall Street Journal, July 8, 2012.
www.bbc.co.uk/news/world-middle-east-16511685
www.theatlantic.com/technology/archive/2011/01/the-inside-story-ofhow-
  facebook-/responded-to-tunisian-hacks/70044
www.milligorusarsiv.com/videolar/file.php?f=5
www.memrijttm.org/content/en/blog personal.htm?id=6098&param=UPP
www.aljazeera.com/indepth/features/2011/07/20111725145048574888.
html
http://world.silkapp/com /page/Tunisia
http://www.inss.org.il/publications.php?cat=21&incat=&read=6963
http://www.ft.com/intl/cms/s/0/f5508056-da2f-11e00144feab49a
html#axzz228uvUSU6, July 30, 2012
http://www.emirates247.com/eb247/economy/uae-economy/arab-food-gap-
  crosses-180bn-over-pastdecade-2010-06-27-1.259717

Books

Bartal, Y. *The Fedayeen Emerg, The Palestine-Israel Conflict, 1949–1956.* Bloomington, 2011.
Hatina, Meir, and Uri Kupferschmidt. *The Muslim Brothers: A Religious Vision in a Changing Reality.* Tel Aviv: Hakibbutz Ha-Meuchad, 2012.
Israeli, Raphael. *Islamikaze: Manifestations of Islamic Martyrology.* London: Frank Cass, 2003.
Israeli, Raphael. *The Spread of Islamikaze Terrorism in Europe.* Vallentine Mitchell, 2008.
Israeli, Raphael. *Poison: Modern Manifestations of a Blood Libel.* Lexington Books, 2002.
Israeli, Raphael. *Blood Libel and Its Derivatives.* Piscataway, NJ: Transaction Publishers, 2012.
Israeli, Raphael. *The Oslo Idea: The Euphoria of Failure.* Piscataway, NJ: Transaction Publishers, 2012.
Kobrin, Nancy, and Phyllis Chesler. *The Banality of Suicide Terrorism: The Naked Truth About the Psychology of Islamic Suicide Bombing.* Potomac Books, 2010.
Khumeini, Ayatullah. *The Islamic Republic.*
Qut'b, Sayyid. *Ma'rakatuna ma'a al-Yahud* (*Our War against the Jews*), 7th ed. Beirut, 1986.
Yang, C. K. *Religion in Chinese Society.* Berkeley, CA: University of California Press, 1967, pp. 294–340.
Weissbrod, Amir. *Turabi: Spokesman of Radical Islam* (Hebrew edition). Tel Aviv: Dayan Center, 1999.

Articles

Barkan, L. "The Islamic Movement in Israel: Switching Focus from Jerusalem to the Palestinian Cause," *Inquiry & Analysis Series,* report no. 628, Middle East Media Research Institute, Washington, DC, July 30, 2010.

Eran, Oded. "Jordan's Internal and External Pressure Cooker," *INSS Insight* no. 358, July 31, 2012.

Guzansky, Yoel, and Benedetta Berti. "Instability and State Weakness: The 'Post-Revolutionary' Challenge in the Arab World," http://www.dayan. tau.ac.il.

Hadzivokovic, Vesna et al. (eds.). *Chronicle of Announced Death,* 1993, Belgrade, p. 52.

Horovitz, David. "A Commentary," *Times of Israel,* July 9, 2012.

Israeli, Raphael. "The Islamic Movement in Israel," *Jerusalem Letter,* Jerusalem Center for Public Affairs, Oct. 15, 1999.

Kawach, Nadim. "Arab Food Gap Crosses $180bn over Past Decade," *Emirates 24/7,* June 27, 2010. http://www.emirates247.com/eb247/ economy/uae-economy/arab-foodgap-crosses-180bn-over-pastdecade-2010-06-27-1.259717.

Kedar, Mordechai. "The Brothers and the Muslims," *Israel Against Terror,* June 28, 2012.

Lappin, Yaakov. http://web.archive.org/web/20100428140334/http://eng. akpati.org.tr/english/lifestory.html

Makovsky, Michael, and Blaise Misztal. "Commentary," *Wall Street Journal,* July 8, 2012.

Marcus, Itamar, and Baraba Crook. "Antisemitism among Palestinian Authority Academics," in *Post-Holocaust and Antisemitism,* no. 69, June 1, 2008, The Jerusalem Center of Public Affairs.

Marcus, Itamar, and Nan Jacques Zilberdik. "The Muslim Brotherhood's Patient Jihad," *Jewish Ideas Daily,* July 25, 2012.

Meital, Y. "The Muslim Brothers in Egypt at the End of the Mubarak Era," in Hatina and Kupferschmidt, op. cit., pp. 147–169.

Qasmi, Ali Usman. "God's Kingdom on Earth? Politics of Islam in Pakistan 1947–69," *Modern Asian Studies,* 44, 6 (2010), pp. 1197–1253.

Savyon, A., and Y. Mansharof. "A Commented Article," MEMRI.

"Turkey Ramps Up Kurdish Offensive," August 2, 2012. http://online.wsj.com/ article/SB10000872396390443545504577565122536657382.

Weissman, Y. "Fundamentalism and Democracy in the Discourse of the Muslim Brothers in Syria," in Meir Hatina and Uri Kupferschmidt, *The Muslim Brothers: A Religious Vision in a Changing Reality.* Tel Aviv: Hakibbutz Ha-Meuchad, 2012, pp. 125–146.

Index

Y

Yasin, Sheikh Ahmed, 256. *See* Gaza.
Yazedi, Ayatuallah, 185
Yemen, 1–2, 7, 11, 16, 23, 28, 30, 60, 63, 68, 76, 78, 108, 171, 179, 205ff
    Abyan area, 209–10
    Ansar al-Shari'a in —, 210
    — General Popular Congress, 212
    Sa'da, 208–10
    San'a, 174, 206, 208
    South —, 208
    — Supreme Court, 212
Yugoslavia, 220ff

Z

Zakat, 17
Zarqawi (Master al-Qa'ida terrorist), 275
Zaydi/Houti (see also Shi'a and Yemen), 23, 206, 210
Zia-ul al Haqq, General, 136
Zionism, 20, 99, 107, 112, 263
    Anti —, 84ff, 184, 187, 188, 232
    Zionist State, 252
Zoroastrians, 53
Zuckerberg, Mark, 73, 138